THE UNITED STATES AND MULTILATERAL INSTITUTIONS

This book brings together a wide range of experts to examine United States policy in intergovernmental institutions such as the World Bank, GATT and IMF.

World politics in the post-Cold War world has become increasingly institutionalized. However, the role of international organizations has been overlooked in much of the literature on international regimes to date. This book aims to fill the gap by providing a comprehensive examination of United States policy in areas ranging from international trade to human rights.

Margaret Karns and Karen Mingst set their detailed policy examination within a sophisticated theoretical framework, looking at the reasons why patterns of continuity and change differ so greatly among issue areas, and from one organization to another.

The book will appeal to both introductory students and to graduate students of Strategic Studies and of International Relations, and especially those taking courses on international organizations.

Margaret P. Karns is associate professor of political science and director of the Center for International Studies at the University of Dayton. She is also a faculty associate at the Mershon Center of the Ohio State University.

Karen A. Mingst is associate professor of political science at the University of Kentucky.

THE UNITED STATES AND MULTILATERAL INSTITUTIONS

Patterns of changing instrumentality and influence

Edited by
Margaret P. Karns
and
Karen A. Mingst

MERSHON CENTER SERIES ON INTERNATIONAL
SECURITY AND FOREIGN POLICY, VOLUME V

London and New York

First published 1990
by Unwin Hyman, Inc.

New in paperback 1992
by Routledge
11 New Fetter Lane, London EC4P 4EE

Simultaneously published in the USA and Canada
by Routledge
a division of Routledge, Chapman and Hall, Inc.
29 West 35th Street, New York, NY 10001

Typeset in 10/12pt Times by Fotographics (Bedford) Ltd
and printed in Great Britain by the University Press, Cambridge

British Library Cataloguing in Publication Data

The United States and multilateral institutions: patterns of changing
instrumentality and influence.—(Mershon Center series on international
security and foreign policy; v. 5)
1. Relations with United States
I. Karns, Margaret P. II. Mingst, Karen, A. III. Series
341.2
ISBN 0-415-08110-6

Library of Congress Cataloging in Publication Data

The United States and multilateral institutions: patterns of changing
instrumentality and influence/edited by Margaret P. Karns and Karen A. Mingst.
Includes bibliographical references.
ISBN 0-415-08110-6
1. International agencies. 2. United States—Foreign relations—1981–
1. Karns, Margaret P. II. Mingst, Karen A., 1947–
JX1995.U576 1990
341.2—dc20
89-38334 CIP

Contents

Acknowledgments

Academic collaboration is a slow and often tortuous task, a product of both enthusiasm and frustration. This volume is no exception. We have met and worked in such diverse settings as the modern public library building adjacent to the Mission at San Juan Capistrano, the shores of Frenchman's Bay, Maine, and the Quality Inn on the Ohio River in Cincinnati. There have been spans of time when each of us was working on other projects in Europe and Africa. It survived the births of two children and a teenager's navigation of the high school years.

The coauthored chapters are very much joint enterprises benefiting from our lengthy discussions as well as the comments of others. We have also worked in tandem editing others' contributions. We believe the integration of the whole owes a great deal to that close collaboration and to the willingness of all the contributors to accept our suggestions for changes in their chapters.

We are most grateful for the generous financial support of the Mershon Center at Ohio State University and its director, Charles F. Hermann, the editor of this series. The financial and in-kind support of the Midwest Consortium for International Security Studies of the American Academy of Arts and Sciences and the Johnson Foundation made it possible to bring all the contributors together with other academics and practitioners at the Wingspread Conference Center, Racine, Wisconsin, January 28–30, 1987. These sessions were invaluable in providing opportunities for critical review and lively discussion of the framework and case study chapters and, hence, contributed to the achievement of an integrated volume. We are also grateful to Marian Rice of the American Academy's Midwest office and Rita Goodman, former vice president of the Johnson Foundation, for their encouragement and assistance.

In addition to the contributors to this volume, participants in the Wingspread Conference included academic colleagues Charles F. Hermann, Chadwick Alger, Charles Lipson, Stephen Krasner, and Mark W. Zacher. The experience of the following policy participants brought valuable perspectives to the discussions: John E. Fobes (former deputy director general of UNESCO), Samuel De Palma (former assistant secretary of state for International Organization Affairs), Edward Luck (president, UNA-USA), and Margaret E. Galey (staff consultant, Committee on Foreign Relations, U.S. House of Representatives). We are grateful for their willingness to give their time, insights, and critical comments to the refinement of the overall framework and the substance of the individual case studies. In addition, the support of the Midwest Consortium for International Security Studies of the American Academy of Arts and Sciences enabled us to include five graduate students from Midwest institutions whose participation enlivened the discussion: Lisa L. Condit (Indiana University), Christopher Holoman (University of Chicago), Jennifer Holt (University of Chicago), Geoffrey Martin (Purdue University), and Suneeta Misra (Ohio State University).

We also made use of opportunities for presentations at meetings of the International Studies Association in 1987 and 1988. Draft chapters benefited from comments of Gene M. Lyons, Lawrence S. Finkelstein, Michael G. Schechter, and John M. McDonald.

We owe a special thanks to Charles Hermann, whose enthusiasm and support helped to sustain us through the project's long gestation. We are also grateful to our respective institutions, the University of Dayton and the University of Kentucky, for in-kind assistance. Lin Daniels at the Mershon Center lent her expert word-processing skills to the entire manuscript.

Finally, we are indebted to our families for their patience ("Will your book ever get out?") and encouragement.

Margaret P. Karns
Karen A. Mingst

Glossary

ABM	antiballistic missile system
ACDA	(U.S.) Arms Control and Disarmament Agency
ACTN	(U.S.) Advisory Committee on Trade Negotiations
AEC	Atomic Energy Commission
AID or	
USAID	(U.S.) Agency for International Development
AIDS	Acquired Immune Deficiency Syndrome
APWG	Action Plan Working Group
ASP	American Selling Price (agreements)
CAME	Conference of Allied Ministers of Education
CAP	(European Community) Common Agricultural Policy
CCC	(U.S.) Consumer Credit Corporation
CFA	(World Food Program) Committee on Food Aid Programs and Practices
CFS	(Food and Agriculture Organization) Committee on Food Security
CGIAR	Consultative Group on International Agricultural Research
CIMMYT	Centro International de Mejoramiento de Maize y Trigo
CR	(United Nations Educational, Scientific and Cultural Organization) Committee on Conventions and Recommendations
DISC	Domestic International Sales Corporations
DNG	(United Nations Educational, Scientific and Cultural Organization) Drafting and Negotiating Group
DOE	(U.S.) Department of Energy
DOS	(U.S.) Department of State
EBF	(International Atomic Energy Agency) Extra-Budgetary Funds
ECOSOC	(UN) Economic and Social Council
EEC or **EC**	European Economic Community; after 1972, European Community
EFF	(International Monetary Fund) Extended Fund Facility
EPTA	(United Nations) Expanded Programme of Technical Assistance
ERDA	(U.S.) Energy Research and Development Administration, later the Department of Energy
FAO	Food and Agriculture Organization
FIRA	(Canadian) Foreign Investment Act
FVA	(U.S. Agency for International Development) Bureau for Food for Peace and Voluntary Assistance
FY	fiscal year
GAO	(U.S.) General Accounting Office
GATT	General Agreement on Tariffs and Trade
GF	(International Atomic Energy Agency) General Fund
GNP	gross national product

GSP	generalized system of preferences
IAEA	International Atomic Energy Agency
IATA	International Air Transport Association
IBRD	International Bank for Reconstruction and Development, more commonly known as the World Bank
ICAO	International Civil Aviation Organization
IDA	International Development Association
IEA	International Energy Agency
IFAD	International Fund for Agricultural Development
IFC	International Finance Corporation
IGCP	International Geological Correlation Program
IGO	international governmental organization
IICI	Institut International de Cooperation Intellectuelle
ILO	International Labor Organization
IMF	International Monetary Fund
INF	intermediate-range nuclear forces
INFCE	International Nuclear Fuel Cycle Evaluation Program
INFCIRC	International Atomic Energy Agency (document designating system of safeguards)
INGOs	international nongovernmental organizations
INTLO	(U.S.) International Nuclear Technical Liaison Office
IPDC	International Program for the Development of Communications
IOC	Intergovernmental Oceanographic Commission
IRRI	International Rice Research Institute
ISG	(IAEA and U.S.) Inter-Agency Steering Group for International Safeguards
ITO	International Trade Organization
ITU	International Telecommunications Union
IWC	International Wheat Council
LASCAR	Working Group on Large Scale Automated Reprocessing
LDC	less developed country
LWR	light water reactor fuel
MAB	Man and Biosphere Program
MFA	Multifibre Arrangement
MFN	most favored nation (treatment)
MITI	(Japan) Ministry of International Trade and Industry
MSA	(U.S.) Mutual Security Act
MTN	Multilateral Trade Negotiations
NASAP	(U.S. Department of Energy) Non-Proliferation Alternative Systems Assessment Program
NATO	North Atlantic Treaty Organization
NIC	newly industrializing country
NIEO	New International Economic Order
NMMSS	U.S. Nuclear Materials Management and Safeguard System
NPT	Treaty on the Non-Proliferation of Nuclear Weapons
NRC	Nuclear Regulatory Commission
NSC	U.S. National Security Council
NSF	(U.S.) National Science Foundation
NSG	Nuclear Suppliers Group
NTB	nontariff barrier

NWICO	New World Information and Communications Order
OAS	Organization of American States
OAU	Organization of African Unity
OECD	Organization for Economic Cooperation and Development
OES	(U.S. Department of State) Bureau for Oceans, Environmental, and Scientific Affairs
OIHP	Office International d'Hygiène Publique
OMA	Orderly Marketing Arrangement
OMB	(U.S.) Office of Management and Budget
ONUC	United Nations Operation in the Congo
OPEC	Organization of Petroleum-Exporting Countries
PAC	political action committee
PAHO	Pan American Health Organization
PANA	Pan African News Agency
PLO	Palestine Liberation Organization
POTAS	(U.S.) Program of Technical Assistance to Safeguards
PMS	Plutonium Management Study
PNEs	peaceful nuclear explosives
PPC	(U.S. Department of State) Bureau for Program and Policy Coordination
RECOVER	REmote COntinuous VERification
RFCC	Regional Nuclear Fuel Cycle Center Project
SAGSI	Standing Advisory Group on Safeguards Implementation
SALT II	Treaty on the Limitation of Strategic Offensive Arms
SAWG	(U.S. and IAEA) Safeguards Agreement Working Group
SIPRI	Swedish International Peace Research Institute
SIR	Safeguards Implementation Report
STI	(U.S. Department of State) Bureau for Science and Technology
TA	technical assistance
TAC	(International Atomic Energy Agency) Technical Assistance Committee
TSCC	Technical Support Coordinating Committee
UN	United Nations
UNCTAD	United Nations Conference on Trade and Development
UNDOF	United Nations Disengagement Observer Force
UNDP	United Nations Development Program
UNEF	United Nations Emergency Force
UNESCO	United Nations Educational, Scientific and Cultural Organization
UNFICYP	United Nations Force in Cyprus
UNICEF	United Nations Children's Fund, originally known as UN International Children's Emergency Fund
UNIDO	United Nations Industrial Development Organization
UNIFIL	United Nations Interim Force
USDA	United States Department of Agriculture
USTR	United States Trade Representative
VER	Voluntary Restraint Agreement
WCARRD	World Conference on Agrarian Reform and Rural Development
WFC	World Food Council
WFP	World Food Program
WIG	Western Information Group

WHA	World Health Assembly
WHO	World Health Organization
WPFC	World Press Freedom Committee

CHAPTER ONE

The United States and Multilateral Institutions: A Framework for Analysis

Margaret P. Karns
Karen A. Mingst

The period since the end of World War II has been marked by the proliferation of multilateral institutions, including international governmental organizations (IGOs) and international nongovernmental organizations (INGOs), to facilitate and promote international order and cooperation. Explanation of the bases and patterns of international interactions requires understanding both of why states find it in their interest to cooperate with one another and of the reasons they choose different means to achieve a measure of order and collaboration in an otherwise anarchic environment.

In recent years scholars have adopted the term *regime* to encompass the variety of formal and informal multilateral arrangements. Yet few attempts have been made to specify the role of formal international governmental organizations within regimes or to link system-level theories of regimes and cooperation with national-level processes and behavior. If regimes and IGOs matter, there must be a two-way flow of influence—a dynamic relationship between them and member state policymaking processes and behavior.

This volume focuses on the United States and multilateral institutions, particularly on U.S.-IGO relationships, based on the hypothesis that institutions make a difference in international interactions because they are utilized by and have influence on even the most powerful states. IGOs in particular have often played key roles in the creation and maintenance of regimes, and it is the organizations within regimes to which governments belong, around whose work bureaucracies are often themselves organized

1

and driven, and whose budgets require governmental decisions on contributions. Patterns of IGO instrumentality and influence need not be constant, but changes in such patterns will shape the evolution of both organizations and the regimes in which they may be embedded. Consequently they will also shape the nature of international order and cooperation.

Although the United States played a key role in the establishment and development of many IGOs in the early postwar period, since the 1960s American willingness and ability to exert leadership and influence have eroded. The United States withdrew temporarily from the International Labor Organization (ILO) under the Carter administration and threatened similar action in the International Telecommunications Union (ITU) and the International Atomic Energy Agency (IAEA). Congress reduced appropriations for IGO contributions in some cases and mandated withholding funds in others. Hence contrary to the trend of "multiplying entanglement"—that is, the proliferation of IGOs and INGOs since World War II (Jacobson et al. 1986)—U.S. commitment to IGOs appeared to decrease. A sequence of actions by the Reagan administration including rejection of the Law of the Sea treaty, opposition to the World Bank's promotion of energy conservation, and withdrawal from the United Nations Educational, Scientific, and Cultural Organization (UNESCO) further fueled debate in the policy arena over the role of IGOs in U.S. foreign policy. Yet the Reagan administration, after its early hostility toward many organizations, discovered the value of many multilateral institutions and the potential for institutional reform. These developments in the policy arena therefore make an examination of the interplay between IGOs and U.S. foreign policy timely. They underscore the variations over time and, for an individual member state, the utility and impact of specific institutions as vehicles for multilateral cooperation.

By analyzing patterns of changing instrumentality and influence in U.S.-IGO relationships and by seeking explanation of those patterns across a variety of organizations and issue areas, we seek to increase understanding of the dynamics of state-IGO relationships. This is an important step in examining the impact of IGOs and regimes on collective behavior at the international level, as well as the sources and nature of regime change. Examination of the two-way flow of influence with reference to one state and several IGOs will also illuminate this specific aspect of the interactions between domestic and international affairs.[1] These concerns lead us to pose four questions:

1. How has the use of IGOs as instruments of U.S. policy changed over time?

2. How have the constraints and influence of IGOs on the United States changed over time?
3. Why have these changes occurred?
4. What are the policy implications for the United States of these patterns of changing influence?

Investigation of these questions requires further specification of the relationships among IGOs, regimes, and international cooperation and of the two-way flow of influence between IGOs and member states. In this chapter we lay the conceptual foundation for the series of case studies of U.S.-IGO relationships that follow and propose four alternate sources of explanation for the patterns of changing IGO instrumentality and influence. We turn initially to elaborate on the role that IGOs and regimes play in the patterns of interaction among states.

IGOs, Regimes, and Cooperation

The term *regime* has been commonly used by scholars in recent years to encompass the "sets of implicit or explicit principles, norms, rules, and decision-making procedures around which actors' expectations converge in a given issue area" (Krasner 1982b: 1). It has been argued that regimes "change patterns of transaction costs and provide information to participants, so that uncertainty is reduced" (Axelrod and Keohane 1985: 249–50). They make more information available to governments, thereby affecting decision makers' perceptions of self-interest and their calculations of the costs and benefits of alternative choices (Keohane 1984: chap. 6). Although the processes of international governance, of creating order and patterns of cooperation, are not limited to the activities of such formal organizations (Kratochwil and Ruggie 1986: 759–60), IGOs are the most easily identifiable of the various multilateral arrangements encompassed by regimes.[2]

IGOs *may* play key roles in the creation and maintenance of regimes. The charters of IGOs incorporate principles, norms, rules, decision-making processes, and functions for the organizations that formalize these aspects of a regime. The organizations' decision-making processes may then be used by member states for further norm and rule creation, for rule enforcement and dispute settlement, for the provision of collective goods, and for supporting operational activities. Through regularized processes of information gathering and analysis, IGOs "improve the quality of information governments receive" (Keohane 1984: 244). They "bring governments into continuing interaction with one another, reducing the incentives to cheat and enhancing the value of reputation" (p. 245).

Not all organizations perform all of the aforementioned functions, and the manner and extent to which they carry out particular functions varies. As instruments of foreign policy, they provide forums for legitimating viewpoints, principles, and norms. States (and other actors) may also use those forums for perpetuating conflict and blocking cooperation. IGOs encourage coalition-building and linkage among issues. IGOs have also been used to facilitate the interactions of governmental and nongovernmental personnel, leading to the development of transnational networks that have become important parts of many regimes.

As central components of many regimes, IGOs not only create opportunities for their member states but also exercise influence and impose constraints on their members' policies and the processes by which policies are formed. IGOs affect member states by setting international and, hence, national agendas and forcing governments to take positions on issues. They subject states' behavior to surveillance through information sharing. They encourage the development of specialized decision-making and implementation processes to facilitate and coordinate IGO participation. They embody or facilitate the creation of principles, norms, and rules of behavior with which states must align their policies if they wish to benefit from reciprocity. Particularly in pluralist societies, IGO-created norms and principles may be used by domestic groups to press for changes in national policies. Informal transgovernmental and transnational networks and coalitions have developed largely out of the necessities and opportunities of interaction within specific IGOs, becoming important parts of many regimes (Keohane and Nye 1977: 234).

IGOs as well as international regimes may contribute to the creation of "habits of cooperation" through the repetition of patterns of behavior over time.[3] States may be "socialized" by regular involvement in the activities of IGOs and related processes of multilateral interaction and policy coordination. Habits of cooperation build on individual learning and socialization.[4] They are related to the roots of obedience to international law in habits of law-abiding behavior and desires to maintain a reputation for the same.[5] Habits of cooperation may be reinforced through the support of domestic groups for certain norms and rules and through bureaucratic changes that create organizational stakes in particular IGOs—that is, in working in and through certain IGOs.

Formal organizations are particularly instrumental in the formation and stability of habits of cooperation by institutionalizing regular meetings, processes of information gathering and analysis and of dispute settlement, and operational activities. To be sure, as in domestic political arenas, various networks of governmental and nongovernmental officials will be useful in moving policy initiatives along and ensuring that the processes of governance are not blocked. Thus in periods of institutional paralysis (or perceived misdirection), informal patterns of organization and ad hoc multilateral groups can ensure that international cooperation does not cease entirely. Over the longer term, however, within many regimes institutional development, especially of formal organizations, is critically important to the maintenance of durable means for providing a measure of predictability in the behavior of other actors, managing conflicts, and addressing the expanding agenda of international problems.[6]

If IGOs are potentially key mechanisms for creating and sustaining patterns of international cooperation, they must in some ways and to some extent influence even the largest, most powerful states in the system. To conceptualize IGOs in particular as instruments of actors' policies is to see them as means to get other actors to change their behavior, to redefine their interests, and to accept certain constraints. Of necessity IGOs must also be seen as influencers, not only of others' behavior but of one's own; that is, there must be some degree of reciprocity (Keohane 1986). As social exchange and power theory suggest, how much one must reciprocate depends on the extent to which one's own preferences predominate in the exchange. Thus utilizing IGOs to affect the behavior of others involves, in turn, being constrained by those very institutions and by the ways others use them. Even if the value of a particular IGO for regime maintenance erodes over time because of the emergence of new organizations or issues, the habits and patterns of cooperation it has helped to create should facilitate the development of other avenues of cooperation, including ad hoc mechanisms. Crises, on the other hand, may well force states to find new ways of using and even strengthening IGOs. It is to the question of the changing importance of IGOs to the United States, in particular, that we now turn.

Changing Relationships between the United States and IGOs

That the United States emerged from World War II as the dominant political, economic, and military power in the international system is widely recognized. International organizations were an important part of this international system structure, organizations designed by the victors (at least in rhetoric) to eliminate war and its causes and to create a liberal international economic order. As the dominant power, the United States played a key role in promoting the establishment of many IGOs, both in the planning phase during the war and in the early days of the organizations' development.[7] For example, it was the United States that sponsored the Uniting for Peace Resolution, thereby increasing the role of the General Assembly.

IGOs offered a way to create structures compatible with American notions of political order and through which to promote U.S. political and economic interests. Although support for such institutions was not necessarily assured (witness the failure to approve the charter of the proposed International Trade Organization in 1948), governmental and public commitment were generally strong. The predominance of Americans in many secretariats and the relatively large share of operating and program funding contributed by the United States reinforced American influence over policies and programs flowing from many IGOs. Inevitably, however, the United States found that it could not always control outcomes within various IGOs. Its predominance was also bound to diminish with time; such is the fate of any power whose dominance is based in part on the postwar weakness of others. In addition, the dramatic transformation of the international system through the process of decolonization and resulting changes in the size, composition, and orientation of many IGO memberships could not help but alter the organizations themselves. Especially in the United Nations in the 1970s, the United States found itself increasingly on the defensive. Its control over agendas slipped; its ability to mobilize votes across all issues eroded; its close ties and influence within secretariats were reduced by the assertion of greater autonomy. U.S. support for international organizations was tested by programs and activities regarded as detrimental to American interests.[8]

It is important to recognize that this change in the U.S. position is quite relative; only when the U.S. role is compared with its position in the early postwar years is a change discernible. Across a broad spectrum of IGOs, the United States remains a major actor whose ability to shape IGO actions and, through them, the behavior of others makes it one of the most important members. Furthermore, although the United States has acted both unilaterally and bilaterally regardless of its influence in relevant IGOs, multilateralism has been an important norm of postwar U.S. foreign policy.

IGOs as Instruments of American Policies

Member states of an IGO can use the organization as a vehicle by which to conduct their foreign policy—that is, as a policy instrument to influence other international actors. Doing so entails building the necessary coalitions of support from other member states. Through IGOs, as the case studies explore more fully, the United States has sought to create regimes, legitimate its policies, avail itself of information, settle disputes, enforce rules, and undertake problem-solving activities.

The United States was actively involved in drafting the charters of many postwar organizations, thus influencing the shape of both the formal organizational structures and the regimes that emerged. Among the latter are the international trade regime negotiated through the General Agreement on Tariffs and Trade (GATT), the international monetary regime formalized in part by the International Monetary Fund (IMF), and the nuclear nonproliferation regime established with the creation of the International Atomic Energy Agency. The United States has not consistently used IGOs for purposes of regime change, however. For example, it strongly supported the negotiation of codes dealing with nontariff barriers to trade within GATT, thereby expanding the scope of the GATT-based international trade regime. Yet the United States largely excluded the IMF from any role in the floating exchange rate system that emerged in the mid-1970s.

From the beginning of the postwar period, the United States used IGOs for collective legitimation of its own actions, particularly in crisis situations such as the Cuban missile crisis, and for delegitimizing the actions of others that it opposed, such as the British, French, and Israeli occupation of Suez and the Soviet invasion of Afghanistan. Since 1960 the United States has found it increasingly difficult, if not impossible, however, to muster the necessary majorities in organizations such as the UN or Organization of American States (OAS). Nonetheless in the Iran hostage crisis the United States used both the UN Security Council and the International Court of Justice to condemn Iran's actions, clearly showing that it had not forgotten the value of IGOs for collective legitimization of its policies.

Given the strength of the United States' own information-gathering and analytical resources, IGOs have generally been less useful for these purposes to the United States than to other states. Nevertheless the opportunities for interaction that IGOs provide enhance information about the behavior of other states and, hence, predictability. Greater interdependence has increased the value to the United States of the information-gathering capabilities of organizations such as the International Energy Agency (IEA) and the Organization for Economic Cooperation and Development (OECD) and the opportunities afforded for surveillance of others' behavior.

The United States has always had high regard for the potential value of at least the dispute settlement mechanisms of IGOs. Willingness to use those mechanisms to settle conflicts to which the United States has been a party has varied widely, however. When those mechanisms have been linked to regimes with clearly defined sets of rules and standards—such as in health care, trade, and shipping—the likelihood of employing them has been greater because of the strength of legalism in the American political culture. The politicization of many IGOs and the lack of consensus on basic norms in the security area have reduced the value of the UN and OAS, for example, for dispute settlement.

The United States has clearly played a key role in initiating and supporting many IGO-based operational activities in all regimes. Although others often benefit more directly from the alleviation of problems such as disease, hunger, and environmental degradation, UN peacekeeping operations have uniformly been regarded as important instruments of American policies, as has the IAEA's safeguards system. In the 1980s the United States strongly supported the increased role of the World Bank in structural adjustment lending.

The perceived utility of individual IGOs and regimes for the United States has been strongly shaped by the ability of American representatives to influence procedures and outcomes. Changes in many IGOs have made it more difficult for the United States to use them as instruments of U.S. policy and have necessitated changes in techniques of statecraft. The United States has frequently had to bargain more to convince other countries' delegates as well as secretariat personnel that a specific course of action was desirable or appropriate, to offer trade-offs among linked issues, and to accept compromise outcomes. In defending its interests and those of close friends, the United States has been less reluctant to use its veto power in the UN Security Council, for example (Stoessinger 1977). In many regimes and issue areas the United States has supported the creation of ad hoc multilateral groups, such as the Group of 5, the London Suppliers Group, and the Quadrilateral Group, to facilitate the management of particular tasks and to supplement or circumvent established IGOs. What is the relationship, then, between variations in the patterns of IGO instrumentality and patterns of IGO impact on U.S. policies and policymaking processes?

The Impact of IGOs on U.S. Policies and Policymaking Processes

To argue that IGOs influence national policies and policymaking does not presume that IGOs are "superior" to states, although states may relinquish authority in certain areas as functionalism has always presumed. IGOs are not "elements of a new international order beyond the nation state" (Keohane 1984: 63) but elements of such an order of, by, and for nation-states. As integral parts of the contemporary international system and potentially important nonstate actors, they have become yet another international source of domestic politics (Gourevitch 1978). They not only enlarge the possibilities of multilateral diplomacy but add to the constraints and costs under which the United States operates. We are specifically concerned with the impact on U.S. foreign policy behavior and decision-making processes of IGO-generated rules and norms, of surveillance through information sharing, and of IGO secretariats' actions and of agendas, as well as with adaptations in decision-making and implementation processes required for effective participation and with the influence of IGOs on domestic groups. We contend that these influences have grown over time.

A limited number of IGOs have the capacity to enact rules and interpret their application through dispute settlement and supervisory processes. Where they do, however, rule-creating and supervisory decisions such as flow from GATT, the IAEA, or the World Health Organization (WHO) directly affect national laws and regulations. To fulfill their legal obligations to these organizations, states have to incorporate IGO rules through legislation or regulatory pronouncements. In the case of the United States, IGO rules have often coincided with existing national rules.[9] But IGOs have increasingly produced rules that the United States has viewed as inimical to its interests, putting U.S. policymakers on the defensive or in opposition.

More indirectly, IGOs' roles in information sharing and surveillance affect U.S. policies. By making members' behavior more transparent, these processes generate pressure for changes in policies that are perceived as incompatible with collective interest in order and stability. Particularly in the last decade, for example, U.S. macroeconomic policies have been subjected to sharp criticism in the OECD and IMF. Growing interdependence has increased U.S. sensitivity to the actions of others and the need for more information on the existing and future policies of other states. Increasingly IGOs may serve as the "transmission belts" for such information and hence have an indirect impact on American policies. Furthermore, as the U.S. government has reduced its own information-gathering activities in a number of areas to cut expenditures, its dependence on IGO sources has risen.

The most pervasive, though not necessarily the most important, way that IGOs may affect national policies is by establishing agendas for national bureaucracies. The hundreds of meetings, conferences, and regular and special sessions of IGOs that take place each year may force governments to mobilize resources to study issues not previously on the national agenda or to form responses on issues in which they have little interest, thus promoting the pretense of policies. During the 1950s and 1960s the frequent initiatives taken by the United States to shape IGO agendas limited the reciprocal potential for IGO influence on U.S. decision-making agendas because most issues were already on the agenda of the American government. Some bureaucratic and budgetary changes were required to provide the infrastructure for participation and the resources for effecting policy goals and financial commitments.

Since the early 1970s particularly in global, universal membership IGOs, the Group of 77 has frequently set agendas, proposing regulatory activities generally regarded as outside the scope of the federal government's powers. The debate over codes of conduct for transnational corporations exemplified the problem IGO agendas could create for the United States. The growing use of IGOs by other states to serve their interests combined with decreased U.S. control over agendas have forced American bureaucrats increasingly to deal with items they would otherwise have ignored.

In addition, member states such as the United States adapt their decision-making and implementation processes to accommodate IGO participation, creating representational structures and allocating budgetary resources.[10] In the early postwar period such bureaucratic and fiscal changes had little impact on overall policy. Growth in the number of IGOs and increased differentiation of issues have led to the multiplication of agencies within the U.S. government dealing with aspects of the same issue area. Interagency and ad hoc groups have been created to coordinate representation and decision making in areas of overlapping responsibility.

Finally, IGOs may appeal to the agendas and concerns of domestic nongovernmental groups. Such groups, so pervasive in pluralist societies, are important actors in the political process, influencing members of Congress, bureaucrats, and decision makers. The number of such groups in the United States has increased significantly in recent years. Their strategies for promoting their own interests, forming coalitions, and utilizing links to IGOs have become more sophisticated. For example, antiapartheid groups in the United States, spurred by international efforts to effect change in South Africa and by desire to influence U.S. government policies, have begun to have an impact at federal, state, and local levels of government and in the private sector (Love 1985).

Debate over the role of multilateralism in U.S. foreign policy has been fueled by the perceived decrease in the utility of IGOs as instruments of U.S. policies and the perceived increase in the constraints IGOs impose on the United States. Having suggested key ways in which the relationships between the United States and IGOs may be changed, we now explore alternative explanations for these changes.

Contending Explanations for Changes in Instrumentality and Influence

If changes have occurred in the relationships between the United States and IGOs, how can these changes be explained? We consider four alternative explanations: the decline in the overall power of the United States, characteristics of the particular issue areas, properties of specific international organizations, and domestic political factors. The relative adequacy of each of these explanations and the linkages among them are likely to vary among cases. Other factors, including exogenous environmental variables, may provide additional explanatory power in specific cases.

Overall Decline in U.S. Power

The most all-encompassing explanation for change is that the overall power of the United States has declined relative to that of other nations,[11] adversely affecting its ability to influence outcomes and making it more sensitive—even vulnerable—to IGO influences. Thus some of the changes in America's relationships with IGOs may be linked to larger shifts in the relative power (particularly economic and military) of the United States and other nations. This explanation is predicated on the argument that the United States was willing "to invest resources in institutions in order to ensure that its preferred rules [would] guide the behavior of other countries" (Keohane 1984: 46). In other words, IGOs offered a way of creating structures compatible with American notions of political and economic order and favorable to the promotion of American interests. Thus U.S. support of IGOs was designed to nurture and guarantee American political and economic dominance based on the notion of the "rightness" and universal applicability of American ways of doing things and American interests. U.S. dominance ensured that there was a high degree of congruence between the U.S. worldview and its strategies for multilateral cooperation. Indeed, as Nicholas noted, the "latent magnetism of American power" was often sufficient basis for influence particularly in the United Nations (1975: 200). The difficulty of changing decision-making structures ensured compatible outcomes for a long time to come—even after the ability of the United States to gain majorities for its preferred outcomes declined. The positive use of financial resources influenced the implementation of IGO outputs as well as the very structure of many organizations.

During the 1970s, however, there was a decline in the United States' relative economic and military position. World trade increased in importance to U.S. GNP while both U.S. trade and U.S. GDP were declining as percentages of world totals. The margin of U.S. military superiority has also declined relative to others as evidenced by comparisons of U.S. and Soviet military capabilities, the increased capabilities of many developing countries, and the increased share of the burden of alliance defense borne by the European members of NATO. This decline in relative resources has affected the ability of the United States to control outcomes generally and altered the patterns of instrumentality and influence in some IGOs.

The relative economic and military decline of the United States was symbolized in the rise of Organization of Petroleum-Exporting Countries (OPEC) in the economic sphere and the U.S. withdrawal from Vietnam in the military arena. The less developed countries (LDC), with the impetus of "cartel power," tested and challenged the United States in many international forums in the 1970s, adding a plethora of new items to many IGO agendas (adding new IGOs as well). Their demands for a New International Economic Order (NIEO) confronted the United States with a debate over the very structure of the international economic system that the United States had helped to shape. Theirs was a quintessentially multilateral strategy: the cohesion of a large group of states (the Group of 77) utilizing the global IGOs wherein one-state, one-vote decision processes maximized their impact (Hart 1983; Krasner 1985).

Simultaneously the U.S. debacle in Vietnam was widely perceived as confirmation of decreased American ability and willingness to exert power and evidence of the erosion of consensus within the United States on the broad goals of American foreign policy. As Holsti and Rosenau suggest,

> The war in Vietnam fostered a situation reminiscent of the 1930s when there was little agreement on such basic issues as the nature of the international system, America's national interests and the most likely threats to them, and the appropriate strategies to promote these interests. (1986: 376)

The erosion of America's preponderant economic and military capabilities, however, has not meant the end of the United States' ability to exert influence and leadership; to apply what are still in most cases superior resources to ensure desired ends. Oye (1987) notes that "as direct control over the actions of other nations becomes difficult, the prosperity and security of the United States increasingly depend on how other nations define their interests and how the United States adjusts to its changing position in the international system" (pp. 20–21).

As a result at least *some* IGOs are more likely to influence U.S. policies and to affect policymaking processes to a greater extent. Some IGOs have become more salient instruments of American policy; others, less. The techniques for utilizing IGOs as instruments of U.S. policies are likely to continue to change as U.S. power to affect outcomes diminishes.

Yet the decline in overall American power is itself a subject of debate.[12] Russett (1985: 230) argues that although there has been some decline in America's economic power base, "cultural hegemony provides long-term influence that persists. . . . It is among the primary reasons why a decline in dominance over material power has not been reflected in an equivalent loss of control over outcomes." If this view holds, then some IGOs should be just as useful as instruments of American policies in the 1980s as in the 1950s but should have more influence on U.S. policies. The changes in patterns of instrumentality and influence may reflect alterations in the nature of the issue area, however, or in the characteristics of the IGO itself, rather than the decline of American power.

Issue Area Characteristics

David Baldwin (1979: 193) has suggested, "It is time to recognize that the notion of a single overall international power structure unrelated to any particular issue-area is based on a concept of power that is virtually meaningless." If there is no uniform pattern of change across issues, issue area characteristics may explain U.S.-IGO relationships better than a general theory of declining power.

Although a number of different categorizations have been proposed, issue areas have typically been distinguished along substantive lines: security, economics, and social welfare.[13] Like other scholars who have used this distinction, we suggest that IGOs functioning in the same issue area—for example, economics or security—may have more in common with one another than with those functioning in other issue areas and that characteristics of each issue area shape both policy processes and outputs. If this contention is valid, we would expect the patterns of IGO instrumentality and influence to be more similar within a given issue area than across different areas.

Within issue areas two dimensions appear to be most relevant in explaining changing relations between the United States and IGOs: the content of the ideology prevalent among the majority of member states and secretariat, and the degree to which U.S. national interests are affected by activities of the IGO. The U.S. ability to affect IGO outcomes hinges on the congruity between American ideology and that of the dominant coalition(s) in IGOs as well as on the extent of American interest in the particular issue area and, hence, in the work of a particular IGO.

The United States has consistently promoted economic and political liberalism domestically and internationally. Economic liberalism is based on the belief that economic relations are basically harmonious both between domestic actors and "true national interest and cosmopolitan economic interest" (Gilpin 1975: 26). The goal of economic activity is maximization of *global* welfare, best achieved when there is separation between politics and economics and an open trade system. "The state should not interfere with economic transactions across national boundaries" (Gilpin 1975: 26). However, the state is instrumental to the achievement of political liberalism. Both at home and abroad the state ought to promote belief in democracy, freedom, equality, progress, and perfectibility of human institutions. The United States had assumed global responsibility as the guardian of freedom and morality (Crabb 1976: 35–36; Kegley and Wittkopf 1987: 40) Such beliefs, though certainly not consistently articulated across time, administrations, or issue areas, have motivated U.S. support of postwar global organizations whose charters embodied these principles.

Increasingly in recent years the United States has tended to adopt the rhetoric of liberalism in its efforts to counteract policies approved by the numerically dominant coalitions within a number of IGOs and promoted by secretariats in some cases. In the economic area the Group of 77 has supported principles and policies calling for more authoritative allocation, believing, according to Krasner (1985: 5), that economic regulation can soften market failure and ensure predictable policies not achievable under liberalism. In the political area this same coalition has challenged the notion that the United States has a monopoly on ensuring democracy, freedom, or equality. The stated goals of the coalition include efforts to reshape IGO structures to give them greater influence over outcomes and to promote their own approaches to these values. In the face of this ideological conflict, it is inevitable that the U.S. ability to influence the numerically dominant coalitions in many IGOs has declined and that the likelihood of such coalitions producing norms and even rules unacceptable to the United States—as happened with the Law of the Sea—has grown. This has, in turn, fueled doubts in the United States about the utility of many IGOs.

Certainly the intensity and relative importance of interests may vary over time. Security-related interests (territorial integrity, protection of key allies) may be primary[14] given that for any nation, the costs of inattention to security or the risks of "defection" are great. Beyond basic issues of security, however, the priority attached to different issue areas is likely to vary as exogenous circumstances make the issue more or less salient to foreign policy decision makers and to different domestic groups. Thus changes in American priorities over time may mean that what the United States seeks to achieve through its participation in IGOs and the extent to which it is influenced change also. The patterns of IGO instrumentality and influence may be shaped by fluctuations (or constancy) in the issue area salience. Within the threefold categorization of issue areas, the U.S. government continues to attach greatest importance to security issues because of the perceived Soviet threat, somewhat less but increasing importance to economic issues, and considerably less to social welfare issues. Hence IGOs that predominantly deal with social welfare rather than security issues are considered less salient instruments of American policies and have less impact.

The relevance of issue area to the explanation of change depends, then, on the degree of congruity between the ideology of the United States and that of the dominant coalition within an IGO and on the degree of American interest in the issue area. Changes in either dimension will likely alter American perceptions of the utility of particular IGOs for achieving American objectives. However, as was noted earlier, the issue area will also influence the nature and structure of IGOs in that area. Therefore such characteristics of IGOs offer another explanation for changing patterns of IGO instrumentality and influence.

Characteristics of the IGO

Three characteristics of IGOs are likely to be salient to the relationships between the United States and IGOs: membership, role and composition of secretariats, and tasks. The process of decolonization and the resulting increase in the number of independent states have augmented the memberships of all global IGOs and have also contributed to growth in the number of IGOs. The resulting changes in voting patterns and dominant coalitions have been amply discussed elsewhere, as have changes in the composition and backgrounds of secretariat personnel and the types of outputs sought from many IGOs (Jacobson 1984). Although the United States was part of the dominant coalition in almost all IGOs on most issues until the early 1960s, increasingly in many organizations since then it has been more frequently in the minority and frequently isolated. Under such conditions one would expect to see changing patterns of instrumentality and influence. In cases in which the United States remains part of a dominant coalition, it is most likely because of limited membership or the nature of its voting arrangements (weighted or restrictive). In such cases there may be less perceptible changes in the patterns.

The geographic background, education, and training of the secretariat personnel may also be important in explaining patterns of instrumentality and influence. Secretariats composed largely of specialized, technical personnel performing essentially nonpolitical tasks would be expected to be relatively immune from the effects of shifting political coalitions and ideologies. However, other secretariats whose personnel have non-technical backgrounds would be more likely to reflect, if not represent, changing constituencies. Increased geographic diversity alone is unlikely to be important.

The character of the executive head is also an important factor.[15] In particular, how much autonomy does a director-general have? Does he use the authority of his office and the political resources to act independently? Or has he been at the beck and call of coalitions of member states? Effective leadership requires consideration of both the coalition(s) that dominates voting in the organization and the coalition that provides the bulk of financial resources.

Finally, IGO tasks, like those of governments and other organizations, can be grouped into categories. The tasks include information gathering, analysis, and dissemination; rule creation and enforcement; and redistribution of resources. The types of tasks and their expected effects may also be factors explaining the patterns of U.S.-IGO participation. Although many IGOs gather and disseminate information, some IGOs are largely devoted to these discrete tasks from which all states may benefit at relatively low political cost. Except when politically charged information such as that on human rights violations is at stake, these IGO activities do not usually provoke opposition from members, including the United States. If IGOs engage in regulatory tasks, making and enforcing rules or standards, however, their impact is likely to be greater for member countries or affected subgroups. The United States has accepted and even promoted some regulations as necessary aspects of regime building (for example, GATT rules) or standard setting (such as international health regulations). Some regulations may impinge on the largely unregulated activities of special groups (for example, multinational corporations) with mixed effects. Finally, if the tasks of an organization involve technology and resource transfers such as those proposed within the NIEO, they are likely to be hotly contested because such outputs are often designed to change the fundamental bases of the institutions themselves and, by altering the rules of the game, to redistribute power.

IGO structures and characteristics have themselves changed in response to the demands of new dominant coalitions. Some IGOs have shifted from predominantly information-gathering to more regulatory and redistributive tasks. When such changes have occurred, the United States may have found organizations less useful for American policy objectives and their outputs more at odds with American preferences. And as IGOs take more actions of a redistributive or regulatory nature, "the U.S. policy-making process tends increasingly to embrace more actors in order to accommodate the growing number of national interests affected by these issues" (Rapkin and Avery 1982: 233). Thus domestic political factors become more important to explanations of the patterns of interaction between the United States and specific IGOs.

Domestic Political Factors

The dynamics of American domestic political processes provide numerous possibilities for explaining patterns of change in instrumentality and influence. We have singled out three potentially powerful factors: changing relations between the executive and legislative branches of government, changing involvement of interest groups, and differences across presidential administrations.

The relationship between the legislative and executive branches may alter the decision-making process, thereby affecting foreign policy outputs. Although the separation of powers was established by the Constitution, the relative power of the branches has varied. In recent years as a consequence of the Vietnam War and Watergate, Congress has reasserted its prerogatives and imposed constraints on the freedom of the executive branch to conduct foreign policy. Among other actions, Congress has more closely scrutinized appropriations for IGOs. Studies from the General Accounting Office (GAO) have analyzed U.S. participation in IGOs, examining such questions as whether the IGO has performed its specified task in preparation for replenishment discussions, whether U.S. suggestions for evaluation have been implemented by various IGOs, and whether American citizens have benefited from U.S. participation in the IGO.[16] The Kassebaum Amendment of 1983 captured the depth of congressional skepticism of the value of the UN system as a whole by stipulating that the United States should pay no more than 20 percent of the annual assessed costs of the organization and its specialized agencies. The legislation also mandated the withholding of at least 20 percent of 1987 contributions unless weighted or restricted voting procedures were adopted for budgetary matters.[17] Much to the surprise of many in the Reagan administration, the UN passed a reform package in December 1986 that even then President Reagan hailed as "a historic step." For the foreseeable future, however, regardless of changes in the UN and its agencies or the attitudes in the White House, Congress is likely to see contributions to IGOs as sources of cuts in the budget deficits.

In addition, Congress has attached amendments to appropriations bills binding U.S. representatives in IGOs to particular policies. For example, in the case of the multilateral development banks, the Gonzalez Amendment (1972) required American representatives to oppose loans to countries that expropriated American investments. The Harkin Amendment (1976) required representatives to vote against loans to countries that consistently engaged in gross violations of internationally recognized human rights (Schoultz 1982; U.S. Senate 1977). Congress has linked appropriations to guidelines concerning the role of women and environmental considerations. In short, although Congress has always harbored a degree of skepticism, even opposition, to multilateralism, these sentiments have grown since 1970, fueled by a sense that in at least certain prominent cases such as the UN and UNESCO, the United States has been funding organizations in which the majorities were distinctly hostile to the United States. Thus the general effect of a more assertive Congress has been to limit U.S.-IGO involvement and to make the United States a less flexible international actor.

Likewise, domestic interest groups may be responsible for the changing U.S.-IGO relationships. The traditionally pluralistic nature of interest group involvement in American politics has been augmented in recent years by the emergence of new groups, including political action committees (PACs). As Ornstein and Edler (1978: 5–6) note,

> In the 1970s, as a result of the turmoil of Vietnam, Watergate, and other political upheavals, the American political process became more decentralized, more active, more open to public scrutiny and pressure, and more diffused generally. Interest groups responded with a concomitant increase in numbers as well as in the scope and intensity of political activity.

This increase in the number, scope, and intensity of political activity may have also had effects on U.S.-IGO relationships. When an issue is put on an IGO agenda and the U.S. government is in the process of determining its position, interest groups may try to influence that position, lobbying both the legislative and executive branches. In recent years as IGOs have considered more regulatory and redistributive policies and activities that would impinge on specific interests, domestic groups have become quite active, trying to convince the U.S. government to vote for or against the items. Yet the role of domestic groups is highly issue- and IGO-specific. Therefore, it is not possible to say that the proliferation of active domestic groups in the United States has changed U.S.-IGO relations in one direction. What does seem evident is that such activity increases the perception of others in the world that there is often sharp division and lack of consensus about U.S.-IGO policy no matter what position the administration assumes.

Finally, differences between presidential administrations account for some of the variation. The policy debate over the U.S. role in IGOs and the U.S. approach to multilateralism more generally came sharply to the fore after the election of Ronald Reagan. Although the catalysts for change were present fully a decade earlier, the issues crystallized during the Reagan administration with the rejection of the Law of the Sea Convention, the lone negative vote against WHO's infant formula code, the withdrawal from UNESCO, the administration's negative attitude toward multilateralism, and its reevalutation of U.S. participation in a number of IGOs.

Whether any of these three domestic political factors actually improves our explanation of the patterns of change in IGO instrumentality and influence will depend on the strength of commitment to influence U.S. multilateral policy and ability to mobilize constituencies for such issues. During the immediate postwar years, when the United States could fairly well count on success in using IGOs and IGO influence on the United States itself was nominal, the commitment or motivation of domestic political actors, including the Congress and domestic interest groups, to become involved with multilateral issues was probably low. When the United States faced more challenges to its interests and domination and IGOs brooked proposals unpopular in the United States, the motivation of the Congress, the executive branch, and domestic groups to intervene increased. Thus the trend toward democratization in U.S. foreign policy has resulted in more active participation in both the formulation and content of that policy.

The changing patterns of U.S.-IGO relationships are unlikely to be explained by a single set of factors. Some of the developments that have contributed to the erosion of America's relative economic and military capability have also been reflected in changing issue area and IGO characteristics and in shifting domestic political factors. To assess the relative potency of the four clusters of explanatory variables and to explore their interrelationships requires the elaboration of both the similarities and differences in the patterns of influence and instrumentality in different IGOs and regimes. We therefore turn to a brief discussion of methodology that will be applied in the remainder of this volume.

Methodological Approach

We have chosen to use case studies of U.S. participation in a number of different IGOs to determine whether there has in fact been a change in the U.S. use of IGOs as instruments of policy and in IGOs' influence on the United States. The IGOs are drawn from three broad issue areas: security (UN, IAEA, NATO, and OAS), economics (GATT, IMF, and World

Bank), and social policy (WHO and UNESCO). In addition, with respect to human rights and food, the focus is on the regime rather than any one IGO because several IGOs deal with related aspects of the problem.

Each of the case studies examines the questions regarding patterns of instrumentality and influence, seeking to determine how those patterns may have changed since 1970. Each seeks explanation of the patterns in one or more of the four clusters of explanatory variables: declining relative power, characteristics of the issue area and of the IGO, or domestic political factors. Thus in the language of Alexander George, we seek "structured focused comparison"—focused "because it deals selectively with only certain aspects of the . . . case" and "structured because it employs general questions to guide the data collection and analysis." Yet as George wisely suggests,

> Asking the same questions of each case does not prevent the investigator from asking specific questions of each case as well to bring out idiosyncratic features that are of possible interest in and of themselves, if not also for theory development. (1979: 61–62)

The case studies explore the nature, degree, and sources of change in the relationships between the United States and various IGOs or regimes. Why, when, and how has one state in particular—and a uniquely important one at that—chosen international organizations as instruments of its statecraft? What influence have multilateral institutions had on U.S. policies and policymaking processes? What patterns emerge within and across the various IGOs and regimes examined? How do these patterns enhance conceptual understanding of the relationships among states, IGOs, and multilateral cooperation? Answers to these questions will illumine the dynamic two-way flow of influence between national and international arenas.

Notes

1. For an insightful new approach to such interactions, see Putnam (1988). Earlier treatments include Haas (1958), Rosenau (1969), Katzenstein (1976), and Gourevitch (1978).

2. The concept of international regime is not universally accepted. For a critical review, see Strange (1982). There has also on occasion been both a tendency to posit a regime where none can be said to exist on the basis of the accepted definition, and also a danger of reifying regimes as actors. See Rosenau (1986).

3. The concept of "habit" in international affairs appears in a number of more recent works of James N. Rosenau. See, for example, Rosenau (1986). For a related discussion, see Young (1986).

4. The literature on learning and socialization of IGO delegates and representatives is

voluminous. See, among others, Alger (1965), Karns (1977), Riggs (1977), Ernst (1978), and Peck (1979).

5. On the subject of obedience to international laws and rules, see, among others, Cohen (1981) and Henkin (1979).

6. The importance of institutions in political development is discussed in Huntingon (1968).

7. The creation of IGOs also served domestic political purposes for the United States. Among those was the creation of a "web" of international "entanglements" that made it difficult for future administrations to return to more isolationist policies (private communication from Lawrence S. Finkelstein).

8. Inis L. Claude (1967) once suggested that the test of U.S. support for international organizations would come when the United States found itself in the position of losing and of being asked to support programs and activities which it regarded as detrimental to its interests. That support was tested by a variety of "shocks" at the UN, UNESCO, ITU, ILO, and elsewhere in the 1970s.

9. On the congruence of many international with national (U.S.) rules, see Henkin (1979) and Keohane (1984).

10. For some interesting and suggestive work on the effects of interdependence on national policymaking structures and budgets, see Sundelius (1984).

11. The literature of American dominance or "hegemony" is large. See, among others, Kennedy (1987), Keohane (1980), and Krasner (1982a).

12. For debate over whether American hegemony has declined and its implications, see Russett (1985), Snidal (1985), and Huntington (1988–89).

13. On the subject of issue areas, see Lowi (1964), Zimmerman (1973), Potter (1980), and Mansbach and Vasquez (1981).

14. Protagonists of the "realist" perspective in the "great debate" of the early postwar period charged the "idealists," however, with denigrating the vitalness of those interests.

15. On the roles of IGO executive heads, see Siotis (1963), Gordenker (1967), and Cox (1969).

16. See, for example, U.S. General Accounting Office (1981), U.S. Report to the Congress by the Comptroller General (1978, 1980).

17. Public Law 99-177 (99 Stat. 1037) Kassebaum Amendment to Senate 1342, Department of State Authorization 1983), Public Debt Limit Increase; Balanced Budget and Emergency Deficit Control Act of 1985. For an assessment of the goals and effects of both the Kassebaum and Gramm-Rudman Amendments, see Williams (1987: 95–105).

References

Alger, Chadwick F. (1965). "Personal Contact in Intergovernmental Organizations." In Herbert C. Kelman, ed., *International Behavior: A Social-Psychological Analysis*. New York: Holt, Rinehart & Winston, 523–47.

Axelrod, Robert, and Robert O. Keohane (1985). "Achieving Cooperation under Anarchy: Strategies and Institutions." *World Politics*, 38(October), 226–54.

Baldwin, David A. (1979). "Power Analysis and World Politics: New Trends versus Old Tendencies." *World Politics*, 31(January), 161–94.

——— (1985). *Economic Statecraft*. Princeton: Princeton University Press.

Claude, Inis L., Jr. (1967). *The Changing United Nations*. New York: Random House.

Cohen, Raymond (1981). *International Politics: The Rules of the Game*. New York: Longman.

Cox, Robert W. (1969). "The Executive Head: An Essay on Leadership in International Organization." *International Organization*, 23(Spring), 205–30.

Crabb, Cecil V., Jr. (1976). *Policy-Makers and Critics: Conflicting Theories of American Foreign Policy*. New York: Praeger.

Ernst, Manfred E. (1978). "Attitudes of Diplomats and the United Nations: The Effects of Organizational Participation on the Evaluation of the Organization." *International Organization*, 32(Autumn), 1037–44.

George, Alexander L. (1979). "Case Studies and Theory Development: The Method of Structured, Focused Comparison." In Paul Gordon Lauren, ed., *Diplomacy: New Approaches in History, Theory, and Policy*. New York: Free Press, 43–68.

Gilpin, Robert (1975). *U.S. Power and the Multinational Corporation: The Political Economy of Foreign Direct Investment*. New York: Basic Books.

Gordenker, Leon (1967). *The UN Secretary General and the Maintenance of Peace*. New York: Columbia University Press.

Gourevitch, Peter (1978). "The Second Image Reversed: The International Sources of Domestic Politics." *International Organization*, 32(Autumn), 881–911.

Gowa, Joanne (1986). "Anarchy, Egoism, and Third Images: The Evolution of Cooperation and International Relations." *International Organization*, 40(Winter), 67–86.

Haas, Ernst B. (1958). *The Uniting of Europe: Political, Social, and Economic Forces, 1950–1957*. Stanford: Stanford University Press.

——— (1983). "Regime Decay: Conflict Management and International Organizations, 1945–1981." *International Organization*, 37(Spring), 189–256.

Hart, Jeffrey (1983). *The New International Economic Order*. New York: Macmillan.

Henkin, Louis (1979). *How Nations Behave: Law and Foreign Policy*. 2d ed. New York: Columbia University Press.

Holsti, Ole R., and James N. Rosenau (1986). "Consensus Lost, Consensus Regained? Foreign Policy Beliefs of American Leaders, 1976–1980." *International Studies Quarterly*, 30(December), 375–409.

Hopkins, Raymond F. (1976). "The International Role of 'Domestic' Bureaucracy." *International Organization*, 30(Summer), 405–32.

Huntington, Samuel P. (1968). *Political Order in Changing Societies*. New Haven, CT: Yale University Press.

——— (1988–89). "The U.S.—Decline or Renewal?" *Foreign Affairs*, 67(2), 76–96.

Jacobson, Harold K. (1984). *Networks of Interdependence: International Organizations and the Global Political System*. 2d ed. New York: Alfred A. Knopf.

Jacobson, Harold K., William M. Reisinger, and Todd Mathers (1986). "National Entanglements in International Governmental Organizations." *American Political Science Review*, 80(March), 141–60.

Karns, David A. (1977). "The Effects of Interparliamentary Meetings on the Foreign Policy Attitudes of United States Congressmen." *International Organization*, 31(Summer), 497–514.

Karns, Margaret P., and Karen A. Mingst (1987). "International Organizations and Foreign Policy: Influence and Instrumentality." In Charles F. Hermann, Charles W. Kegley, Jr., and James N. Rosenau, eds., *New Directions in Foreign Policy*. Boston: Unwin Hyman, 454–74.

Katzenstein, Peter J. (1976). "International Relations and Domestic Structures: Foreign Economic Policies of Advanced Industrial States." *International Organization*, 30(Winter), 1–45.

Kegley, Charles W., Jr., and Eugene R. Wittkopf (1987). *American Foreign Policy: Pattern and Process*. 3d ed. New York: St. Martin's Press.

Kennedy, Paul (1987). *The Rise and Fall of the Great Powers: Economic Change and Military Conflict from 1500 to 2000*. New York: Random House.

Keohane, Robert O. (1980). "The Theory of Hegemonic Stability and Changes in International Economic Regimes, 1967–1977." In Ole R. Holsti, Randolph M. Siverson, and Alexander George, eds., *Change in the International System*. Boulder, CO: Westview Press, 131–62.

——— (1984). *After Hegemony: Cooperation and Discord in the World Political Economy*. Princeton: Princeton University Press.

——— (1986). "Reciprocity in International Relations." *International Organization*, 40(Winter), 1–27.

Keohane, Robert O., and Joseph S. Nye, Jr. (1977). *Power and Interdependence: World Politics in Transition*. Boston: Little, Brown.

Krasner, Stephen D. (1982a). "American Policy and Global Economic Stability." In David P. Rapkin and William Avery, eds., *America in a Changing World Political Economy*. New York: Longman, 29–48.

——— (1982b). "Structural Causes and Regime Consequences: Regimes as Intervening Variables." In Stephen D. Krasner, ed., *International Regimes*. Ithaca, NY: Cornell University Press, 1–21.

——— (1985). *Structural Conflict: The Third World against Global Liberalism*. Berkeley: University of California Press.

Kratochwil, Friedrich (1984). "The Force of Prescriptions." *International Organization*, 38(Autumn), 685–708.

Kratochwil, Friedrich, and John Gerard Ruggie (1986). "International Organization: A State of the Art on an Art of the State." *International Organization*, 40(Autumn), 753–76.

Love, Janice (1985). *The U.S. Anti-Apartheid Movement: Local Activism in Global Politics*. New York: Praeger.

Lowi, Theodore (1964). "American Business, Public Policy, Case Studies, and Political Theory." *World Politics*, 16(July), 677–715.

Mansbach, Richard W., and John A. Vasquez (1981). *In Search of Theory: A New Paradigm for Global Politics*. New York: Columbia University Press.

Nicholas, H. G. (1975). *The United Nations as a Political Institution*. 5th ed. London: Oxford University Press.

Ornstein, Norman J., and Shirley Edler (1978). *Interest Groups, Lobbying, and Policymaking*. Washington: Congressional Quarterly Press.

Oye, Kenneth A. (1987). "Constrained Confidence and the Evolution of Reagan Foreign Policy." In Kenneth A. Oye, Robert J. Lieber, and Donald Rothchild, et al., *Eagle Resurgent: The Reagan Era in American Foreign Policy*. Boston: Little, Brown, 3–39.

Peck, Richard (1979). "Socialization of Permanent Representatives in the United Nations: Some Evidence." *International Organization*, 33(Summer), 365–90.

Potter, William C. (1980). "Issue Area and Foreign Policy Analysis." *International Organization*, 34(Summer), 405–28.

Putnam, Robert D. (1988). "Diplomacy and Domestic Politics: The Logic of Two-Level Games." *International Organization*, 42(Summer), 427–60.

Rapkin, David P., and William P. Avery (1982). "America in the World Political Economy: Prognoses, Prescriptions, and Questions for Future Research." In William P. Avery and David P. Rapkin, eds., *America in a Changing World Political Economy*. New York: Longman, 227–40.

Riggs, Robert E. (1977). "One Small Step for Functionalism: UN Participation and Congressional Attitude Change." *International Organization*, 31(Summer), 41–50.

Rosenau, James (1969). "Toward the Study of National-International Linkages." In James Rosenau, ed., *Linkage Politics: Essays on the Convergence of National and International Systems*. New York: Free Press, 44–63.

—— (1986). "Before Cooperation: Hegemons, Regimes and Habit-Driven Actors in World Politics." *International Organization*, 40(Autumn), 849–94.

Russett, Bruce (1985). "The Mysterious Case of Vanishing Hegemony: Or, Is Mark Twain Really Dead?" *International Organization*, 39(Spring), 207–32.

Schoultz, Lars (1982). "Politics, Economics and U.S. Participation in Multilateral Development Banks." *International Organization*, 36(Summer), 537–74.

Siotis, Jean (1963). *Essai sur le Secretariat Internationale*. Geneva: Droz.

Snidal, Duncan (1985). "The Limits of Hegemonic Stability Theory." *International Organization*, 39(Autumn), 579–614.

Stoessinger, John G. (1977). *The United Nations and the Superpowers: China, Russia, and America*. New York: Random House.

Strange, Susan (1982). "Cave! Hic Dragones: A Critique of Regime Analysis." In Stephen D. Krasner, ed., *International Regimes*. Ithaca, NY: Cornell University Press, 279–96.

Sundelius, Bengt (1984). "Foreign Policy Making in the Nordic Countries: An Introduction." *Cooperation and Conflict*, 19, 87–120.

U.S. Senate, Staff Report to the Subcommittee on Foreign Assistance of the Committee on Foreign Relations (1977). *U.S. Policy and the Multilateral Banks: Politicization and Effectiveness*. Washington, DC: U.S. Government Printing Office.

U.S. General Accounting Office (1981). *Status Report on U.S. Participation in the International Fund for Agricultural Development* (GA1.13; ID-81-33, March 27). Washington, DC: U.S. Government Printing Office.

U.S. Report to the Congress by the Comptroller General of the United States (1978). *Independent Review and Evaluation of the Asian Development Bank* (GA1.13; ID-81-30, April 21). Washington, DC: U.S. Government Printing Office.

—— (1980). *American Employment Generally Favorable at International Financial Institution* (GA1.13; ID-81-3, December 10). Washington, DC: U.S. Government Printing Office.

Williams, Douglas (1987). *The Specialized Agencies and the United Nations: The System in Crisis*. New York: St. Martin's Press.

Young, Oran (1986). "International Regimes: Toward a New Theory of Institutions." *World Politics*, 39(October), 104–22.

Zimmerman, William (1973). "Issue Areas and Foreign Policy Process: A Research Note in Search of a General Theory." *American Political Science Review*, 67(December), 1204–12.

CHAPTER TWO

U.S. Military Security Policies: The Role and Influence of IGOs

Harold K. Jacobson

Throughout the period since World War II international governmental organizations have played an important though not exclusive role in U.S. military security policies and have exerted significant influence on these policies. U.S. security has traditionally been defined as preserving the territorial integrity and political independence of the United States, protecting U.S. interests abroad, and promoting a global milieu in which the U.S. economy and polity could prosper. When governmental officials have gone beyond this abstract conception, U.S. security has been defined pragmatically in response to particular perceived threats.

The role of IGOs in U.S. security policies during the post–World War II period has evolved in response particularly to U.S. perceptions of threat and to the changing character of IGOs, especially as these changes have impinged on the ability of the United States to prevail within the relevant institutions. International governmental organizations have affected the way in which the United States has defined its security and the choices that the United States has made with respect to the security policies it has pursued. IGOs have ameliorated some U.S. security problems but have also exacerbated others, at least in the short run. This chapter explores these issues.[1]

The Vision and Reality of the Post–World War II Order

In the abstract vision that the United States had for the postwar order, the United Nations was to be the centerpiece of U.S. security policy.

Consequently the U.S. government devoted considerable effort to establishing the UN (U.S. Department of State 1950). The adjective *abstract*, however, is a crucially important qualification because the United States placed emphasis on the UN in postwar planning in the absence of any clearly perceived threat to U.S. security. Even then, however, although the UN was designed to promote a milieu favorable to U.S. interests, it was viewed as a tool rather than a constraint on U.S. policy, and it was always seen as only one of many foundations of a postwar order.

The UN Charter contained ample evidence of U.S. (and others') hesitancy to commit itself to the new institution and of a strong U.S. desire to retain substantial freedom of action to pursue whatever security policies it might choose (Russell 1958). Article 107 allowed the United States to conclude World War II without reference to the UN. Articles 23 and 27 permitted the United States to block UN action by casting a veto in the Security Council. Article 51 permitted the United States to take individual and collective self-defense action.

It was also clear that the United States had no intention of allowing the United Nations to be the sole international institution that would deal with security issues. The United States always favored special institutional arrangements to deal with security in the Western Hemisphere, the area traditionally proclaimed and generally regarded as the U.S. sphere of influence. Chapter VIII on Regional Arrangements was included in the UN Charter to permit this.

Despite U.S. hopes that the United Nations would ensure its own and global security, as U.S. policymakers increasingly perceived a specific threat to U.S. security in place of the undefined threat for which the United Nations had been designed, the organization's inadequacy as an instrument to deal with this problem became more and more apparent. U.S. security policy had to be redefined; the UN could no longer be the centerpiece.

Starting as early as the closing days of World War II, growing numbers of U.S. policymakers came to believe that the Soviet Union sought to expand its power and influence and that such expansion would constitute a serious threat to U.S. security (Gaddis 1972). By mid-1947 containing the Soviet Union had become the dominant motif of U.S. security policy. When the Soviet Union detonated a nuclear device in 1949 and began to develop an arsenal of nuclear weapons that would give it the capacity to attack and devastate the continental United States, the USSR posed an unprecedented threat to U.S. security. Never before had U.S. territory been so vulnerable. Preventing a Soviet nuclear attack on the United States became a singularly important goal of U.S. security policy.

Goals and Instrumentalities of U.S. Security Policy

In the new, more specific definition of U.S. security that was developed in the late 1940s and early 1950s, three clear goals emerged: (1) preventing a nuclear attack on the United States; (2) maintaining close ties with Canada, Western Europe, and Japan—the states that had the greatest industrial potential and with which the United States had the most extensive trading relationships—and keeping these states out of the Soviet orbit; and (3) promoting alignment with the West among Third World states, or at least ensuring their neutrality between East and West and ensuring that conflicts among these states did not spark a direct Soviet-American clash.

U.S. policymakers maintained that these three goals were oriented toward promoting the same basic concept of an international political order that the United Nations had been designed to serve: an international order that protected the territorial and political integrity of its component sovereign states, outlawed change through violence, and promoted peaceful change (Truman 1956). The United Nations as originally conceived, however, assumed Soviet-American cooperation. In contrast, the instrumentalities chosen to implement the three specific goals assumed substantial Soviet-American conflict. In pursuing its three major security goals the United States made ample use of the latitude that the UN Charter allowed for taking actions outside the UN and creating additional institutions.

U.S. policymakers saw IGOs as being only marginally relevant to the first goal: preventing a nuclear attack on the United States. They saw U.S. unilateral policies and U.S. strategic nuclear forces as the most reliable mechanisms for pursuing this task. These policies were justified as falling within the legitimate self-defense actions permitted under Article 51 of the UN Charter.

A newly created, completely unanticipated, and unique IGO—the North Atlantic Treaty Organization (NATO)—became the principal instrument for promoting the military security of Canada and Western Europe; a bilateral alliance was chosen to protect Japan. Established in 1949, NATO is a bureaucratized and institutionalized peacetime alliance, something never previously attempted. U.S. policymakers maintained that the creation of NATO and other alliances were also justifiable actions within the terms of Article 51.

Created in 1948 to provide a broad framework for inter-American cooperation, the Organization of American States (OAS) was directly relevant to the third goal. The OAS fit the definition of the regional organization contained in Chapter VIII of the Charter.

The UN continued to have a role in U.S. security policy, primarily as an instrument for achieving the third goal, though it and the agencies of the

UN system were also used to some extent in pursuit of the other two goals. In contrast to the original U.S. vision of the postwar order, the UN's actual role in U.S. efforts to gain security was greatly diminished.

By 1950 the basic goals of U.S. security policy had been defined, and multifaceted and differentiated roles had been set for several IGOs in strategies to obtain these goals. These roles were more varied than that envisaged for the UN in U.S. postwar planning, and they were designed so that the relevant institutions would be able to make decisions in circumstances when the UN could not because of the Soviet Union's veto power. NATO was a military alliance designed to counter a perceived threat in a specified geographical area. OAS was simultaneously an alliance against extraregional threats, a geographically limited collective security system, and a multipurpose IGO with a broad mandate.

Because these varied roles stemmed from the incapacity of the UN to implement the broad security role originally assigned to it in U.S. plans, this chapter has a broad focus rather than concentrating on only one institution or role. This allows the possibility of asking in the concluding section whether the United Nations could assume a role in U.S. security policy closer to that contained in the vision of U.S. postwar planning should the Soviet-American conflict abate. Moreover, there is a seamless quality to security policy. One aspect inevitably has ramifications for other aspects. Because of its broad focus the chapter is more a survey than an in-depth analysis. Its purpose is to show the overall role of IGOs in U.S. military security policy, how the United States has used them as instruments, and how being part of them and using them has influenced the course of U.S. policy. Even with its broad focus, however, the chapter does not cover all aspects of U.S. security policy—only those that are essential to considering the role of IGOs.

The three broad goals that were defined in the late 1940s and early 1950s have remained relatively constant in the ensuing decades. We turn now to examine in detail the role that IGOs have played in U.S. efforts to achieve them, the extent to which these roles have remained constant or changed, and explanations for the extent of constancy and change. Both the use of IGOs by the United States and the influence of these IGOs on the United States will be considered. The course of U.S. policy over the several decades with respect to each of the three goals will be described, then explanations for the extent of constancy and change will be explored.

The Modality of Exploring Change and Constancy in U.S. Policy

Chapter 1 posed the question of whether or not U.S. involvement in IGOs had changed and then offered four possible explanations for such changes.

According to the framework presented, changes in use of IGOs could be explained by (1) the overall decline in U.S. power relative to that of other countries that has occurred during the postwar period; (2) characteristics of the issue area, particularly with respect to the content of the dominant ideology and the degree of national interest in the issue; (3) the characteristics of the IGOs, especially their membership, the composition and role of their secretariats, and the character of their policy outputs; and (4) domestic political factors, including changing relations between the executive and legislative branches of government, changing involvement of interest groups, and differences between presidential administrations.

Given the central role of power in security issues, one might expect the first explanation to have particular potency; thus it is important to consider it carefully. To test the possibility that whatever changes might have occurred in the role of IGOs in U.S. security policy are the result of the overall decline in relative U.S. power, the description of U.S. efforts with respect to each of the goals will be divided at roughly 1970. Although the decline in U.S. power relative to that of other states has been gradual, it was substantially greater before 1970 than since that time.

In 1950, by all conventional measures U.S. power relative to that of other states was clearly overwhelming. Two aspects of U.S. power can be cited to illustrate the point. The U.S. gross national product constituted almost a third of the world product. The United States had some 450 operational nuclear warheads; no other state had such a capacity. Although U.S. relative power declined substantially during the next two decades as those states that had been devastated by World War II rebuilt their economies and as the Soviet Union and other states developed arsenals of nuclear weapons, the U.S. lead during this period remained so substantial that these decades have generally been regarded as the era of U.S. dominance.

By 1970 U.S. power relative to that of other states had declined significantly. The same two aspects of power can be used for comparison. In 1970 the U.S. gross national product was only slightly more than a quarter of the world product. In 1970 the United States had 4,000 operational nuclear warheads and 2,260 strategic delivery vehicles, but the Soviet Union had 1,800 nuclear warheads and 1,745 strategic delivery vehicles. Although U.S. relative power continued to decline after 1970, the decline, especially in the economic realm, was less precipitous than it had been in the preceding two decades. In 1980 the U.S. GNP was 22 percent of the world product. The United States had 10,100 nuclear warheads and 1,946 strategic delivery vehicles, and the Soviet Union had 6,000 warheads and 2,482 strategic delivery vehicles. With respect to the strategic balance, by 1970 both sides had achieved a second-strike capability, and by 1980 it was generally conceded that the Soviet Union had achieved strategic parity with the United States. Because of the relatively rapid decline in U.S. relative power from 1950 until 1970 and the more gradual decline thereafter, 1970 can mark the beginning of the period when the United States was no longer in the dominant position that it occupied in the immediate aftermath of World War II. By 1970 other major powers had recovered from the effects of war, and international politics entered what could be regarded as a more normal era (Organski and Kugler 1980: 137–44).

The year 1970 is also a convenient dividing point for exploring whether or not changes in U.S. use of IGOs might be related to changes in the IGOs themselves. During the 1960s the universal membership agencies of the UN system and other broad membership IGOs such as the Organization of American States were substantially changed by an influx of newly independent states (Claude 1967). During the 1960s more colonies gained independence and joined the UN and its affiliated agencies than in any preceding or subsequent decade. At the beginning of 1960 the UN had 89 members; by the end of 1969 this total had swelled to 126. Between 1970 and 1988 the UN's membership grew to only 159. The Third World caucus, the Group of 77, was formed in 1964. By 1970 the Third World's influence in the UN, its affiliated agencies, and other broad membership IGOs had more or less reached the high level at which it would remain in the coming years.

There is no similar breaking point for the second explanation, that concerning the characteristics of the issue area. U.S. security goals that were set in the late 1940s and early 1950s have remained relatively constant. The broad framework of world politics in which the Soviet-American conflict has been the dominant feature has also been relatively constant.

Concerning the last explanation—domestic factors—temporal divisions are easy to establish with respect to which party controlled which branch of government. Democrats were in the White House from the outset of the postwar period until 1953, from 1961 until 1969, and from 1977 to 1981. Republicans occupied the White House during the intervals from 1953 to 1961, 1969–1977, and from 1981 to at least 1993. Democrats have constituted the majority in the House of Representatives from the outset of the postwar period until 1947, 1949–1953, and since 1955. Democrats controlled a majority of seats in the Senate from the outset of the postwar period until 1947, 1949–1953, 1955–1981, and since 1987. If these changes significantly affected U.S. security policy concerning IGOs, policy shifts would coincide with the dates of these changes.

Other domestic factors, such as the role of interest groups and the mood of the country, do not fit as easily into neat temporal divisions. However, by 1970 the United States was clearly determined to withdraw from Vietnam, and the consequences of the Vietnam War for the American polity were beginning to be felt. Debate over the substance and modalities of U.S. security policies continued even after the end of American involvement in Vietnam.

With this background we turn to a historical examination of the role of IGOs in pursuing each of the three major goals of U.S. security policy.

Preventing a Nuclear Attack on the United States

Negotiations to establish international controls for nuclear energy were the first task that the United Nations undertook (United Nations General Assembly 1946). Within a short time, however, these negotiations foundered, making it doubtful that international governmental organizations could have a substantial role in protecting the United States against the dangers of a nuclear attack.

Restricting the Transfer of Knowledge and Material

Initial U.S. policy with respect to nuclear weapons continued the unilateral restriction on the dissemination of knowledge about the fabrication of nuclear weapons, as it had done during World War II. The United States offered to share this knowledge, however, with an international authority it proposed in the Baruch Plan presented in 1946. These negotiations failed, so the question of actually transferring the knowledge of nuclear technology never arose (Bechhoefer 1961). Whatever it might have done in the event of a different outcome, the United States has continued its policy of restricting the dissemination of knowledge about the fabrication of nuclear weapons to the present day.

As a limited number of other countries developed a capacity to fabricate weapons and many more developed nuclear industries, the United States successfully sought to enlist them in efforts to restrict the transfer of knowledge about the fabrication of nuclear weapons and to restrict the transfer of technology relevant to this process. As will be discussed in a subsequent section, emphasis on the restriction of the transfer of knowledge and materials became even more pronounced in the 1970s than it had been previously or has been in the 1980s.

With the USSR's development of an arsenal of nuclear weapons, first publicly evidenced by the Soviet nuclear detonation in 1949, it was apparent that additional policies beyond merely restricting information would also be required. The more the Soviet arsenal grew, the more pressing the need became to develop these policies.

Deterrence

By the mid-1960s when the Soviet Union had about six hundred nuclear warheads, the U.S. government settled on maintaining an assured second-strike capability—the ability to launch a devastating nuclear attack against the USSR even after suffering a Soviet nuclear attack—as the crucial element of its policy designed to deter a direct nuclear attack. International governmental organizations played virtually no role in the debate that led to the adoption of this policy or in the subsequent debates about what military forces would be required to maintain a second-strike capability (Gaddis 1982; Huntington 1961). Nor did IGOs play a role in the debate about whether defensive measures against strategic nuclear weapons were feasible and, if they were, whether they would contribute to or weaken deterrence.

As the USSR's strategic nuclear capability continued to grow in the 1960s and 1970s, so did U.S. concern with preventing a Soviet attack on the United States. In response to this concern, the United States sequentially pursued two quite different policies.

Superpower Arms Control and the Military Buildup

The first of these policies stressed arms control or efforts to limit the military capabilities of both sides. This strand of U.S. policy dated from the early efforts to control nuclear energy. Its first success, however, was the signing in 1963 of the partial ban on the testing of nuclear weapons (Jacobson and Stein 1966), and most of its major achievements were registered in the 1970s (Carnesale and Haass 1987). The Treaty on the Limitation of Anti-Ballistic Missile Systems which the United States and the Soviet Union signed in May 1972 was one of the first. The treaty was based on the belief that if neither side developed an extensive ABM capability, both would have an assured second-strike capability and hence strategic nuclear weapons would not be used.

At the same time that the ABM Treaty was signed, the two states signed an interim agreement that committed them not to add to the strategic capabilities in their inventories or under construction pending the negotiation of a treaty that would establish a quantitative cap on these capabilities. The Treaty on the Limitation of Strategic Offensive Arms (SALT II) was finally completed and signed in June 1979 but has never been ratified.

Postwar U.S. military buildups have occurred in three waves. Even before the SALT II Treaty was completed, the United States launched a buildup that paralleled earlier ones in the 1950s and 1960s. The modernizing and augmentation of the U.S. strategic nuclear arsenal began under the Carter administration and was accelerated during the first part of the Reagan administration. In addition, the Reagan administration inaugurated the Strategic Defense Initiative in 1983, a major research effort directed toward developing a defensive capability against ballistic missiles.

IGOs have played only a modest role with respect to these U.S. policies. The arms control treaties were negotiated bilaterally with the USSR and have been verified by technical means under U.S. and Soviet national control. The concepts on which the treaties were based were developed within the United States or in conjunction with the Soviet Union. The U.S. military buildup in the 1980s resulted from unilateral U.S. actions as a response to needs that were perceived primarily in the United States (though perhaps also in NATO), as the subsequent section will make clear.

Continuing calls in the United Nations and other IGOs for the superpowers to reduce their arsenals may have served as a stimulus to the negotiations between the Soviet Union and the United States and may have reinforced pressure within the two countries for negotiations, but they surely were not the primary motivating force for these talks. The limited role and influence of IGOs with respect to U.S. policy designed to prevent a nuclear attack on the United States was readily apparent in the 1950s and 1960s and has remained unchanged since 1970.

Limiting the Proliferation of Nuclear Weapon Capabilities

IGOs have, however, played an important role in U.S. policies designed to prevent a nuclear attack on its territory by limiting the spread of nuclear weapons—that is, by limiting the number of countries that could implement such an attack. President Dwight D. Eisenhower proposed in 1953 in his "Atoms for Peace" address that an international agency be created that would diffuse knowledge about nuclear energy and also ensure, through the establishment of a system of safeguards, that this knowledge would be used only for peaceful purposes. The International Atomic Energy Agency (IAEA), which was established as a specialized agency of the United Nations in 1957 and which is the subject of chapter 3 in this volume, was the direct result of this address. It became a principal component of U.S. nonproliferation policy (Scheinman 1987), particularly through the safeguards system that went into effect in 1963.

A second principal component of U.S. nonproliferation policy, negotiating a treaty to limit the proliferation of nuclear weapons, was pursued in the United Nations itself. In the 1950s legal limitations on the spread of nuclear weapons were a feature of both Soviet and U.S. disarmament proposals. The impetus for a treaty on nonproliferation resulted from Swedish and Irish proposals that were adopted by the UN General Assembly in 1961. Although the United States initially opposed the Swedish resolution on the grounds that it might interfere with NATO plans for the creation of a multinational nuclear force within the alliance, by 1964 U.S. policy shifted and President Lyndon B. Johnson proposed that negotiations to conclude a nonproliferation treaty be conducted in the United Nations. Negotiations began in 1965 and were concluded in 1968. The Treaty on the Non-Proliferation of Nuclear Weapons (NPT), which resulted from these negotiations, entered into force in 1970. The NPT and the IAEA have been two of the principal instruments on which the United States has relied to limit the spread of nuclear weapons.

For a period in the 1970s the United States pursued several initiatives primarily outside the framework that the agency provided. The Indian detonation of a nuclear device in 1974 heightened concern in the United States about the proliferation of nuclear weapons capability, and the oil crisis increased interest in nuclear energy. The United States took three actions in response. First, it sought to work with other states that supplied nuclear materials to establish guidelines so that safeguards obligations would not be undercut as a consequence of commercial competition. The London Nuclear Suppliers Group, which was established in 1974 as a result of the U.S. initiative, completed its first set of guidelines in 1977. Second, the United States called for an international investigation of the nuclear fuel cycle to determine if some technologies posed greater dangers of proliferation than others, and it took the lead in 1977 in establishing the International Nuclear Fuel Cycle Evaluation Program (INFCE). The IAEA secretariat provided technical support for the INFCE and was the forum to which some of the conclusions of the program were referred. Third, in 1978 the United States adopted the Nuclear Non-Proliferation Act, which mandated that to receive nuclear materials from the United States, countries would have to comply with more rigorous standards than had been applied in the past and that, in particular, they would have to accept safeguards on all of their nuclear facilities. These actions are discussed in more detail by Schiff (chapter 3).

The International Atomic Energy Agency was not more centrally involved in U.S. nonproliferation policy during the 1970s because U.S. policymakers wanted to move more quickly than they thought they could if the United States acted only within the agency and because they wanted to take stronger actions than they thought the majority of IAEA would approve.

In the 1980s IAEA was again given a more central role in U.S. policy. The experience of the 1970s had demonstrated that some U.S. objectives were unattainable or were attainable only if the United States was prepared to accept conflict with other nuclear-supplier states and suffer some commercial handicaps. Moreover the problems that these objectives had been designed to minimize appeared less immediate and dangerous than they had in the 1970s. Among other things, the shift from a global energy shortage to a global energy surplus made states less eager to rush to develop nuclear power facilities.

The experience of the 1970s demonstrated again what was already apparent in the 1950s. Even when the United States had overwhelming power, it could not achieve its goals with respect to limiting the proliferation of nuclear weapons through unilateral actions. It was certainly not able to do so in the 1970s when its power was relatively diminished. Although the IAEA has not always produced the results the United States sought, it would be hard to argue that since 1970 the agency has been substantially less responsive to U.S. nonproliferation interests than it was in the preceding period. Those IAEA actions that have most disturbed the United States have largely been symbolic and have involved condemnations of Israel.

Several points can be made about IGOs and U.S. nonproliferation policy. First, because the objective of limiting the spread of nuclear weapons applied to all states and involved intrusive inspection procedures, the United States sought to gain broad legitimacy for its objectives by utilizing IGOs with potentially universal membership—the United Nations and the International Atomic Energy Agency—as the principal instruments through which it pursued its policies. The United States could not obtain its goals through unilateral action or through limited-membership organizations.

Second, U.S. policy aimed at limiting the spread of nuclear weapons has been relatively constant. The IAEA has always been central in this policy, even in the 1970s, when there was a flurry of U.S. initiative outside of the agency.

Third, even in the period when the United States had overwhelming power, it had to make concessions to other states to attain its objectives. Examples include Article VI of the Non-Proliferation Treaty in which the states that possessed nuclear weapons pledged to engage in good faith negotiations to reduce their nuclear arsenals and the guarantee given by the United States, the Soviet Union, and the United Kingdom to the UN Security Council that nuclear aggression or the threat of nuclear aggression against a state that did not possess nuclear weapons and adhered to the NPT would require immediate action by the council, especially its permanent members. Using IGOs as policy instruments almost inevitably implies making concessions to gain consensus or majority support. But there is little evidence in the record that the United States has had to make significantly greater concessions in IAEA as time progressed despite the vast expansion in the agency's membership.

Fourth, actions of international organizations such as the UN General Assembly resolutions sponsored by Ireland and Sweden contributed to the U.S. consideration and ultimate adoption of a course that it initially opposed: negotiating a nonproliferation agreement independent of agreement on broader arms control and disarmament measures. In this sense the UN performed an agenda-setting role. Proceedings in the UN were a factor in the U.S. considering and ultimately adopting a course of action that it had initially rejected.

Fifth, as will be described in the following section, security policies that the United States was pursuing in one organization (NATO) at least initially constrained the security policies that it could pursue in another (the UN).

Finally, to the extent that the capacity to develop nuclear arsenals has spread since 1945, this spread occurred largely before the nonproliferation regime was in place. The Soviet Union detonated a nuclear device in 1949, the United Kingdom in 1952, France in 1960, and the People's Republic of China in 1964. Beyond these five states, only India has publicly admitted to conducting a nuclear explosion and is the only state to have done so since the creation of the nonproliferation regime. U.S. nonproliferation objectives have largely been met, and IGOs have been crucial factors in this success.

Alliance with the West

In contrast to the rather limited role of international governmental organizations with respect to preventing a nuclear attack on the United States, NATO became the cornerstone of American policy with respect to a major portion of the second U.S. security goal: maintaining close ties with Canada and the states of Western Europe and ensuring that these states did not fall under Soviet control. NATO joined the United States, Canada, and ten Western European states—Belgium, Denmark, France, Iceland, Italy, Luxembourg, the Netherlands, Norway, Portugal, and the United Kingdom—in a military alliance. In 1952 Greece and Turkey joined the alliance, and in 1955 the Federal Republic of Germany was admitted to membership. Spain has been the only additional country to join NATO, becoming a member in 1982. Because of its importance as an instrument for achieving a key security goal, NATO has also played a major role in shaping U.S. military strategy.

NATO and U.S. Military Strategy

In 1950 the NATO Council adopted a forward strategy, deciding that the military defense of Western Europe should be attempted as far to the East as possible to protect the maximum number of Western European states. That same year NATO began assembling a military force designed to implement this decision. Since then U.S. military policies and those of the alliance have been inextricably linked (Fox and Fox 1967; Osgood 1962). A substantial portion of U.S. military forces have been committed to NATO, either being deployed in Europe or designated as potential reinforcements for Europe.

When NATO military strategy was initially set, it was clear that the Soviet Union and its allies had substantial superiority in conventional weapons. In May 1952 at the meeting of the NATO Council in Lisbon, military force goals were established that would have brought NATO's conventional forces roughly to the level of those of the USSR and its allies. It soon became apparent that these goals were unrealizable, at least in the short run. Indeed, they have never been met or even approximated.

The doctrine of "massive retaliation," enunciated by Secretary of State John Foster Dulles in 1954, was partly designed to compensate for this weakness in Europe. The doctrine implied that a Soviet conventional attack in Europe might be met with a U.S. nuclear attack on the USSR. In 1956 the NATO Council adopted massive retaliation as the alliance's official military strategy.

The U.S. policy of developing tactical nuclear weapons, including a neutron weapon, had a similar goal of compensating for Western weakness in conventional forces (Kissinger 1957). The United States started deploying tactical nuclear weapons in Europe in 1953, and tactical nuclear weapons have been fully integrated into NATO military strategy since then.

With the adoption of the doctrine of massive retaliation and the deployment of tactical nuclear weapons close to the dividing line between East and West in Europe, the United States became committed to having the option of initiating the use of nuclear weapons at a fairly early stage in a European armed conflict. The United States might have adopted such a military strategy even had it not been a member of NATO, but its membership in NATO was clearly a factor pushing it toward this strategy.

Various American policymakers have sought to reduce the pressure to use nuclear weapons, especially during the early stages of a conflict. In

1962 Secretary of Defense Robert S. McNamara announced that the United States would move toward a military strategy of "flexible response." According to this strategy, Western conventional forces would be built up so that a Soviet conventional attack could at least be met initially without resort to nuclear weapons. As McNamara later put it, the use of nuclear weapons would be "late and limited" rather than massive and early (McNamara 1986: 24). At the NATO Council meeting in May 1962 he proposed that flexible response replace massive retaliation in NATO's official military strategy. The NATO Council finally accepted this proposal in 1967.

Many European members of NATO were then and have remained reluctant to deemphasize the role of nuclear weapons in alliance strategy for fear that doing so would weaken the deterrence effect of the alliance. Nor have they been willing to bear the costs of supporting conventional forces adequate to balance those of the Soviet Union and its allies. Furthermore, from the European perspective, a large-scale conventional war in which their territories might be overrun and then liberated, as occurred in World War II, could be almost as destructive as a nuclear war. Therefore, European members of NATO have preferred a strategy that might reduce the probability of war occurring even though it might increase the amount of destruction that would occur if war should break out. The United States, on the other hand, which would be relatively isolated from a conventional war in Europe but is vulnerable to strategic nuclear weapons, has had a different outlook. Nevertheless because of its commitment to NATO, successive U.S. administrations have not felt that they could renounce the possibility of initiating the use of nuclear weapons; a no-first-use pledge would seriously compromise NATO military strategy. The difference between the U.S. and European perspectives has been a persistent source of tension in the alliance (Bundy et al. 1982; Schwartz 1983; Steinbrunner and Sigal 1982).

France has compounded U.S. difficulties with respect to both nuclear and conventional force strategies. French strategic nuclear forces have never been included in the NATO command structure. They could be launched by a unilateral French decision and could trigger a broader nuclear exchange. France withdrew its conventional forces from the NATO integrated military command in 1966. The absence of French participation makes planning a NATO defense in depth difficult and creates additional pressure for the early use of nuclear weapons.

Just as it did in the 1950s and 1960s, U.S. membership in NATO has continued to have crucial consequences for U.S. military strategy in the 1970s and 1980s. Flexible response has remained the central doctrine of U.S. and NATO military strategies. In addition, because the United

States and NATO have continued to regard NATO conventional forces as inferior to those of the Warsaw Treaty Organization, they insisted on retaining the option to initiate the use of nuclear weapons.

NATO as a Lever in the U.S. Political Process

NATO's role and influence have extended beyond the basic identity between U.S. and NATO military strategies. In the 1970s some elements of the U.S. military forces remained stable and others, which had been built up during the Vietnam conflict, declined. By the mid-1970s several officials in the U.S. Department of Defense, including some who were appointed when the Carter administration took office, thought the United States should increase its military forces. In his campaign for the presidency, however, Carter pledged to decrease the military budget, and there was a substantial group in the Carter administration and in Congress who favored a decrease.

As part of their strategy to mobilize a coalition to support the policy they advocated, those favoring an increase in U.S. military forces put the issue of growing Soviet and Warsaw Treaty military forces on the NATO agenda. In the discussions that ensued they were able to obtain a decision in May 1977 at the ministerial session of the NATO Defense Planning Committee committing the members of the alliance to a five-year program of building up NATO's military strength (Brzezinski 1983). Specifically, members pledged to increase their military budgets by approximately 3 percent per year after discounting for inflation. This decision was subsequently endorsed by the NATO heads of state and government when they met as the NATO Council in May 1978 in Washington. U.S. Defense Department officials were able to use this commitment as supporting argument in their efforts to obtain an increase in the U.S. military budget.

Only in the Carter administration's third budget (fiscal year 1980), however, did the U.S. military budget increase in constant dollars, and then by 2.1 percent. Because of inflation, the military budget actually decreased in years 1978 and 1979 by 0.1 and 1.2 percent, respectively. NATO's European members came closer to fulfilling their pledge.

In this instance U.S. membership in NATO was a resource that a segment of the U.S. government could use in its efforts to secure adoption of the policy that it favored. In another instance other NATO countries raised a concern that the United States virtually alone had the resources to meet.

Intermediate-Range Nuclear Forces

In the late 1970s the USSR began deploying SS 20 missiles on its European territory. These intermediate-range weapons carrying multiple warheads were capable of striking targets throughout Western Europe. NATO did not have a comparable weapon system. The SS 20s threatened the ability of NATO to initiate the use of tactical nuclear weapons; if NATO used tactical nuclear weapons, the Soviet Union could respond by attacking major European targets with SS 20s and still keep its strategic nuclear weapons in reserve to deter a U.S. strategic attack on the USSR. The SS 20s had a coercive effect on NATO's European members: if the Soviet Union should threaten to use them, NATO could only respond by threatening to use strategic nuclear weapons, a step everyone realized a U.S. president might be reluctant to take. The United Kingdom and France, of course, had national nuclear arsenals that could be used to deter Soviet use of the SS 20s, but to threaten their use would risk national annihilation, a step that might not be taken for defense of anything other than their own territory. The SS 20s were particularly menacing to NATO's member states that did not possess nuclear weapons and especially to the Federal Republic of Germany.

The Soviet deployment of SS 20s occurred at the same time that the Soviet Union was coming closer to attaining strategic parity with the United States, if indeed it had not achieved parity by then. The growing size of the USSR's strategic arsenal increased doubts that the United States would respond to a Soviet attack on Western Europe that would surely invite nuclear retaliation against the United States. This combination of developments and their implications for the ability of the United States to deter an attack on Western Europe contributed to the belief in the United States that the U.S. strategic nuclear arsenal needed to be modernized and augmented.

A NATO decision led the United States to accept a commitment to develop a capability in Europe to respond to the SS 20s. In an address at the International Institute for Strategic Studies in January 1979, Chancellor Helmut Schmidt called for a NATO response to the Soviet deployment of SS 20s. In December of that year NATO adopted a two-track strategy. It decided to deploy 108 Pershing II launchers and 464 ground-launched cruise missiles. It also endorsed arms control negotiations between the United States and the USSR concerning land-based, long-range, theater nuclear missile systems and stated that the objective of such negotiations should be limitations on these systems based on the principle of equality between sides.

Whether or not the United States would have chosen to deploy such weapons in Western Europe in the absence of strong pressure on the part of its European allies for a response to the Soviet deployment of SS 20s is moot. In any case, the initiative for the move came more from Europe than from the United States. The deployment of Pershing II missiles in the Federal Republic of Germany beginning in 1983 meant that U.S.-controlled nuclear weapons that could reach major parts of the USSR were located very close to the line dividing Eastern and Western Europe, a location that would create strong pressure for their early use should military violence break out in Europe. The 1979 NATO decision therefore had profound implications for U.S. military strategy, but it also prompted new arms control efforts.

Starting in 1981 the United States pursued negotiations with the Soviet Union to limit both sides' intermediate-range nuclear forces. The negotiations were tumultuous and volatile and were broken off by the Soviet Union for a time after deployment of the Pershing II and cruise missiles began in 1983. The talks were resumed in 1985; in 1987 the Soviet Union accepted President Reagan's zero option proposal: that both sides eliminate their intermediate-range nuclear forces. A treaty to this effect was signed in December 1987 and ratified in 1988.

NATO has thus had a unique and important agenda-setting role in U.S. military strategy and security policy, in addition to serving as the principal instrument for obtaining one of the major security goals of the United States. Indeed, U.S. and NATO interests and policies have been so intertwined that they are frequently indistinguishable.

Intertwined Interests and Polices

The linkage between the United States and NATO has been effected and symbolized by key personnel. A U.S. general has always been the NATO Supreme Allied Commander. The first Supreme Allied Commander, General Dwight D. Eisenhower, was elected to be the thirty-fourth president of the United States, serving from 1953 to 1961. Many other U.S. military officials who have held positions in NATO have subsequently held high offices in the United States; indeed, within the U.S. military forces, service in an international role has been a prerequisite for promotion to general officer rank. The interchange of personnel has been an important factor in maintaining the close links between U.S. and NATO military policies; U.S. military officers and civilian officials have implemented NATO policies and in doing so have been socialized to appreciate NATO problems and concerns. Of course, the basic reason for the linkage—and the cause of the personnel interchange—was the fundamental decision made in the 1940s that the security of Western Europe was vital to U.S.

security. Bureaucratic adjustments made in response to this fundamental decision ensured the socialization.

The interchange of personnel has been shaped by the broad context within which it has occurred. The United States has always been the most powerful member of the alliance and the only one capable of matching or exceeding Soviet strength in nuclear weapons. This has been the basis of U.S. influence in NATO. Even during the 1950s and 1960s, however, the United States could not alone determine the policies of the alliance; it always had to take account of the views of other member states. If these states chose not to follow the American lead, as in the case of France, there was nothing the United States could do. On the other hand, when the United States wanted to pursue a particular military course, such as adoption in the 1960s of the flexible response strategy or in the 1980s of the Strategic Defense Initiative, it was generally able to convince its NATO allies to go along and, if necessary, endorse the course it had chosen. This endorsement by other member governments, however, has never been automatic or necessarily prompt. U.S. influence in NATO, always substantial though never absolute, has been relatively constant.

The U.S. role in NATO has consistently involved bearing a substantial share of the burden of the alliance's military forces, a share that came to seem increasingly disproportionate to many Americans as Western European states recovered from the effects of World War II and prospered (Calleo 1987). From time to time efforts have been made, especially by members of Congress, to reduce the U.S. contribution to NATO's military effort. Administrations of both parties have resisted these efforts. To a certain extent the American contribution to NATO reflects the familiar collective goods proposition. If the largest member of a group has an interest in having the collective good provided, it is likely to make a disproportionate contribution toward the provision of that good. Given the United States' strong interest in ensuring the military security of Western Europe, the United States may still have been justified in bearing more than its proportionate share of the burden for Western defense. In the absence of NATO, some Western European countries might not have mounted any military effort, or only a modest one, so the real U.S. choice may not have been between a disproportionate and a fair share of the military burden but rather between disproportionate shares of varying dimensions.

As noted earlier, the alliance has had a profound impact on the definition of the United States' own military strategy, particularly in committing it to reliance on nuclear weapons in a conflict in Europe to counter Soviet conventional forces and to the first use of these weapons. The United States has had to shape its military strategy to European conditions and take into account the perspectives of its alliance partners. The alliance has also influenced U.S. policies by setting the agenda, as in the case of the Soviet deployment of SS 20s and the two-track strategy of INF deployment and arms control negotiation.

In sum, it is difficult to imagine a closer interaction between a country's policies in a given sector and an international institution than that between U.S. military policies and NATO—a relationship that has endured for almost four decades with little change.

Having examined the role of IGOs in U.S. security policy with respect to protecting American territory and that of its closest allies, we now shift our attention to the Third World.

U.S. Security and the Third World

In the revised and specific definition of U.S. security goals that emerged in the late 1940s, the United Nations became particularly relevant to protecting and advancing U.S. interests in the Third World—a role played also by the Organization of American States. During the 1950s and 1960s both were useful instruments of U.S. policies, but support was not uniformly forthcoming in either. At times the United States acted outside of the framework of any IGOs, including these two, even though their mandates made them relevant to the problem at issue. After 1970 U.S. use of both institutions as instruments became more problematic; their members were less inclined to favor courses of action advocated by the United States. Both the United Nations and the Organization of American States have also had some impact on U.S. policies, especially when they were employed as instruments for these policies, but the two institutions have influenced American policies even when they and the United States have been in conflict. The role of these organizations in U.S. security policy was not predetermined but was shaped gradually and pragmatically in response to emerging situations.

UN Peacekeeping Efforts

In 1950 the United Nations provided a framework with wide legitimacy for U.S. efforts to defend the Republic of Korea and for mobilizing other states to assist in this task. After the North Korean attack on South Korea, the United States quickly decided that it should contribute militarily to defending South Korea (Wolfers 1954). A desire to uphold the UN Charter's commitment to protect the territorial integrity and political independence of all states was one of the factors contributing to this decision, along with the desire to enhance the credibility of the U.S. commitment to containment and especially the guarantee to NATO. Thus U.S. membership in the UN contributed to the definition of U.S. interests.

The fact that the Korean War was fought under UN auspices, however, had at most a marginal impact on U.S. military operations (Goodrich 1956). The U.S. commanding general in Korea was designated as the UN commander, but his orders came directly from Washington.

In 1956 when, as an outgrowth of the controversy over the Egyptian nationalization of the Suez Canal, Israel, France, and the United Kingdom attacked Egypt, the United Nations provided an instrument for limiting and ending the violence. The conflict posed a dilemma for the United States. It either had to oppose Israel and its NATO allies, the United Kingdom and France, or to allow the UN prohibition against the use of force and the tripartite decision guaranteeing the borders in the region to be violated, thereby alienating Egypt and other Third World States. The dilemma resulted in part from U.S. membership in two IGOs.

The United States led the United Nations to call for a ceasefire and for a withdrawal of the Israeli, French, and British forces from Egyptian territory and also to deploy a UN peacekeeping force—the United Nations Emergency Force (UNEF)—to separate the belligerents. UNEF was broadly seen as a device for limiting the conflict, for preventing its geographical spread and the escalation of violence.

From 1956 through 1967 the United States relied on UNEF as one of the principal instruments to maintain peace in the Middle East. In 1967, however, the Egyptian government requested that UNEF be withdrawn from Egyptian territory. Because the force could not be deployed on a country's territory without its consent, UNEF was withdrawn even though the United States would have preferred that it remain. Shortly thereafter Israel launched an attack that ultimately led to its gaining control of all of the Sinai peninsula including the Sharm el Sheikh base, all of Jordan's West Bank, and a major part of Syria's Golan Heights. The UN Security Council first called for a cease-fire and then attempted to define the terms of a settlement in Resolution 242 which, among other things, called for Israel to withdraw from the occupied territories. The United Kingdom took the lead in shaping and crafting this resolution so that it would be acceptable to both the United States and the Soviet Union.

UN peacekeeping forces were also deployed in 1960 in the Congo when Belgium intervened militarily shortly after granting the colony independence. The request for UN forces came from the Congolese government but was strongly supported by the United States. The United Nations Operation in the Congo (ONUC) entailed the actual use of military force to quell secessionist movements in the country. ONUC's mission and financing became major issues of contention. The force was withdrawn in 1964. U.S. efforts to require that all members provide financial support for ONUC were unsuccessful. The USSR and France, among others, refused to pay.

Despite the Congo experience, UN peacekeeping forces were deployed on Cyprus in 1964. The UK request for a UN force followed an effort to create a NATO force. The United Nations Force in Cyprus (UNFICYP) has remained there since it was first deployed, remaining even during the violence that resulted from the coup d'état staged by Greek officers and the Turkish intervention of 1974. The costs of the force have been met by the governments of the countries providing the military contingents and by voluntary contributions, particularly from the United States.

When violence resumed in the Middle East in October 1973 as a consequence of the Egyptian and Syrian attack on Israel, the United States relied heavily on the United Nations in its efforts to restore peace. The United States and the Soviet Union jointly requested an urgent meeting of the Security Council and jointly submitted the proposal to the Security Council calling for a cease-fire. When fighting continued despite the Security Council decision, the United States refused an Egyptian request that the United States and the Soviet Union dispatch troops to the area to enforce the cease-fire and instead supported the proposal of the non-aligned members of the Security Council to establish a new UN peace-keeping force. The nonaligned initiative led to the creation of the second United Nations Emergency Force (UNEF II), which remained in place until July 1979 following the signing of the Camp David peace treaty between Egypt and Israel.

Although fighting between Israel and Egypt subsided following the Security Council call for a cease-fire, tension in the area of Golan Heights, where Israeli forces now occupied even more territory, remained high. In early 1974 the situation became increasingly unstable, and firing between the two sides intensified. Henry Kissinger, then U.S. Secretary of State, undertook a mediation mission that led to a disengagement agreement (Kissinger 1982). This agreement was monitored by a UN Disagreement Observer Force (UNDOF) created by the Security Council in response to a U.S. proposal. UNDOF has remained in place on the Golan Heights since it was created.

In March 1978 in retaliation for a commando raid by forces of the Palestine Liberation Organization, Israeli military forces invaded and occupied southern Lebanon. Acting on the basis of a U.S. proposal, the UN Security Council called for respect for the territorial integrity of Lebanon within its internationally recognized borders and decided to establish a United Nations Interim Force (UNIFIL) in southern Lebanon that would confirm the withdrawal of Israeli forces and assist the government of Lebanon in establishing its authority in the area. UNIFIL has also remained in place since it was created.

The Camp David treaty between Egypt and Israel had provided for UN forces to supervise the implementation of the treaty's security arrangements, and it had been envisaged that UNEF II would perform these tasks. The Palestine Liberation Organization (PLO), many Arab states, and the Soviet Union opposed the Camp David treaty because it did not provide a comprehensive settlement to the Arab-Israeli conflict. Because of their opposition, the Security Council did not extend UNEF II's mandate, which lapsed in July 1979. The United States continued efforts to obtain a UN force to monitor the Camp David accord, but it was unsuccessful. As a consequence, in 1981 Egypt and Israel signed an agreement providing for the creation of a Multinational Force and Observers. The agreement, which the United States signed as an observer, provided that a U.S. civilian would head the force, that the United States would contribute an infantry battalion of about a thousand personnel, and that the United States would pay approximately 60 percent of the initial costs of the force.

U.S. forces had already been deployed in the Middle East. As a consequence of the second Egyptian-Israeli disengagement accord that was signed in 1975, the Sinai Field Mission, a civilian observation group of approximately four hundred personnel, was stationed along the truce line to operate an electronic observation post. They were stationed in the Middle East again as part of the International Peacekeeping Force in Beirut in 1982 in the aftermath of the Israeli invasion of Lebanon.

Thus on three occasions starting in 1975 the United States deployed its own forces in the Middle East, in part because an agreement to establish a UN force could not be obtained. The PLO, several Arab states, and the Soviet Union objected to the type of force that Israel and the United States wanted.

This stalemate reflects a deeper disagreement about what would constitute a desirable settlement to the Arab-Israeli conflict. Many Arabs insist that there can be no solution that does not provide for the creation of a Palestinian state. Yet Israel is unalterably opposed to this. Although this disagreement was just as strong in the 1950s and 1960s, it has become more prominent in the United Nations since the 1970s, and UN proceedings and actions have been more anti-Israeli. This has contributed to American disenchantment with the UN. It has also, however, been a factor in the United States becoming more concerned about the Palestinian problem.

The decreased use of UN peacekeeping forces in the late 1970s and early 1980s is related more to the change in UN composition than to the decline in the relative power of the United States. As the UN's membership has expanded, more and more states have been added that are sympathetic to the Arab position. The longer the conflict has been unresolved, the more frustrated Arabs who feel that their interests are ignored have become. The United Nations is one of the few arenas in which they can prevail. The Soviet Union has chosen to support the Arab side, and it would like to play a major role in any Middle East settlement. In sum the political composition of the UN and the character of the Arab-Israeli conflict have both changed, making the United Nations a less convenient and dependable instrument for U.S. purposes. The decline in U.S. relative power may be a factor in these developments, but it is surely not the dominant explanation.

Even though the United States did not originate the concept of UN peacekeeping forces or introduce many of the proposals for their deployment, it came to place heavy reliance on them. They provided useful instruments for limiting and ending violent conflicts and thereby helped to forestall possible Soviet interventions. All of the major forces were deployed in the aftermath of decolonization. They helped the United States escape the dilemma of having to side with either its NATO allies (the former colonial powers) or the newly independent countries, or, in the case of Cyprus, with one NATO ally against another. Useful as they were in limiting and ending violence, the peacekeeping forces and the UN broadly often made little contribution to resolving the disputes that had led to the violence. The underlying dispute thus continued to be of concern to the United States. Sometimes in supporting UN peacekeeping actions the United States had to adjust its policies in directions that it might not otherwise have favored, directions that limited its freedom in dealing with the underlying disputes. For example, from the U.S. perspective, by supporting the demand for the creation of a Palestinian state, the UN exacerbated the Arab-Israeli conflict.

The late 1980s brought a sudden resurgence of interest in UN peacekeeping activities. In September 1987 Mikhail Gorbachev, General Secretary of the Communist party of the Soviet Union, published an article in *Pravda* and *Isvestiia* entitled "The Realities and Guarantees of a Secure World" (Gorbachev 1987) in which he called for several measures to strengthen the UN system. Many of these involved reversals of long-standing Soviet policies. Most important, he called for a development of the UN's peacekeeping capacity. In 1988 the Soviet Union announced its intention to pay its overdue contribution to peacekeeping operations. In an unprecedented move, a UN monitoring force was built into the agreement for the Soviet withdrawal from Afghanistan. Both the United States and the Soviet Union supported the creation of a UN force to monitor the cease-fire between Iran and Iraq. Simultaneously and for the first time, the

UN forces were utilized in interstate conflicts that were not part of the aftermath of decolonization. Further, in 1989 a UN force went into operation in Namibia, as provided for in Security Council Resolution 435 (1978).

How extensive the resurgence of UN peacekeeping activities will be is difficult to forecast. The shift in the Soviet Union's attitude is of major significance. How the Third World and the United States will act is not yet clear. The U.S. experience with forces created outside of the UN framework in the 1970s and early 1980s was not notably successful. The failure of the United States to pay its own assessed contributions to the United Nations, however, made any extension of UN activities problematic.

The Organization of American States

The Organization of American States has played a somewhat different and functionally broader, though geographically more specific, role from that of the United Nations in U.S. strategy in the Third World. The United States has sought to use the OAS as an instrument to deal with conflicts among OAS members. It has also sought to use it as an instrument to fight the spread of Marxist regimes in the Western Hemisphere.

In the 1950s and 1960s the United States supported the referral to OAS of several disputes, especially those among Central American states, and facilitated the organization's mediation efforts. Within the framework of the legitimacy provided by OAS sponsorship, the United States often played a crucial role in these mediation efforts. Keeping disputes within the OAS also meant keeping them out of the United Nations and thus away from the UN Security Council, where the Soviet Union would have a voice and a veto (Claude 1964).

In responding to the Cuban missile crisis, for example, the United States obtained OAS endorsement for its naval blockade of Cuba. Then in 1964, on U.S. urging, the OAS expelled Cuba. Only Mexico among OAS members continued to maintain diplomatic relations with Cuba. When the United States intervened militarily in the Dominican Republic in 1965 to prevent what the Johnson administration perceived as an attempt to establish a Marxist government, its contingent formed the core of an OAS multilateral military force.

Even when the OAS was useful to the United States as an instrument for obtaining its security goals in the Western hemisphere, the other member states did not completely share the U.S. government's views about the purposes of the institution. They tended to see the organization more as a device for restraining U.S. unilateral interventions and as a vehicle for obtaining U.S. economic assistance. The more the United

States used the OAS for its purposes, the more it had to accept a commitment to abide by the organization's doctrine of nonintervention and the more pressure it felt to provide economic assistance to Latin American states. Indeed, the Alliance for Progress was in part a response to this pressure. It was also not coincidental that the program was introduced after Castro came to power in Cuba.

The role of the Organization of American States in U.S. security policy since 1970 has been substantially less than it was in the 1950s and 1960s. When the Sandinistas came to power in Nicaragua in 1979, the United States could not use the OAS to isolate the regime the way it had done when Castro assumed power in Cuba. The OAS in fact disapproved of U.S. efforts to overthrow the Sandinista regime. When the United States invaded Grenada to overthrow the government that had been established by a military coup and to prevent Grenada from becoming more closely aligned with Cuba and the Soviet Union, it did not seek OAS endorsement of the action but instead relied on the request of the Organization of Eastern Caribbean States. The UN Security Council voted to deplore the U.S. military action in Grenada.

What explains U.S. difficulty in the 1970s and 1980s in utilizing the OAS as an instrument of its security policy? To some extent perhaps it can be explained in terms of the decline in the U.S. relative power. Many states in the Western Hemisphere became stronger in relation to the United States, and virtually all became less economically dependent on the United States than they had been previously—or at least they knew they had more choices in international trade and financial matters—so they were in a better position to oppose U.S. policies if they chose to do so. U.S. difficulties with the OAS were compounded by American support of Britain in the Falklands war.

Like the membership of the UN, that of the OAS expanded, and mobilizing a majority in the OAS has been more difficult for the United States in the 1970s and 1980s than it was in the preceding two decades. Many members of OAS, including several of those that joined since 1970, have governments that are more to the left and more nationalistic than had been the case. These governments are less anticommunist than their predecessors and more insistent on maintaining the traditional OAS doctrine of nonintervention.

The Doctrine of Nonintervention

Beyond dealing with specific disputes, IGOs seek to influence the milieu within which international politics occurs. Both the UN and the OAS and international institutions generally have stood squarely behind the doctrine of nonintervention, with strong rhetorical support from the United States. Successive U.S. administrations have affirmed the importance of the principle of ncnintervention for a peaceful world and have used this principle to condemn the actions of others. The United States may have itself been affected by the principle, though not always abiding by it in practice. If it were possible to use collective action as a way of legitimating intervention, the United States would, as we have seen in the account of OAS activities, pursue that course. If this were not possible, however, through the early 1970s the United States did not hesitate to intervene unilaterally.

The United States intervened unilaterally in Iran in 1953 to restore the shah to power and in Guatemala the following year to topple the Arbenz regime. The latter intervention followed an unsuccessful U.S. attempt to induce the OAS to condemn the Arbenz regime. International institutions were not involved in the Vietnam War, either in the initial French effort to maintain control or in the later U.S. effort to prevent the Communists from assuming power in South Vietnam. The United States was impervious for several years to pleas from various agencies of international institutions, including the UN Secretary-General, to limit and end its interventon in Vietnam.

The United States has shown less of a propensity to intervene unilaterally in the Third World since it withdrew from Vietnam in 1975. This shift in American policy seems to have been primarily the consequence of the way the U.S. foreign policy elite has interpreted the Vietnam experience, rather than a gradual socialization to norms that have been articulated by the UN, the OAS, and other international institutions (Holsti and Rosenau 1984).

In the 1980s the United Nations demonstrated a renewed willingness to condemn Soviet actions and the actions of Soviet allies. The United States favored and encouraged this. The UN condemned the Soviet invasion of Afghanistan and the Vietnamese invasion of Cambodia/Kampuchea. These actions underscored the fact that because the U.S. definition of its own security interests involved preserving the territorial integrity and political independence of Third World states, U.S. purposes were served when IGOs supported nonintervention. Promoting the principle of nonintervention advanced the U.S. objective of attaining a global milieu in which the U.S. economy and polity could prosper. The realization of this benefit may have reinforced the reluctance within the U.S. government to take actions that would break the norm; certainly it is difficult to use the norm as an instrument to condemn others when one's own conduct is also in violation.

Reflections on the Role and Influence of IGOs in U.S. Security Policies

Because the major features of the postwar international system, especially the Soviet-American conflict, became apparent in the late 1940s, U.S. security policy and the role and influence of IGOs in this policy have been relatively constant. What changes have occurred have mainly been in U.S. uses of international institutions to obtain its security goals in the Third World.

The decline of U.S. relative power, broadly defined, has not had many consequences for U.S. security policies, especially as they have related to IGOs. One explanation for this may be that although by several measures U.S. relative power has declined, this decline has not fundamentally altered the bipolar character of the principal challenge to U.S. security. Since the cold war began, the Soviet Union has been the only state that could directly attack the United States. Issues affecting this relationship have been and remain essentially bilateral. IGOs have had and continue to have little influence on the relationship. The Soviet Union's achieving parity with the United States may have affected the relationship between the two countries, but it has not affected the place of IGOs in this relationship.

Although U.S. relative power has declined in a general sense, in relationship to its closest allies, Japan, and the members of NATO U.S. military power is as dominant in the 1980s as it was thirty years earlier. The members of NATO are as dependent on the U.S. nuclear guarantee as they were in the 1950s. The only way in which the situation has changed is that since the Soviet Union achieved strategic parity with the United States in the late 1970s, there may have been more questions about the U.S. willingness to use strategic nuclear weapons for the defense of Europe, but there were questions about this even in the 1950s. However much doubts may have increased about the U.S. nuclear guarantee, neither Japan nor the members of NATO have thus far taken action significantly to lessen their reliance on this guarantee. Therefore the bargaining strength among the Western states on security issues has remained quite constant, and NATO's actions have reflected this.

The constancy of the role and influence of IGOs in U.S. security policy appears, then, primarily to be the consequence of the special character-istics of the issue area, as spelled out in the preceding paragraphs and in the introductory section of this chapter. The U.S. definition of the challenge to its security has been constant, and IGOs have been assigned relatively fixed roles within the context of this definition. The issue area is also crucial because its characteristics determine which components of power are relevant. Although overall U.S. power resources may have declined, power relevant to U.S. policy concerning IGOs in this issue area has not changed much, and the relationship between power and policy has been close.

To the extent that changes have occurred in the role and influence of international governmental institutions in U.S. security policy, they have been in those aspects of this policy that have involved the Third World. Members of both the UN and the OAS have been less receptive to U.S. policies than they were in the 1950s and 1960s. This seems to be primarily attributable to changes in the membership of these organizations, changes in the composition of their member governments, and changes in the character of the security problems being considered. There were also signs, however, toward the end of the 1980s that the UN at least could become more amenable to U.S. objectives, given the experience in Afghanistan and the Persian Gulf.

Throughout the post–World War II period, then, U.S. security policy has included actions pursued through and outside international governmental organizations. The preference for unilateral action has varied, though not systematically in relation to U.S. relative power defined in either broad or issue-area-specific terms. The United States acted unilaterally when it had overwhelming power, and it has continued to act unilaterally when it has been relatively much weaker. The most significant unilateral action was the U.S. involvement in the Vietnam War from 1964 through 1973. Neither Democratic nor Republican administrations have consistently demonstrated a preference for unilateral actions or for multilateral action through IGOs. Democratic administrations were responsible for escalating U.S. unilateral military intervention in Vietnam, but Republican administrations have also undertaken unilateral military interventions.

Domestic factors within the U.S. polity generally do not explain much concerning the role and influence of IGOs in U.S. security policy. Administrations have changed, as have congressional-executive relations, but these changes have done little more than modify stylistic emphases. No significant changes in U.S. policy coincide with the dates of these changes. The only domestic factor to have had an apparent and significant impact is the domestic reaction to the Vietnam experience, which has contributed to inhibiting U.S. military intervention in the Third World, and thus moved the United States in the direction of complying with the norm of nonintervention, at least during the late 1970s.

Whatever the exact balance between unilateral actions and actions pursued through international governmental organizations, the latter have always been important components of U.S. security policy. The UN,

IAEA, OAS, and NATO have all played vital roles, and each of these institutions has had an influence on U.S. policy. Given the way in which the United States has defined its security, each of these institutions has been vital.

The United States has used these organizations as instruments to obtain its goals: (1) preventing a nuclear attack on the United States; (2) maintaining close ties with Canada, Western Europe, and Japan and keeping these states out of the Soviet orbit; and (3) promoting alignment with the West among Third World states—or at least ensuring their neutrality between East and West—and ensuring that conflicts among these states did not spark a direct Soviet-American clash. The United States has sought and gained legitimation in IGOs for its objectives and actions. It has pushed the institutions to take collective action that would have greater legitimacy than unilateral U.S. action. When it has utilized IGOs as instruments, the United States has had to adjust its policies so that they would gain majority support within the organizations. Through their agenda-setting capacity, the organizations have forced the United States to pay attention to issues that it might have preferred to ignore or minimize. In the case of NATO, U.S. participation has involved a substantial bureaucratic and policy adjustment as well as socialization of key personnel.

Unless the United States were to define its security interests in sharply different terms, it is unlikely that the role of IGOs in U.S. security policy would change significantly. Their place is more the function of the U.S. definition of its security interests and the nature and composition of the respective organizations than of U.S. relative power, broadly defined, or the preferences of administrations in power. The shifts in Soviet policy that began in the late 1980s, however, opened up the possibility of a reversal at least to some extent of the decline in U.S. uses of the United Nations. Should these shifts in Soviet policy blossom into major changes that would result in a transformation of the Soviet-American relationship, then the role of IGOs in U.S. security policy might become significantly different. Indeed, the original vision of great power cooperation in the United Nations might be revived.

Notes

1. I gratefully acknowledge the assistance of Cheryl L. Shanks in the preparation of this chapter. I also appreciate the advice and suggestions of the editors and other contributors. Work on this chapter was supported by funds provided to the Center for Political Studies by the John D. and Catherine T. MacArthur Foundation.

2. In an article published in *Foreign Policy*, Richard Ullman revealed that the United States has provided covert assistance to French nuclear forces since 1973. Ullman also indicates that in return for this assistance France had agreed in event of war in Europe to coordinate operations of French forces with NATO forces. Plans called for the use of French facilities to funnel U.S. reinforcements to Europe and for communications. These revelations change significantly the picture of French relations with the United States and NATO. Ullman argues that the covert program "may well have been the factor that caused de Gaulle's successors to bring France most of the way back into the alliance" (Ullman 1989: 33).

References

Bechhoefer, Bernard G. (1961). *Postwar Negotiations for Arms Control*. Washington, DC: Brookings Institution.

Brzezinski, Zbigniew (1983). *Power and Principle: Memoirs of the National Security Adviser, 1977–1981*. New York: Farrar, Straus, and Giroux.

Bundy, McGeorge, George F. Kennan, Robert S. McNamara, and Gerard Smith (1982). "Nuclear Weapons and the Atlantic Alliance." *Foreign Affairs*, 60(4), 753–68.

Calleo, David P. (1987). *Beyond American Hegemony: The Future of the Western Alliance*. New York: Basic Books.

Carnesale, Albert, and Richard N. Haass, eds. (1987). *Superpower Arms Control: Setting the Record Straight*. Cambridge, MA: Ballinger.

Claude, Inis L., Jr. (1964). "The OAS, the UN, and the United States." *International Conciliation*, no. 547, 3–67.

—— (1967). *The Changing United Nations*. New York: Random House.

Fox, William T. R., and Annette Baker Fox (1967). *NATO and the Range of American Choice*. New York: Columbia University Press.

Gaddis, John Lewis (1971). *The United States and the Origins of the Cold War, 1941–1947*. New York: Columbia University Press.

—— (1982). *Strategies of Containment: A Critical Appraisal of Postwar American Security Policy*. New York: Oxford University Press.

Goodrich, Leland M. (1956). *Korea: A Study of U.S. Policy*. New York: Council on Foreign Relations.

Gorbachev, Mikhail (1987). "The Realities and Guarantees of a Security World." New York: USSR, Mission to the United Nations, Press Release No. 119, September 17, 1987.

Holsti, Ole R., and James N. Rosenau (1984). *American Leadership in World Affairs: Vietnam and the Breakdown of Consensus*. Boston: Unwin Hyman.

Huntington, Samuel P. (1961). *The Common Defense: Strategic Programs in National Politics*. New York: Columbia University Press.

Jacobson, Harold K., and Eric Stein (1966). *Diplomats, Scientists, and Politicians: The United States and the Nuclear Test Ban Negotiations*. Ann Arbor: University of Michigan Press.

Kissinger, Henry A. (1957). *Nuclear Weapons and Foreign Policy*. New York: Harper Brothers.

McNamara, Robert S. (1986). *Blundering into Disaster: Surviving the First Century of the Nuclear Age*. New York: Pantheon.

Organski, A. F. K., and Jacek Kugler (1980). *The War Ledger*. Chicago: University of Chicago Press.

Osgood, Robert Endicott (1962). *NATO: The Entangling Alliance*. Chicago: University of Chicago Press.

Russell, Ruth B. (1958). *A History of the United Nations Charter.* Washington, DC: Brookings Institution.

Sauvant, Karl (1981). *The Group of 77: Evolution, Structure, Organization.* Dobbs Ferry: Oceania.

Scheinman, Lawrence (1987). *The International Atomic Energy Agency and World Nuclear Order.* Washington, DC: Resources for the Future.

Schwartz, David N. (1983). *NATO's Nuclear Dilemma.* Washington, DC: Brookings Institution.

Steinbrunner, John D., and Leon V. Sigal, eds. (1982). *Alliance Security: NATO and the No First Use Question.* Washington, DC: Brookings Institution.

Truman, Harry S. (1956). *Memoirs.* New York: Doubleday.

Ullman, Richard H. (1989). "The Covert French Connection." *Foreign Policy,* 75 (Summer), 3–33.

United Nations General Assembly (1946). *Resolutions Adopted by the General Assembly during the First Part of Its First Session.* Resolution 1, pp. 9–10. London: United Nations.

U.S. Department of State (1950). *Postwar Foreign Policy Preparation, 1939–1945* (Department of State Publication 3580, General Foreign Policy Series 15). Washington, DC: U.S. Government Printing Office.

Urquhart, Brian (1972). *Hammarskjold.* New York: Alfred A. Knopf.

Wolfers, Arnold (1954). "Collective Security and the War in Korea." *Yale Review,* 23(4), 481–502.

CHAPTER THREE

Dominance without Hegemony: U.S. Relations with the International Atomic Energy Agency

Benjamin N. Schiff

The International Atomic Energy Agency (IAEA) began operations in 1957 after four years of effort by the United States to achieve multilaterally what it could not do by itself. Prior to 1952 the United States had pursued a policy of nuclear technology denial, but the Soviet Union's test of a nuclear device in 1949 demonstrated that policy's failure. Likewise, pressure from Great Britain to resume atomic energy cooperation terminated by the United States after World War II made denial politically untenable, leading to a resumption of cooperation under the 1952 revision of the Atomic Energy Act of 1946. President Eisenhower's "Atoms for Peace" speech to the United Nations in December 1953 denoted the adoption of a policy of controlled technology dissemination. Eisenhower called for the creation of an organization to manage international development of peaceful uses for atomic energy. The IAEA—a modified version of the organization Eisenhower envisioned—was intended to promote and control the international dissemination of nuclear technology.

Since the beginning of the IAEA the United States has been its most important member. However, the United States does not absolutely control outcomes in the IAEA, nor has its role in the IAEA been immune to the kinds of changes in U.S. influence that have occurred in other multilateral organizations. Several factors explain the changing pattern of influence in the IAEA. The general decline in U.S. dominance in the international system is mirrored in the IAEA, as the newly independent Third World countries in the organization have reduced the U.S. ability to muster automatic majorities. The character of the issue area also changed.

Although it has proved impossible to prevent the spread of the technology, the common U.S.-Soviet recognition of nuclear proliferation's threat has led to the delineation of regime rules. The domestic politics of U.S. nonproliferation and IAEA policies have changed, but not in a single direction. They have varied between quiet acceptance of executive branch use of the agency to pursue its purposes and general skepticisim over the agency's utility. Typically Congress has challenged administration assurances that the IAEA is adequate to the control task. Sometimes different parts of the executive branch itself have disagreed over the appropriate course of IAEA diplomacy.

Multilateralism has become a constraint on U.S. nuclear policy as well as an asset to it. Limits imposed by multilateralism cannot be avoided; however, room for maneuver remains. The IAEA has not always been the best vehicle for pursuing U.S. nonproliferation objectives. As a consequence the United States has created other forums and occasionally pursued unilateral courses of action. But it keeps returning to the IAEA, seeking legitimacy for agreements reached in ad hoc groups, trying to build consensus around its unilateral policies, and pressing to expand the IAEA's mandate and operations.

This chapter is composed of five parts. First, the international role and the structure of the IAEA are described. Second, I discuss U.S. use of the IAEA for its nonproliferation policy and actions the United States has taken to mold the agency into an effective tool. Third, IAEA influences on U.S. policies and policymaking are outlined. Fourth, alternative explanations of the changing U.S.-IAEA relationship are considered. Finally, I describe the implications of this relationship for multilateralism in U.S. foreign policy.

Role and Structure of the IAEA

The IAEA is the organizational core of an international nuclear nonproliferation regime whose rules are spelled out in a network of treaties, bilateral and regional obligations, and informal agreements. The regime's norms are that the proliferation of nuclear weapons is bad, though some states individually seek to obtain the capability; nuclear technology and its dissemination are desirable, though nuclear power's economic viability and political acceptability vary from country to country; universality of membership in the regime is desirable and obligations within the regime should be reciprocal, if not equal.[1]

Within this broad consensus, countries pursue different national priorities. The United States played a key role in establishing the agency and has labored to extend the regime to prevent the spread of nuclear weapons. Since 1963 the United States and USSR have agreed on the principle of on-site inspection of nuclear facilities in countries without nuclear weapons. The two superpowers subsequently worked in concert to extend the regime—a unique example of U.S.-Soviet cooperation in a world still divided by the cold war.

Developed nonnuclear weapons states have generally not worried as much as the United States about nuclear proliferation. They have used the IAEA for information exchange networks and for international diplomatic and commercial contacts. However, proliferation concerns and commercial interests do overlap for them. Exporters of nuclear technology need a stable regulatory environment (preferably at low levels of intervention, but at least a level that minimizes political intrusion into trade flows) in order to maximize their nuclear exports. And they have generally assented to U.S. nonproliferation initiatives, including the incremental expansion of IAEA responsibilities, in order to deter the United States in part from taking more extreme unilateralist positions.

For developing countries the regime generally and the IAEA in particular offer opportunities to demand increased international technology transfers. The superpowers' concerns with proliferation have helped developing countries to obtain nuclear-related training, materials, and hardware. They have accepted the proffered exchange of technology transfer for monitoring and control.

IAEA forums present opportunities for national politicians and technocrats to meet with their foreign counterparts and discuss issues important to the IAEA and the nuclear regime in general. The agency is governed by its General Conference and Board of Governors. The annual General Conference, in which each member state has one vote, approves the agency's budget and program, elects the director general, and discusses issues that confront the agency. The Board of Governors, currently composed of thirty-five members, meets several times during the year and is the policymaking body of the agency. Board members are elected according to a formula for regional representation and leadership in nuclear technology. The board is dominated by the thirteen states most advanced in nuclear technology and most influential in establishing the agency. The General Conference's selection of the director general is subject to board approval (IAEA 1959; U.S. House of Representatives and Senate 1977: 43–58).[2]

In 1957 when the IAEA was established, the United States succeeded in setting up a framework within which international nonproliferation norms and rules could evolve. Since 1957 the United States has usually been able to mold the agency to its purposes, though the difficulty of achieving successes in these efforts has varied considerably depending on how much U.S. policies have challenged the interests of other member states.

IAEA as an Instrument of U.S. Policy

The primary tenet of U.S. nonproliferation policy is that international stability is undermined when additional countries develop nuclear weapons capabilities. The United States has worked to create an international regime to carry out as much of this policy as possible, seeking to create rules and legitimate or delegitimate other states' activities under the regime's norms. U.S. policy entails (1) thwarting other countries' nuclear weapons development; if they appear to be proceeding, (2) pressuring them to stop; if they appear to have developed to an explosive, (3) preventing them from testing it; and if they test an explosive, (4) discouraging them from deploying weapons. The United States uses the IAEA to carry out parts 1 and 2 of the policy.

Technology control is at the crux of the regime's activities. IAEA safeguards are intended to deter by threat of detection the development of weapons by states that submit to IAEA safeguards. If the safeguards fail to deter development, at least they can warn the rest of the international community that a country is failing to adhere to international nonprolifera-tion norms. Information about countries' compliance with those norms is the collective good that the IAEA produces. IAEA technical assistance is a benefit offered in exchange for states' accepting the rules of the regime. Since passage of the 1978 U.S. Nuclear Non-proliferation Act, the United States has required technology recipient states to accept IAEA safeguards on all of their nuclear facilities as a condition of supply. (This condition, however, has not always been fulfilled because of the use of a presidential waiver in cases affecting the "vital security interests" involved in continued supplies to, for instance, India.)

In its quest for international technology controls, U.S. nonproliferation policy confronts commercial rivals for and consumers of nuclear exports. It tries to minimize commercial confrontation by negotiating multilateral agreements. It tries to bring consumers into the regime by convincing them of the threat of nuclear proliferation and, to the extent possible, by making it difficult for them to acquire nuclear technology unless they can accept the regime's rules. The United States gambles that disseminating the technology helps it to retain moral influence, if not actual control, over the path taken by new entries into the nuclear marketplace; the IAEA holds the bets.

From 1963 until 1973 nonproliferation diplomacy was relatively stable.

U.S. commercial interests were promoted by the Atomic Energy Commission. The IAEA and other forums were used to seek agreement over controls and the direction of nuclear technology transfer and development. The IAEA promoted nuclear technology. Negotiations beginning in 1961 led to the Treaty on the Non-proliferation of Nuclear Weapons (NPT), which went into effect in 1970. The treaty spelled out the rules of the regime. Under the NPT countries that had no nuclear weapons promised not to acquire or develop them, and states with weapons technology promised not to transfer it to nonnuclear countries. The IAEA was to verify that peaceful installations were not turned to military purposes.

Since the early 1960s U.S. commentators had predicted that dire consequences would follow from nuclear proliferation (Beaton and Maddox 1962). But with IAEA safeguards beginning in 1963, the NPT in 1970, and more extensive safeguards to follow, the United States was relatively complacent about the problem until 1973.

Then, with the skyrocketing price of oil changing the nature of the energy issue area, plans were laid for a massive expansion in use of nuclear power in most industrialized countries. The expansion of nuclear power would require great increases in uranium fuel for the current generation of reactors, and projections indicated that such fuel would become scarce. Its price rapidly escalated. One way to resolve the fuel shortage problem was to develop breeder reactors, which would produce large quantities of plutonium for use as fuel. But the same plutonium could be diverted for conversion to weapons. Just as the breeder began to look like a reasonable technological solution to the fuel problem, evidence emerged that even in the existing world where access to plutonium was quite limited, threats of nuclear proliferation were increasing.

Israel was rumored to have begun assembling weapons in the early days of the 1973 Yom Kippur War. Nuclear weapons were reportedly being developed in Taiwan, South Africa, India, and South Korea. Then in 1974 India tested its "peaceful nuclear explosive" (Spector 1984: 31–38).[3] The U.S. gamble appeared to be a losing one. For the next six years the United States undertook a variety of steps to shore up what it perceived as an inadequate regime. It pressed the IAEA to improve safeguards. The agency and other forums were used to create new agreement over regime norms and rules, on the future of nuclear technology transfer and development, and for tighter control on existing programs.

These efforts were politically costly. The United States roused enmity when it tried (successfully) to deter France from selling reprocessing equipment to Pakistan (Spector 1984: 74–75, 78–80); (unsuccessfully) to derail a giant German-Brazilian reactor deal (Gall 1976; Lowrance 1977);

and (successfully) to influence Japan to slow reprocessing and subject it to international safeguards (Rochlin 1979: 125). New export limitations were eventually agreed on, IAEA operations were improved, and by the mid-1980s a degree of international amicability had returned to nonproliferation diplomacy (Beckman 1985: chaps. 9–10).

Safeguards: Monitoring International Rules

When the United States began its Atoms for Peace program in 1954, it required recipients of nuclear technology to sign agreements for cooperation guaranteeing that transfers would be used exclusively for peaceful purposes (Atomic Energy Act of 1954). In 1963 the United States and Soviet Union finally reached agreement over proposed IAEA safeguards (Schiff 1984: chap. 3). In 1965 the system (known by its IAEA document designation, INFCIRC/66) went into effect. It required that equipment, materials, or technology transferred through the agency would be monitored to ensure they were not diverted to military purposes. Parties to transfers not directly involving the IAEA could contract with the IAEA to verify compliance with peaceful uses guarantees. When INFCIRC/66 came into effect, the United States converted its bilateral safeguards agreements to IAEA trilateral agreements. At first INFCIRC/66 covered only nuclear reactors of limited sizes. The United States successfully pressed to include larger reactors, reprocessing, and enrichment technology. The final version of the system (INFCIRC/66/Rev. 2) went into effect in 1968 (Fischer and Szasz 1985: Appendix IV; IAEA 1965).[4]

At the same time that the United States sought extension of the INFCIRC/66 system within the IAEA, it also pursued negotiations in the Eighteen Nation Disarmament Conference on the proposed NPT to convert the implicit rules of the regime into explicit treaty guarantees. When the NPT was opened for signature and ratification (1968), the United States pressed for a second safeguards system to carry out NPT Article III. Under that article all nuclear facilities in nonnuclear signatory states were to be inspected by the IAEA to verify compliance with the treaty.

Two years of negotiations produced agreement on the new safeguards system, INFCIRC/153 (Fischer and Szasz 1985: Appendix V; IAEA 1972). Experts from the Federal Republic of Germany led in developing the system, ensuring that the FRG would join the NPT and fulfilling the Soviet Union's primary objective for the NPT. Although INFCIRC/153 laid out procedures for safeguards of NPT signatories' nuclear facilities, it did not specify when safeguards would be "triggered" for transfers from NPT signatories to nonsignatories of the treaty. Given that several nuclear consumers had not signed the treaty, this became a major U.S. concern. The United States sought supplier agreement on a "trigger" list. Because the Europeans were less concerned about proliferation than the United States, were more worried about competitive advantage, and regarded the spread of technology as inevitable, they were reluctant to agree on the list. The United States feared that without it, loose safeguards restrictions would become bargaining chips in the increasingly fierce competition for international nuclear sales.

In 1971, an IAEA committee (the Zangger Committee) was formed to seek agreement on what transfers would be considered sensitive. The negotiations failed. France, Belgium, Italy, and Switzerland refused to agree to an official IAEA trigger list.

Supporters of the list, led by the United States, went ahead with their own list, informing the agency and having it publicize the information in a 1974 communiqué, INFCIRC/209 (SIPRI 1975: 17–19 and Appendix 1). The United States thus used the IAEA to publicize the regime rules it sought (unsuccessfully) to establish under IAEA auspices.

Having failed within the IAEA, the United States then created its own forum outside. In 1976 the United States brought together a secret Nuclear Suppliers Group (NSG) and pressed for a common safeguards policy. The group, including the INFCIRC/209 holdouts, agreed on a trigger list in 1978 and again published it through and hence legitimated it by notifying the IAEA of the agreement. It was issued as an IAEA document (INFCIRC/254; see Fischer and Szasz 1985: Appendix IX). Resorting to the Suppliers Group showed the United States could not achieve its objectives through the agency's representative organs. However, its use of the IAEA to publicize the outcome of the trigger list discussions demonstrated its desire to use the IAEA to legitimate its activities.

Domestic political factors combined with changes in the international arena to shape U.S. nonproliferation policies in the mid-1970s. Specifically India's nuclear test in 1974 led to congressional review of those policies and IAEA activities. The Senate Committee on Government Operations criticized past U.S. laxity on export standards and challenged the effectiveness of IAEA safeguards. In 1976 the IAEA established the Standing Advisory Group on Safeguards Implementation (SAGSI), which issued the first annual Safeguards Implementation Report (SIR) the following year. In order to report on implementation, the agency's safeguards division defined new, quantifiable objectives for the system, introduced new equipment for evaluating compliance, and reported its results in the SIRs (IAEA 1975–79, 1977a).

At the same time, the United States worked with the secretariat to bring the first safeguards system (INFCIRC/66/Rev.2) into conformity with methods and routines developed for INFCIRC/153, thereby simplifying the IAEA's task. States that had not signed the NPT and were still safeguarded under INFCIRC/66/Rev.2 complained that the United States was seeking to tighten restrictions through the back door of the IAEA secretariat instead of through the proper political channels.

To help implement the improved safeguards system, U.S. Energy Research and Development Administration (ERDA, later the Department of Energy) and Arms Control and Disarmament Agency (ACDA) safeguards technologies were transferred to the IAEA. National laboratories participated in the U.S. Program of Technical Assistance to Safeguards (POTAS), the products of which were transferred to the IAEA. The United States contributed directly to IAEA safeguards technological development, aside from support through the IAEA regular budget. Table 3.1 shows the level of U.S. regular budget and special contributions to the agency's safeguards program as reported in a 1984 General Accounting Office study.

After 1983 Department of Energy (DOE) contributions continued

TABLE 3.1
U.S. Financial Support to International Safeguards ($ millions)

	1977	1978	1979	1980	1981	1982	1983	Total
IAEA Safeguards								
Regular budget[a]	7.95	12.03	14.83	18.26	19.86	23.20	29.53	125.66
U.S. share, regular safeguards budget	4.32	3.66	4.64	6.01	6.83	7.01	8.21	40.70
Additional Support								
DOE[b]	2.40	3.40	4.50	7.14	6.60	6.50	6.50	37.04
ACDA[c]	.41	1.89	.96	1.60	1.25	.34	.30	6.74
NRC	.00	.15	.09	.44	.08	.16	.23	1.14
POTAS	5.42	3.80	5.58	4.10	4.10	4.00	4.50	31.50
Subtotal U.S.	8.23	9.24	11.12	13.27	12.03	11.00	11.53	76.41
Total U.S.	12.55	12.90	15.76	19.28	18.86	18.03	19.74	117.12

SOURCE: IAEA safeguards figures: IAEA, *Annual Budget* reports; U.S. information, GAO (1984).

[a] IAEA figure includes regular budget allocations only.

[b] Note from GAO study: "Includes funds for all DOE domestic safeguards research and development and for supporting IAEA inspections at selected U.S. nuclear facilities. Thus, includes more than just IAEA-needed safeguards equipment. . . . Figures reflect only program activities carried out under DOE international rather than domestic support. The products of these DOE efforts are largely transferred to IAEA through POTAS. . . . Figures include technology research and development and systems analyses for policy assistance to apply IAEA safeguards at U.S. nuclear facilities." This indicates that the amounts are overstated as seen from the IAEA standpoint, but they do include projects that the United States deems relevant for IAEA purposes.

[c] Note from GAO study: "Includes a project called RECOVER (REmote COntinuous VERification) which IAEA perceived as having applicability to IAEA safeguards, but never reached the stage of development required for IAEA use and therefore was never officially accepted for safeguards use."

at approximately a level of $6.5 million per year; the ACDA and Nuclear Regulatory Commission (NRC) contributions remained at very low levels. As the IAEA continued to increase safeguards funding, so also funding of the Program of Technical Assistance to IAEA Safeguards (POTAS) increased. According to reports filed by the executive branch to Congress under the Nuclear Non-proliferation Act of 1978, POTAS funding grew as noted in Table 3.2.

TABLE 3.2
Program of Technical Assistance to IAEA Safeguards (POTAS) Funding
and IAEA Safeguards Regular Budget (1982–88) ($ millions)

	1982	1983	1984	1985	1986	1987	1988
POTAS	3.35	3.74	3.74	5.00	5.58	5.26	5.13
IAEA	23.20	29.53	27.30	30.99	39.90	43.79	49.49*

SOURCE: President's report to Congress on nonproliferation activities under Section 601 of the NNPA, 1982–88, from U.S. Department of State, Office of Nuclear Technology and Safeguards, Bureau of Oceans and International Environmental and Scientific Affairs (1989); IAEA, biennial *Budget and Programme* reports.
    * Budgeted.

The direction of U.S. pressure to extend and refine safeguards has been consistent since the IAEA's founding, but the intensity of that pressure increased following the events of 1973–74. The United States pushed much harder to tighten the system after the shocks of 1973–74. When European states' competitive interests stymied agreement on the trigger list, the United States moved outside of the IAEA to shape the negotiations. The United States used multiple diplomatic channels to respond to the increasingly complex negotiating environment. IAEA operational capabilities remained vital to the United States, and it used the agency to confer legitimacy on U.S. initiatives. The Atoms for Peace trade-off had exchanged control for assistance. As the United States tried harder to extend controls, it had to pay increasing attention to the technology transfer side of the equation—that is, activities to uphold the other side of the control-for-benefits bargain.

Technical Assistance: IAEA Operations to Uphold the Nuclear Bargain

At the time of its founding, the IAEA was quicker to implement technical assistance activities than to carry out safeguards measures because there was no disagreement over assistance. It could be restricted to uses of atomic energy that had no military ramifications, and no countries felt threatened by the "payoff" side of the exchange of control for technology transfers. The enticement for agreement to control preceded development of the controls themselves.

The agency's technical assistance program expanded rapidly when the United States phased out its Atoms for Peace program in the early 1960s, with former recipients turning to the IAEA to fill the gap. They became the initial and major IAEA technical assistance clients. U.S. withdrawal from its bilateral assistance program was a demonstration that it successfully dominated the agency. The United States could count on the IAEA to carry out its policy direction.

As the 1960s progressed, nonnuclear developing countries became increasingly concerned that IAEA technical assistance was not keeping pace with the increase in safeguards activities. The United States reacted when it became concerned that assistance was not enough to motivate states to accept safeguards. In the mid-1970s developing countries began resisting U.S. and IAEA initiatives to tighten safeguards, demanding that increases in technical assistance keep pace with safeguards so that *both* sides of the control-for-transfer bargain would be upheld. By the late 1970s the United States was pressing for large increases in the agency's technical assistance budget and sought to improve the administration of the technical assistance program in order to respond to the LDC's demands (Interviews at ACDA and Department of State 1984).

Table 3.3 shows that the technical assistance budget substantially increased during the late 1970s and 1980s. To avoid the statute's restriction that there be no discrimination for political reasons among recipients of General Fund assistance, the United States and other contributors began channeling money into technical assistance through "extrabudgetary" funds rather than the General Fund. Such funds could be earmarked for particular projects or countries so that donors created additional rewards for states that signed the NPT.

As shown in Table 3.3, U.S. influence on technical assistance as measured by its proportion of the combined budget and of extrabudgetary funds grew and then fell during the late Carter and Reagan administrations. Although U.S. concern about proliferation peaked during the Carter administration, it was pursuing policies in several forums in addition to the IAEA, and thus its concern is not reflected in an increase of its share of the IAEA's budget. Early efforts to reinforce the IAEA through extrabudgetary contributions first gave the United States a disproportionately large share in these earmarked funds, which then declined as other states followed the U.S. example. Under Reagan U.S. funding levels held relatively constant, demonstrating the administration's reduced interest in the IAEA because, given inflation, the value of the U.S. contribution declined in real terms. At the same time, other states continued to

TABLE 3.3
U.S. Contributions to IAEA Technical Assistance Programs 1975–87,
General Fund and Extrabudgetary Funds ($ millions)

	Total TA Funds	Total GF	Total EBF Donations	U.S. GF Donation (% GF)	U.S. EBF Donation (% EBF)	U.S. Total IAEA TA (% Total)
1975*	5.69	4.5	1.19	1.24 (27.6)	.51 (42.9)	1.75 (30.8)
1976*	6.87	5.5	1.37	1.52 (27.6)	.63 (46.0)	2.15 (31.3)
1977*	8.15	6.0	2.15	1.65 (27.6)	1.20 (55.8)	2.85 (35.0)
1978	9.96	7.1	2.86	1.75 (25.1)	1.04 (36.4)	2.79 (28.3)
1979	11.44	8.8	2.64	2.13 (24.2)	1.08 (40.9)	3.21 (28.1)
1980	13.27	10.6	2.67	2.63 (24.8)	1.16 (43.4)	3.79 (28.8)
1981	16.56	13.0	3.56	3.12 (24.0)	1.22 (34.3)	4.34 (26.2)
1982	20.41	16.0	4.41	4.00 (25.0)	1.37 (31.1)	5.37 (26.3)
1983	27.30	19.2	8.10	4.69 (24.4)	1.83 (22.6)	6.52 (23.9)
1984	28.16	27.2	5.96	5.50 (24.8)	1.40 (23.5)	6.90 (24.5)
1985	30.68	25.2	5.48	6.50 (25.8)	1.76 (32.1)	8.26 (26.9)
1986	34.60	27.9	5.70	7.01 (25.1)	1.15 (20.2)	8.16 (23.6)
1987	35.90	30.2	5.70	8.21 (27.2)	1.5 (26.3)	9.71 (27.0)

SOURCES: IAEA *Bulletin*, 27(2), 10; IAEA, Annual *Report on Technical Assistance*; IAEA, Annual *Accounts* documents.
GF = General Fund: voluntary contributions; EBF = Extrabudgetary Funds: contributions outside GF.
* Not strictly comparable to later years because of accounting procedures.

increase their contributions. The United States was less willing to bear a disproportionately large share of the costs of multilateralism, especially under an administration suspicious of international organizations.

The United States has been concerned with the technical assistance program mostly because assistance might help to gain adherents to the NPT and to IAEA safeguards and could help to influence an international nuclear technical elite to adopt the U.S. perspective on nuclear energy and its threat. At first the IAEA program was merely a multilateral successor to the old U.S. bilateral program. With time it evolved into a program largely devoid of direct U.S. influence, except that the United States has supported the program to uphold that side of the assistance-for-control exchange. As U.S. nonproliferation proponents became increasingly dissatisfied with the level of assurances they could gain through the exchange as it was structured, they pressed for studies and agreements that would create consensus over the future course of nuclear development.

Planning the Nuclear Future: Legitimating and Verifying Limits to Nuclear Development

Until the early 1970s the United States used the IAEA to promote nuclear power in developing countries. Then as fears of proliferation grew, it reversed course and tried to quell interest in parts of the fuel cycle that it considered to be proliferation threats, using the IAEA to explore possibilities for new international controls. When its actions inside the IAEA and through domestic legislation created too much suspicion, the United States pursued its policies outside the agency but sought to use the IAEA to legitimate its views.

In the late 1960s and early 1970s the United States and IAEA were still promoting nuclear power reactors for use in developing countries. The United States made available to the IAEA a set of computer programs developed by the Brookhaven National Laboratory for energy demand modeling; it also carried out a series of nuclear power "market surveys" intended to provide developing countries with the information they needed to understand the potential for nuclear energy development (IAEA 1973). The surveys were intended to create demand for small reactors and to show reactor manufacturers that a market existed.[5] As the United States became more concerned with proliferation threats, its interest in the market surveys declined and criticisms of their methodology mounted.

A second major study undertaken by the IAEA reflected the changed U.S. priorities. By 1975 shortages of nuclear fuel were being predicted because of projected increases in demand for nuclear energy and decreases in the availability of fuel. One possible solution was chemical extraction of plutonium from spent fuel and its recycle in light water reactors. The problem was that increased plutonium availability would increase the risk of weapons proliferation.

U.S. State Department and ACDA officials thought that the risks of plutonium recycling might be reduced if reprocessing facilities were placed under multinational control. International centers could reduce motivations to develop and deploy reprocessing in nonnuclear countries and could be safeguarded more easily than multiple-nation installations. The United

States urged the IAEA to look into the possibilities for multilateral fuel reprocessing centers, and it responded by initiating the Regional Nuclear Fuel Cycle Center (RFCC) project. The RFCC report was issued in 1977 (IAEA 1977b). By that time U.S. enthusiasm had dissipated. The Carter administration feared that planning for reprocessing under any auspices would exacerbate the problem.

As U.S. and IAEA officials became more concerned about the products of reprocessing, they realized that international control would be necessary not only of the facilities but also of the materials produced by the centers: uranium and plutonium separated from spent fuel. The IAEA began a smaller-scale study on plutonium management in 1977–78 (IAEA 1977c). The decline in nuclear fuel demand and the apparent diseconomies of reprocessing made the RFCC and PMS studies obsolete by the early 1980s.

By 1977 U.S. manipulation of the enriched uranium supply (Brenner 1981: chap. 2), unilateral abrogations of enrichment contracts, efforts to create suppliers' agreement over the "trigger list," and the pending domestic Nuclear Non-proliferation Act, which threatened to impose sanctions on countries not complying with U.S. demands for "full-scope safeguards," had roused serious opposition to and suspicion of further U.S. nonproliferation initiatives. Seeking to increase the priority of non-proliferation considerations in other states' decision making about their nuclear programs, the United States initiated a planning exercise outside the IAEA. The high levels of suspicion about U.S. initiatives meant that gaining agreement on the study within the agency's legislative organs would not be possible.

Instead the United States invited countries to join it in the International Nuclear Fuel Cycle Evaluation (INFCE). Officially not a negotiation but a technical exercise, INFCE technical discussions were shaped by the national nuclear commitments of participating states. The United States sought agreement on a nuclear future that would reduce proliferation threats. It argued (against European and especially French opposition) that power demand would grow more slowly than previously predicted, and thus there was no urgent need to build nuclear fuel reprocessing plants or breeder reactors. It urged agreement on definitions of "sensitive" technologies and encouraged exporters to promote safer technologies. It tried to convince others to research and develop proliferation-resistant nuclear technologies to replace the current generation of equipment.

INFCE participants developed national positions, then contributed to joint reports in multinational working groups.[6] The national positions on the growth of nuclear power, the export trade, technological change, and the seriousness of the proliferation threat differed considerably. The working group discussions became highly charged.

The IAEA's primary role in INFCE was to provide secretariat staffing, meeting places, and technical support for the working groups and to publish the final report. The agency also wound up representing the otherwise underrepresented developing countries by contributing to INFCE a study of the nuclear technology needs of developing countries. IAEA involvement in INFCE was funded by special contributions from participating states.[7]

INFCE was successful in raising proliferation concerns, especially among the European nuclear supplier states. It was in that sense the climax of activist U.S. nonproliferation efforts that had grown throughout the 1970s.

By the end of the decade the United States had pressed its non-proliferation policies with considerable success despite resistance from European and developing states. The objectives it had pursued in the 1970s, however, were harder to attain. It continued to set the agency's agenda and increased its contributions of technical expertise and funds. When necessary, it stepped outside the agency to pursue policies it could not push forward within the IAEA. It remained committed to the agency, especially at working levels within the bureaucracy, even as the Reagan administration came into office with less concern about proliferation than its predecessors and less commitment to working within international organizations.

The United States retained significant influence in the IAEA even as the environment in which it pursued its nonproliferation policies grew more turbulent. Although other countries gained in their influence within the IAEA, this influence did not translate into important constraints on the United States. The IAEA's effects on U.S. policy have generally been expected and accepted by the United States as a price for using this multilateral organization to influence other states. Nonetheless, the IAEA has been an important part of the environment that has shaped U.S. nuclear nonproliferation and nuclear energy development policies.

IAEA Impact on the United States

Since 1957 U.S. policy and organization in the nuclear nonproliferation field has been predicated on the existence of the IAEA as a major—but not the exclusive—channel for influence in the regime. Changes in U.S. policy and decision making cannot be attributed exclusively to the IAEA, but the agency is an important part of the environment to which it has responded. Decision-making processes and domestic nuclear and inter-national nonproliferation policy have been affected by the IAEA—the concrete manifestation of regime norms and rules that the United States seeks to uphold and extend—but the IAEA has been less an overt source of influence than a major target of policy. Affecting the IAEA and other states has required policies that the United States would probably not have undertaken had it been operating without concern over multilateral management of the threat of nuclear proliferation.

Adapting U.S. Decision-Making Processes

Like any other international organization, the IAEA pressures the U.S. bureaucracy simply by its existence. Its schedule and annual agenda create a set of deadlines and topics requiring decisions. U.S. agencies with relevant statutory or customary responsibilities need to agree on the agency's budget and program direction, and technical expertise needs to be organized to contribute to policy and program reviews and initiatives. The more important nonproliferation has been for the United States, the greater the IAEA's impact on its decision-making bureaucracies: decision makers have had to figure out how to get what they want through the IAEA or how to create other venues by which to circumvent its limitations.

The U.S. mission to the IAEA is formally instructed by the secretary of state. Before the Energy Reorganization Act of 1974[8] the AEC's international programs division dominated policymaking toward the IAEA, and AEC personnel seconded to the U.S. mission were the primary U.S. link to the agency. After the AEC was abolished other bureaucratic actors became increasingly important, although initially former AEC people, transferred into the Department of State, continued to dominate.

By the late 1970s bureaus in the State Department and Arms Control and Disarmament Agency played the major role in U.S.-IAEA policy. The State Department's Bureau for International Organizations continued to coordinate formulating the secretary of state's instructions to the U.S. mission, but policy was actually made collaboratively by the Bureaus for Science and Technology (STI), Oceans and International Environmental and Scientific Affairs, ACDA's Non-proliferation Bureau (later under Reagan, an amalgamated Bureau for Weapons and Nuclear Control), sometimes the National Security Council (NSC) staff, and, on particular issues, bureaus within the Departments of Defense and Energy and the Nuclear Regulatory Commission. Varying degrees of latitude have been left to the U.S. Mission in Vienna, but its influence has declined since the days of the AEC.

The agency's annual cycle of meetings structures the agenda of U.S. nonproliferation policymakers. Member states use the occasions of the General Conferences to pursue not only IAEA but also other nonproliferation business. Bilateral demarches and extraordinary diplomatic efforts such as the London Supplier's Group and the INFCE became independent of the IAEA cycle once they acquired their own momentum, but informal consultation over such initiatives routinely take place at regular IAEA meetings. In addition, the ongoing support programs for the IAEA such as POTAS require domestic preparation and backing.

INFCE was initiated in the Carter administration by the office of Deputy Undersecretary of State for Security Assistance, Science and Technology Joseph S. Nye. It absorbed the efforts of large numbers of people in the Departments of Energy, State, and ACDA who developed working papers on technical aspects of alternative nuclear fuel cycle futures and possible institutional innovations to limit proliferation. INFCE working groups were also the users of a Department of Energy study of the comparative proliferation resistances of alternative nuclear fuel cycles called the Non-proliferation Alternative Systems Assessment Program (NASAP); (U.S. Department of Energy 1979).

A second programmatic consequence of U.S. policy toward the IAEA is the Department of Energy, ACDA, and national laboratory work for the POTAS. The relevant safeguards development work at the national laboratories is geared specifically toward IAEA uses (U.S. General Accounting Office 1984).

Unlike the safeguards case, there has been little bureaucratic attention to and coordination of contributions to the IAEA's technical assistance program. Until its dissolution the AEC international division cursorily examined IAEA Technical Assistance Committee (TAC) proposals for technical assistance funding and occasionally criticized some of the projects or requested modifications. After 1974 ERDA and later DOE took over the task, but there was no standing interagency mechanism or custom for tailoring U.S. responses to the TAC reports, for proposing innovations in the program, or for integrating contributions into larger nonproliferation and foreign policies.

In 1985, recognizing that the technical assistance side of the IAEA equation is very important, representatives of the Department of State, ACDA, Nuclear Regulatory Commission, and Department of Energy agreed to coordinate their activities in this area.

DOE continued to take the lead in examining IAEA proposals for the program of technical assistance, but U.S. participation in IAEA non-safeguards activities has been handled through the International Nuclear Technical Liaison Office (INTLO) run by the Argonne National Laboratory in Washington, D.C., under contract to the Department of State. The INTLO coordinates nominations of U.S. citizens to short-term IAEA technical meetings; manages U.S. offers of fellowships, experts, and training projects to the IAEA and coordinates selection of personnel for them; and scrutinizes projects proposed for footnote "a" funding (that is, funds to the IAEA in excess of the voluntary technical assistance contribution) by the United States. The INTLO stays in close contact with the U.S. mission to the IAEA in Vienna (Interview 1985).

Domestic decision-making structures have also grown up around U.S. efforts to improve IAEA safeguards and to implement IAEA safeguards in U.S. facilities. In 1976–77 an interagency mechanism was established to coordinate U.S. policy on safeguards. At the top of the bureaucratic pyramid is the Inter-agency Steering Group on IAEA Safeguards (ISG), consisting of deputy assistant secretary or office director-level representatives from the State Department, ACDA, DOE, NRC, NSC, and, depending on the issues involved, the Department of Defense.

In 1976–77 two working groups were established by the ISG. The first was the Action Plan Working Group (APWG) to coordinate a U.S. effort to formulate and implement a program of activities to improve IAEA safeguards operations and credibility. The APWG continues to operate, coordinating safeguards involvement of U.S. agencies with the IAEA and serving as the base for consultations over safeguards with U.S. allies.

The second group was the Technical Support Coordinating Committee (TSCC), consisting of experts from State, DOE, ACDA, and the NRC; it oversees the U.S. voluntary Program of Technical Assistance to IAEA Safeguards. POTAS itself is administered for the Department of State by the International Safeguards Program Office at Brookhaven National Laboratory. The State Department also contracts with Brookhaven's Technical Support Organization for safeguards technical expertise, contributions to POTAS, and technical back-up for the U.S. representative to the Standing Advisory Group on Safeguards Implementation (SAGSI; Kessler 1989: 6).

Also under the ISG are the Working Group on IAEA Safeguards Staffing (WGISS), which "coordinates efforts to recruit U.S. citizens to work on the IAEA safeguards staff," and the LASCAR (Large-Scale Automated Processing) Working Group, "which coordinates activities in support of the international effort to develop safeguards technology" (U.S. Department of State 1989: 24).

Prior to establishment of these interagency efforts, the United States had made a commitment in 1980 that served to expand activities under the ISG. In 1967 the United States had offered to allow the IAEA to safeguard some civilian installations to show reluctant European states that signing the NPT would not create commercial disadvantages for them (Hauk 1985: 13, 17). It took long negotiations between the United States and the IAEA following the offer to reach agreement on implementation procedures. The agreement came into force in 1980. Then in 1981 the United States set up another group under the ISG, the Safeguards Agreement Working Group (SAWG), to monitor and coordinate implementation of U.S. safeguards obligations and to circulate the results of the safeguards inspections to concerned American agencies. The SAWG includes a Subsidiary Arrangements Negotiating Team that negotiates with the IAEA specifications for the safeguards activities to be carried out at each U.S. nuclear facility (Kessler 1989: 3–4).

Domestic Policy Effects of Changing Rules and Norms

Until 1973–74 domestic nuclear policy had very little to do with nonproliferation efforts. The AEC's international division dominated policy but was essentially promotional in its attitude toward nuclear trade. Domestic decisions did not have to be made with much concern about their international ramifications because objectives at the two levels of policy were congruent.

As U.S. concern about proliferation increased, the government became aware that other states reacted to what it did domestically as well as internationally. The United States became concerned with the "demonstration effect" of its domestic nuclear policies. As its relative power declined, the United States sought to demonstrate that the policies it advocated for others were policies it was willing to implement at home. The demonstration effect, it hoped, would promote nuclear control as it had once promoted nuclear power development.

Under the Ford and Carter administrations, therefore, the United States took a number of domestic steps aimed at supporting international policy. To undermine the argument that Peaceful Nuclear Explosives (PNEs) might be useful for digging canals, stimulating natural gas recovery, or creating lakes, the United States terminated its own PNE testing program (Cornell University 1975). U.S. pressure then led to dissolution of the IAEA division established to consider how PNE services could be carried out under international auspices.

To demonstrate U.S. willingness to undergo the same sacrifices that nonnuclear states made for the purpose of verifying compliance with the NPT, in 1967 the United States accepted the principle of IAEA safeguards on its civilian facilities even though under the NPT it had no such obligation. When implementation finally began in the early 1980s, the United States guaranteed that the costs of implementing safeguards in the United States would not affect contributions to the agency; the costs would be borne by the United States and the program used as a testing ground for safeguards instrumentation and accounting innovations.

To support its nonproliferation stance, the United States terminated large-scale nuclear fuel reprocessing and breeder reactor development. From the early days of the AEC through the Nixon administration it had been assumed that light water reactor (LWR) fuel should be reprocessed (extracting unburnt uranium and newly created plutonium from spent fuel) to provide additional fuel for current-generation reactors, reduce the volume of high-level radioactive waste, and prepare the industry for breeder reactors. By 1975 projected demand for nuclear fuel had radically declined as costs of reactors climbed, energy demand projections fell, and concern about proliferation increased. A Ford administration ERDA study argued that reprocessing could not be economically justified for current reactor fuel cycles, and that because there was no near-term fuel shortage, breeders (which create nuclear fuel from otherwise nonfissionable Uranium 238) were not imminent (Brenner 1981: 101–8). Although massive investments had already been made in the Barnwell (South Carolina) reprocessing plant and the Clinch River (Tennessee) breeder reactor, the Carter administration followed the study's lead and reversed the Nixon-era reprocessing policy, mothballing the Barnwell plant and doing all it could to terminate the breeder program. The Barnwell and Clinch River projects remain moribund a decade later.

These measures were the domestic concomitant of international efforts to discourage other countries from moving to fuel cycles that the United States considered highly dangerous from a proliferation standpoint. It cannot be said that the IAEA directly influenced the United States in these decisions; in fact, because the IAEA retained the dual promotional and control roles that had been divided within the U.S. bureaucracy, its reports and secretariat tended to be more promotionally oriented than the Carter administration's control-oriented policies.

International Policy Effects of Changing Rules and Norms

U.S. nonproliferation multilateralism reduced the international legitimacy of its own unilateral efforts. The norms to which the United States subscribed in pushing IAEA involvement in international nuclear control could be upheld only if the United States subscribed to them in its own policies. Having pressed for creation of INFCIRC/66 and its revisions and ultimately the NPT safeguards system under INFCIRC/153, the United States could no longer demand direct access to recipient countries' nuclear facilities unless they failed to adhere to the safeguards system and the NPT. U.S. support for the two safeguards documents and the method of their negotiation also limited the degree to which the United States could legitimately push for tighter controls through other means.

The United States discovered the costs of relinquishing its claim to unilateralism during the 1970s when it attempted to push for tighter safeguards and export controls. It confronted supplier and consumer countries that pointed to the existing system and the consensus that created it as the primary reason unilateral U.S. pressure could legitimately be resisted. The United States was accused of unilateralism, imperialism, trying to create a "suppliers' cartel," and acting in bad faith (Lellouche 1981).

On the other hand, the multilateralization of safeguards expanded the scope of nonproliferation rules by trying to establish that nuclear safeguards were a technical, not a political, issue and should therefore be protected from transient political influence. International consensus implied a lack of political disagreement. IAEA safeguards provided the United States with the opportunity to pursue its own safeguards agenda under the legitimating cloak of multilateralism.

The same quality existed in the technical assistance area. When the IAEA was established as an internationalized successor to the U.S. Atoms for Peace program, IAEA assistance was envisioned as a benefit that would help to motivate states to join the agency. The United States ended its bilateral assistance programs and tacitly replaced it with IAEA assistance. Although the Atoms for Peace assistance program technically lived on for a few years, IAEA secretariat personnel dealing with technical assistance in the early 1960s saw the end of the program as a deliberate U.S. effort to shift the burden (and thus the benefits of the "payoff") to the IAEA (Interviews 1977).

Multilateralization of technical assistance through the IAEA reduced the value of the assistance as a diplomatic tool of the United States. The old Atoms for Peace program had been used to reward friendly states and to create incentives for nonaligned countries to cooperate with the United States. In contrast, the IAEA statute explicitly prohibits discrimination on political grounds among its members.[9] Thus the agency may not differentiate between signatories and nonsignatories of the NPT in distributing technical assistance projects. Seeking to build incentives into the provision of technical assistance to promote NPT signature and to reward those states that have signed the treaty, this statutory provision has become something of a burden to the United States and other NPT proponents.

Beginning in 1953 the United States pursued a policy of multilateralism to achieve its objectives for nuclear control, but in the 1970s it stretched the norms of the regime by trying unilaterally to reshape the rules of national behavior. The IAEA remained a useful tool but at times an exasperating one.

Explaining the Changing U.S.-IAEA Relationship

Rising U.S. concern about nuclear proliferation and concomitant efforts to strengthen the regime resulted from changes in the distribution of international power generally and nuclear technology in particular. U.S. dominance in the nuclear field declined because of the nature of the problem that defines the issue area: it has proved impossible to prevent completely the spread of nuclear technology. Domestic factors have played an important role in U.S. responses to that reality. As U.S. decision makers became increasingly concerned about the proliferation threat, they questioned the effectiveness of the IAEA and attempted to tighten international nonproliferation standards and to infuse the regime with their own perspectives, through the agency when possible.

Because of the structure of the IAEA, some of these measures were easier to execute than others. The United States remains the single most powerful influence within the IAEA, as it does in other international organizations. In comparison with other IGOs, however, its dominance is less diminished by the rise of the Third World bloc, and its policy objectives and willingness to use the IAEA for its purposes remain consistent.

Declining Power and Issue Area Characteristics

Declining U.S. hegemony in the nonproliferation regime is most dramatically demonstrated by the increasing number of states that are approaching nuclear weapons capabilities and the increased number of nuclear technology suppliers (Spector 1984, 1985, 1987). Despite these trends, international acceptance of nonproliferation norms continues. The primary effect for the United States is that it has to consider the requirements of consensus building and protecting IAEA institutional credibility in order for the agency to remain an effective adjunct to U.S. policies. The United States no longer commands easy majorities in the General Conference or the Board of Governors. As a consequence the United States has become more careful in its diplomacy and has on occasion gone outside the organization to pursue its nonproliferation policies.

The trend of declining U.S. hegemony in the IAEA is inevitable given the development of other states' economic, scientific, and technological capabilities. The dangers of having a large number of nuclear armed states are commonly accepted. Understanding this threat has led to a unique regime in which some states accept severe intrusions on their sovereignty in the form of international safeguards. U.S.-Soviet agreement over the dangers of proliferation has made this practically the only area of international disclosure in which East-West conflict is absent. Global ideological agreement, if not pragmatic acceptance, that retarding proliferation is desirable makes this an arena in which continuing international cooperation is likely. The nonproliferation regime may be one whereby the decline of a dominant power reveals an underlying structure of behavior attributable to states discovering their common interests in global stability. If consensus can be reached in the absence of a hegemon, it may represent more stable agreement than when forced by a dominant state. Gaining action in the contemporary nonproliferation regime may be more difficult than when the United States fully dominated it, but agreements now reached should be as robust as or more than before.

In some respects declining dominance in the nonproliferation regime is an indicator of U.S. success, in much the same way that its declining economic dominance is partly the product of successful postwar reconstruction efforts. During the late 1960s licensing agreements with companies in the OECD states led to European nuclear technological independence. In the early 1970s manipulation of nuclear fuel supplies and the Nixon administration's effort to "privatize" the nuclear fuel industry created artificial fuel shortages that led to development of independent European enrichment and reprocessing industries. This undermined the U.S. near-monopoly position in nuclear fuel supply and reduced U.S. leverage (Brenner 1981: chap. 2).

Developing countries—seeking political independence, regional power, scientific modernization, and frequently lacking energy resources—came to consider nuclear technology a vital element of military and civilian modernization and sought technology transfers. Atoms for Peace, then IAEA technical assistance, international conferences on the peaceful uses of atomic energy, and commercial transactions accelerated the dissemination of nuclear technology to developing states.[10]

The United States gambled that disseminating technology willingly would help it retain moral influence, if not actual control, over the path taken by new entries into the nuclear marketplace. When it appeared to be losing the gamble, the United States sought tighter technology transfer limits, greater supplier consensus, and more effective IAEA safeguards. The new policies were costly to international goodwill, especially in Europe. U.S. influence became more difficult to wield; however, U.S. initiatives remained relatively successful (Nye 1984).

The decline in U.S. domination did not result in a loss of U.S. influence in the agency. It had to be more adroit in its initiatives within and to move outside the IAEA to press some objectives that did not command wide support inside the agency. U.S. largesse provided access to the secretariat, and U.S. technological methods were adopted by the agency. Expanded monetary and technological aid to the safeguards program helped the agency to improve verification procedures and increase credibility even as it struggled to keep pace with the expansion of nuclear facilities around the world.

The United States has become less dominant within the IAEA but is still the most influential member state. Its decline in domination coincided with its increasing desire to manage the spread of nuclear technology: the mid-1970s were watershed years in many respects. In the IAEA U.S. dominance, when measured against its easy ability to gain its ends, declined in part because its objectives became more ambitious: this explains the need occasionally to depart from the IAEA's universalistic halls for more manageable ad hoc meetings such as the NSG and INFCE.

The United States continues to be the primary actor contributing to the regime's collective goods. At its most expansive, the collective good is the control of nuclear proliferation. In a more limited sense, the collective good is information about the nuclear status and intentions of other states. When the United States has been more worried about controlling proliferation or guaranteeing that the regime verified that nuclear technology was being used exclusively for peaceful purposes, it has paid the prices of diplomatic unpopularity and increased financial contributions to the IAEA. When other states have agreed with the United States, the burdens have been more widely shared. In some cases when the United States has found that the IAEA could not serve its purposes, it has taken actions against the agency (as in the representational battles to be described) or outside the agency (as in the NSG), demonstrating that its commitment to the agency is limited. These threats of defection have proved to be effective means for increasing influence within the organization, counteracting declining U.S. dominance. The limits of U.S. leverage in the IAEA are partly products of organizational characteristics that the United States established in 1956–57.

IGO Characteristics

The structure of the IAEA has assisted the United States in maintaining a high degree of influence. When the United States pressed for establishment of the IAEA, it recognized that its control of international nuclear development was limited and would decline. The 1956 draft statute of the IAEA guaranteed that the agency would be controlled by its Board of Governors, dominated by the states most developed in nuclear technology. Although the nonnuclear states tried to shift the balance in power away from the board toward the General Conference and tried to add members to the board to dilute nuclear state power, the rules of the conference enabled the powerful states to resist successfully (Bechhoefer 1959).

As the number of IAEA members increased and their geographical distribution shifted, the Third World bloc and regional groupings of states demanded that the governing board be enlarged and that the weight of permanent members be effectively reduced. Under this pressure the board has been enlarged three times, diluting nuclear supplier states' power. Further increases in the size of the board might jeopardize their domination. With its present thirty-five members, of which thirteen are permanent, the board has already attained a size the United States considers unwieldy and inefficient, but it retains its ability to form a blocking coalition (Interviews 1975–86).

The increased number of states represented in the IAEA's General Conference has opened it to political issues not directly connected to nonproliferation. The United States has struggled to maintain the "technical" qualities of the agency, resisting what it considers inappropriate politicization, and seeking to ensure that decisions are made on criteria whose definition it has dominated. As its dominance decreased, the United States has had an increasingly difficult time in resisting politicization, and has finally resorted to explicit opposition and threats of withdrawal from the agency when actions it disapproves are taken. Because the IAEA and its members need U.S. support if the agency is to carry out its mandate, the United States remains very influential.

During its first few years, the United States and the Soviet Union clashed over admission of NGOs as observers to the IAEA (IAEA 1957–61). These ritualized East-West political conflicts disappeared once the United States and Soviets agreed on the role of the IAEA. Recent representational battles over South African and Israeli participation in the IAEA show that North-South political issues have come to the forefront, and that the IAEA is not purely the creature of the United States. However, the United States can wield considerable influence on political issues if it is willing to step back from unconditional support of the agency.

As the only African state with a nuclear program, South Africa was a founding member of the IAEA Governing Board. Although its regional technological leadership remained unquestioned, challenges to its position on the board began in the mid-1960s. Its detractors charged that South Africa's white minority government was illegitimate and thus could not represent the country or the African region. In 1977 South Africa's critics finally succeeded, electing Egypt to the board over U.S. objections. Since then South Africa has not been seated at the General Conference or permitted to participate in IAEA committees or working groups. The

United States considers this inappropriate politicization of the agency (Interviews 1975–86; Scheinman 1985: 36).

Israel's status within the IAEA has been the other major representational issue. In September 1981 the General Conference condemned Israel's bombing of the Iraqi reactor in Baghdad. At subsequent General Conferences Iraq has moved to expel, suspend, or at least condemn Israel. In 1982 Iraq successfully amended the report of the General Conference credentials committee to reject seating of the Israeli delegation. The conference was to end in about an hour, so the action was purely symbolic. The United States and several other countries walked out.[11]

The United States subsequently withheld contributions to the agency and withdrew from participation for about five months while it undertook a "reassessment" of U.S. participation in the agency. This was the third reassessment by the United States of its participation in the agency. U.S. representative to the IAEA Richard Kennedy declared the United States was prepared to return to the agency if other countries would "return this agency to its status as an effective international technical organization" (Kennedy 1983). At the end of the five-month period, the U.S. study reaffirmed the value of the IAEA to its policies despite demands from congressional supporters of Israel that harsher steps be taken.

In subsequent years Iraq continued its efforts to condemn and expel Israel, and the United States spent enormous effort to fight the movement. In 1985 partly because of inept Iraqi diplomacy, the General Conference accepted Israeli assurances and adopted a Norwegian motion that laid the issue to rest. U.S. actions on the Israeli issue upheld U.S. opposition to what it saw as politicization of the IAEA.

Another source of stability in the U.S.-IAEA relationship lies in considerable influence in the IAEA secretariat. As the largest contributor to the agency and the country with the most trained people in fields relevant to the agency's work, the United States has provided the bulk of the secretariat staff. The flow of U.S. personnel has transferred U.S. views, especially on safeguards, directly into the IAEA. The officials who return from Vienna to U.S. government service bring first-hand knowledge of the agency's problems and capabilities. The friendly relationship between the agency secretariat and U.S. officials and experts continue to provide political and technical support for the agency from the U.S. executive branch.

This has continued despite the concern of the present director general, Hans Blix, for Third World states' interests. The United States appears to appreciate Blix's ability to build Third World consensus and has found that the director general's diplomacy has simplified rather than (as some had feared) complicated the pursuit of U.S. interests (Interviews 1984–85). Blix's initiatives for increased technical assistance coincide with U.S.

desires that the benefits of the safeguards-for-technology transfer bargain be upheld. U.S. interests in keeping developing countries happy with the IAEA have outweighed its concern that the focus of attention has somewhat shifted.

U.S. financial predominance in the budget has strongly influenced the IAEA, setting priorities among agency programs by providing financial, expert, and technological support to the agency's safeguards program. The safeguards budget rapidly increased following the 1963–64 U.S.-Soviet agreement and accelerated again after 1970 when the NPT came into effect (IAEA 1963–87; Schiff 1984: chap. 3).

While the United States has pressed for expansion of the safeguards budget, Third World states have sought commensurate increases in technical assistance supplied through the IAEA. Initially the technical assistance budget of the IAEA was much larger than the safeguards budget, but by the early 1960s technical assistance grew much more slowly. By the late 1960s developing countries demanded that a balance be maintained between the size and rate of growth of the two budgets, arguing that because the two duties of the IAEA were of equal importance, they should receive similar support (GOV/ORs; Scheinman 1985: 51–52; Schiff 1984: chap. 4).

The overall percentage of the IAEA regular budget contributed by the United States has declined, but the United States remains the largest single donor. Seeking increases in the safeguards budget in 1975, the United States pushed through a revision of the funding formula so that safeguards contributions for relatively poor countries would be frozen. This decreased their opposition to safeguards budget growth considering it would cost them nothing, and it was impossible to object to technical improvements in safeguards. Although the direction of U.S. policy toward the IAEA appeared relatively consistent when viewed from the vantage point of other countries, conflict has repeatedly arisen within the U.S. government over how best to use the IAEA for its own purposes.

Domestic Factors

The executive branch has reviewed U.S. commitment to the IAEA three times since the agency's inception: in 1962, 1972, and 1982. Each report essentially confirmed the finding of the first: that the IAEA is "the most effective means" for carrying out policies of technical dissemination and safeguarding. With each report corroborating the findings of the first, the importance of the IAEA to U.S. policy was reaffirmed (Astin 1972; Kennedy 1983; Smyth 1962).[12] These reviews were motivated largely by congressional concern over U.S. nonproliferation policy and the IAEA's capabilities. But the operational-level influences on the IAEA have been generated primarily from issues that emerged within the executive branch of the U.S. government.

As nuclear proliferation gained centrality in U.S. foreign policy in the early 1970s, and after ERDA and NRC were created in 1974, the Department of State took over leadership in U.S. policymaking toward the agency. The State Department and ACDA built up technical and political expertise in the nonproliferation field with transplanted experts from AEC and officials returning from the IAEA. ACDA managed to maintain a central role in nonproliferation during the second Nixon administration and into the Ford years even though the director of the ACDA, Fred Ikle, was largely thwarted by Secretary of State Henry Kissinger from effective action in other arms control areas. The expertise of Ikle's staff and Kissinger's focus on strategic arms limitations left ACDA comparatively free to act in the nonproliferation area (Clarke 1979: 49).

Even with an increased interest in nonproliferation because of the Indian explosion and other events of the early and mid-1970s, coordination of IAEA policymaking remained poor. Under the Carter administration U.S. policy, while still perhaps chaotic, became less reactive and more innovative. IAEA policy was spread among the ACDA Non-proliferation Bureau (with a technical and a political division) under Charles Van Doren, the Department of State's powerful OES, State's Office of the Special Ambassador for Non-proliferation Affairs (Gerard Smith), and Joseph Nye's office dealing with nuclear nonproliferation as deputy to the Under Secretary of State for Security Assistance, Science and Technology.

The changes of the mid-1970s in U.S. nonproliferation policy, culminating with the 1978 Nuclear Non-proliferation Act, resulted from executive branch concerns that were supported and stimulated by congressional action. The Congress, in turn, was reacting partly to a confluence of interests within domestic environmentalist groups between opposition to nuclear power reactors in the United States and concern over the effects of nuclear exports on the proliferation threat. As noted earlier, the Indian nuclear test in 1974 galvanized outside critics and congressional skeptics about U.S. nonproliferation policies. Congressman Bingham and Senators Ribicoff, Symington, and Glenn led major investigations of U.S. policy leading to the 1978 act and amendments to U.S. foreign aid legislation, calling for cutoffs of aid to countries that did not comply with U.S. requirements for "full-scope" (NPT-type) safeguards (Beckman 1985).[13]

By the end of the Carter administration, adverse reactions to U.S. policies, especially the Nuclear Non-proliferation Act, had led to moderation in U.S. demands and a decline in major policy demarches in the nonproliferation area. On February 1, 1980, the *New York Times* quoted candidate Reagan as saying "I just don't think it's any of our business" in reference to U.S. efforts to keep nuclear weapons from spreading to additional countries. When the Reagan administration took office, non-proliferation in general and the IAEA in particular appeared to be threatened with reduced priority within the foreign policy apparatus. Falling relative levels of U.S. extrabudgetary contributions to the IAEA substantiate this observation, although they are at least partly caused by the new generosity of some other countries (notably Italy). But by the beginning of its second term, the Reagan administration had fought off attacks on the agency generated by pro-Israel congresspeople, maintained the POTAS and other assistance programs for the agency, and continued to affirm publicly the centrality of the IAEA to U.S. policy.

A nominally more independent IAEA still depended on U.S. contributions to its safeguard program and continued to administer extra-budgetary assistance to technical assistance projects. The new director general takes Third World objectives more seriously than did his predecessor, but the United States has recognized that this contributes to maintaining the utility of the agency. Because of its technological leadership and financial support, the United States has continued to dominate IAEA policies. Reductions in hegemony necessitate flexibility of maneuver in the agency. Increases in flexibility require improved internal coordination to develop and execute nonproliferation policies effectively.

Lessons for Multilateralism in U.S. Policy

The United States will not be able to return to the days of monopolistic control of nuclear supplies or international deference to its policies. To maintain influence in the IAEA, it will have to continue to convince other states that some actions could cause the United States to reduce or withdraw its support of the agency. Conversely, in order for the United States to avoid damaging the agency or losing its own influence by being overly aloof, it will also need to demonstrate an ability to compromise, to respond positively to other states' efforts to develop consensus, and to articulate its commitment to the IAEA as a coordinate body, not simply as an adjunct of U.S. hegemony.

Having led in establishing the agency, the United States continues to set the agency's technical and institutional agendas in part because it has had more new ideas and suggestions than any other state. Responding to the chaotic circumstances of the mid-1970s, U.S. experts proposed, and the United States assisted in funding streamlined and rationalized agency operations. The United States pressed for improvements in safeguards and technical assistance programs because of, as well as despite, its declining hegemony. The market surveys, the RFCC study, and the plutonium management study demonstrated, regardless of their conclusions, the influence of U.S. analyses in determining what kinds of activities the IAEA should consider.

In creating the IAEA, the United States endorsed multilateralist norms that eventually came to restrict and shape its nonproliferation diplomacy and to influence the shape of its domestic decision making. By persisting in its efforts to use the IAEA as a major channel for its nonproliferation diplomacy, the U.S. government indicated its conviction that the benefits of multilateral nonproliferation efforts outweighed their international and internal costs. Although U.S. influence has declined, the IAEA still serves the purposes for which it was founded, binding both the general membership and a sometimes reluctant United States into the multilateral norms of the nonproliferation regime.

Disturbances within the regime, such as the set of events of the early 1970s, caused changes in U.S. policy toward the IAEA. The policies that emerged were produced by an executive branch under pressure from Congress. But IAEA policy per se has not been very interesting to popular politicians or to powerful domestic interest groups and thus has been isolated from domestic U.S. policies much as its technical nature has helped to isolate it from ambient political issues at the international level. IAEA effects on the United States have been caused by the need to coordinate U.S. policy in order to be effective at the international level, not by IAEA restrictions on U.S. sovereignty. As U.S. leverage has declined, it has had to be better organized internally to gain its international objectives.

Changes in the power distribution among IGO members will not necessarily modify regime norms or rules that underpin multilateral cooperation. Building consensus within organizations may be more difficult as hegemonic leadership declines—as has happened to a limited extent in the IAEA—but the organization will also be less vulnerable to the demands of the hegemon. Assuming underlying consensus over norms and rules, greater equality among members may contribute to organizational stability. The IAEA does not appear to be suffering from the decline in U.S. dominance; it is adjusting to an increase in genuine multilateralism.

Notes

1. For discussion of the nuclear nonproliferation regime and an analysis of the IAEA using regime concepts, see Schiff (1984: chap. 1).

2. The structure of the IAEA is laid out in the statute, available in IAEA (1959) and U.S. House of Representatives and Senate (1977: 43–58). The board was expanded three times, increasing developing state representation.

3. For congressional and international reaction, see Beckman (1985: 217–18).

4. INFCIRC/66 was revised twice to include reactors of larger size and then enrichment facilities. It is commonly known as the final version of the revised document, INFCIRC/66/ Rev.2 (1968).

5. It was considered that 600 megawatts of electrical power (MWe) was the maximum useful size for small electrical grids. By this time reactor manufacturers were concluding that to compete effectively with alternative energy sources, reactors built in the 1970s would have to be in a unit size range of 1000 MWe. But for LDCs, 1000 MWe was far too large to be efficiently integrated into poorly interconnected and underdeveloped electrical grids.

6. At the INFCE organizing conference the forty states and four IGOs participating were Algeria, Argentina, Australia, Austria, Belgium, Brazil, Canada, Czechoslovakia, Denmark, Egypt, Finland, France, German Democratic Republic, Federal Republic of Germany, India, Indonesia, Iran, Ireland, Israel, Italy, Japan, South Korea, Mexico, Netherlands, Nigeria, Norway, Pakistan, Philippines, Poland, Portugal, Romania, Spain, Sweden, Switzerland, Turkey, USSR, United Kingdom, United States, Venezuela, Yugoslavia, and representatives of the IAEA, the Commission of the European Communities, the International Energy Agency (of the OECD), and the Nuclear Energy Agency (OECD). By the end of the conference, sixty-six nations had participated. Beckman (1985: 359–63) has a very useful discussion of the internal U.S. politics of INFCE.

7. The United States was particularly concerned with fuel supply assurances and the threat of reprocessing. For a history of U.S. policy in the wake of the U.S. Nuclear Non-proliferation Act of 1978, the 1980 Review Conference of the Parties to the NPT, and the activities of the IAEA's Committee on Assurances of Supply, see Van Doren (1983).

8. Energy Reorganization Act of 1974, P. 93–438, 88 Stat. 1233. See Beckman (1985) for an excellent account of the issues.

9. Statute Article XI, "Agency Projects" lists a long set of criteria by which proposed projects are to be evaluated. They are all technical/economic/scientific criteria. Within IAEA forums, this has been taken to mean that no distinction can be drawn on other bases.

10. Beginning in 1954, Geneva Conferences on the Peaceful Uses of Atomic Energy served as forums for a new U.S.-Soviet competition. They each tried to demonstrate leadership in nuclear technology by declassifying large amounts of previously secret technical information. For a history of the U.S. attitude toward declassification and international cooperation, see Nieburg (1964).

11. This description of events at several Geneva Conferences comes from U.S. officials and is corroborated by unclassified Department of State reporting cables; George P. Shultz, unclassified letter to Speaker Thomas P. O'Neil, Jr., House of Representatives of March 1, 1983.

12. The Smyth Report (1962) reviewed the first four years of the IAEA's activities, evaluated its usefulness in promoting U.S. objectives, and made recommendations about future U.S. policy and activities. It urged that the United States recognize the IAEA as "the most effective means by which the United States can carry out" its policy of technology dissemination, called for transfer of bilateral U.S. agreements for technology transfer to the IAEA "wherever practical," and asked that the United States secure international agreement that the IAEA was the most appropriate instrument to carry out international safeguards, establish health and safety standards, provide technical assistance, develop liability and indemnification practices, carry out international research, and promulgate waste management standards. Astin (1972), evaluating U.S. relations with the IAEA in the wake of the NPT coming into force, essentially reiterated the findings of the earlier study, stressing the

need to keep balance between the control activities and the technology transfer activities. It called for special budgetary practices that would allow the United States to contribute to the IAEA at levels beyond the limits being imposed on other international organizations, and pressed for domestic technological and regulatory research to back up IAEA development efforts. Kennedy (1983) summarized the latest report, written in response to congressional unhappiness with the political battle over Israeli representation in the IAEA that had erupted following Israel's bombing of an Iraqi reactor in 1981. After five months, the report again reaffirmed the importance of the IAEA to U.S. policy.

13. In particular, Representative Bingham and Senators Ribicoff, Glenn, and Symington played major roles in moving legislation forward that resulted in the 1978 Nuclear Non-proliferation Act and amendments to U.S. foreign aid legislation prohibiting aid to countries that appeared to be developing nuclear weapons. The best and most thorough description of Congress involvement is Beckman (1985).

References

Astin, Allen W. (1972). "International Atomic Energy Agency: An Appraisal with Recommendations for Future Policy." Report to the Secretary of State, February 2.

Atomic Energy Act of 1954. PL 83-703, 68 Stat. 619.

Beaton, Leonard, and John Maddox (1962). *The Spread of Nuclear Weapons.* New York: Praeger.

Bechhoefer, Bernard G. (1959). "Negotiating the Statute of the IAEA." *International Organization*, 13(1), 38–59.

Beckman, Robert L. (1985). *Nuclear Nonproliferation: Congress and the Control of Peaceful Nuclear Activities.* Boulder, CO: Westview Press.

Brenner, Michael J. (1981). *Nuclear Power and Non-proliferation: The Remaking of Policy.* New York: Cambridge University Press.

Clarke, Duncan (1979). *Politics of Arms Control: The Role and Effectiveness of the U.S. Arms Control and Disarmament Agency.* New York: Free Press.

Cornell University, Program on Science, Technology and Society (1975). "Analysis of the Economic Feasibility, Technical Significance, and Time Scale for Application of Peaceful Nuclear Explosions in the U.S., with Special Reference to the GURC Report Thereon." Report to the U.S. Arms Control and Disarmament Agency. Ithaca, NY: Author.

Fischer, David, and Paul Szasz (1985). *Safeguarding the Atom: A Critical Appraisal.* London: Taylor & Francis for SIPRI.

Gall, Norman (1976). "Atoms for Brazil, Dangers for All." *Foreign Policy*, 23(Summer), 155–201.

Gulf Universities Research Consortium (1975). "PNE Activity Projections for Arms Control Planning." Galveston, TX: Author.

Hauk, Frank (1985). "The U.S. Voluntary Safeguards Offer: History and Scope." IAEA *Bulletin*, 27(2).

IAEA (1957–61, 1975–79). GOV/ORS Oral Records of the Board of Governors Meetings. Vienna: Author.

———(1959). *Multilateral Agreements* Legal Series #1. Vienna: Author.

———(1965). "The Agency's Safeguards System." INFCIRC/66. Vienna: Author.

———(1972). "The Structure and Content of Agreements between the Agency and States Required in Connection with the Treaty on the Non-Proliferation of Nuclear Weapons." Vienna: Author.

—— (1974). "The Export of Nuclear Materials and of Certain Categories of Equipment and Other Material." INFCIRC/209 (3 September). Vienna: Author.

—— (1973). *Market Surveys for Nuclear Power in Developing Countries: General Report.* Vienna: Author.

—— (various years). *Annual Report.* Vienna: Author.

—— (1977a). *Annual Report for 1976*, Document GC (XXI)/580. Vienna: Author.

—— (1977b). *Regional Nuclear Fuel Cycle Centers.* 2 vols. Vienna: Author.

—— (1977c). "International Management and Storage of Plutonium and Spent Fuel." Internal document (photocopy). Vienna: Author.

—— (1978). INFCIRC/254. In David Fischer and Paul Szasz (1985). *Safeguarding the Atom: A Critical Appraisal.* London: Taylor & Francis for SIPRI.

—— (1985). *The Agency's Budget for 1986.* Vienna: Author.

Interviews conducted by the author in Washington (1975, 1977–79, 1984–86) and Vienna (1976, 1977).

Kennedy, Amb. Richard T. (1983). "U.S. Completes Assessment of IAEAs." Statement to the Governing Board of the IAEA. Department of State *Bulletin* (March), 79. Washington: U.S. Government Printing Office.

Kessler, J. Christian (1989). "A State Department Perspective on IAEA Safeguards." *Journal of the Institute of Nuclear Materials Management*, 17(4).

Lellouche, Pierre (1981). "Breaking the Rules without Quite Stopping the Bomb: European Views." *International Organization*, 35(1), 39–58.

Lowrance, William (1977). "Nuclear Futures for Sale: From Brazil to West Germany, 1975." *International Security*, 1(2), 147–66.

Nieburg, Harold (1964). *Nuclear Secrecy and Foreign Policy.* Washington, DC: Public Affairs Press.

Nye, Joseph P., Jr. (1984). "Sustaining Non-proliferation in the 1980s." In James A. Schear, ed., *Nuclear Weapons Proliferation and Nuclear Risk.* New York: St. Martin's Press, chap. 5.

Rochlin, Gene I. (1979). *Plutonium, Power and Politics: International Arrangements for the Disposition of Spent Nuclear Fuel.* Berkeley: University of California Press.

Scheinman, Lawrence (1985). *The Non-proliferation Role of the International Atomic Energy Agency: A Critical Assessment.* Washington, DC: Resources for the Future.

Schiff, Benjamin N. (1984). *International Nuclear Technology Transfer: Dilemmas of Dissemination and Control.* Totowa, NJ: Rowman and Alanheld.

SIPRI (1975). *Safeguards against Nuclear Proliferation.* Cambridge: MIT Press.

Smyth, Henry D. (1962). "Report of the Advisory Committee on U.S. Policy toward the IAEA." Washington, DC: Department of State.

Spector, Leonard (1984). *Nuclear Proliferation Today.* New York: Vintage.

—— (1985). *The New Nuclear Nations.* New York: Vintage.

—— (1987). *Going Nuclear.* Cambridge, MA: Ballinger.

U.S. Department of Energy (1979). *Nuclear Proliferation and Civilian Nuclear Power: Report of the Nonproliferation Alternative Systems Assessment Program.* 9 vols. Washington, DC: Author.

U.S. Department of State, Office of Nuclear Technology and Safeguards, Bureau of Oceans and International Environmental and Scientific Affairs (1989). "President's Report to the Congress under Section 601 of the Nuclear Non-Proliferation Act of 1978." Washington, DC: U.S. Government Printing Office.

U.S. General Accounting Office (GAO) (1984). Report B-215047 "New and Better Equipment Being Made Available for International Safeguards" (NSIAD-84-46, June). Washington, DC: Author.

U.S. House of Representatives, Committee on International Relations, and U.S. Senate, Committee on Governmental Affairs (1977). *Nuclear Proliferation Factbook*. Washington, DC: U.S. Government Printing Office.

Van Doren, Charles (1983). "Nuclear Supply and Non-proliferation: The IAEA Committee on Assurances of Supply." Congressional Research Service Report No. 83-202 S. Washington, DC: Library of Congress.

• CHAPTER FOUR •

The United States and the International Monetary Fund: Declining Influence or Declining Interest?

Miles Kahler

At first glance, U.S. relations with the International Monetary Fund provide an ideal test of both the hypothesis that the pattern of American relations with international organizations has changed and of the alternative explanations advanced for that change. There can be no question that the IMF was principally an American (or Anglo-American) creation or that the Bretton Woods institutions did more than simply serve a legitimating function (they controlled substantial resources). More than any other postwar international organization, the International Monetary Fund was viewed by successive American administrations as a linchpin of the international economic order.

Explanations for changes in the U.S. relationship with the IMF that are based on relative American power can be evaluated with some precision; weighted voting within the IMF provides a measure that can be matched against other indicators of influence. Nevertheless, two alternative explanations provide a more satisfying explanation of American behavior toward the organization: the characteristics of the international monetary issue area and the domestic politics of the United States. Despite the apparently central position of the IMF compared with other international organizations, changes in the international monetary regime after 1971–73 led the United States to explore alternative means of advancing American interests. Two were particularly appealing: "great power" cooperation through the Group of Five (G-5) and later the Group of Seven (G-7), and reliance on the private financial markets, subject only to modest intergovernmental oversight. The presence of these alternatives strongly influenced the American posture toward the Fund.

American relations with the IMF have also been shaped by features of American domestic politics. As Joanne Gowa (1983) has argued, the high value placed on domestic economic goals has propelled American policy toward unilateralism rather than sustaining existing international regimes. That hierarchy of goals, coupled with the weight of the United States in private financial markets and with laissez-faire ideology, has reinforced American preferences for market solutions. In the 1980s ideology and resources combined to thrust the IMF, quintessentially technocratic and apolitical, into a national debate over international economic organizations. That debate revolved around a request for additional resources in 1983; at a time of budgetary stringency, the U.S. commitment to international organizations was defined as never before by the desire to reduce resource commitments. The IMF was attacked from the left and the right; its plight suggested deeper changes in American political ideology and commitment to internationalist solutions.

Through all the fluctuations of U.S. interest in the International Monetary Fund, the characteristics of the organization served to keep the United States from abandoning the IMF altogether. A well-qualified staff of mainstream economists—most from industrialized countries—offered the United States an instrument that appeared reliable; that reliability was reinforced by a structure of weighted voting and special majorities that limited the decline of American influence within the organization. Although the need for additional resources provided a periodic opportunity for critics to attack the organization, its relatively low demand for budgetary outlays enhanced its attractiveness.

The following account of U.S. relations with the International Monetary Fund will also attempt to assess the IMF's influence on American policy. Separating the influence of an organization (the IMF) from the influence of the rules of the game or regime in the international monetary system is very difficult; even more complicated is the pressure—only weakly institutionalized—from other monetary powers. It could be argued that the International Monetary Fund is both more and less capable than other international organizations of influencing American policy. It does possess the resources and expertise to influence governments; however, its prescriptions concern economic policies of the highest political importance, not narrowly defined regulations or matters of expert consensus. The central position of the United States in the international monetary and financial system further reduces IMF leverage.

Measuring influence over time—whether American influence on the Fund or Fund influence on the United States—is difficult. In examining the influence of the United States on the International Monetary Fund, three indicators are employed: *staff selection* (particularly the managing director), *policy parameters* (for example, looser or tighter conditionality in IMF lending), and *individual country programs*. In determining the level of U.S. influence in the organization, evidence that expressed American preferences are not matched in any of these areas will be of particular importance. The manner in which American influence is exercised is of equal importance: Does the United States bargain intensively for favorable outcomes or do they seem to happen automatically?

Analyzing IMF influence on U.S. policy is more problematic, for it is difficult to separate the influence of an organization like the IMF from the influence of the rules of the game or the international monetary regime. One way to measure organizational influence is to assess the degree to which the stated prescriptions of the IMF match those of winning economic policy coalitions within the American government. An even stronger test would estimate whether the IMF is critical to that coalition. A different and weaker measure of IMF influence on American policy would set aside such direct tests and instead investigate the wider agenda of policy choices offered to the United States by the existence of the Fund. Measuring influence in both directions is hampered by the confidentiality that surrounds relations between the IMF and member governments. Although I have tried to confirm my findings with more than one source, estimates are necessarily imprecise.

Three periods have been chosen for closer examination. The first is the period usually described as the apogee of American hegemony in international economic affairs, from World War II until the erosion of the Bretton Woods gold exchange system of fixed parities in the late 1960s. The second period extends from acceptance of floating exchange rates following the failure of global reform efforts through the advent of the Reagan administration in 1981. This period has often been cited as exemplifying the relative decline of American influence, particularly in international economic affairs. Finally, the years of the Reagan administration deserve independent consideration. Renewed emphasis on American power in international politics coupled with domestic political change had significant implications for U.S. relations with many international organizations. The Reagan administration marked a sharp break with the past in its initial skepticism toward the IMF (a skepticism that disappeared with the debt crisis), but it also epitomized the growing difficulty that preceding administrations had experienced in mobilizing support to commit resources to international organizations. It is timely to ask now whether American support for international organizations as one means to strengthen state cooperation in an international market economy has been impaired or whether despite changes in the American international position international organizations remain a principal means to legitimate American intervention in the international economy.

The United States and the Early IMF:
The Very Model of Hegemony?

The preeminent role of the United States in shaping the International Monetary Fund is well documented. Although the Bretton Woods organizations had emerged from hard bargaining between Britain and the United States, the disparity in financial resources between the two powers guaranteed greater weight to American preferences despite the brilliance and negotiating skill of John Maynard Keynes (Gardner 1980). The United States had seriously underestimated the disequilibrium in the postwar international economy, however, and in the face of economic crisis in Western Europe, massive financing through the Marshall Plan over-shadowed the new international organizations. During the immediate postwar years the Bretton Woods institutions were largely bypassed.

Although they were hardly central instruments in postwar recon-struction, the United States actively pressed its preferences and policies within the organizations. The selection of the IMF's managing director provides a clear picture. Although each of the managing directors has been European (according to a convention that remains in place today), the United States took the lead in appointing the first managing director. When a managing director's accomplishments did not meet American expectations, the United States made it clear that it would not support a renewal of his tenure (Interview July 15, 1985). As late as 1963 Pierre-Paul Schweitzer was nominated by the American executive director (Interview July 18, 1985). In each of these cases, however, there was little resistance from the other key players—Britain or the other European countries.

Americans were pervasive in the early staff of the organization, creating an annual "chorus of complaints," according to one veteran, until the national balance shifted. Most important was the deputy managing director, who by convention has always been an American and, since Frank Southard's appointment in 1962, has always been the former American executive director. The deputy managing director has also been a "Treasury man", reinforcing the close ties between that agency of the U.S. government and the IMF. In the case of the deputy managing director and other key staff appointments, however, there is no evidence that nationality served as a back door to influence within the Fund. The United States also supported an informal rule, established early on, that allocated the positions of area department heads to a representative of the region in question. Although the appointments of most important functional departments (research, for example) were sounded out with key executive directors (including the United States), it was also quickly established that appointments below that level were the prerogative of the managing director and staff.

The United States was a principal initiator of policy changes during the early years, and it never lost an open policy conflict. The crucial principle of IMF policy established at this time was the attachment of conditions to the use of Fund resources, commonly referred to as conditionality. On the issues of conditionality and exclusion of recipients of Marshall Plan aid from IMF drawings, the United States found the ten European countries—the deficit countries of the period—among its opponents. In deciding one of the rare foreign policy questions that arose in this early period, the expulsion of Czechoslovakia from the organization in 1954, the United States confronted the opposition of virtually the entire board.[1] Such open conflict, pitting the United States against most of the organization's members, was rare, however.

In the determination of parameters for country programs—size of drawing and conditions attached to the various tranches—approval by the United States was critical, and in the first decade of the IMF negotiations between the United States and countries seeking assistance sometimes excluded the Fund staff. As Southard (1979: 19–20) describes,

> In the 1950s the U.S. voice in the Fund was decisive—indeed a task of the U.S. Executive Director was to keep that voice muted so as not to frustrate Board and Management/staff activity. The practical question in those years, in any prospective large use of Fund resources, was whether the United States would agree—and the answer was usually obtained by direct inquiry.

The negotiations between the United States and Britain that resulted in Britain's 1956 drawing were the most significant example of the central U.S. role in setting the terms and amounts of financing available through the IMF. American negotiators, believing that the British request for $750 million was insufficient, agreed to a $1.3 billion drawing by Britain. The operation was successful in large measure because the United States decided to go "all out" (Southard 1979: 20).

Nevertheless, from early in the organization's existence, the IMF's staff began to exercise its autonomy, and the Executive Board restrained its own attempts to revise country programs. Countries lost the right to approve staff country papers before they were brought to the board; programs also had to have the approval of the staff and managing director before consideration by the board. Efforts to regain this right of appeal to the board over the heads of the staff have continued to the present, but the rule has not been successfully breached. The United States supported these expansions of staff autonomy. In part it had no choice; meticulous design of country programs required a level of expertise and information that executive directors and their staffs could not provide. In part the United States knew that national governments could shape the general outlines for country programs in board discussion and decisions; a key example was Brazil's forcing of rule clarification after Britain's drawing in 1968.[2]

The formal basis of American influence within the organization has been twofold: the weighted system of voting, which allocated quotas and voting shares according to formulas, that reflected international economic influence, and the changing pattern of special majorities, which subjected decisions of particular importance to an effective U.S. veto.[3] In the early years, given the relative share of the American quota, weighted voting was most important to American influence within the organization. As the economic weight of the United States in the world economy declined, and with it the American quota share within the IMF, special majorities grew in significance. The importance of quota share and special majorities does not mean that formal votes have typically been used in the IMF. In most cases the managing director, as chair of the Executive Board, has created as broad a consensus as possible while taking into account the quota shares represented by different constituencies. The United States favored the trend away from recorded votes as another means of disguising its preponderant influence (Southard 1979: 5–6).

Whatever the formal system of decision-making rules, the American contribution of resources and its importance to effective implementation would have required its consent, at least in the first two decades after 1945. The IMF structure of rules, however, legitimated the award of greater influence to the United States; it also legitimated growing influence in the organization *for others* based on the same criteria. In certain cases the decision-making rules of the Fund, which assigned so much weight to the United States, made all the difference. For example, in the case of Czechoslovakia it was clear that the United States with a few allies could carry the day over uniform opposition from the Europeans. American financial power could also be exercised outside the IMF, however. In the principal test of wills with Britain in this period, American unwillingness to support the pound during the Suez crisis in 1956 seems to have been critical in the British decision to withdraw from Suez. The IMF was unnecessary for sending the desired signals in that instance.

Despite the evidence of American dominance during the first twenty years of the IMF's existence, it is important to note significant limits on

American influence even during this period. Certain conventions on staff appointments have already been described. Gradually as the organization's staff lost its American or Anglo-American coloration, another convention became accepted: staff representation should roughly match quota share. On policy questions, where the American view seemed to triumph again and again, other members could threaten to leave the organization or simply permit it to lapse into inactivity. The United States had to decide whether it wanted to force its policy preferences at every turn or whether by doing so it endangered the legitimacy of an organization that served its broader interests. Its dilemma became more pressing as its relative weight in the organization declined. Finally, the United States accepted that country programs would not be extensively revised in meetings of the Executive Board. How far it attempted to exert its influence outside the board room in particular cases is difficult to determine. One feature did restrain such intervention, however: the Treasury Department jealously guarded (and guards) its control of American relations with the Fund. Other government agencies that might attempt to politicize the IMF for broader foreign policy goals tended to be excluded from direct access to it. As noted earlier, only the Czechoslovakian case is a clear example of such politicization during the period of greatest American influence.

Even in these years of American predominance, the United States found it valuable to veil its power through conventions that convinced other countries that the rules of the game were reasonably fair or at least better than no rules at all. The United States bargained more than its predominance might have predicted.

Before and after Smithsonian: Declining Influence or Declining Interest?

During the 1960s as European weight in the international monetary system and discontent with America's dominance grew in tandem, the United States saw the IMF as an important bulwark of its position. In debates about persistent American deficits or creation of a new reserve asset, it was the Europeans, and particularly the French, who evidenced a distrust of the IMF. The organization was perceived as dominated by the "Anglo-Saxons", and the rapid growth of the European economies was reflected in voting shares only with a substantial lag. The Europeans preferred clublike organizations of the industrialized countries (such as the G-10) in which they enjoyed greater symmetry of influence vis-à-vis the United States. The Europeans also ensured that significant decisions under the First Amendment to the IMF Articles of Agreement required a special majority of 85 percent, granting the European Community an effective veto over those decisions (Gold 1977: 38). In resisting European desires for a less universal arena, the United States enjoyed tacit support from the developing countries and from the Fund management and staff (Solomon 1982: 72–73, 76, 135).

The American decision to close the gold window in August 1971 signaled a major upheaval in international monetary affairs; it also marked a sharp, if temporary, break in American support for the International Monetary Fund. Whatever its surprise and drama, however, the 1971 decision was one in a series of decisions by the United States indicating its dissatisfaction with the existing international monetary regime. That disillusionment persisted in the failed reform exercise of 1972–74 and the much looser system of managed floating that was codified in the Jamaica Agreement of 1976 and the Second Amendment to the Fund's Articles of Agreement. American disenchantment necessarily implied a more critical attitude toward the organization that embodied the existing rules of the game in international monetary affairs.

At least three different reasons for the change in American attitudes toward and influence within the IMF can be proposed, however. First, hegemonic stability theory predicts that with a *decline in relative economic power* of the United States, American attachment to existing regimes would wane and the web of international cooperation would fray. A second explanation views American policy in the 1970s as determined by declining *interest* in the International Monetary Fund, whose influence in the financial and monetary universe of the 1970s was reduced by *changes in the issue area* of international monetary relations. With looser rules of the game, the enforcer of those rules became less central. Rules governing exchange rates were not the only ones to change. Financing from the Euromarkets through private banks became far more important to deficit countries, and the role of the IMF in financing current account deficits became peripheral for all but the poorest developing countries or those without access to the private markets. For some countries the importance of private finance coupled with looser international monetary rules pointed to new forms of intergovernmental cooperation. The emergence of alternative means of monetary cooperation only loosely connected to the Fund reinforced other changes in international monetary relations. Chief among these was the G-5, which brought together the major economic powers in informal and secret discussions.

Changes in *American domestic politics* were a third reason for reduced U.S. interest in the IMF. Those who preferred unilateral policy initiatives and a market-based international financial system to a system based on interstate rules and international organizations were increasingly vocal.

Gowa (1983: 22–23) has argued convincingly that domestic political dynamics biased American foreign economic policy in a "nationalist direction"; policymakers were unwilling to subordinate either domestic economic policy goals or external security goals to maintaining a particular set of international rules. John Odell (1982: 341–42) has noted the importance of the "Chicago" strand in American willingness to risk a floating exchange rate regime. Similar arguments grew in importance during the 1970s and undermined support for organizing international economic relations through intergovernmental organizations or rules. The culmination of this trend came with the Reagan administration, but it underlay the self-confidence of bankers and others who took a benign view of the private financial markets. The invisible hand of the market was regarded as superior to the all-too-visible hand of international civil servants.

Although it may not be the only explanation for changed American relations with the IMF, evidence of shrinking American influence was apparent in the organization during the 1970s. Managing directors could not be selected or retained over an American veto: the United States demonstrated its dissatisfaction with Pierre-Paul Schweitzer in a public and unprecedented manner (DeVries 1985: 1005). Nevertheless, the United States played a smaller role in selection procedures during the 1970s. In choosing Schweitzer's successor, the U.S. executive director was not at the center of the process. Of greater significance was the growing importance of the G-9, the executive directors representing the developing countries. They vetoed the nomination of Emil van Lennep as managing director; his history at the OECD suggested too great an attachment to industrial country interests. The Executive Board then settled on Johannes Witteveen. In choosing the successor to Witteveen, the G-9 sought involvement in the procedures of selection before the informal floating of names through an informal board meeting; they also challenged but then conceded the convention that the managing director should be a European (Interviews July 9, 18, 1985). Most recently the choice of Michel Camdessus as managing director remained largely a European decision, although the United States indicated that Camdessus was an acceptable candidate.

The bases of support for policy decisions are harder to decipher given the consensual nature of most Fund decisions and the closely held character of Executive Board discussions. Nevertheless, it was clear by the 1970s that even on major policy issues the United States needed the backing of other key players within the International Monetary Fund. As described earlier, the Europeans have used the instrument of special majorities to ensure their power to veto key decisions. Special majorities—

essentially exceptions to the general rule that decisions in the Fund were made by majority vote—grew in importance from the First Amendment of the Articles (1969) to the Second Amendment (1978). Under the Second Amendment, with "one exception and one qualification," two special majorities—70 and 85 percent—were required for decisions of particular significance. The effect of these majorities was to require additional bargaining in an organization that had already accepted the convention of consensus decision making.

Expansion of the use of special majorities to protect national positions within the IMF merely codified a trend that had been apparent since the 1960s. The First Amendment itself resulted from bargaining between the United States and the Europeans; the bargain that finally produced the Jamaica Accords and the Second Amendment to the Articles of Agreement was struck between the United States and France (Dam 1982: chap. 8). Bargaining with the Europeans also characterized other initiatives affecting the organization of the international monetary system, such as the aborted effort to establish a substitution account in the late 1970s. On minor issues within the IMF itself, the United States now found itself on occasion in the minority. One long-time observer of the Executive Board recalled the first time the United States was on the losing side, on a staff salary matter in the early 1970s. He remarked at the time that once the spell of American influence was broken, matters would never be the same in American relations with the organization.

Although the United States was forced into more intensive bargaining within the IMF and could now find itself in a minority on certain policy matters, special majorities also protected its dominant position against precipitous erosion. As the quota power of the United States (its positive capability to influence Fund policies) declined, the role of the special majorities (representative of its negative capabilities to prevent policy change) grew in significance. The share of U.S. and U.K. quotas, which had dominated the fund in 1946 (56 percent), had declined to 27 percent in 1983; the U.S. quota alone dropped from 38 to 20 percent (Lister 1984: 68–70). After its voting share dropped below 20 percent, the special majority of 85 percent became particularly important.[4]

The consequences of special majorities, however, were not simply a regime of "negative hegemony" in which the United States could at least arrest change that it found distasteful. The special majorities regime also gave similar power to other national actors (blocs of countries) within the IMF, particularly the Europeans and the developing countries (when they were able to act collectively). Given the broad consensus that was usually sought by the managing director for important policy decisions, this new regime was characterized by the need for coalition-building and bargaining, sometimes producing complicated package deals. One such example occurred after a lengthy Executive Board discussion in December 1983 in which a compromise package was designed that encompassed rates of remuneration (special majority of 70 percent) and enlarged access to Fund resources (special majority of 85 percent). More recently in 1986 a similar compromise was designed to balance the IMF's budget by increasing the charges for using Fund resources and reducing the rate of remuneration paid to creditors. Although the United States enjoyed considerable leverage because of its voting share, it had to engage in active logrolling and bargaining to mobilize a majority on issues that concerned it. The United States remained the only *single* country with this level of bargaining power, but depending on the issue, the Europeans and the G-9 were also capable of wielding voting power. As Lister (1984: 94) notes, "Increasing awareness of the role of special majorities has spread throughout the Fund's membership, partly because smaller countries participating in voting blocs have now gained a better grasp of how such blocs can exercise veto powers in specific circumstances."

Concurrent with power shifts among nations within the IMF has been the changing role of management and staff. Influence here depended on the agenda and skill of individual managing directors, but the Executive Board would rouse itself from time to time to exert control by the national governments as a group over the actions of the staff. The policy initiatives of management and particularly the preeminent role assigned to the staff in country programs made it possible for a different sort of bargain to be struck by the United States: one between an activist management and the U.S. government. In assessing the influence of the United States on particular country programs, it is such tacit bargains that seem most important given the principle of uniformity of treatment and the stated opposition of the United States to intervention in bargaining between other countries and the Fund.

Although the pattern of bargaining among member states and between those states and the staff changed as American voting weight declined within the IMF, those changes were overshadowed by the aforementioned shifts in American attitudes toward the Fund. The months following August 1971 seemed to signify that the United States would reconstruct the international monetary system without the International Monetary Fund. The Fund staff seemed helpless in confronting the gathering crisis in 1971; Secretary of the Treasury John Connally made it clear that consultation with the IMF was not part of his program. The managing director of the IMF, Pierre-Paul Schweitzer, was told of the U.S. decision to close the gold window only thirty minutes before President Nixon's speech. During preparation for the Smithsonian Conference in late 1971, the IMF was

distinctly on the sidelines (Southard 1979: 37–42). Relations between
Schweitzer and the U.S. Treasury remained chilly, and the United
States ultimately failed to support a new term for the managing
director.

Although American relations with the IMF recovered after the
Connally years, the relative importance of the Fund during the 1970s in
overseeing the exchange rate system was clearly reduced; countries were
now free to choose their own exchange rate systems, and the introduction
of Fund surveillance seemed to imply "a backing away from the view that
officials are better able than the market to determine the correct exchange
rate for a currency" (Dam 1982: 265). As financing of current account
deficits increasingly shifted toward commercial banks, the IMF's role
seemed limited to providing finance for poorer members who could not
turn to the private markets and to providing a seal of approval (the
"catalytic role") for policy changes that would reassure private creditors.
The latter was an important role, particularly after commercial banks
discovered that they could not impose their own conditionality, but the
number of large debtors in trouble in the 1970s remained small. Although
one could attribute the decline in the Fund's role to the erosion of a rule-
based regime and a decline in American (or any single power's) influence
(within the international monetary regime), one might well agree with
Alexander Kafka (1976: 18) that the "real reason why no more was
accomplished was simply that no compelling need was felt for anything
more." There was no "disastrous rise in internationally antisocial
action."

Although the evolution of the international monetary sphere reduced
American interest in the IMF and offered other instruments for international collaboration, the Fund was not dissolved or set aside. The
characteristics of the organization served to sustain it and ultimately to
reinstate it as a center of international monetary negotiations. In particular
its professionalism and relatively small size enabled it, with appropriate
leadership, to innovate in ways that enhanced its utility for the principal
monetary powers. This was clear even in 1971, when it appeared to be
excluded. Although the preparatory negotiations for the Smithsonian
Conference were carried out under the G-10 and not the Fund, Schweitzer
and the staff participated in the meetings and prepared papers for the
conference (Southard 1979: 41). The IMF ultimately served as the umbrella
for study of reform of the international monetary system. The resulting
changes were approved as amendments to the Articles of Agreement, not
as a new institution.

The Reagan Administration:
Skepticism, Belated Support, Politicization

The Reagan administration's relations with the IMF deserve separate scrutiny. They extended several trends in U.S. disengagement that have already been noted, particularly a distinct skepticism regarding the value of intergovernmental cooperation in the international financial and monetary arena and an even more pronounced belief in the stability and efficiency of private market solutions. With the beginning of the debt crisis in 1982, however, the Reagan administration found the International Monetary Fund to be a useful instrument of American policies at a time of considerable strain on the international financial system. Its willingness to countenance a renewed though circumscribed activism on the part of the IMF abruptly met another trend: resistance within the American Congress to granting greater resources to the Fund through a quota increase. The administration became embroiled in the most ideological and overtly political debate over the International Monetary Fund since Bretton Woods, one that did not augur well for enhanced American support for the institutions of postwar economic internationalism. The second Reagan administration and the tenure of Treasury Secretary James Baker continued the turn toward international monetary and financial collaboration on the part of the United States both for managing exchange rates and dealing with the debt crisis. The Baker Plan, announced in October 1985, reinforced the central role played by the IMF in debt crisis management; in efforts to encourage exchange rate realignment, however, the Fund seemed to play a secondary role as the monetary powers struck bargains outside the organization.

The first eighteen months of the Reagan administration were marked by an accentuation of the market orientation that had been favored by administrations during the 1970s. In managing the floating exchange rate system, the Reagan administration continued to endorse market forces as the determinant of exchange rates among the major industrial countries. The rise of the dollar against other major currencies beginning in 1980 scuttled the substitution account discussions even before Reagan took office, and arguments that the United States should take action to realign exchange rates were quickly dismissed: the definition of "disorderly market conditions" after 1981 was to be very narrow.

The change in the U.S. position on the Fund's financing role, particularly for developing countries, seemed even more dramatic. The managing director of the IMF, Jacques de Larosière, was far more activist than his immediate predecessors and also more disposed to increase the IMF role in developing countries. Particularly after the second oil shock in

1979, he worked to expand Fund financing of the ensuing current account deficits. The scale of involvement with the poorest developing countries, particularly in sub-Saharan Africa, grew, and in the eyes of some the IMF seemed to be edging toward a new role in medium-term development finance.

Expansion of access to Fund resources (the policy of enlarged access) and what seemed to be very weak conditionality in some of the post-oil shock programs had already stirred disquiet among Executive Board members from the industrial countries. That disquiet extended from the policies being pursued to the belief among board members that the managing director and staff were setting policy rather than implementing policies directed by the board and IMF members. Under the Carter administration, concerns over loosening conditionality and expanding access to Fund resources were balanced by a desire to maximize the financial resources directed toward the developing countries. For the Reagan administration both the policy and the organizational shifts were objectionable, and the administration's agenda quickly led to a collision with the management and with the developing countries.

The Reagan administration's view of the IMF might be labeled "classical": to the degree that a public organization was necessary in financing current account deficits, its role should be strictly limited. In this view the International Monetary Fund was originally designed as a short-term lending institution, and recent trends toward longer-term financing—such as the Extended Fund Facility and extended periods of adjustment—only served to blur that primordial role. To the degree that nations required longer-term financing, the often-stated American view was that they should turn to established lending institutions such as the World Bank or (the preferred course) to the private financial markets. Given this view of the Fund's role, in the context of flexible exchange rates the resources required by the IMF were limited; hence in its first year the Reagan administration opposed a quota increase for the Fund, and, even in the midst of the debt crisis, opposed a new allocation of special drawing rights.

Less finance meant sharper adjustment, and that too fitted with administration preferences. The policies instituted under de Larosière had conceded a portion of the developing countries' case that they required a lengthier period of adjustment in the face of such external shocks as the oil price increases. To the Reagan administration, lengthier adjustment seemed to mean no adjustment in many cases; reduced financing forced hard and necessary policy choices on unwilling governments. Conditionality should be tightened rather than loosened; the balance between financing and adjustment had to be shifted in favor of the latter.

These preferences for a narrower IMF role also implied a reassertion of national governments' control over policy. The Reagan administration clashed with the managing director early on, at the 1981 Interim Committee meeting in Gabon. The managing director had put forward a name for chairman of the Interim Committee at the meeting, a step that was clearly viewed as out of line by the U.S. Treasury. Personal relations worsened between the new administration and the Fund's management. In reining in the Fund, the Reagan administration quickly found allies among the governments of other industrialized countries. On certain policy questions, such as tightened conditionality, a new consensus was even more easily achieved: the U.S. position was shared by the Federal Republic of Germany, the United Kingdom, Japan, and often by the Netherlands. The new conservative orthodoxy that prevailed among industrialized countries during the 1980s found expression in the G-5 consensus within the IMF. Other aspects of the U.S. agenda, such as its opposition to use of Fund resources before exhausting commercial credits (the reasoning behind American opposition to the EEF proposed for India in 1981) found much less support.

To many outsiders the pronounced changes in IMF conditionality after 1980 were evidence of continuing American dominance of the organization's policies. John Williamson (1982: 44–51) has presented convincing evidence that such a shift did in fact take place, particularly in the number of high-conditionality arrangements. Nevertheless, it would be more accurate to describe the role of the United States as a vocal focus for a coherent industrialized country program to shift Fund policies after 1980. The United States required and received support for the new line from Germany, Britain, and Japan in particular.

The United States and its allies had hardly begun to shift IMF policies, however, when the declaration of a moratorium on debt servicing by Mexico in August 1982 forced yet another change, toward endorsing renewed activism on the part of the IMF. The Mexican rescue and its aftermath resulted in renewed governmental intervention, led by the United States, and collective measures to ensure adequate financing for troubled debtors in exchange for tough adjustment programs monitored by the Fund.[5] Although the U.S. Treasury had been slow to recognize the impending crisis, it quickly pieced together a financing package for Mexico; the role of the Federal Reserve under Chairman Paul Volcker grew partly because of its expertise on Mexico and its connections to the country and partly because of the prominent role played by private banks in the crisis (Kraft 1984; Lipson 1986: 227–31).

In the face of apparent weaknesses in private financial markets and with the support of the United States, the IMF assumed a role that went beyond issuing its characteristic "seal of approval" to catalyze private lending to countries undertaking an adjustment program. To ensure adequate financing for successful adjustment programs, the Fund became the linchpin in constructing financing packages for the major debtors, withholding its endorsement until it was assured of a "critical mass" from both commercial banks and governmental creditors. Thus the IMF's endorsement of a country's economic policies served not only to reassure lenders but also to guarantee a certain level of finance to support the policies. This innovation of "involuntary" or "concerted" lending was, by all accounts, the idea of Managing Director Jacques de Larosière. U.S. support for such an interventionist innovation was a striking endorsement of the Fund by those who had previously attempted to limit its role. In this instance the characteristics of the issue area served to revive a prominent role for the International Monetary Fund, just as it had reduced its role in the 1970s: reliance on private finance introduced instabilities and threats to the international financial system. When those threats reached large American financial institutions, the United States (and other industrialized countries) were compelled to act, and the International Monetary Fund became their chosen instrument.

As the IMF and its staff became absorbed in tying together debt reschedulings and adjustment in an ever-lengthening list of countries after 1982, the Reagan administration held to the other parts of its agenda for the IMF: the need for tightened conditionality in all Fund programs as well as an emphasis on the short-term nature of lending. Given the IMF's central role in maintaining confidence in the international financial system, however, it did concede the need for additional resources in the form of a quota increase. That decision brought a surprising political conflict at a time when the Fund's public profile was higher than ever before.

The tortuous path through Congress of the proposed increased contribution by the United States to the International Monetary Fund has the characteristics of a melodrama. Its significance for future American support of international organizations remains controversial.[6] From its introduction in March 1983 until final passage in November of that year, the intense opposition stimulated by the proposed quota increase was in part conjunctural, produced by a deep recession and the intent of a Democratic House of Representatives to use this issue—any issue—to wring concessions from the Reagan administration. In this case the concessions were, first, a housing bill and, second, closer surveillance of international lending by the banks.

Other aspects of the controversy may have signaled deeper changes, however, ones that point to increasing difficulty for international organizations that require resources to be allocated periodically by the United

States. First, the ideological changes mentioned earlier figured prominently in the debate. Despite the Reagan administration's shift in position to support for the IMF, the usual hard core of Republican opposition to international organizations and foreign aid remained. This conservative opposition in Congress has been a constant for most of the postwar era. Centrist internationalists, both Republican and Democrat, confronted a *liberal* opposition in this case as well: free marketeer Howard Ruff appeared in strange alliance with consumer advocate Ralph Nader. What were the sources of liberal disenchantment? The key issue that cemented this coalition was a populist one: hostility toward the money center banks that were viewed as the cause of the debt crisis. Other issues also fed liberal reluctance to support the IMF. Hard times (the bill was presented in the depths of the 1981–82 recession) were linked to international competition, which was in turn linked to financing provided by the Fund and the banks. Later in the debate an IMF loan to South Africa nearly delivered the Black Caucus to the opposition.

These sources of discontent among normally internationalist supporters of the IMF point to a second conclusion about the domestic politics of internationalism. The internationalization of the American economy should, it might be argued, produce *greater* support for organizations that claim to promote international economic cooperation. Instead, those groups hurt by internationalization may deflect that injury onto the organizations; those who benefit from the organizations' role may not be ideal political allies. Large commercial banks were the core of support for the IMF bill, but they did not take a prominent public stance because their support would probably have hurt chances of passage.

Weighing the persistence and depth of these changes in American politics is difficult. The narrowing of political support for economic internationalism is likely to remain a permanent feature of American politics, however, increasing the costs for any administration in supporting an international organization such as the IMF.

IMF Influence on the United States: The Privileges of Position

Using either of the strong measures of organizational influence on the U.S. government demonstrates that the influence of the IMF on American policy has been slight and that little change in that influence has occurred over time. The limited extent of Fund influence—despite relatively high regard for the competence of its staff—has been demonstrated repeatedly, even during the years of reduced American influence within the organization. Most dramatic were the efforts of Managing Director Schweitzer to

influence the course of American policy and negotiating stance in 1971—
efforts that were, in the words of John Odell (1982: 272), "shrugged off."
(Schweitzer probably paid for his unprecedented public admonitions when
the United States failed to support a renewal of his tenure.) Gowa's
(1983) account of the decision to close the gold window vividly illustrates
the weakness within the U.S. government of those who defended the
Bretton Woods rules of the game in August 1971. Only Arthur Burns,
chairman of the Federal Reserve Board, argued for equating respect for
the existing system and the maintenance of international economic
cooperation. For the other presidential advisers and for Nixon himself,
"momentum . . . had gathered behind the idea that the Bretton Woods
system was encroaching on an objective sacrosanct to the most powerful
members of the Nixon administration . . . the maintenance of U.S.
autonomy in decision making" (Gowa 1983: 159–60).

Later episodes confirmed the Fund's impotence in the face of strongly
held American preferences. Managing Director de Larosière and the IMF
staff were enthusiastic supporters of the substitution account in the late
1970s, a plan to reduce the dollar overhang in the international monetary
system by a mechanism of exchanging dollars for SDRs. The plan
ultimately foundered on disagreement between the United States and
other members of the G-5 over sharing the cost of the scheme, a conflict
that the assiduous IMF efforts could not bridge (Gowa 1984: 673). During
the early 1980s, despite constant Fund arguments that the United States
should reduce its fiscal deficit in the interests of global economic recovery,
American economic policymakers refused to budge from their combination of tax reductions and increased military spending.

The reasons for the IMF's limited influence are twofold. First, from its
earliest years the Fund's influence over policy in any country that is not
using Fund resources has been slight (Southard 1979: 13–14, 44–45). A
Fund program is the key lever that gains IMF entry into the policymaking
process. Although the United States has drawn on IMF resources, it has
never had an upper-tranche, high-conditionality program with the IMF.
Without such a program the Fund must rely on Article IV consultations,
relatively anodyne meetings between Fund staff and member governments
that result in a report that is discussed by the Executive Board. The Article
IV procedures do provide a narrow avenue of surveillance of member
states' policies, including the United States. Given that the reports are not
made public and that Executive Board discussions are also confidential, the
policy impact is often slight. During certain episodes of international
economic disarray, the Fund's policy advice has been useful to the U.S.
Treasury and its allies in internal political battles. Any ammunition is
useful in such battles, however, and no policymaker interviewed could

detect an occasion in which IMF support or intervention was critical to the winning side.

Second, IMF influence on American policy is reduced by the predominant role of the Treasury in setting U.S. international monetary policy. The executive director reports to the Treasury; most of his staff is seconded from the Treasury. The Treasury serves as an effective gatekeeper in relations between the American government and international financial organizations; other agencies, with the exception of the Federal Reserve (which has played a particularly prominent role during the debt crisis), may be briefed but are rarely consulted in setting U.S. policy.

The policy predominance of the Treasury muffles Fund influence in at least two ways. Although the executive director may define his role in part as conveying IMF views to the U.S. government, his point of contact is restricted to a single agency. Building an intragovernmental coalition parallel to Fund positions is thus made more difficult. The Treasury itself may not be the key player in every case, and its attitude toward the international rules of the game may be ambivalent. As Gowa (1983: 109) notes, the Treasury has retained its prominent policy position by following the priorities of successive presidents and most domestic interest groups, "an ordering that subordinates the demands of the international monetary order to the imperatives of domestic economic policy and foreign security policy." That ordering was clear not only in the early 1970s but also during most of the Reagan administration, when the Treasury's hostility toward Fund prescriptions was apparent.

Less demanding tests of influence on American policy suggest that the arenas of international monetary cooperation associated with the Fund—the Interim Committee and the annual meeting—do serve a modest agenda-setting function within the U.S. government (Widman 1982: chap. 4). Under an activist managing director, the IMF can also propose innovations that are accepted by the United States and other industrialized countries; involuntary lending in late 1982 is the best example. Through such innovation the Fund may widen the range of choice for the United States and other countries, offering cooperative solutions that were not previously available. The case of the substitution account demonstrates, however, that underlying conflicts of interest may not be overcome by even the cleverest device proposed by an international organization.

The United States and the IMF—Influence and Its Limits

Hegemonic stability theory attempts to link changes in the international system with the decline of a dominant power such as the United States.

The relative decline of the United States as an economic power is reflected by changes in its IMF quotas. As noted earlier, the U.S. relative share has declined from 38 percent in 1946 to just under 20 percent in the 1980s. This account has suggested two important qualifications, however, to any attempt to link American relations with the International Monetary Fund to that simple portrait of decline.

First, the dominance of the United States in the "hegemonic period" was not so great as the figures might suggest. Clearly its views carried great weight on policy questions, but even then bargaining was necessary, particularly on important issues such as conditionality. Not only did the United States find it necessary to bargain in order to win the consent of other members, but it also conceded a measure of autonomy to the managing director and staff for reasons of efficient decision making and enhanced legitimacy. Consultation on all but the top staff appointments was foregone; country programs were designed by the staff and only the staff. Executive directors representing the United States or other countries could only hope to influence those programs through Executive Board discussions.

Second, the influence of the United States within the IMF in the 1970s and 1980s remained high, protected by the regime of special majorities that gave greater importance to coalition building and broad consensus. Its influence over staff appointments remains that established in the 1950s, although the proportion of Americans on staff declined with the American quota. In the design of country programs, the United States has repeatedly told foreign governments that it will not intervene in negotiations between the Fund and member governments. It is clear nonetheless that the United States (and other major countries) can still influence programs for friends and clients at the margin. In considerable measure American influence over country programs is awarded by financing that the United States provides independently of the IMF. U.S. intervention is limited, however, by American interest in utilizing the Fund as a buffer in awkward bilateral relations, imposing economic conditions that the United States would find it hard to impose bilaterally. Finally, on policy questions, where American preferences seem to have received a new hearing at the Fund in the 1980s, American influence is highly dependent on a policy coalition linking most of the major industrial countries. Although the United States has been most vocal in advocating its classical view of the Fund's role, Germany, Japan, and the United Kingdom have often been eager to support American initiatives.

In determining U.S. relations with the IMF, however, American influence in the organization has been less important than the perceived usefulness of the Fund as an instrument of American policies in the international economy. Changes in the international monetary and financial issue area during the 1970s and 1980s produced two rival means of advancing American interests that competed with the IMF's rule-based and universal arena: informal cooperation among the industrialized countries (in the G-5 and later the G-7) and reliance on the private financial markets. One of those competitors, the private markets, suffered a serious setback with the onset of the debt crisis in 1982. The other— "great power" bargaining—remains the critical arena for determining exchange rates among the G-5 (as demonstrated by successive accords, beginning with the Plaza Agreement in September 1985). Since the Versailles Summit of 1982, the IMF has been more closely associated with G-5 cooperation. As part of multilateral surveillance, the managing director has attended meetings of the G-5 ministers.

Domestic politics has, in turn, influenced the attractiveness of each of these alternatives. Support for the IMF by recent administrations has been beset by ideological opposition to economic internationalism and by increasing difficulty in extracting resources from Congress. Both of these domestic developments grew in importance during the 1980s.

Conclusion

Despite the IMF's renewed prominence in the early 1980s, its close relations with the United States and its key role in the international financial system may not persist. Much of its new-found prestige grew from the debt crisis. As the crisis lingered on for most of a decade, the Fund approach to debt crisis management came under increasing criticism. With the Baker Plan the United States endorsed adjustment with growth as a goal but offered little in the way of additional financing to realize the new approach. By the late 1980s both debtors and banks appeared to be searching for a new model that would end the cycle of low growth, growing debt, and endless renegotiation. Debt write-offs became thinkable, as did moratoria on debt payments (such as that declared by Brazil in early 1987). With the ungluing of a strategy of debt crisis management that had been overseen by the International Monetary Fund for most of the decade, one future role of the organization is uncertain.

Even more significant for the future relations of the United States and the IMF was the organization's role in the management of exchange rates and, more broadly, the surveillance of macroeconomic policy. Discontent with the system of floating exchange rates has grown among the developing and industrialized countries in the 1980s; that discontent surfaced latest in the United States. Nevertheless, the tenure of Treasury Secretary Baker marked a turning in American attitudes toward coordination of economic policies to achieve a different exchange rate equilibrium. Up to this point, however, cooperation has emerged through a combination of unilateral policy initiatives, bilateral bargaining, or agreements within the G-5 or G-7. The IMF has played a relatively peripheral role. The threat that a club of industrialized countries will supersede the Fund in fact, if not in law, remains significant; it is a threat that has been beaten back repeatedly by the IMF since the formation of the G-10 twenty-five years ago.

Even if the Fund plays a more prominent role in negotiations over economic policy and exchange rate coordination, the asymmetry between Fund influence over developing countries and its influence on the large industrialized countries will remain. Paul Volcker (cited in Solomon 1982: 250) once recounted a story told to him in Southeast Asia: "When disagreement arose between the IMF and member countries on the need for policy changes, if the country was small, it fell into line; if it was large, the IMF fell into line; if several large countries were involved, the IMF disappeared." The question of the Fund's ability to exercise surveillance over (or influence) the economic policies of even its most powerful members is important for more than theoretical reasons. As described earlier, its record to date has been disappointing, particularly in mobilizing international pressure to influence U.S. policy. A mechanism for the coordination of national economic policies—or at least the elimination of their inconsistencies—continues to elude national governments. As the United States confronts a high level of international indebtedness and a potentially painful adjustment of its own, the Fund may provide a useful means of disguising American weakness, just as in an earlier period it disguised American strength. Despite its highly publicized involvement in the Third World debt crisis, it is this issue and the development of the IMF's ability to influence the strong as well as the weak that will decide the usefulness of the Fund in the fifth decade after Bretton Woods.

Notes

1. In the deciding vote on this issue, the opponents abstained (Horsefield 1969: 363). The American executive director at the time, however, conceded that "there is no doubt that the majority felt is was unwise to force the issue" (Southard 1979: 14).

2. See Southard (1979: 9–11). In that case representatives from the less developed countries including Brazil, though agreeing that a standby arrangement in support of the sterling need not include any phasing of drawings, did urge a subsequent review of terms for standby arrangements to ensure equitable treatment of all members (Southard 1979: 31–33).

3. For a detailed analysis of the effects of the IMF's voting system on its decision making, see Lister (1984).

4. On the changes in special majorities under the Second Amendment, see Lister (1984: chap. 4) and Joseph Gold (1977).

5. An account of international innovations for dealing with the debt crisis is given in Kahler (1986) and Lipson (1986). Details of the Mexican episode are drawn from Kraft (1984).

6. The best summary account of the year-long progress of the IMF quota increase is U.S. House of Representatives (1983: 11–133). I have also used interviews with congressional staffers and other participants in the debate, as well as an excellent unpublished account by Karen Shaw, "Lobbying for a Bank 'Bail-Out': How a Bill Beat the Odds."

References

Dam, Kenneth (1982). *The Rules of the Game*. Chicago: University of Chicago Press.

Dell, Sidney (1981). *On Being Grandmotherly: The Evolution of IMF Conditionality*. Princeton, NJ: International Finance Section, Princeton University.

DeVries, Margaret Garritsen (1985). *The International Monetary Fund, 1972–1978: Cooperation on Trial*, vols. II, III. Washington, DC: International Monetary Fund.

DeVries, Margaret Garritsen, and J. Keith Horsefield (1969). *The International Monetary Fund, 1945–1965*, vol. II. Washington, DC: International Monetary Fund.

Gardner, Richard (1980). *Sterling-Dollar Diplomacy*. New York: Columbia University Press.

Gold, Joseph (1977). *Voting Majorities in the Fund: Effect of Second Amendment of the Articles*. Washington, DC: International Monetary Fund.

Gowa, Joanne (1983). *Closing the Gold Window: Domestic Politics and the End of Bretton Woods*. Ithaca, NY: Cornell University Press.

——— (1984). "Hegemons, IOs, and Markets: The Case of the Substitution Account." *International Organization*, 38(4), 661–84.

Horsefield, J. Keith (1969). *The International Monetary Fund, 1945–1965*, vol. I. Washington, DC: International Monetary Fund.

Kafka, Alexander (1976). *The International Monetary Fund: Reform without Reconstruction?* Princeton, NJ: International Finance Section, Princeton University.

Kahler, Miles (1986). "Politics and International Debt: Explaining the Crisis." In Miles Kahler, ed., *The Politics of International Debt*. Ithaca, NY: Cornell University Press.

Kraft, Joseph (1984). *The Mexican Rescue*. New York: Group of Thirty.

Lipson, Charles (1986). "International Debt and International Institutions." In Miles Kahler, ed., *The Politics of International Debt*. Ithaca, NY: Cornell University Press.

Lister, Frederick K. (1984). *Decision-Making Strategies for International Organizations: The IMF Model*. Denver, CO: University of Denver.

Odell, John S. (1982). *U.S. International Monetary Policy: Markets, Power, and Ideas as Sources of Change*. Princeton, NJ: Princeton University Press.

Shaw, Karen (n.d.). "Lobbying for a Bank 'Bail-Out': How a Bill Beat the Odds." Unpublished manuscript.

Solomon, Robert (1982). *The International Monetary System, 1945–1981*. New York: Harper & Row.

Southard, Frank (1979). *The Evolution of the International Monetary Fund*. Princeton, NJ: International Finance Section, Princeton University.

U.S. House of Representatives, Committee on Foreign Affairs (1984). *Congress and Foreign Policy, 1983*. Washington, DC: U.S. Government Printing Office.

Widman, F. Lisle (1982). *Making International Monetary Policy*. Washington, DC: Georgetown University Law Center.

Williamson, John (1982). *The Lending Policies of the International Monetary Fund.* Washington, DC: Institute for International Economics.

World Bank (1985). *Annual Report.* Washington, DC: World Bank Publications.

CHAPTER FIVE

The World Bank and U.S. Control

William Ascher

The relationship between the World Bank and the U.S. government is a story of ambiguous separation. Critics frequently cast the World Bank as the creature and servant of U.S. interests; other observers emphasize the clashes between the U.S. government and the Bank. With the exception of the complicated issue of the state's role in development, the "development advice" expressed by the World Bank has typically been quite similar to the development strategies advocated by the U.S. government, although both have changed over the years. There has been a steady *coevolution* of development approaches that makes the question of who is leading and who is following a moot point. The two thus have had a complex, evolving relationship that is part symbiosis, part two-way influence, and part struggle over the Bank's autonomy of action.

During the 1970s and 1980s the relationship between the World Bank and the United States has been particularly strained. These strains developed largely out of disillusionment with multilateral aid on the part of both members of Congress and the executive branch. They increased during the 1980s when the Bank's lending elevated the role of the state sector in the developing countries, to the dismay of the Reagan administration. These developments, however, have been part of a longer struggle for control over the Bank's direction, which has coincided with the decline of U.S. economic and political hegemony. The period of Robert McNamara's presidency (1968–81) was a crucial one for understanding the change in the U.S. relationship to the World Bank. It was a period of the Bank's greatest expansion when many American officials came to see the Bank as having betrayed the United States. In turn, efforts by the Bank's leadership and staff to maintain their autonomy from the U.S. government account for a good portion of the Bank's structure, actions, and problems.

Thus the argument of this chapter is that the World Bank's leadership and staff have developed a "protective shell" of beliefs and practices that insulate the Bank from U.S. pressures but often create problems for the Bank's functions as an international development institution. These reactions to U.S. pressure are interesting beyond the policy problems they create. First, it is striking that an international organization, constituted through a formal agreement among its founding nation-state members, is shaped not only by the particulars of this agreement but also by its subsequent interactions with these nation-states. Second, it is troubling that the established instruments of nation-state control over multilateral lending do not seem to satisfy the U.S. government. The American commitment to "multilateralism" has been brought into question by the U.S. stance toward the Bank since the beginning of the McNamara presidency. Indeed, the U.S. commitment to multilateralism when that means something more than disguised bilateralism has always been problematic.

I will first examine the evolution of the U.S.–World Bank relationship, then focus on how the commonalities and divergences of the United States and World Bank outlooks have arisen. Finally, an analysis of *how* the reactions of the World Bank to U.S. pressure have created problems in both Bank projects and policy advice leads to some recommendations for modifying the U.S.–World Bank relationship.

Historical Evolution of the U.S.–World Bank Relationship

The World Bank was largely the brainchild of the United States and Great Britain in their efforts to shape the post–World War II international economic order. The Bretton Woods agreements established both the International Monetary Fund and the World Bank in 1944. Many other countries, including developing nations, were involved in the deliberations, but the United States and Western Europe dominated. The initial priority of the World Bank (officially the International Bank for Reconstruction and Development) was indeed reconstruction, and very little effort was devoted to aiding developing countries until the U.S. Marshall Plan ensured Western European recovery.

The initial rationale of the World Bank was to provide a vehicle for channeling U.S. private investment into Europe, not to provide official U.S. aid. Given the reluctance of private investors to place their capital abroad after the defaults of the Great Depression and the dislocations of war, the official endorsement and guarantee of the World Bank's soundness by the United States was more important than the U.S. funds, contributed along with those of other member nations, to capitalize the Bank. When reconstruction was no longer a priority of the World Bank and development economics fastened on the provision of capital as the key element for Third World growth, the rationale shifted in terms of the target but remained a matter of facilitating the movement of private capital.

Although the World Bank was not established fundamentally as an aid institution, participation by the United States and other member nations did permit the Bank to lend at lower than commercial interest rates. And this modestly concessional nature of World Bank loans permitted the Bank to find borrowers even when it imposed conditions—ranging from broad economic policy to the specific conditions of funded projects. The World Bank thus lent predominantly for large projects, but its advice and pressure have influenced both project design and general macroeconomic policy—for example, in insisting on currency devaluations and better-balanced budgets.

In its early years the World Bank was quite open about its efforts to influence the economic policies of borrowing governments. As David Baldwin noted in his assessment of the Bank's political nature twenty years ago, the World ‚Bank's second *Annual Report* (1946–47) candidly announced the Bank's objective of "exerting a 'helpful influence' on member governments in order to persuade them to remove trade barriers and adopt sound financial programs." The third *Annual Report* (1947–48) elevated this objective as a higher measure of the Bank's effectiveness than the number or volume of its loans (Baldwin 1965: 77–78).

In addition to these overt efforts to influence governments to follow liberal guidelines, the International Finance Corporation (IFC) was established in 1956 as a World Bank affiliate dedicated to encouraging *private* enterprise by lending directly to private firms. Although IFC lending has never amounted to even a tenth of the World Bank's total loan volume, it has sent a steady signal of the Bank's orientation.

With the completion of postwar reconstruction and the increase in the number of independent, developing countries, pressure built for multilateral *aid* to developing countries. The United States and other developed countries, however, remained leery of schemes to channel massive official development aid through the United Nations; thus the World Bank's "soft" loan facility was established in 1960. Although the Bank is nominally affiliated with the United Nations system in practice, it is totally autonomous from the UN and represented in the minds of Western officials a more sober and tough-minded overseer of multilateral aid.

Labeled the International Development Association (IDA), this soft loan facility is actually wholly operated by the same structure that processes the World Bank's "hard" loans. But IDA loans bear no interest, are payable in fifty years, and have a ten-year grace period. Only countries with very low per-capita income are eligible for IDA loans, which obviously approximate straightforward aid. Given that the bulk of IDA funds must be provided by contributions from the governments of developed nations in periodic "replenishments," the United States plays a key role. U.S. contributions have ranged from 42 percent at the beginning to 25 percent in the eighth, most recent, replenishment (World Bank 1982: 6; 1987: 29). In addition, other donors have made their contributions contingent on the U.S. government's willingness to appropriate funds. Thus although the IDA obviously increases the scope of World Bank operation and its capacity to provide capital for the world's poorest nations (IDA lending has typically been around $4 billion annually in the 1980s), the need for IDA replenishment clearly increased the dependence of the World Bank Group—that is, all of the World Bank's lending facilities—on the donor nations and particularly on the United States.

U.S. Expectations

From its founding in the late 1960s, because of the importance of the U.S. role, the World Bank was viewed by many largely as an appendage of the U.S. government, one the United States could use to achieve its objectives. The U.S. government itself viewed the Bank as that part of the international financial system channeling capital to less developed countries in exchange for "credit-worthy" economic performance.

During these early years Bank policy prescriptions coincided so closely with policy prescriptions preferred by the U.S. government that the Bank was widely viewed as a spokesman for the U.S. administration. For example, the Bank's insistence that India devaluate its currency in the mid-1960s was seen as "sparing [the United States] the unsavory epithets of . . . 'aid with strings,' 'arm-twisting political pressures,' etc." (Patra 1966: 238). The World Bank has been viewed as a convenient enforcer precisely because it was not formally an agency of the U.S. government. "To avoid giving Indian nationalism too much offense, [President Lyndon] Johnson seems to have let the Bank do most of the tough bargaining" (Mukerjee 1966b: 603). Similarly, on the issue of Indian and Pakistani military spending, the *Far Eastern Economic Review* theorized that "aid-givers prefer to speak through the Bank, because its neutral and apparently technical advice may be less offensive to national sentiments than direct intervention by the United States" (Mukerjee 1966a: 634).

The U.S. commitment to use the World Bank as a major channel for multilateral capital transfer has endured across time, although the extent of the commitment to transferring capital to developing countries has varied according to both the state of the U.S. economy and the ideology of the U.S. administration.

The flow of U.S. *aid* via the bilateral and multilateral channels has fluctuated considerably, as shown in Table 5.1. Although U.S. bilateral aid grew steadily during the Eisenhower administration, U.S. multilateral aid was minimal. Those contributions took an immediate and sustained fourfold increase—even in real terms—after 1960, however, and accounted for more than a third of all developed country multilateral aid. Still, multilateral aid was a very small proportion of U.S. aid, never amounting to even 10 percent of the total U.S. economic aid under the Kennedy administration. During the Nixon administration a dramatic shift of U.S. aid to a more multilateral focus occurred. As U.S. bilateral economic aid drifted down, multilateral aid increased even in real terms.

TABLE 5.1
U.S. Economic Aid

	Bilateral (millions US $)	Multilateral (millions US $)	U.S. Share of Developed Countries Multilateral Aid (%)
1950–55 (avg.)	1,058	60	36 (1956)
1960	2,545	256	39
1965	3,349	69	20
1970	2,657	393	35
1975	2,941	1,066	28
1980	4,366	2,772	30
1985	8,182	1,221	16

SOURCE: Organization for Economic Cooperation and Development, *Flow of Financial Resources in Less-Developed Countries 1956–63* (Paris: OECD, 1964), pp. 134 & 149 (old series); Organization for Economic Cooperation and Development, *Flow of Financial Resources to Developing Countries* (Paris: OECD, 1973), p. 447; and Organization for Economic Cooperation and Development, *Development Cooperation*, various issues (Paris: OECD, various years, new series).

The Carter administration enacted sizable increases in both bilateral and multilateral aid. In several years multilateral aid constituted nearly two-fifths of the total. Under the Reagan administration total U.S. economic aid continued to increase, at least through 1985. An early initiative by Budget Director David Stockman to gut the Bank contributions because of its support of "state planning efforts" and its "emphasis on programs fostering income redistribution" was ultimately turned back

(Sanford 1982: 74–75). All U.S. administrations have looked to the World Bank as the primary channel for multilateral assistance and lending, despite fluctuations in the commitment to, and levels of, multilateral aid.

Although the United States was increasing its contributions to multilateral aid, and even increasing the relative balance between bilateral and multilateral assistance in favor of the multilateral channels, the U.S. *share* of total multilateral aid fluctuated, as evidenced in Table 5.1. Other developed countries were assuming more of the burden generally, and the United States no longer accounted for the lion's share of multilateral aid funding. Simultaneously the Bank increased its autonomy and became truly multilateral largely through the leadership of President Robert McNamara. U.S. influence over the Bank declined.

The McNamara Watershed

In 1968 President Lyndon Johnson selected Robert McNamara, the controversial former secretary of defense, as World Bank president. McNamara had far more public visibility than former Bank presidents. He deviated sharply from the previous avoidance of public sector industrial projects. Almost immediately the Bank abandoned its official taboo against publicly controlled development corporations and development banks lending to state industrial projects. The straightforward argument was that because some governments preferred public sector institutions and private sector capital or profitability was often lacking for projects that governments wanted to support, the World Bank should endorse the trend to "widening options" (World Bank 1976: 13). State-owned industries quickly assumed a major role in the World Bank project portfolio (Ayres 1983; Hurni 1980).

By 1973 McNamara had not only launched an expansion of Bank operations and shown himself to be as independent-minded as ever, he also undertook a highly visible reorientation of the Bank's lending to "poverty alleviation" projects that focused on rural development, provision of social services such as health care, and urban slum upgrading. With all of these new initiatives, the World Bank Group's lending increased fivefold from 1968 to 1981 in *real* terms, discounting for inflation (Ayres 1983: 7).

In the early 1970s U.S. policymakers were also modifying their approach to bilateral development aid in the direction of poverty alleviation. Congress approved so-called New Directions legislation in U.S. foreign assistance in 1973 (Mathieson 1981; U.S. Congress 1973), the same year as McNamara's famous Nairobi speech committing the World Bank to helping "the poorest of the poor." It is very interesting, however, that a careful reading of McNamara's 1971 and 1972 annual addresses reveals striking similarities to the 1973 Nairobi speech in emphasis and argument (McNamara 1981). One implication is that the New Directions legislation was *preceded* by McNamara's shift to a direct poverty alleviation focus. Clearly by the early 1970s McNamara was regarded as an authority on development issues within the American establishment. He helped to shift both the World Bank and U.S. bilateral aid toward poverty alleviation.

However, another implication in the fact that 1973 is "remembered" as the year of the World Bank's shift to poverty alleviation is that this dating results more from the coverage of U.S. and World Bank public stances than from any concrete changes in Bank policy that year. This was apparently because of both coevolution and blurring of the boundaries between the Bank and the U.S. administration in the eyes of many observers.

In the mid-1970s the development orientation of both the World Bank and the U.S. government also began to change with respect to the primacy of securing capital for projects. The "takeoff" that some expected would result from massive investment had not materialized in the majority of developing countries. Rising energy prices only demonstrated the vulnerability of their industrialization strategies. Those that had industrialized the most, such as Brazil and Mexico, faced mounting international indebtedness.

Questions over the efficiency of using capital in the context of "distorted" policy regimes led to an emphasis on general *policy* adjustments, the elimination of state-enforced economic distortions, and the adoption of export promotion policies. By the end of McNamara's presidency in 1981, the Bank was reemphasizing private sector lending and had embarked on structural adjustment lending. The latter entails a very different role for the World Bank in several respects. The structural adjustment loans are typically much larger than project loans; they are of shorter term; and they engage the Bank in a different level of dialogue with the borrowing countries. Traditional project-based lending is based on expertise in microeconomics and engineering, whereas the "conditionalities" of structural adjustment lending rely on macroeconomic expertise and assessments of general economic policy.

Only in the wake of the 1982 world debt crisis did the Reagan administration recognize the importance of this new role for the Bank and permit significant increases in the World Bank's capitalization to enable it to *lend* at a higher level. Subsequently various U.S. initiatives—for example, the Baker plan—have called for a far bigger leap in the Bank's lending to help the relatively more developed debtor nations. In addition, both the Treasury Department and Congress have looked to the World

Bank to play a major role in covering the short-term balance-of-payments problem of developing countries beset by debt crises. Thus the structural adjustment lending, begun in a tentative way during the 1970s, has more recently been seen as a source of immediate hard-currency liquidity akin to the loans of the International Monetary Fund.

It may seem ironic that the Reagan administration, which began with the impulse to cut back on U.S. financial obligations to the World Bank, ended up advancing a bolder role that indeed brought the Bank into competition with the IMF. It is unclear, however, that use of the World Bank as a channel of short-term financial resources means a restored commitment to multilateral development aid.[1] Moreover, the U.S. administration (and, for that matter, other member governments) seemed far less concerned with the long-term coherence of the World Bank's mission than with the convenience of using the Bank as an instrument to attack the debt crisis.

The Reagan administration was both critical of Bank programs that supported the public sector and supportive of efforts to strengthen the Bank's influence on recipients. For example, David Stockman, director of the Office of Management and Budget, testified in 1981 in favor of deep cuts in IDA appropriation (a position subsequently reversed by the Reagan administration that year). He complained that "IDA has supported state planning efforts to some countries and in recent years has placed a major emphasis on programs fostering income redistribution." Yet Stockman went on to argue, "IDA has not been vigorous in using the leverage inherent in its large lending program to press recipients to redirect their economies toward a market-orientation" (quoted in Sanford 1982: 75). Thus ironically the Reagan administration also advocated a stronger role for the World Bank in its insistence that the Bank apply leverage and conditionality more aggressively to pressure recipient governments to rely more on free markets. A more aggressive stance by the World Bank on behalf of the U.S. administration's vision of free-market development could decrease the Bank's autonomy from the U.S. government.

Members of Congress have exhibited two broad patterns of behavior in dealing with the World Bank: linking loans to noneconomic criteria and curbing excessive swings in Bank support by successive administrations. In the first instance, in the mid-1970s congressional oversight committees broadened their interest in the impact of the World Bank beyond the issues of the volume of multilateral lending (Sanford 1982: chap. 5). With the expansion of congressional staffing, the capacity to review the World Bank's impact on poverty, environment, appropriate technology, human rights, the role of women, and so on increased dramatically. With the growing realization that the World Bank had the capacity to impose conditionality or to withhold loans, congressional committees began to press for greater attention to these concerns on the part of the Bank and the recipient governments. For example, growing concern over human rights in the 1970s resulted in legislation that barred the U.S. executive director from voting in favor of loans to countries in "gross violation" of human rights, although implementation was left to the discretion of the executive branch. However, it is important to bear in mind that the power of Congress to enforce its will on the World Bank is not very great; the success of the human rights legislation and even the impact of U.S. abstentions or negative votes on loans are not terribly significant (U.S. Senate 1977: 17).

Congress has also tilted against both administrations that have been enthusiastic about multilateral aid and those that have been reluctant to support such aid. This pattern does not suggest legislative contrariness or obstructionism as much as the middle-of-the-road character of the U.S. Congress and its reactions to wider swings by the executive branch. Thus when Presidents Johnson and Nixon were expanding the volume of aid available to the World Bank, Congress appeared to be more hesitant; when the Reagan administration gave early signals of massive cutbacks, Congress seemed more supportive. As the effort to resolve the U.S. budget deficit grows, this dialectic may become even more pronounced.

The United States had a variety of means for exerting influence over the Bank in addition to its substantial contributions. Executive-legislative relations have relatively little impact on some of these, however.

Devices of U.S. Control over the World Bank

The devices available to the United States for controlling the World Bank can be ranked according to how formally they fit into the official or conventional oversight mechanism. The most obvious and conventional source of influence is through the U.S. executive director, who, with the executive directors chosen by other member countries, has formal authority over all Bank decisions made under the Articles of Agreement (Article V, Sections 1, 2). The U.S. executive director has more voting power than any other but less than a majority.

The U.S. executive director reports to the secretary of the Treasury. Administration policy is, however, not exclusively in the hands of the Treasury Department. In 1973 the Working Group on Multilateral Assistance was created to include representatives from the State Department, Commerce Department, International Development Cooperation Agency, Federal Reserve, and Export-Import Bank, as well as Treasury.

The group is chaired by Treasury officials. The range of agencies involved and the variety of their major concerns go far in explaining why U.S. pressure on the World Bank has gone beyond strictly financial issues.

Occasionally the U.S. executive director abstains from voting for a loan; even more rarely the U.S. director votes against a loan. Because these are the only "hard data" on U.S. pressure on the Bank, such actions have commanded more attention than they are worth. Most of these formal "no" votes and abstentions occur when the American executive director is prohibited by U.S. law from supporting aid to a country that has expro-priated U.S. property or is judged to be in violation of human rights standards (Sanford 1982: chaps. 3, 8). But these U.S. votes do not kill projects that have come that far in the World Bank's approval process; negative votes and abstentions merely signal the U.S. disavowal of support for that loan. When the U.S. government is adamantly opposed to World Bank lending to a given country and successfully blocks such lending, the result is more likely to be that loan proposals simply do not make it through the process to the point of Executive Board decision. Thus Robert Ayres (1983: 57) notes that even without effective U.S. vetoes,

> There is no doubt, however, that the U.S. government retains an extremely preeminent role in the operations of the Bank. The Bank's operations in Peru were minimal following the nationalization of the International Petroleum Company by the government of Juan Velasco in 1969. The Bank made no new loans to Chile under Salvador Allende from 1970 to 1973. Nor did it loan to Peronist Argentina from 1973 to 1976. McNamara agreed there would be no additional lending to unified Vietnam following the domestic political controversy in the United States attendant upon an IDA credit to that country in fiscal 1979.

The most important role of the U.S. executive director is to convey U.S. government priorities and concerns, in formal Executive Board delibera-tions and informally as well. Even when the executive director votes in favor of a loan, he may suggest changes to future loan proposals. Any signal of displeasure by the U.S. executive director has an almost palpable impact on the Bank leadership and staff, whether the signal is an explicit complaint or simply the executive director's request for information on a problem. This is also true, though to a lesser extent, when other executive directors send comparable signals, but the World Bank is particularly attuned to the mood of the U.S. administration. Criticisms or even neutral comments about the Bank from the U.S. president, the Treasury secretary, senators, and others reverberate throughout the institution. Yet clearly the basis for this healthy respect for U.S. power goes beyond the weight of the U.S. vote.

A second, nearly formal device is the privilege of the U.S. president to select the president of the World Bank based on a general understanding rather than the Articles of Agreement. The impact of this has been magnified by the fact that most presidents have been prominent former government and financial officials. The Americans chosen as World Bank presidents have never been totally subservient, however (Mason and Asher 1973: chaps. 3, 4). The desire of the United States to make the Bank a strong institution required the selection of strong presidents. Even A. W. Clausen (president from 1981 to 1986), who came from the private sector, had the standing to be a forceful and independent-minded leader, although an apparent lack of clear direction and adverse world economic conditions prevented him from making much of a mark. An American president is more likely to be aware of U.S. concerns and to think like a U.S. insider. By the same token, however, an American insider will know better how to manipulate the U.S. government. Hence the selection of Barber Conable, a former U.S. congressman, to succeed Clausen signaled a recognition of the importance of congressional support for Bank replenishments.

We might expect the large number of American personnel on the Bank's staff to be a vehicle for U.S. influence. Yet this is not only difficult to demonstrate, it is also increasingly moot. Whereas 64 percent of professional staff were U.S. citizens in 1950, by 1968 it was 31 percent, and 24 percent by 1987.[2] Perhaps more important—and yet almost totally unexamined—is the influence of American and other Western universities in training World Bank professionals of many nationalities. The commonality of economic ideology that similar training provides, however, does not leave the U.S. government with greater control in any direct sense.

As noted previously, probably the most important source of pressure that the United States has wielded is the threat to withhold IDA replenishment. Yet such withholding means far more than simply reducing how much the World Bank can lend. It threatens the jobs of some World Bank personnel, the morale of the Bank's leadership and staff, and the Bank's overall stature. The system of allocating personnel according to the magnitudes of lending in different sectors and regions is disrupted by unpredictable IDA cutoffs. IDA cutoffs also constitute the most graphic symbol of the Bank's dependence on member governments, particularly the United States.

The first IDA replenishment, finalized in 1964, went smoothly and in fact was instigated by the United States and other industrial countries before the Bank board, leadership, or staff had formulated a position on the issue. But the second replenishment was finalized only after interminable wrangling in the U.S. Congress. Every subsequent replenishment, coming three years apart, faced congressional opposition and sometimes the administration's desire to reduce the U.S. share (Sanford 1982: 60–69, 158–71, 204–14). By the 1980s President Reagan's reluctance to provide the full U.S. replenishment resulted in long delays and reductions in American contributions, corresponding cutbacks in the contributions by other governments, and ultimately billion-dollar reductions in already programmed loan commitments.

Many factors have entered into the U.S. government's hesitation to fund IDA, not the least of which has been the simple concern over U.S. budget deficits. But in expressing its qualms about contributing to the IDA, U.S. officials have not hesitated to point out what they considered World Bank *policy* flaws. The threat of denying IDA replenishment has thus become explicitly linked with specific objections about World Bank actions. This gives the U.S. government policy leverage inasmuch as no matter how much World Bank officials might deem these criticisms part of the theatrics of the U.S. budget process, they can hardly escape the conclusion that reversing these policies would increase (albeit to an unknown degree) the probability of U.S. funding.

It is ironic that just as the U.S. government traded control in order to establish the World Bank as a more significant actor in development assistance, the World Bank's autonomy has been somewhat compromised by its expansion of IDA aid to the poorest countries and the consequent dependence on periodic replenishments. Thus automony has had to be sought through other means.

The World Bank's Devices in Pursuit of Autonomy

From the beginning the leadership of the World Bank has frequently expressed its desire for autonomy from the United States. For example, its first president, John J. McCloy, insisted that executive directors desist from interfering with daily Bank operations. The leaders anticipated that autonomy from the United States might make it easier to get the Bank's recommendations accepted by other national governments. Even if the World Bank were a U.S. government agency, organizational theorists would predict that the Bank would seek some degree of autonomy (Ascher 1983). There is more prestige in being "international" civil servants. And Bank leadership and staff, many of whom were not Americans, had little desire to be subservient to the United States. It should not be surprising, then, that the Bank's leadership and staff have developed countermeasures to the U.S. government's own devices of control. The Bank's devices include perfectionism in its projects, a rigorous apoliticism, and a high volume of lending.

Perfectionism

One of the most striking developments of the McNamara era was the increased "perfectionism" of the World Bank's projects, project appraisal mechanisms, and reports. Although the Bank shifted from infrastructure and industrial projects toward rural development, even its rural development projects have been, at least on paper, ultrasophisticated—large in scale, elaborate in design, and highly technical.[3]

The review process has also become more hierarchical (according to widespread staff perceptions), with emphasis on highly polished reports and elaborate efforts by the Bank's management to enforce "quality control" of the reports. Management involvement thus increases with the Project Brief review, the Issues/Decision process, and reviews of the various report stages. One of the most commonly heard complaints within the World Bank—and one that is often blamed for low staff morale—is that this review process is too hierarchical, with higher levels of management applying a repetitive series of assessments on specific projects without adding to the quality of design (as distinct from its presentation). Reviewers basically focus on the soundness of what the report contains rather than on what is left out, and they take the project design more or less as given (as opposed to more preliminary management intervention). Thus they may be sacrificing the opportunity to provide the greater scope of their experience and concerns.

This review process clearly has its disadvantages. It does not engage top managers very much in the project identification stage, which is the best opportunity to involve senior staff with the clout to pressure governments to shape their overall project portfolios in conformity with the Bank's ideas about appropriate development strategies. Reviewers become increasingly removed from the reality addressed by the projects. Finally, the imperative to write polished reports in a timely fashion often discourages innovation.

The allure of this otherwise problematic emphasis on the polish of the reports is that it leaves the overseers of the Bank—the executive directors—without much of a toehold to criticize. Although individual executive directors may have first-hand knowledge of the conditions facing the project, collectively the executive directors are even further removed from the actual context and thus have to rely on the project report. The polish of the reports discourages exploration of potential problems, alternative approaches, or even the very structure of the Bank itself.

Thus the World Bank's projects, though sometimes controversial, have not been the marginal projects that otherwise would have been neglected. The large size of the projects, involving elaborate coordination and often several different governmental entities, makes them often prone to administrative problems. The very sophistication of the models on which they are based limits opportunities for criticism, especially from the executive directors, thus promoting the Bank's autonomy.

Similarly, the World Bank tendency to be monolithic in its policy *advice* limits critical review. Country economic reports do not explore the likely consequence of the range of policy options contemplated by the government; they tend to focus almost exclusively on the Bank's preferred strategy for that country. Although some emphasis on the virtues of adopting the Bank's advice is inevitable and unobjectionable, the advisory function is not well served by ignoring other options. But again, this uniformity, enforced upon considerable diversity of opinion among Bank personnel, leaves the executive directors and outside critics with less leverage to second-guess the Bank leadership and staff. With no other strategy elaborated, the executive directors are in a weak position to argue against the Bank's preferences.

Thus compared with the pre-McNamara years, World Bank executive directors are left with relatively little to do. The prominence of individuals appointed by governments to represent them on the Executive Board has declined because governments feel less compelled to appoint a high-powered figure given the diminished responsibilities. The decline in the opportunities for executive directors to have a substantial impact on project decisions is reinforced by the decline in the directors' status. Ironically the decline of Board control is a factor in inducing the United States to intervene through other channels.

Yet the Bank's perfectionism has also helped to maintain its prestige and standing within U.S. and other government circles enhancing its influence on national development programs. For example, the World Bank's focus on rural development since the early 1970s has legitimated the continuation of the U.S. Agency for International Development's (AID) own focus on rural development. The Bank's strategies and its economic assessments are likely to be regarded as more expert than those of any other institution. When it sours on a country—as, for example, when it cut lending to the Marcos regime in the Philippines in the early 1980s—the Bank sends a clear signal both to private sector corporations and banks and to governments. The result is likely to be cuts in private sector and bilateral aid as well. Thus perfectionism has enhanced the World Bank's autonomy from the United States and other governments, but it has also increased its influence on public and private decision makers. It has also reinforced the Bank's efforts to resist pressure to introduce political considerations—for example, human rights violations or expropriation of foreign assets into lending decisions.

Apoliticism

The World Bank has long taken the public position that it is totally nonpolitical. Any other stance might weaken the Bank's ability to challenge the legitimacy of these U.S. pressures. Bank officials have invoked the Articles of Agreement stipulating that neither political considerations nor the nature of the borrowing country's regime can be taken into account. This argument, by no means obvious given the many ways the Articles could be interpreted,[4] serves the dual purpose of avoiding attacks for actions that the Bank does take and fending off pressures to take other actions. The Bank's image of political neutrality in assessing the economic prospects of a country affects others' acceptance of its decision to increase or decrease support for a country as neutral, expert judgments rather than as decisions based on U.S. political or strategic interests.

This need to take an apolitical stance as a matter of principle, however, has the unfortunate effect of stifling concerns that arise in both project work and policy advice. The stance of political impartiality limits more aggressive efforts to promote poverty alleviation, or to pressure governments into improving their project portfolios or their macroeconomic policies. It is conceivable that the Bank would have introduced human rights criteria on its own had external demands not made the Bank adamantly resist such pressure.

This apolitical stance has also handicapped the Bank's analysis of borrowers' credit-worthiness and project feasibility. Naturally decisions on a country's lending ceilings or the feasibility of particular projects will reflect political assessments, but in this "nonpolitical" environment they are made "off the cuff" by Bank leadership that is often far removed from the situations in the countries.

Apoliticism extends further into the Bank's historic ambivalence toward using its leverage to shape borrowers' economic strategies. The Bank's annual reports are a useful barometer of changing trends. Early reports trumpeted the Bank's role in "helpful persuasion." By 1954–55 the Bank congratulated itself for having

> consistently urged attempts to settle defaulted external debt, to put economic and fiscal policies on a sound footing, and to direct public investment in such a way as to promote, rather than to obstruct or displace, the flow of private capital. While the Bank has not insisted as a condition of lending that final solutions be reached in matters of this kind, it has required appropriate evidence that progress in the desired direction is being made. (World Bank 1955: 35)

By the 1960s, however, these sections were absent from the annual reports, replaced by sections on technical assistance. This new emphasis also provided a means for the Bank to initiate and help develop projects, but it was, significantly, cast as a technical matter rather than one of pressuring governments to do certain types of projects. From 1973 on, the annual reports dropped altogether the discussion of the Bank's role in pressuring even for sound economic criteria. Again, this does not mean that the Bank desisted entirely from using its leverage to press for policy changes; pressure was less open than it could be. Many Bank staff members, leery of departing from the model of neutral international civil servants, were ambivalent about promoting what they believed were optimal development strategies.

The reluctance of World Bank leadership and staff to go beyond the technocratic mode may at first seem to contradict the activism of the Bank during McNamara's presidency. But in fact there was a growing distinction between the Bank presidency and the rest of the Bank (Ascher 1983: 422). Moreover, the Bank's activism flowed into some channels but not others.

McNamara himself was not neutral—he would commit the Bank to poverty alleviation and leave the Bank's staff to carry out the mandate. His decision to emphasize new project areas such as integrated rural development, rural education, and urban slum upgrading was a bold departure especially given that the state-of-the-art development expertise was shaky at best. The perfectionism required of Bank project design and approval, however, combined with the staff's reluctance to push governments into greater investments in these areas apart from the Bank's own projects, did not sustain McNamara's bold initiatives. And although McNamara made political decisions—that is, decisions based on political assessments—in setting the lending limits for borrowing governments, the facade of neutrality was maintained.

There were three costs to this approach. One was the cynicism directed against an institution led by an obviously political president and yet one trying to maintain a neutral image. A second cost was the increasing separation between the Bank staff and the unpredictable "Man on the 12th Floor." For a staff consisting of many individuals who had held positions of considerable responsibility before coming to the World Bank, working for a "thunderbolt-throwing" leader while being subjected to numerous constraints and an often oppressively picky review process was demeaning and ultimately sapped much of their enthusiasm and dedication.

The third and most tangible cost was a preoccupation with the Bank's own project portfolio. Apoliticism with respect to borrower countries' non-Bank projects and the Bank's activism with respect to its own ventures left the Bank's own projects as the dominant focus of attention. This preoccupation was also motivated directly by outside criticism that (unfairly) focused on the Bank's project portfolio and argued that the Bank ought not to focus so heavily on infrastructure or industry when so much poverty existed in rural areas.

By 1980 the Bank found itself increasingly thrust into the role of giving policy advice—in part an abdication of political neutrality. Structural adjustment lending has involved macroeconomic policy changes in exchange for lending to cover balance-of-payments deficits. There was much concern that structural adjustment lending was the province of the International Monetary Fund; certainly its adoption by the World Bank was not uncontroversial. Yet the Bank had resisted earlier pressures to do much the same thing, and it was only after strong support for the idea came from the Board of Governors and the executive directors in the 1979 annual meeting that the Bank proceeded with this activity. Even then senior Bank officials took pains to emphasize the precedents. E. Peter Wright, senior advisor in the Development Policy staff, provided figures showing that the World Bank had been involved in "program lending" since the very beginning. He then argued that "lending for structural adjustment is thus a neutral extension of program lending." To counter the problem that the Articles of Agreement require all lending to be for specific projects "except in special circumstances," Wright invoked the precedents of countries receiving program loans in 1976–79 for similar balance-of-payments reasons: import earnings decline because of falling commodity prices and increased export burdens resulting from higher-priced oil (Wright 1980: 22). In effect the Bank downplayed its structural adjustment lending initiative. Perhaps the low-key approach in the Bank reflected its desire to avoid the appearance of pressure from the United States considering that the Reagan administration had been such an ardent supporter of policy reform lending.

Sheer Magnitude of Lending

If the Bank is to stand up to U.S. pressures without engaging in new functions other than those actively pressed upon it, then the path of least resistance is simply to boost the volume of Bank lending. The expansion to $12 billion annually under McNamara had the ironic effect both of accommodating the widely recognized need to help in recycling petro-dollars and of making the World Bank a bigger actor and hence (in theory) a greater force to reckon with. But this expansion itself has serious liabilities. The need to move so much money has made it very difficult to entertain small prototype projects that could focus the Bank's potential for innovation and creativity. The Bank's bargaining power over governments' policies is actually reduced when borrowers realize that the Bank has to come up with sufficient loans. To carry this volume of loans, the Bank had to turn to state enterprises, a choice that was, right or wrong, inconsistent with its traditional private sector approach. Finally, processing nearly three hundred major new projects each year has meant that the Bank staff has expanded dramatically at the cost of the most close-knit intimacy of the World Bank of earlier days. A larger staff may contribute to the Bank's standing as an actor in its own right, but it also makes control a greater challenge for the Bank's leadership. Thus the Bank's efforts to exert autonomy have affected the character of the World Bank as an organization. They have contributed to some troublesome distortions in its operations, including the types of projects it has supported and its commitment to private enterprise.

U.S. pressures on the World Bank in turn reflect both the Bank's ambiguous links with the U.S. government and the ambivalence of that government over time toward multilateral aid. What factors help to explain this relationship of ambiguous separation, marked as it is by symbiosis, mutual influence, and struggle for control?

Explaining Ambiguous Separation: The World Bank and U.S. Objectives

The persistence of a commonality of outlook on a wide range of issues between the United States and the World Bank does not prove that the U.S. government dictates World Bank policy. Yet that commonality is rooted in the neoclassical training of economists both at the Bank and in the U.S. government. It is continually reinforced by the Bank's political and financial circumstances. Moreover, the role of the World Bank as disciplinarian of aid recipients puts it in the position of insisting on sober economic policy and efficient projects—the same position typically advocated by the United States and other donors. The commonality of interests and outlook is also reinforced by the fact that many economically advisable reforms are politically unpopular within the recipient countries, leaving their governments reluctant to carry them out. Thus it is common for "outsiders," whether bilateral aid donors such as the U.S. government or multilateral donors such as the World Bank, to join in denouncing the political "sacred cows" such as subsidies to key business enterprises, overvalued currency, and tax loopholes and to call for economic efficiency over political expediency. The opportunity to use aid as a source of leverage in pursuit of these reforms puts aid donors on the same side.

Although the commonality of outlook has been reinforced by the importance of the United States in the formation and operation of the World Bank, other factors must be taken into account. These range from the evolution of development economics to the orientations of developing countries on the issue of how to bargain with international financial institutions such as the World Bank and the International Monetary Fund.

An intriguing puzzle in the relationship between the United States and the World Bank is why, in spite of the commonality of outlooks and other devices of control, the U.S. government has apparently become less content to allow the World Bank to act autonomously. Why would U.S. government officials want to intervene directly in an institution whose credibility, morale, and effectiveness rest at least in part on its independence? The answer can be framed by considering domestic political factors.

Domestic Political Sources of Change in the U.S.–World Bank Relationship

Given the fact that the World Bank was structured by the United States and headed by an American, what political factors can explain the need of the United States to exert control? An obvious answer lies in the separation of power in the U.S. government. Enthusiasm for the World Bank in the executive branch has often been countered by congressional uneasiness. This has reflected the clash between the internationalism that was particularly strong in the Johnson and Nixon administrations (hence the early years of McNamara's presidency) and the parochialism of some members of Congress. Although the Treasury Department was often able to get support for the Bank from the relevant authorizing committees in the House and Senate whose members shared an internationalist perspective, it ran into trouble with appropriations committee members who questioned either the importance of foreign aid in general or the benefits to the United States of aid channeled through multilateral institutions. Multilateralism requires a commitment both to foreign aid and to the principle of conveying this aid through channels that do not give direct credit to the United States as its source. At any point in time some members of Congress will oppose one or more of these commitments.

Until the 1980s, however, Congress had always approved the authorization requests for all multilateral development banks (U.S. Congressional Budget Office 1980: 90). Beginning in 1980 Congress cut IDA replenishment. This shift reflected much more than merely congressional parochialism. As early as the Nixon administration, the executive branch has expressed qualms about the relative share of the U.S. contribution. By the time of the Carter administration, and far more so under the Reagan administration, second thoughts about the basic logic of multilateral aid became much more prominent. Robert L. Ayres (1983: 61) has observed that by 1980,

> Opposition to a larger role for the Bank . . . did not appear to be made on the grounds of requisite financial probity but politically. Much of the opposition to the further growth of the World Bank came from those who wished to reverse the growth of multilateralism.

Indeed, it has been difficult for the World Bank to respond to some of these actions of U.S. policymakers precisely because there is a component of simple disengagement. Ironically, the devices of control based on withholding resources gain additional credibility because some U.S. actors are interested in reduced involvement as an end rather than as merely a ploy to gain greater control.

Understanding the significance of the shift in U.S. thinking about multilateral aid requires further probing of the logic behind it and the shift in the Bank's own role as a multilateral aid-giving institution.

The Logic of Multilateral Aid

The logic of multilateral aid is rather subtle. On purely altruistic grounds, it makes sense to permit a country to receive aid unencumbered by the political interests of the donor or, at least, to reduce the politically motivated leverage of any given donor. But why should the donor forego the opportunity to pursue its own interests? There are three possible practical rationales. The first is to induce other donors to contribute in much the same way in order to increase the volume of aid devoted to approved purposes. As long as the multilateral institution does what a particular donor endorses, that donor can enjoy the magnification of its own desired aid impact. Collective aid also reduces the scope of other countries' pursuit of political interests via their aid.

The second rationale is to influence the policies of the aid recipient in the desired directions but without incurring the costs that often arise from direct and heavy-handed attempts at influence. Here, too, the utility of influence via multilateral aid obviously diminishes as the multilateral institution's initiatives depart from the preferences of the donor government.

The third rationale is to allow for a "division of labor" between bilateral and multilateral targets or objectives. If, for whatever reasons, the U.S. government finds it expedient not to focus bilateral aid on particular countries, and yet it is in the interest of the United States for that country to receive development assistance, then multilateral aid may be the alternative. If assistance for a particular objective such as population planning would arouse strong domestic opposition as a focus for bilateral aid, it may still be pursued through multilateral aid. In other words, rather than having multilateral aid replicate the targets and objectives of bilateral aid, it may be complementary to the orientation of bilateral aid.

The problem, of course, is that departures in objectives between donor and aid institution do occur. Any independence of mind on the part of the multilateral institution's officials will be expressed in their decisions. If there are several major donors, the officials cannot accommodate only one at the risk of jeopardizing the participation of the others. Thus the gains to donors of operating through multilateral channels come at the cost (or risk) of losing some degree of control over where their money goes. A key question, then, is what determines whether a major donor government can tolerate the departures? More specifically, why has the tolerance of the U.S. government eroded?

It must be understood that these rationales for multilateral aid were not very relevant when the World Bank was established. The executive directors, and particularly U.S. Director Emilio Collado, were prepared to run the World Bank as if they were the executive committee of a commercial bank. Once John J. McCloy insisted that he would not accept the Bank presidency unless the power of the executive directors—particularly the U.S. director—was sharply curtailed, however, the separateness of the World Bank decision-making emerged. Even then, however, the Bank's importance in the grand scheme of things was not terribly great, and the "grey insiders"—Presidents McCloy, Black, and Woods—rarely took actions or articulated positions that were perceived in the United States as running counter to U.S. preferences or interests. The World Bank, though formally multilateral and to a certain degree autonomous, did not exert its autonomy in ways that aroused second thoughts on the part of the American executive branch. The large proportion of U.S. funding and voting strength and the orientation of Bank presidents as "part of the U.S. team" allowed the United States to treat the Bank as if it were an appendage with a multilateral appearance.

Thus another way of viewing the issue is to date the birth of the World Bank as a genuinely multilateral institution from 1968, the appointment of Robert McNamara and the increased volume of loans. Whereas before the McNamara era the Bank's lending volume was relatively small, McNamara made it big enough for any departure from U.S. government preferences to matter. The decision to make the World Bank significantly more multilateral, in the sense of effectively ending the virtual guarantee that the Bank and the U.S. government would take the same position, was a fascinating decision. Although the true motivations behind President Johnson's choice of McNamara cannot be definitely proven, in the context of flagging U.S. confidence that uncoordinated bilateral efforts could adequately deal with the development problem, the Johnson administration must have understood that the selection of a strong World Bank leader meant relinquishing some control over the shaping of development aid.[5]

There was, of course, another option, at least in theory. If the bilateral aid of the various industrial nations was perceived as inconsistent and ineffective, the United States could have provided the inducements for other donors to coordinate more effectively. The United States even could have supplied far more aid on its own. Clearly this was not an option given the economic strain of the Vietnam War. Furthermore, the U.S. government did not see the payoff to American economic interests in the Third World as sufficiently rewarding to warrant underwriting development to a greater extent than before.

U.S. support for a larger and more truly multilateral role for the World Bank may also be explained by changes in the international economic and political system associated with the decline of U.S. hegemony (Keohane 1984). Hegemonic stability theory holds that once that dominant or "hegemonic" power no longer derives major benefits from the international economic system, because of either slipping political control or economic competition, it loses the incentive to bear the costs of maintaining the system. The Johnson administration, so painfully confronted with the impossibility of being the world's policeman, was willing to reduce control over this particular multilateral institution. Such an action obviously stopped short of abandoning responsibility for aid but relieved the United States of full responsibility for leading the aid effort. Contrary to the usual interpretation of the significance of the decline of hegemony—that it is more difficult to establish an international regime in the absence of one country willing to provide the inducements and negative sanctions to enforce compliance with it—the international aid regime in this case was allowed to expand through a more autonomous World Bank. Thus the United States encouraged an IGO to act more autonomously in order to reduce its own commitment to look after the economies of developing countries.

Conclusion

Multilateralism under the control of a hegemonic power is not much different from disguised bilateralism. As long as the hegemon can rely on the multilateral agency to send the same message, or to send a desired message that would have been awkward to send through bilateral channels, multilateralism is a sophisticated way of making the hegemon's message less offensive and of magnifying its impact by putting the force of the multilateral agency and other member states behind the message. Once multilateral institutions become autonomous in fact as well as in form, however, their appeal to the United States is bound to wane. The cost of using the institution as an instrument of policy rises, and there is declining incentive to induce other actors to make that institution conform to U.S. preferences. Thus by cutting some of the strings controlling the activities of the World Bank at a time when the U.S. commitment to carry the burden of financing Third World development was diminishing, the United States was also opening the way to cutting its own commitment to the Bank. Thereafter the executive branch became increasingly reluctant to support full IDA replenishment; U.S. executive directors more frequently vetoed or abstained from voting on loans to countries at odds with the United States; the U.S. share of World Bank capitalization and, hence, U.S. voting strength shrank.

Furthermore, tolerance for complementarity (as opposed to similarity) to development aid has diminished as doubts about the multilateral aid approach have risen. The agenda of the multilateral agency seems increasingly divergent from that of the bilateral agencies, particularly considering that public opinion holds the government responsible for the orientation of the multilateral agency. Complementarity can be achieved by allowing the multilateral agency to set its own agenda. Bringing it into line with bilateral aid objectives naturally requires greater exertion of control.

Some effort on the part of the United States to rethink the status of multilateral aid seems essential. Jonathan Sanford (1982) has pointed out that the U.S. government gets further in quiet consultation and negotiations over the IDA replenishments than in confrontational voting. More important, the efforts of the United States to reexert control over the Bank have fueled the Bank's struggle for autonomy and affected the basic character of the organization, contributing to distortions in its operations. Recognition of these problems may well lead to a reconsideration of the U.S. position. Certainly the increased interest of the Reagan administration in the possibilities of using the World Bank to promote structural adjustment and reduced statism suggest that in spite of the struggle over the Bank's autonomy, it is still important for furthering American policy objectives.

Notes

1. Note that the argument for low IDA commitments persists even as the argument for World Bank "shorter-term" lending mounts. See the testimony in U.S. House of Representatives (1986).

2. Figures were obtained from the IBRD Personnel Department. The first two figures are reported in Mason and Asher (1973: 880).

3. Attitudes of World Bank officials were explored in 60 formal interviews with Bank officials in 1980 and 1981, reviews of Bank memoranda, and numerous informal discussions with Bank officials and staff in the period 1981–87.

4. Article IV, Section 10 states, "The Bank and its officers shall not interfere with the political affairs of any member, nor shall they be influenced in their decisions by the political character of the member or members concerned." This can be interpreted simply as a prohibition against either making decisions discriminating against particular kinds of regimes or making decisions in order to support or undermine a given regime.

5. How much of what happened can be attributed simply to the idiosyncracies of World Bank history—for example, to the uniqueness of Robert McNamara as the man who not only expanded the Bank's operations but also carved out its increasingly assertive and even defiant position? McNamara's uniqueness certainly must be acknowledged, but it does not provide a separate explanation for the World Bank's autonomy. The commitment to multilateralism is to be found in choosing a man as prominent and headstrong as McNamara as the institution's president. The U.S. government's decision to put McNamara astride an institution with rapidly growing assets, responsibilities, and prominence reflects a deliberate effort to strengthen multilateralism. The subsequent decisions to endorse expansions of the World Bank's role were further reflections of this orientation.

References

Ascher, William (1983). "New Development Approaches and the Adaptability of International Agencies: The Case of the World Bank." *International Organization*, 37(3), 415–39.

Ayres, Robert L. (1983). *Banking on the Poor*. Cambridge: MIT Press.

Baldwin, David (1965). "The International Bank in Political Perspective." *World Politics*, 18(1), 68–81.

Hurni, Bettina (1980). *The Lending Policy of the World Bank in the 1970s: Analysis and Evaluation*. Boulder, CO: Westview Press.

Keohane, Robert O. (1984). *After Hegemony: Cooperation and Discord in Political Economy*. Princeton: Princeton University Press.

Mason, Edward, and Robert Asher (1973). *The World Bank since Bretton Woods*. Washington, DC: Brookings Institution.

Mathieson, John A. (1981). *Basic Needs and the New International Economic Order*. Washington, DC: Overseas Development Council.

McNamara, Robert S. (1981). *The McNamara Years at the World Bank: Major Policy Addresses of Robert S. McNamara 1968–81*. Baltimore: Johns Hopkins University Press.

Mukerjee, Dilip (1966a). "Cat and Mouse." *Far Eastern Economic Review* (June 30), 634–35.

——— (1966b). "Currency in Crisis." *Far Eastern Economic Review* (June 23), 602–5.

OECD (1964). *Flow of Financial Resources in Less-Developed Countries 1956–63*. Paris: Author.

——— (1973). *Flow of Financial Resources to Developing Countries*. Paris: Author.

——— (various years). *Development Cooperation*, various issues, new series. Paris: Author.

Patra, Saral (1966). "With Hope High." *Far Eastern Economic Review* (May 5), 238–9.

Sanford, Jonathan (1982). *U.S. Foreign Policy and Multilateral Development Banks*. Boulder, CO: Westview Press.

U.S. Congress (1973). *United States Foreign Assistance Act, 1973*. Washington, DC: U.S. Government Printing Office.

U.S. Congressional Budget Office (1980). *Assisting the Developing Countries: Foreign Aid and Trade Policies of the United States*. Washington, DC: U.S. Government Printing Office.

U.S. House of Representatives, Subcommittee on International Development Institutions and Finance Committee on Banking, Finance, and Urban Affairs (1986). *Third World Debt Legislation*. Washington, DC: U.S. Government Printing Office.

U.S. Senate, Staff Report to the Subcommittee on Foreign Assistance of the Committee on Foreign Relations (1977). *U.S. Policy and Multilateral Banks: Politicization and Effectiveness*. Washington, DC: U.S. Government Printing Office.

World Bank (1945). *Articles of Agreement of the International Bank for Reconstruction and Development*. Washington, DC.

—— (1947). *Annual Report, 1946–47*. Washington, DC.

—— (1955). *Tenth Annual Report*. Washington, DC.

—— (1976). *Development Finance Companies*. Washington, DC.

—— (1982). *IDA in Retrospect*. Washington, DC.

—— (1987). *The World Bank Annual Report, 1987*. Washington, DC.

Wright, E. Peter (1980). "World Bank Lending for Structural Adjustment." *Finance and Development*, 17(3), 20–23.

• CHAPTER SIX •

Multilateral Diplomacy and Trade Policy: The United States and the GATT

Margaret P. Karns

The huge American trade deficit, trade conflicts with key allies, and increased pressures for protectionist legislation punctuate the importance of trade issues for the United States in the late 1980s. To what extent can the international trade regime centered on the General Agreement on Tariffs and Trade (GATT) serve as an instrument for dealing with these problems? How has the United States used it in the past, and with what effect? How have U.S. trade policies and policymaking processes been influenced by the evolution of GATT?

The international trade regime is unique in that it represents "an institutional arrangement requiring little in the way of organization" (Young 1986: 108). Although the International Trade Organization (ITO) originally proposed in 1948 would have provided the regime with an explicit international organization for trade, the ITO was stillborn. In its absence the GATT has gradually acquired some of the characteristics of an IGO without the benefit of a charter (Curzon and Curzon 1974). The multilateral trade agreement provided a framework of rights and obligations to encourage the expansion of world trade and the resolution of trade disputes among the contracting parties. As John Jackson (1979a: 2) notes, "This uncertain beginning explains many of the deficits and difficulties of GATT. In fact, the GATT has served world trade and economic well-being far better than anyone had a right to expect."

GATT has been a primary instrument of U.S. international economic policy. As the dominant power of the post–World War II period, the United States played a key role in the negotiation of the GATT and has greatly influenced its subsequent development. The very importance of GATT in U.S. policy, however, as well as its rule-creating and supervisory nature, has enhanced its impact on American policy and policymaking processes. Nevertheless, the patterns of instrumentality and influence are not constant over the forty-year period of GATT's existence. Are the changes in those patterns attributable to a decline in American dominance? Alternatively, do they stem from the substantial changes in the nature and structure of world trade, from change in GATT itself, or from domestic political factors? This chapter focuses on the changes in GATT's role as an instrument and influencer of U.S. trade policy and on four sources of explanation.[1] With the eighth round of GATT negotiations under way and the growth in domestic political attention to trade, it is important to determine first whether the evolution of GATT's role makes it still a useful instrument of U.S. trade policy.

GATT as an Instrument of U.S. Policy

American interest in creating a liberal trading system after World War II has been amply reviewed elsewhere. The desire to open up markets previously closed to American goods, to institutionalize norms of multilateralism, nondiscrimination, limited state (that is, government) intervention, and reciprocity, and to promote economic growth through expanded trade are well known (Dam 1970; Finlayson and Zacher 1981; Gardner 1969). Less well known perhaps are the ways in which the United States limited the scope of these norms, the rules in which they became embodied, and the nature of GATT as a rudimentary IGO. However, we need to identify the ways in which the GATT has served as an instrument of American policy before examining the evolution of those patterns of usage.

First, GATT has served as an instrument for creation of the norms, rules, and negotiating processes for a liberal international trade regime compatible with American interests in opening other countries' markets to American goods and promoting the overall growth of world trade. Second, GATT has provided mechanisms for settling trade disputes. Third, GATT has been useful for countering U.S. domestic political pressures for the protection of specific industries and sectors from foreign competition. Fourth, it has been a useful instrument for other American foreign policy objectives, most notably promoting European integration and bringing Japan into the network of Western political and economic relations. To a limited extent the United States has used GATT to respond to demands from the developing countries for accommodation of their economic interests. In these respects GATT, like many other IGOs, has been a vehicle for collective legitimation.

GATT as an Instrument for Regime Creation

The GATT is based on the principles of trade liberalization, non-discrimination (or unconditional most-favored nation [MFN] treatment), and reciprocity, which have laid at the heart of U.S. trade policy since 1934. Central to GATT too are the norms of consultation to resolve disputes and negotiations to reduce trade barriers on a multilateral basis. The "major interests" norm has guided negotiations—that is, the principal negotiations involve the major suppliers and consumers of products (Finlayson and Zacher 1981: 584–93). The results are then "multilateralized."

Since the mid-1960s the norms of nondiscrimination and reciprocity have been modified to permit preferential treatment for developing nations' trade to spur their economic development. Although the application of these principles and norms has been compromised in a variety of other ways from the very beginning, they remain the cornerstones of GATT rules and the GATT-centered international trade regime.

Under GATT rules only tariffs are an acceptable device for protecting markets; import quotas are strictly proscribed. The rules authorize countries to use safeguards to deal with domestic and balance-of-payment problems and to impose special duties to "offset or prevent" dumping of goods at less than market value. A similar, though more ambiguous, provision covers the use of countervailing duties when domestic industries are injured by government subsidies of foreign goods. The negotiated schedules of cuts in tariff levels have been augmented since 1970 by a series of codes dealing with nontariff barriers and trade-related practices.

The United States has played a key role over the years in shaping these rules as well as in their interpretation and application. It has used these rules to serve American policy objectives, even when in doing so it compromised GATT's fundamental principles (or at least compromised the spirit underlying those principles) and, in some cases, sacrificed American economic interests (Krasner 1979). Congress' skepticism, if not opposition, toward GATT and the jealousy with which the legislative branch has guarded its prerogatives with respect to trade have contributed significantly to the ways in which the United States has circumscribed the scope of certain GATT rules.[2] In 1951, for example, Congress imposed import quotas on agricultural goods, forcing Eisenhower to request a waiver of GATT rules under Article XXV. This effectively removed agricultural goods from further negotiations and laid the basis for some of the most troublesome trade problems in the 1980s.

For the United States and many other countries, the periodic rounds of multilateral negotiations to reduce trade barriers are the heart of GATT. The United States has driven the timing of those rounds to a large extent because the executive branch needed congressional authorization to negotiate tariff reductions that could go into effect through presidential proclamation, obviating the need for subsequent legislative approval. The passage of authorizing legislation has determined the timing of initiation of most rounds; the impending expiration of negotiating authority has provided impetus for their conclusion. In addition, restrictions in U.S. trade law, such as the requirement of item-by-item negotiation, determined the form of GATT negotiations. The major interests norm accorded well with U.S. preferences and ensured that the United States as both a principal producer and consumer of many goods heavily influenced the outcome of negotiations. The size of the American market provided incentives to others to negotiate reductions in tariff levels.

U.S. objectives in the successive rounds of GATT negotiations were largely encompassed in authorizations to negotiate reductions of tariffs by 50 percent in 1947, 15 percent in 1955, 20 percent in 1958, 50 percent in 1962, and 60 percent for tariffs above 5 percent in 1974, eliminating entirely those below 5 percent. The reductions that occurred, particularly in U.S. tariffs on industrial products, are widely documented, along with the corresponding expansion of world trade. In addition, quotas on most nonagricultural products were eliminated, thus implementing a basic GATT rule.

Beginning with the Kennedy Round in 1962, U.S. officials regarded GATT negotiations as an important instrument for adapting the GATT system to the creation of the European Economic Community (EEC or, after 1972, EC) and to the needs of the growing number of developing countries. For example, the Trade Expansion Act of 1962 specifically provided authority to negotiate a "trade partnership with the European Common Market" (Preeg 1970: 45) and authorized across-the-board tariff cuts for the first time. In seeking the latter authority, administration officials had noted, "The Common Market countries cannot conduct their negotiations on any basis other than across-the-board cuts" (Preeg 1970: 46). The Kennedy Round produced tariff reductions covering eight times as much trade as the preceding Dillon Round (1960–61) but no general accommodation for the EEC's Common Agricultural Policy (CAP).

As Destler and Graham (1980: 54) have noted, however, "the American system for negotiating tariff reductions became a victim of its own success. Progressively lowered, tariffs affected trade less than 'non-tariff measures.' " The proliferation of nontariff barriers to trade in the late 1960s and 1970s (in part to counter reductions in tariffs and in part because of the expanding role of governments in domestic economies) along with the issues unresolved by the Kennedy Round (most notably agriculture) led the United States to take the lead in preparations for a successor round. Domestic political difficulties delayed passage of the necessary authorizing legislation in the United States, and negotiations on nontariff measures required preliminary study of issues not previously addressed on a multilateral basis. Yet this seventh round of trade talks substantially broadened the scope of the international trade regime even as extra-GATT arrangements narrowed the percentage of goods traded under GATT rules.

In early 1979 the Tokyo Round of Multilateral Trade Negotiations (MTN) concluded with agreement on a set of codes dealing with subsidies, government procurement, customs valuation, technical barriers and standards, and import licensing procedures along with modest further tariff reductions. Arguably, the United States advanced its interests in creating the codes on nontariff measures, but the negotiations clearly demonstrated both the difficulty of the underlying issues and American willingness to compromise the nondiscrimination norm to gain agreement on the codes. Because they were drafted as separate agreements—that is, they are not incorporated into the GATT itself—benefits are open only to signatories. For example, the U.S. legislation implementing the Government Procurement Code states that the United States will offer MFN treatment for an industrialized country only if that country has signed the code and provided "reciprocal competitive government procurement opportunities to United States products" (Krasner 1979: 515). The codes also established new dispute settlement procedures in what one analyst referred to as a "Balkanization of those processes" (Jackson 1979a).

More than with any previous GATT round, the success of the MTN negotiations in accomplishing American objectives of rule creation and trade liberalization depended on the extent to which the codes were directly applied in the laws and administrative practices of their signatories. Such actions would take time; the effects on trade would not be immediately apparent. The Government Procurement Code was regarded as offering the greatest opportunities for trade liberalization, whereas the subsidies code was considered the least effective and, hence, inadequate from an American perspective given the United States' tendency to use government subsidies less than other developed countries.[3] The United States was unable to secure agreement at the last minute on a safeguards code and failed to make much headway in bringing agriculture under the regime, both primary objectives.

In a larger sense, as Winham (1986: 17) notes, the codes "tended to change GATT rules from statements of broad principle to more detailed regulations relating to domestic and international procedures . . . [and] served as an attempt to increase the orderliness, and possibly the fairness, of international trading arrangements, but not necessarily to reduce protectionism." The codes represented significant efforts to increase the transparency of national rules and procedures, information sharing and exchange, and the adoption of uniform systems of customs valuation. They were important steps, therefore, for addressing the proliferation of nontariff barriers to trade, for adapting GATT to the changing nature of trade and the growing role of governments in domestic economies, and for reducing the "scope of arbitrary government constraints on international trade" (Winham 1986: 362). Given the increasing fragmentation of the international trading regime arising from special arrangements for developing countries and sectoral agreements for steel, textiles, and autos that proliferated in the 1970s, Winham (1986: 366) also notes that "an important goal of the Tokyo Round was to maintain control over the international trading system and to build a cooperative structure that would contain competitive actions by individual nations. The task was the management of a relationship, even more than the distribution of specific benefits." The goal was only partially met.

In 1982 increasing competition for markets among the developed countries and from the newly industrializing countries (NICs), as well as disputes fueled by the holes and ambiguities in the MTN codes, led to the first ministerial-level meetings of GATT parties since the early 1970s. Although the initiative for the 1982 meetings came from the European Community, the United States alone submitted items for the agenda, including old issues such as agriculture, safeguards, dispute settlement procedures, and developing state relations, as well as three new ones: trade in services, investment, and high technology, all areas of American strength. The United States was particularly interested in establishing a work program for a code for services (Interview 1983). Studies and discussion of various service sectors were already under way among the developed countries in the OECD.

The ministerial meetings coincided with the worst recession of the postwar period, unprecedented unemployment rates, and rapidly rising debt service costs for developing countries. It was not surprising, then, that U.S. Ambassador William Brock gave the final results a tentative grade of C, commenting, "Perhaps our most important achievement was in keeping the GATT system together and moving in a positive direction" (U.S. House of Representatives 1983: 7–8).

Indeed, the 1982 Ministerial did begin the process leading to a new round of GATT negotiations, the eighth since 1947. U.S. trade officials invested substantial energy in shaping the agenda for the Uruguay Round launched at Punte del Este, Uruguay, in September 1986 to ensure the inclusion of trade in services, agriculture, investment, high technology, and intellectual property. Many GATT members—particularly the developing countries—have opposed negotiation of rules on trade in services, however, fearing competition for their own infant service industries. Negotiations are complicated also by the fact that each sector (such as shipping, tourism, telecommunications) has its own characteristics, and in many countries certain service industries (such as telecommunications) are national monopolies. Agreement to establish a Group for Negotiations on Services came over strong opposition from the developing countries led by Brazil and India and only after the United States threatened to pull out of the Special Session if trade in services was not included. There is no commitment, however, to incorporate any rules on services into the overall GATT framework.

In 1967 more than 80 percent of world trade was estimated to be covered by GATT agreements (Jackson 1967: 250). That percentage has shrunk over the past twenty years, though by how much is a matter of some dispute. Some estimate that it covers about 50 percent of world trade (Interview 1983). Clearly, a fuller picture of the international trade regime and of U.S. trade policy would include the extra-GATT sectoral arrangements that effectively restrict trade: the Multifibre Arrangement (MFA) covering textiles and clothing; restraint agreements covering autos, steel, and semiconductors. U.S. free trade arrangements with Israel, the Caribbean countries, and Canada compromise the U.S. commitment to the principle of multilateralism. GATT is not, therefore, the only means for shaping the international trade regime. In fact, under the Reagan administration the United States openly accepted bilateral, free trade, and sectoral arrangements as legitimate complements to multilateral arrangements.

Because the United States was never receptive to having the United Nations Conference on Trade and Development (UNCTAD) or some other forum acceptable to the developing countries supplant GATT, however, the latter provides the only *institutionalized multilateral process* for negotiating rules for the regime *as a whole*. The rounds of trade negotiations provide political impetus by committing the governments of major countries to the success of the round; they also offer multiple possibilities for trade-offs. Thus it is easier in the United States, at least, to build domestic support for the results of such negotiations than for specific sectoral deals. The benefits in many different areas offset the costs in a few specific areas (U.S. Congress, Joint Economic Committee 1984: 26–28). Yet domestic politics in the United States now require a greater emphasis on "fair" trade along with free trade.

The energy invested by U.S. trade officials in shaping the agendas for the 1982 GATT Ministerial and the Uruguay Round testifies to the continuing importance attached to GATT as an instrument for negotiating liberalization and expanding the scope and strength of the regime. Indeed, the United States has demonstrated increasing interest since the 1960s in using GATT to create more specific rules for a broader array of trade barriers. The American interest in strengthening GATT's dispute settlement mechanisms, to which we now turn, represents a further way in which GATT continues to be regarded as an important instrument of American trade policy.

Dispute Settlement Procedures as an Instrument of U.S. Policy

The American record in using GATT's dispute settlement and avoidance mechanisms reflects in part the importance attached to the role of law in the U.S. domestic economy and the tendency of many lawyers, government officials, and representatives of private businesses "to view the GATT as a judicial system . . . an embodiment not only of the rule of law, but of the enforcement of law, on the international level" (Malmgren 1983: 192).[4] The United States has regarded the dispute settlement procedures as valuable tools for securing clearer interpretations of rules, for seeking change in other nations' trade practices, and hence for promoting both specific American interests and the broad goal of an open, nondiscriminatory international trading system. Table 6.1 illustrates the pattern of U.S. use of GATT dispute settlement machinery, especially the sharp increase in the most recent period, 1981–86.

GATT provides means both for "dispute avoidance" through the use of various escape clauses and for dispute settlement procedures. The articles distinguish between matters that are subject to multilateral surveillance (the balance-of-payments escape clause, provisions dealing with customs

TABLE 6.1
The United States and GATT Disputes

Period	Total Disputes Initiated	Disputes Initiated by the U.S.	Percentage	Disputes Initiated against the U.S.	Percentage
1948–52	25	7	8.0	6	4.0
1953–60	33	6	18.1	5	15.1
1961–68	33	11	33.3	2	6.0
1969–74	21	13	61.9	1	4.7
1975–76	10	5	50.0	1	10.0
1977–80	19	6	31.5	4	21.0
1981–86	55	16	29.0	7	30.9

Note: Data from which this table has been compiled were gathered in an inventory on GATT disputes directed by John H. Jackson at the University of Michigan. I am grateful to Professor Jackson for sharing the data.

unions and free trade areas, and general waivers) and those for which parties are required first to seek bilateral settlement (emergency or safeguard action on imports of particular products, nullification or impairment of specific benefits accruing from GATT membership arising from the action or inaction of a trade partner, and modifications of tariff rates). Article XIX dealing with safeguards for domestic producers injured by import "was, in fact, included in the General Agreement in 1947 in order to accommodate U.S. legislation which it mirrored down to its very phrasing. In view of the dominant position occupied by the United States at that time," the Curzons argue, "it is perfectly understandable that an escape clause specifically tailored to fit U.S. legislation should have no provision for multilateral control." This provision has been exercised rather frequently, they note, particularly by the United States, "to the detriment of the smaller and weaker members and of the trade system itself" (Curzon and Curzon 1976: 205).

In addition to using the Article XIX provisions on safeguards, the United States has availed itself of the Article XXV provisions for general waiver, first in the case of agricultural quotas cited earlier, again in 1968 to cover the U.S.-Canadian Automotive Products Agreement providing for sectoral free trade, and most recently for the Caribbean Basin Initiative.

Articles XXII and XXIII of the General Agreement provide mechanisms for the application and interpretation of previously agreed norms and rules through bilateral or multilateral consultations, or the establishment of a panel to investigate the dispute (Article XXIII). Jackson (1979a: 15) has noted that historically, "many governments have hesitated or refused to invoke the procedures of Article XXIII . . . partly from a lack of faith in the fairness of the process." In the fifty-two cases that led to submission of a panel report, only once was a party authorized to retaliate, and it did not take action.[5]

Despite the weaknesses of the GATT dispute mechanisms, they have been useful to the United States in getting other countries to change their policies, as well as to lay the legal basis for retaliation through application of a countervailing duty. Particularly since the conclusion of the Tokyo Round, the United States has tried to use the procedures to settle disputes over interpretations of the codes and, in some cases, thereby to legislate by interpretation (Hudec 1980; Interviews 1984, 1985).

One of the most acrimonious disputes in which the United States has been involved was the "Chicken War" in the early 1960s when the European Community's Common Agricultural Policy (CAP) was taking shape. The dispute arose after the EC announced a feed grain compensatory levy that would effectively treble the tariff rate over that negotiated under the Dillon Round. The United States threatened to withdraw concessions equivalent to what it considered to be the worth of annual trade in poultry in 1963, a figure the EC disputed (Walker 1964). The dispute over valuation was submitted to a GATT panel, but a compromise was reached through bilateral consultations. The Curzons (1976: 213) note, "The GATT conciliation procedures appear to have made a positive contribution to the preservation of peaceful trade relations between the United States and the EEC at that particular point in time . . . [although] the issue of compensation for the CAP was in fact never settled."

The Chicken War case illustrates the difficulty of using GATT's dispute settlement procedures to settle larger issues of rule interpretation not previously resolved in negotiations. Other GATT parties are seldom willing to accept this approach that has increasingly marked the complaints the United States has brought before GATT panels in the 1970s and 1980s. In the mid-1970s, for example, faced with an EC complaint about a set of U.S. tax provisions for Domestic International Sales Corporations (DISC), the United States filed complaints simultaneously against the Netherlands, Belgium, and France for income tax practices that exempted export sales. It hoped that the disagreement over DISC could be discussed as part of a general examination of indirect tax practices. The U.S. DISC legislation, designed to retaliate against European indirect taxes, was passed in 1971 and allowed a U.S. company to create a U.S. subsidiary. If 95 percent of the latter's receipts consisted of exports, it could defer income tax on 25 percent of profits. The EC regarded this as unfair subsidization of exports. The United States was unsuccessful in its effort to create a single panel for all four disputes and thereby to focus attention on the larger issues of the trade impact of various tax practices (Interviews 1983, 1984; Jackson 1978). In 1982 the GATT Council finally adopted the panel reports, including the negative finding on the DISC case. The United States did not succeed in gaining any settlement of the larger issue of tax practices.

Trade frictions stemming from increased competition for markets, high inflation and interest rates, increased oil prices, and slowing economic growth led to a mushrooming of complaints filed with GATT in 1981 and 1982. The ambiguity of many provisions in the codes negotiated in the Tokyo Round was also a factor. In addition, the Reagan administration adopted an activist approach to solving outstanding trade disputes and pressing for clarification of the new MTN codes. Often the cases involved very small amounts of trade and seemingly insignificant products such as canned fruits, walnuts, and pasta; the complaints related to small technicalities in the rules; the issues were the larger principles underlying ambiguous GATT rules regarding subsidies (pasta) and market shares (wheat flour). A number involved EC practices that had been accepted for twenty years (pasta and citrus fruit). At best, the United States has succeeded in securing marginal openings in European markets.

In another case involving a question of principle, however, the United States secured a major change in Canadian legislation on foreign investment. In early 1982 the United States complained that the newly enacted Canadian Foreign Investment Act (FIRA) violated the national treatment provisions of Article II and threatened to reduce opportunities for foreign investment in Canada—a matter of considerable concern to the United States. The case presaged efforts to stimulate discussion of the need for rules on investment at the November 1982 Ministerial meetings. Following the adoption in February 1984 of the GATT panel report concluding that Canadian practice was inconsistent with Article III:4, Canada brought the FIRA into conformity with GATT. The dispute settlement process was useful in securing change in the legislation of a major U.S. trade partner.

Thus over the years the United States has consistently attempted to use GATT dispute settlement machinery to promote its short- and long-term trade interests. The volume of complaints that the Reagan administration referred to GATT between 1981 and 1984 led critics to charge that many of the cases were poorly prepared and hence not likely to result in clear-cut rulings. One former USTR official (Interview 1983) suggested, "it doesn't make sense to push on things that we left ambiguous because agreement couldn't be reached. Such usage," he noted, "undermines the confidence of the public and Congress in the effectiveness of the GATT." The number of complaints would actually be higher, however, if countries—including the United States—did not tolerate the proliferation of extra-GATT arrangements. Furthermore, complaints from U.S. domestic industries injured by imports or loss of overseas markets from unfair trade practices increasingly have fueled pressures for legislative or administrative protective measures. Although historically U.S. proponents of liberalizing trade have found GATT useful for managing such domestic protectionist pressures, the pattern appears to be changing.

GATT and the Management of Protectionist Pressures

GATT negotiations and dispute settlement procedures, as well as existing rules, have provided U.S. officials with justification for resisting pressure in the Congress and from domestic interest groups to change U.S. trade policy. As one former USTR official commented (Interview 1983), they are "a control device on our own protectionist pressures." GATT's "braking power" derives from the likelihood of retaliation and the opportunities for opening markets. Whether retaliation would significantly harm the United States in material terms has been less important than the fear that once initiated, a cycle of countermoves would be difficult to stop, might unravel the whole framework of international trade, and undo the benefits of liberalization. Thus as Destler (1986: 9–36) has masterfully described, GATT and the trade negotiation process, combined with the necessity for delegating authority to the executive branch, have been part of a system of antiprotectionist counterweights to the natural proclivity of Congress to raise trade barriers in response to pressures (these counter-weights channel most of the pressures away from Congress to the executive branch and GATT).

In early 1979 as the MTN negotiations neared completion, the U.S. Treasury Department's authority to waive countervailing duties on subsidized goods expired. The volume and scope of imports affected was relatively small, but the EC threatened to jeopardize the entire round if the waiver was not extended (Lenway 1986: 109). The GATT negotiations in this case added weight to administration efforts to get Congress to renew the waiver authority (U.S. Senate 1979b). The price, however, was a deal with the textile lobby, which precluded any agreement to lower textile tariffs (Destler and Graham 1980: 62–63).

Another example arose in 1984 with the proposed extension of the manufacturing clause of U.S. copyright law that prohibited imports except from Canada of more than two thousand copies of copyrighted literary and nondramatic works by American authors. The clause, which dated to the nineteenth century, had been grandfathered under the GATT. Legislation passed in 1976 provided for its expiration in 1982. When Congress extended the clause to 1986, the EC filed a complaint. The GATT ruling found that the 1976 legislation had fundamentally altered the clause by adding the termination date, and hence the 1982 extension was ruled illegal. Administration officials argued before Congress that if the United States continued to ignore the panel finding, other countries would not see why they should implement adverse rulings. In addition, failure to implement the ruling would have a harsh effect on administration efforts to gain consideration of intellectual property protection. As Secretary of Commerce Malcolm Baldridge said, "We just can't afford to ignore that the 1982 extension was GATT-illegal. . . . No nation can announce it is going to bring its laws into compliance with GATT requirements, encourage other nations to accept its word, which is what we did in the 1979 multilateral trade negotiations, and then just simply reverse our course" (U.S. House of Representatives 1986: 6). The warnings worked. Congress allowed the manufacturing clause to expire in 1986.

Confidence in the GATT-based trade regime within the United States has eroded, however. A high-level official in the USTR delegation in Geneva commented in 1985 that U.S. trade officials "can't use the old argument of GATT to resist pressures in Congress because the reality appears to be that no one else is doing so" (Interview 1985). Congressional proposals for new trade legislation, which would curb imports and punish partners who maintain high trade surpluses with the United States, proliferated even while the ponderous machinery for the Uruguay Round was being set into motion. In a break with past patterns, Destler (1987: 16) notes, Congress seemed "determined to *legislate* on trade," with little consideration of the effect of legislation on the Uruguay Round. The international consequence may be the erosion of U.S. leadership, for the latter has depended on the willingness and ability of the United States to reduce its own barriers to imports even as it pressed others to do likewise. In the early years of GATT the United States capitalized on that leadership position to use the trade regime for foreign policy objectives other than those specifically linked to trade.

Legitimating General Foreign Policy Objectives

IGOs have often been important tools for collective legitimization of U.S. policies. GATT has legitimated the value of an open trading system; it has provided a forum for generating peer pressure and opposing policies that would close markets. The United States found GATT useful, too, for securing support of broad American foreign policy objectives in the 1950s and 1960s. Since the mid-1960s trade concerns have predominated. The U.S. use of GATT in the 1940s and 1950s to promote economic recovery, European integration, and democracy and a Western orientation in Japan paralleled use of other IGOs for collective legitimation of a range of American policies. In 1955, for example, the United States pressed for the admission of Japan to the GATT. Although successful on the membership question, it was able to persuade only a few other members to lower their barriers to Japanese goods, notably Canada, Denmark, Finland, Italy, Norway, and Sweden. Fourteen members invoked Article 35 allowing refusal of MFN to new members. The objective was sufficiently important that the United States "was willing to give twice as much by way of scheduled concessions as she received" (Lipson 1982: 440) and lowered its tariffs on Japanese textiles even though the barriers of others diverted Japanese exports to the United States.[6]

Similarly, under U.S. pressure both the European Coal and Steel Community and the Common Market went into effect without full scrutiny of their conformity to GATT rules on regional customs unions and free trade areas. The United States also tried to use GATT to encourage the Common Market to act favorably on the British application for membership in the early 1960s. The 1962 Trade Expansion Act provided authority to negotiate the elimination of tariffs on products in which the United States and the Common Market supplied 80 percent of world trade. Only two relatively insignificant items would qualify unless Britain were part of the market (Preeg 1970: 52). Although the United States was unsuccessful, the Kennedy Round, as noted earlier, was regarded as an important vehicle for ensuring continuation of Atlantic political and economic partnership.

In the mid-1960s the large number of newly independent countries brought considerable pressure for changes in the international economic system—including GATT—to accommodate their needs for development. The United States in particular among the developed countries resisted change in the international trade regime. The United States did agree to a generalized system of preferences for developing countries, however, reversing its own trade policy in the process (Meltzer 1976). This very limited and reluctant use of GATT to legitimate the concerns and needs of developing countries represents the last such use by the United States for general foreign policy objectives. The reasons for this shift in instrumentality did not stem from loss of U.S. influence to coalitions of new members or politicization, as happened in so many other IGOs. Indeed, the LDCs' difficulty in exercising influence within GATT had much to do with the formation of UNCTAD and efforts to use that organization to legitimate their own objectives. Rather, the U.S. approach to GATT since the mid-1960s had emphasized American economic and specifically trade interests.

Thus we see subtle shifts in the patterns of GATT's value as an instrument of U.S. policies. The United States has rather consistently found GATT useful for creating the norms and rules of a liberal international trade regime, although like other members, it has increasingly resorted to extra-GATT arrangements to protect key domestic industries injured by imports. GATT is therefore *less central* to the regime than it once was. The United States has provided leadership for the expansion in scope of GATT rules to encompass codes on nontariff barriers and potentially in the future, trade in agriculture, high technology, services, and investment. The United States has also consistently used GATT procedures for dispute settlement but finds itself an increasing target of complaints. GATT's utility for containing domestic protectionist pressures has decreased, as has its value for legitimation of other foreign policy objectives.

Although the patterns of usage have changed over time, GATT clearly remains an important instrument of policy. As Lipson (1982: 446) has suggested, "the connection between regimes and nation-states . . . is mutually conditioning. An ongoing regime forms a significant context for the framing of national policies. Multilateral arrangements and institutions may constrain the policy process, provide new opportunities and sources of support for some policy makers and ultimately influence the choice of national policies." Our discussion thus far of the United States and GATT has already suggested a good deal of reciprocal influence. It is to this reciprocity that we now turn.

GATT Influence on the United States

In analyzing GATT's influence on the United States, we are concerned with (1) the impact of GATT norms and rules on trade-related legislation and regulation in the United States, (2) adaptations in U.S. policymaking and implementation processes arising from participation in GATT, (3) the effects of *other* countries' use of GATT's dispute settlement machinery to bring complaints against the United States, and (4) the GATT's influence on domestic groups. Although extra-GATT arrangements have weakened GATT's influence in a number of key sectors, the direct and indirect effect of GATT on trade barriers, U.S. policymaking processes, and trade-related regulations has broadened over time.

Legislative and Regulatory Effects of the GATT

The nature of GATT as a set of multilateral agreements for the regulation of international trade creates considerable potential for influence on national trade policies and legislation. Although there were early questions about the constitutionality of some aspects of U.S. participation in GATT, over time the periodic renewals of the Reciprocal Trade Agreements Act, recognition by federal and state courts of GATT's validity, presidential proclamations implementing GATT agreements on tariff rates, the Trade Expansion Act in 1962, the Trade Act of 1974, and certainly the Multilateral Trade Agreements Act of 1979 have given domestic legal effect to GATT (Jackson 1967).

The tariff cuts of the first six rounds of GATT negotiations were put into effect through presidential proclamations. The situation was quite different, however, once the focus of GATT negotiations shifted to the proliferating nontariff barriers (NTBs). Indeed, U.S. negotiators in the Kennedy Round had no authority to negotiate nontariff agreements, and Congress rejected the Antidumping Code and American Selling Price (ASP) agreements when they were submitted for approval. The very nature of NTBs means that rules may require substantial changes in domestic law and administrative and regulatory practices. For the United States this has also necessitated changes in the nature of the authorization to conduct negotiations in the first place and in the process by which the United States formulates its negotiating position.

Rejection of two NTB agreements in 1968 dramatized the need to consult members of Congress during negotiations. With tariff negotiations Congress could specify the maximum acceptable cut; with nontariff negotiations the shape and potential impact of an agreement could not be predicted in advance. Yet how could the United States provide adequate assurance to negotiating partners that the results would be accepted by Congress? The 1974 Trade Act specified that if members of Congress were included in the Tokyo Round negotiations, Congress would consider the agreements under expedited procedures. As a result, although the MTN codes had a potentially far-reaching effect on a variety of practices, Congress enacted them in record time in 1979 and 1980, requiring revision only of a section of the Government procurement code that would have precluded federal agencies from reserving certain competitive bidding purchases to businesses owned by blacks and other minorities (Destler and Graham 1980: 65–66).

Because the Tokyo Round codes "tended to change GATT rules from statements of broad principle to more detailed regulations relating to domestic and international procedures" (Winham 1986: 361), they required both the Trade Agreements Act of 1979 and the promulgation of new regulations and administrative practices to give them legal effect. Some of the codes required more changes than others. In many cases the agreements conformed to existing U.S. law and practice. Detailed statements of the requisite changes were mandated by Section 102 of the 1974 Trade Act and issued in mid-1979 along with studies of the impact of MTN on the U.S. economy (U.S. Senate 1979c). For example, the Subsidies and Countervailing Duties Code required the addition of a material injury test, something U.S. trade partners had sought for a long time. The Customs Valuation Code achieved another long-sought change: elimination of the ASP valuation in favor of a generalized system based on transaction value. The Government Procurement Code primarily required adaptations in administrative practice and the Buy America Act of 1954, whereas the Code of Standards and Technical Barriers required none at all (U.S. House of Representatives 1979). As the report of the Advisory Committee on Trade Negotiations (ACTN 1979: 3) noted, "These codes and agreements . . . constitute a kind of legislation—at the international level—whose results will only be seen through its application and interpretation over time." Thus in attempting to minimize the trade effects of the wide variety of domestic regulations and practices that constitute nontariff barriers, GATT rules have reached more deeply into both federal and (occasionally) state law.

GATT's potential legislative and regulatory effects do not stem solely from its rule-creating role. Because GATT dispute settlement machinery can serve as a vehicle for other countries to bring complaints against the United States, adverse panel findings can require changes in national practices. The number of disputes has risen sharply in recent years. Table 6.1 illustrates the rise in complaints against the United States beginning in the early 1960s.

The DISC case was one of the most notable findings against the United States. When the reports were submitted to the GATT Council in November 1976, the United States indicated its willingness to see all four adopted, though it was uncertain whether the Congress could be persuaded to eliminate or revise the DISC legislation (Jackson 1978: 777). After the findings were adopted in 1981, U.S. representatives refused to agree, however, to an EC-sponsored draft decision at the May 1982 GATT Council meeting calling for the United States to "take appropriate action without delay to bring the DISC legislation into conformity with the provisions of GATT" (GATT 1982: 65). Although the United States subsequently informed the council in October 1982 that the administration would seek the necessary changes in the tax law to bring the DISC into conformity, such a change has yet to be made. Ironically, those familiar with the case argue that some of the legislative proposals may also create GATT problems or be more beneficial to U.S. companies than the existing DISC legislation.

The influence of GATT in spurring legislative changes can be closely linked in cases such as DISC to the utility of GATT as an instrument for managing protectionist pressures. Enjoyment of the benefits of reciprocity, expanded markets, economic growth, and prosperity requires willingness to impose costs, to eliminate practices that create unfair advantages for domestic producers. Thus conclusion of the Tokyo Round required extension of the countervailing duty waiver authority; the adverse panel ruling on the manufacturing clause of the copyright law necessitated elimination of the clause if the United States wanted to press others for action on intellectual property issues. Yet GATT's influence is not limited to trade-related legislation and regulations; it has increasingly extended to policymaking and implementation processes.

GATT Influences on Policymaking and Implementation Processes

Until the 1960s the United States had little in the way of policymaking machinery specifically for trade, reflecting the relatively low importance of trade for the American economy. The subsequent changes have, therefore, been quite dramatic (Cohen 1981; Cohen and Meltzer 1982: chaps. 1, 3–5; Destler 1980: chaps. 9–12; 1986).

U.S. participation in GATT and the growing importance and complexity of trade issues have prompted several changes in decision-making and implementation processes for trade: creation and enhancement of the Office of the Trade Representative, regularization of congressional and private sector involvement in trade negotiations, and adaptations in administrative practices. Congress provided for a Special Representative for Trade Negotiations under the Trade Expansion Act of 1962. Cohen (1981: 55) notes, "misgivings on Capitol Hill and in the private sector about the State Department's ability to drive a hard bargain and bring home the most advantageous trade agreement in the then impending Kennedy Round" inspired Congress to create the new position. In addition to designating the representative as the "chief representative" of the United States in all trade negotiations, Congress specified that he chair the trade policy coordinating committees to be established by the president in an effort to provide coherence in trade policy. "In practice it has also been the chief trade negotiator who is responsible for securing congressional support and the necessary supplemental legislation for trade agreements entered into by the executive branch" (Cohen 1981: 56).

The 1974 Trade Act elevated the post of Special Trade Representative to cabinet rank, provided legislative authorization for the supporting office, and extended the authority of the trade policy committees over proposed trade-restricting actions. In 1980 the Trade Representative's office was reorganized, renamed (USTR), given even a broader mandate, and increased in size (Cohen 1981: 56–57). In short, as Goldstein (1986: 180) notes, each time since 1962 that Congress has granted presidential authority for trade negotiations, it has "checked presidential discretion by widening the scope of the trade-related bureaucracy."

The establishment of GATT committees to gather and review information from member countries on implementation of the MTN codes in domestic laws and administrative actions required a more regular presence in Geneva than had previously been necessary. For example, were signatory governments informing foreign contractors of the procedures for bidding on government contracts as required by the Government Procurement Code? Thus after the Tokyo Round a USTR delegation was created in Geneva to handle GATT matters, separate for the first time from the U.S. delegation to the UN and headed by a deputy trade representative with the rank of ambassador.

Implementation of the MTN codes has meant a substantially expanded role for the U.S. Trade Representative's office generally and a variety of changes in administrative practice. For example, USTR is responsible for coordinating domestic implementation of the Government Procurement Code by federal and state agencies as well as private persons. New procedures have been established to inform foreign contractors of U.S. government contract opportunities, to assist American firms in taking advantage of opportunities opened up in other countries, and to monitor foreign implementation. All government departments and agencies are responsible for ensuring that their standards-related activities do not create obstacles to international trade, for accepting foreign tests and certification where possible, and for reviewing other countries' standards for adverse impact on U.S. exports (U.S. House of Representatives 1979).

In addition to new offices and changes in administrative practices, steps have been taken since the early 1970s to increase the involvement of members of Congress and representatives of key industry groups in GATT-related trade policymaking. Winham (1986: 342) argues that such involvement was an important means of managing domestic constituencies, necessitated by the fact that the Tokyo Round "engaged domestic politics more than trade negotiations have ever done in the past." The presence of members of Congress during the Tokyo Round was described by one USTR official as "very helpful." "We could show the negotiating parties the problems of dealing with Congress . . . it also went the other way. Members got some sense of others' views" (Interview 1983). This adaptation in policy process contributed significantly to the ease with which MTN slipped through Congress in 1979. It gave congressional trade specialists a vital stake in the disposition of the agreements.

Yet congressional participation in the 1982 GATT Ministerial meetings was widely regarded as detrimental. Some of those attending got their first exposure to the depth of disputes with the EC over agricultural trade and came away shocked by the extent of the confrontation. A Senate staff member described the Ministerial as an "unmitigated disaster for GATT" (Interview 1983). Clearly this particular adaptation in policy process is not necessarily conducive to positive attitudes toward the GATT. The reasons, however, have more to do with the unpredictability of learning experiences than with the innovation of including members on delegations.

Most members of Congress get little exposure to GATT itself. Their attitudes and behavior are influenced by the administration, trade lobbyists, constituent interests, and the perceived fairness of agreements. A former high-level member of the Tokyo Round team noted, nevertheless, that the process of including members (and, by implication, their staffs) in the GATT negotiations increased their understanding of the complexity of the latter and their knowledge of the provisions of the agreements as well as GATT itself (Interview 1984).

The 1974 Trade Act also established sectoral advisory committees (SAC) that were heavily involved in policymaking during the Tokyo Round. They "expanded the U.S. Government's capacity to deal with constituency groups . . . through internal bargaining" (Winham 1986: 346–47). In addition, the ACTN report was instrumental in smoothing congressional action on the Trade Agreements Act of 1979. Some forty sectoral committees involving over eight hundred people continue to provide an active private sector advisory process. This has necessitated adaptations by USTR to facilitate the effectiveness of the consultations but represents an important indirect impact of GATT on domestic policy processes. A further impact directly on groups themselves can also be discerned.

Thus participation in GATT prompted major changes in U.S. trade policymaking processes in the 1960s and 1970s. With a more developed infrastructure in place, future changes are likely to be concentrated in implementation processes.

GATT Influence on Domestic Groups

Destler (1986: 35) has suggested that the growth of trade facilitated by the GATT-based international trade regime has had a "multiplier effect" on trade pressures. Although the number of beneficiaries of expanding markets for U.S. exports has continued to rise, the number of industries and workers "injured" has also risen. "If trade 'losers' go regularly into politics to seek relief, the trade 'winners' generally stick to business." Hence pressures for protection have steadily increased over the years as more major U.S. industries such as automobiles, consumer electronics, machine tools, and, most recently, semiconductors have been adversely affected by competition. In a number of cases, however, these industries have been denied relief under Section 201 rules because their injury has been judged not to relate only to competition from imports. Nevertheless, their political weight has led to extra-GATT protective measures, weakening the impact of the GATT regime.

Increasingly, the domestic group most affected by GATT may be bureaucracies, however, as the latter replace traditional private sector groups as sources of protectionist pressure. "Modern protectionism," Winham (1986: 392) notes, "consists also of attempts by government bureaucracies to provide advantages for domestic producers through a whole range of sophisticated programs." They gain a stake in those programs and a mission for their agencies. As GATT rules reach deeper into the webs of domestic policies and practices that can affect trade, they may mobilize the opposition of increasing numbers of government bureaucrats, producing "bureaucratic nationalism."

The very nature of GATT therefore ensures some impact on its member states. That effect on the United States (and others) has grown with respect to legislation, regulations, and administrative practices affecting trade. The influence of complaints and panel findings is very situationally specific, though there has been some increase in the number of cases brought against the United States. The trend with respect to decision-making and implementation processes shows marked change since the early 1960s as trade policy has become more important and the complexity of GATT rules has demanded both greater bureaucratization and changes in administrative practice.

In assessing GATT's impact on the United States, how do we reconcile these patterns with the overall decline in GATT's role in managing international trade? Likewise, how do we explain the patterns of both continuity and change in GATT's utility as an instrument of U.S. policies?

Contending Explanations for the Patterns of GATT Instrumentality and Influence

Declining Power

Through much of GATT's existence the economic power of the United States and the size of the American market provided incentives for others to negotiate reductions in tariff levels and to shape the interpretation of norms and rules. American willingness to concede more than it gained in tariff concessions until the Kennedy Round speeded the liberalization of world trade and secured major U.S. objectives. U.S. trade law drove the periodic rounds of GATT negotiations. Restrictions in that law, such as the requirement for item-by-item negotiation prior to 1962 and the waiver for quotas on agricultural imports, circumscribed the scope and form of negotiations.

The major interests norm, as noted earlier, gives predominant weight in GATT negotiations to major powers. For this same reason the creation and expansion of the European Community, as well as the growth of Japan and the NICs, have reduced the competitive advantage and market share of the United States in many sectors and eroded its ability to shape outcomes in GATT.

It is difficult to determine the precise extent to which this is the case, however. Since the early 1970s followership has become as important as leadership to the maintenance and extension of the international trade regime based on GATT. The decline in the United States' relative position (measured in terms of resources, not necessarily control over outcomes) and domestic pressures for "fair trade" have lessened the feasibility of a strategy of one-sided concessions. With the shift of focus from tariffs to nontariff barriers, such concessions have become more difficult to identify in any case. Hence bargaining is tougher. A long-time U.S. trade official noted (Interview 1985) that in order to secure the agreement of Brazil, India, and other developing countries to include trade in services in the Uruguay Round, the United States "had to agree to a lot of things it wouldn't accept at the Havana Conference in 1948 from the LDCs!"

A variant on the theories of the role of power, hegemonic stability theory, has been widely used to explain the dynamics of international regimes, especially in international economic relations. It offers a persuasive explanation for the U.S. role in the creation and early development of GATT (Yarbrough and Yarbrough 1987). Hegemonic stability theory is far less useful in explaining either the changes in GATT itself or in the U.S. relationship to GATT since the Kennedy Round (Keohane 1980; Krasner 1976). As Haggard and Simmons (1987) point out, hegemonic stability theory has the inherent weakness of structuralist theories in its inability to explain the processes of international interactions. It also cannot explain national policy choices, especially when such choices and the patterns of interaction to which they give rise derogate from predicted paths. More to the point, much of the writing on hegemonic stability has ignored the role of rules or regimes in expanding or constraining choice.

To be sure, some of the patterns of U.S. policy vis-à-vis GATT have causal links to the decline of America's relative economic position. For example, the erosion of American ability to shape outcomes in GATT, combined with a growing sense that other countries are not abiding by GATT rules, has contributed to the decreased utility of GATT for managing domestic protectionist pressures and greater demands by the United States for reciprocity. In addition, because trade makes up a greater share of U.S. GNP now than at any time in the past, GATT rules are of greater significance to both foreign and domestic policy. Finally, greater trade competition, the increased importance of trade to the U.S. economy, and domestic pressures have contributed to the rise in the number of disputes and use of the GATT dispute settlement machinery to change the practices of others and to secure clarification of ambiguous rules.

We need to look beyond declining American power, however, for fuller explanation of the continuity and change in the U.S. use of GATT as an instrument of policy and GATT's widened influence on policy and policymaking. Are there characteristics of trade as an issue area that have shaped those patterns? In particular, have changes in international economic relations and in the salience of trade issues been key factors?

Character of the Issue Area

Changes in the international economic environment and particularly in the nature of trade issues account for many of the changes in the ways in which the United States finds GATT useful as an instrument of policy and in GATT's impact on the United States. These include the shift in focus from tariff to nontariff barriers, the proliferation of extra-GATT arrangements (including orderly marketing arrangements [OMAs] and voluntary restraint agreements [VERs]), surplus capacity in key sectors, growth of trade in services, and the increased role of governments in promoting investment and trade.

First, as we have noted, nontariff barriers have made international trade negotiations far more complex and truly multilateral. The variety of such barriers seems almost endless; their close links to domestic social and economic policies mean that negotiations touch sensitive political issues for many countries; their proliferation requires almost continuous surveillance and negotiation and casts doubts on adherence to the goal of an open, liberal trading system. The MTN codes widened and deepened the scope and impact of GATT rules, but their many ambiguities and omissions fueled an increase in complaints and, hence, use of the GATT dispute settlement machinery. This was particularly true for the United States, whose tendency to take a legalistic approach to GATT in the first place led it to use that machinery to try to legislate through interpretation.

Second, the founders of GATT assumed that international negotiations would liberalize trade. They did not anticipate "negotiated protectionism" in the form of bilateral and multilateral arrangements that undermine or go around GATT. Inevitably, the influence of GATT has dwindled with these changes. How much can be attributed to negotiated protectionism is hard to assess. With the exception of the multilateral arrangements for textiles, many OMAs and VERs are temporary protectionist measures and therefore do not mark a permanent retreat from open trade (Aggarwal, Keohane, and Yoffie 1987). Indeed, one author concludes that voluntary restraint agreements will continue to proliferate as a way of dealing with trade problems "without unduly disturbing other profitable trade opportunities or the general GATT regime" (Dunn 1987: 250).

Negotiated protectionism has predominated in sectors with surplus capacity such as steel, textiles, shipbuilding, automobiles, and agriculture (Strange 1979). Because all the developed countries—including the United States—have wrestled with the problems of surplus capacity for a decade or more, the OECD has made structural adjustment the central focus of many of its work programs since 1984 in an attempt to address them. Cowhey and Long (1983) have articulated a theory of surplus capacity to explain the willingness of the United States after 1980 to move in the direction of managed trade for automobiles outside GATT. Only in agriculture has the United States attempted, with little success, to use GATT as an instrument of its policies. Although it sought consensus on the need for change and for multilateral rules governing agricultural trade (and particularly subsidies) through the OECD, the seven-power Venice summit, and now the Uruguay Round, the prospects are uncertain. The increase of trade in services (estimated in 1986 to account for one quarter of the $2 trillion total annual value of world trade; *New York Times* September 21, 1986: 1) also accounts for a significant portion of the trade outside of GATT rules, and its growth has been a major factor in U.S. efforts to include services in the Uruguay Round.

Finally, governments have assumed a greater role in attracting or guiding investment and, hence, in shaping trade flows. GATT rules assumed that government activities would be designed to restrict trade, not promote it. The Subsidies Code was a first step in dealing with government promotion of trade, directly and indirectly. American concern about government and industry collaboration such as through Japan's Ministry of International Trade and Industry (MITI) or European state enterprises underlies many charges of unfair competition. By one estimate 48 percent of world trade in 1980 was managed (Brittan 1982: 546). Yet although charges of unfair trade now fuel domestic pressures for legislated protectionism, investment and subsidies are high on the list of U.S. objectives for the Uruguay Round—evidence of a continuing commitment to GATT as an instrument for rule creation.

In spite of changes in the issue area, GATT has adapted to the shift from tariff negotiations to more complex negotiations of codes for government procurement, subsidies, and, now, ventures into trade in services. Thus for the United States GATT remains at the center of the international trade regime as the only instrument for negotiating *overall* regime rules. To what extent, however, can this continued salience be attributed to GATT's unique organizational character?

Character of the Organization

A striking characteristic of GATT is, in fact, the lack of organizational structure. Technically it is not an international governmental organization. Yet in the vacuum left by the stillborn ITO, GATT developed the essential organizational characteristics: regular meetings of the contracting parties, a small secretariat to service negotiations, and dispute settlement machinery. Much of GATT's institutional development has occurred since 1970, when a council was established to provide intersessional planning and review. Further efforts to enhance consultation and decision making led to creation of the Consulting Group of 18 in 1975 and an informal Quadrilateral Group in 1983, neither of which has been very effective (Meltzer 1988). Each cf the MTN codes added its own set of rule-making and implementation procedures, along with machinery for dispute settlement. This has decentralized and complicated GATT's functioning.

The continuity of these organizational characteristics is striking, particularly by comparison with the changes that have marked most IGOs. The single most important reason for this continuity lies in the *lack* of major change in membership—either size or composition—thanks to the establishment of UNCTAD in 1964. The developing countries did not wish to subject themselves to GATT's disciplines and (correctly) perceived that it could not be "captured" in the way in which so many other IGOs were and shaped to serve their interests. Although gradually some developing countries (and some socialist) have joined GATT, it remains dominated by the major Western industrial trading countries. Membership is now expanding, however, as UNCTAD has proved impotent to manage North-South trade relations. With over one hundred countries participating in the Uruguay Round, negotiations inevitably will be slower and more complicated.

Historically the GATT secretariat has operated under sharply circumscribed powers, unable either to monitor members' policies or to propose initiatives to resolve emerging problems. The preliminary studies of a code for government procurement and, more recently, of codes for trade in services were conducted in the OECD precisely because the GATT secretariat was not specifically empowered to undertake special studies and seemed reluctant to do so (Interviews 1985). The MTN codes have enhanced the secretariat's role with respect to information gathering, and proposals to give them authority for regular reviews of members' trade policies have been under serious consideration (Blackhurst 1988; *New York Times* March 29, 1988).

There is no evidence to suggest, however, that the weakness of the GATT dispute settlement machinery has reduced U.S. willingness to use that machinery. There is evidence that the limited role of the GATT secretariat has influenced U.S. use of the OECD for background studies (Interviews 1985). The latter also enabled the developed countries to gain greater collective understanding and agreement on these matters before they were addressed in the broader forum of GATT negotiations.

It could be argued that GATT has *lost* some of its importance as both instrument and influencer precisely because its character has not changed. When the United States and other parties have preferred to discriminate, to restrict access to their markets, and to manage trade, they have utilized arrangements outside GATT. This enables them to proclaim the importance of GATT's basic norms, whereas the reality is akin to Swiss cheese. In the case of the United States, however, some of the reasons for tolerating departures from GATT rules at home and abroad lie in changing domestic political realities.

Domestic Political Factors

Trade historically has touched both domestic and foreign policy arenas. For reasons of governmental structure and domestic pressures this is particularly true for the United States. Hence any explanation of trade policy and U.S. relations to the international trade regime must encompass domestic political factors (Haggard and Simmons 1987). The constitutional separation of powers and specifically the legislative branch have had a powerful effect on the ways and extent to which the United States could use GATT as an instrument of policy, as well as the potential impact of GATT rules. The legislation authorizing trade negotiations has given political will to both U.S. and other countries' trade negotiators and influenced the timing and duration of successive rounds. Legislation has also defined the parameters of tariff cuts, the basis of valuation of goods, waiver of countervailing duties, and prospects for speedy and favorable consideration of nontariff codes.

The sensitivity of other countries to the domestic political factors shaping U.S. trade policy was clearly demonstrated in 1978 when expiration of the countervailing duty waiver authority held up negotiations until the extension was passed by Congress on April 12, 1979 (Destler and Graham 1980: 62–63). The limits domestic political realities could impose were also amply demonstrated at the close of the Kennedy Round when Congress rejected the agreements on an antidumping code and the American Selling Price on the grounds that U.S. negotiators had no authority to conclude nontariff agreements.

The beauty of the U.S. trade policy system until the 1980s was its ability to neutralize or diffuse the power of all but a few key sectors such as agriculture, textiles, steel, and automobiles. Agriculture being a case unto itself (and subject to GATT waiver at U.S. request), the textile industry has been the most effective in securing protection over the years, requiring successive administrations to appease its interests (Destler 1987: 22). Thus a few industries have influenced U.S. use of GATT, securing either outright exemption, as in the case of agriculture, or extra-GATT arrangements, as in the case of textiles, steel, automobiles, and semiconductors.

As Destler (1986) describes, however, the "old" system has broken down with a consequence that more pressure is focused on Congress.

Simultaneously the scope of pressures has increased significantly because of the expansion of trade as a percentage of U.S. GNP (more workers and industries benefit or suffer from change in the trade balance), the widening trade deficit, the perceived unfair trade practices of others, and executive branch unwillingness to take adequate actions against the latter.[7] Proposals for legislated protectionism have proliferated. Reflecting a widely shared perception of the erosion of the international trading system, Senator William V. Roth, Jr. noted, "the relevance of GATT rules, which are based on a presumption that free markets operate in trading nations, is more and more open to question" (U.S. Congress, Joint Economic Committee 1984: pt. II, 1). Congress has not entirely lost faith in GATT as an instrument for opening markets to U.S. exports, though there is strong sentiment regarding the need for reform of GATT and strengthening of its rules. However, members "are skeptical-to-cynical about what can be accomplished, at least in the absence of tough unilateral actions by the United States" (Destler 1987: 17).

Historically, antiprotectionist groups in the United States have never been numerous or strong. There has been a sharp increase in anti-protectionist activity since the mid-1970s, however, often to counter the pro-protectionist activity in key product areas such as steel, textiles, and footwear (Destler and Odell 1987: 25–59). The "explosion" in capacity for organized political action has been an important factor in transforming trade politics, fueled by growth in the importance of trade to the U.S. economy.

In general changes of administration have had little effect on the U.S.-GATT relationship given that all postwar administrations have affirmed their commitment to the GATT-based free trade regime. The Reagan administration was more willing than its predecessors to pursue complaints through GATT dispute settlement machinery, particularly complaints designed to secure clarification of ambiguous rules. It is difficult to ascertain how much of the increased number of complaints can be attributed specifically to the ideological predilections of the Reagan administration. Certainly an aggressive attitude characterized the administration's approach during the period 1981–83. Just as certainly, many of the disputes arose from the ambiguity of the recently enacted MTN codes. The tempo of rising disputes also owes a lot to the general economic recession in that period. Provisions of the 1974 and 1979 trade laws give USTR and the executive branch less leeway to determine when they will or will not file complaints. Attorneys and companies have gained increased familiarity with those procedures as a cheap remedy for trade problems. Furthermore, the increased awareness of key sectors and industries of the MTN codes and of the various dispute settlement procedures as a result of participation of the sectoral advisory committees in the MTN negotiations was clearly another factor fueling rising complaints (Interviews 1984, 1985).

Thus domestic political factors do provide substantial explanation of the ways in which the United States has continued to use GATT as an instrument for rule creation and dispute settlement. Changes in the trade policy system specifically account for the decreased utility of GATT as an instrument for managing domestic protectionist pressures and for the increased role of GATT in magnifying those pressures. More than ever before in the postwar period, pro- and anti-protectionist groups compete to shape U.S. trade policy. Yet no single set of variables—declining relative power, changing issue area, organizational character, or domestic politics—fully accounts for the patterns of change in the importance of GATT as an instrument of U.S. trade policy or in GATT's impact on U.S. policies and policy processes.

Conclusion

Substantial changes have occurred in the international economic environment since GATT's rules were first drafted, strongly influenced by U.S. interests. The growth of the EC, Japan, and the NICs has decreased U.S. dominance and competitive advantage. Tariff barriers have been reduced to the point that they no longer constitute infringements on trade in most products. Instead, the variety of nontariff barriers enmeshed in domestic social and economic policies have become the primary issues. Slower economic growth, recession, and high unemployment have intensified labor and industry demands for protection in all member states. Surplus capacity in key sectors has contributed to the surge in negotiated protectionism outside GATT as governments have found it more expeditious (and politically easier) to undermine or go around GATT (Strange 1979). Inevitably GATT's influence has dwindled with these changes and trade negotiations have become increasingly difficult. The unsatisfactory outcomes of many disputes brought before GATT as well as the very number threaten the attractiveness and viability of the dispute settlement procedures.

Nevertheless for the United States in particular and other nations, GATT remains "the only game in town" for promoting and maintaining a relatively open *global* trading system. The United States remains the only country with sufficient economic weight and commitment to a liberal, open trade regime to provide leadership within GATT. "Its participation and agreement are necessary if relative openness is to be maintained" (Stein

1984: 386). Whether the United States will exercise the necessary political will or whether it can exercise sufficient influence to move others remains to be seen. Exercising leadership entails not only playing a positive role in promoting the centrality of GATT rules and negotiations in international trade but also refraining from retaliation against others when retaliation might provoke a dangerous cycle of countermoves. It therefore requires the United States "to accept not only the original asymmetric bargain [at the heart of GATT] but also the increased cheating of others at a time when it [the United States] is experiencing an absolute economic downturn." Will the United States, Stein (1984: 383) asks, "keep a bargain it can no longer afford?"

The continuity of U.S. leadership in the initiation of successive rounds of GATT negotiations, including the Uruguay Round, indicates that the United States clearly still regards GATT as highly useful for creating the norms and rules for a global trading regime. This pattern is enforced by the role the United States has played in setting the agendas for negotiation, including efforts to ensure the inclusion of trade in services, high technology, and agriculture in the Uruguay Round. The proliferation of extra-GATT arrangements, however, just as clearly indicates that although the United States still supports and promotes the overall GATT norms, it finds the political and economic costs of applying those across the board too high. Similarly because the MTN codes are technically separate from GATT with benefits open only to signatories, they have compromised a key norm of the GATT-based regime: unconditional MFN. The latter was always more an ideal than a reality, but the shift reinforced the pattern of proliferating bilateral and plurilateral trade arrangements, weakening the multilateral GATT regime.

The erosion of the U.S. predominant position and domestic political pressures, however, require the United States to bargain harder to get what it wants and to seek outcomes that result in a fairer distribution of economic (that is, trade) benefits for the United States. Gone are the days of one-sided concessions accepted for larger political and economic objectives. True to patterns typical of interest group activity and in spite of increased antiprotectionist activity, there is little evidence that U.S. service groups have pressed for the opening of trade in services, though services are estimated to make up roughly 60 percent of U.S. GNP, a significant percentage of current exports and potentially a far greater absolute volume of exports with reduced barriers. Self-interest dictates exploring the possibilities of developing GATT rules to open other countries' markets; studies and discussions continue at the OECD as well, where the codes on capital movements and invisible operations have liberalized developed country markets at least.

The increased importance of trade to the U.S. economy, changes in the nature of trade barriers, and domestic political factors have all contributed to extensive U.S. use of GATT's dispute settlement machinery, although even before 1970 the United States was the single most frequent user of Article XIX provisions (Curzon and Curzon 1976). Domestic protectionist pressures and a more aggressive attitude under the Reagan administration fueled efforts to use those procedures and decreased reluctance to initiate retaliatory measures against others. Frustration has been rising, however, over the difficulty of securing satisfaction in disputes with the European Community. Some of that frustration has led to proposals for strengthening the procedures. The problems lie less with the procedures, however, than in the nature of the EC and particularly of the CAP. Tough retaliatory measures and crisis diplomacy have secured somewhat greater access to European markets for specific American exports, but GATT mechanisms have been no more useful than direct negotiations in securing changes in basic EC practices.

The United States has also found itself the target of an increasing number of complaints and adverse panel findings since 1980. As the DISC case illustrates, the United States is not necessarily inclined to make changes in its own trade-related laws and practices even when those violate GATT rules.

Although GATT has been an important instrument for the United States in managing domestic protectionist pressures, it appears much more questionable that it can continue to be used effectively in this way given demands for trade legislation. U.S. trade officials still perceive GATT negotiations in this light, as do other governments; hence some of the pressure (and support) for the Uruguay Round of negotiations. Containing or defusing domestic pressures, however, has required much more attention to "fair" outcomes since the early 1970s (Krasner 1979: 479). Domestic perceptions of widespread violations by others of GATT rules have eroded support in the United States for both abiding by existing GATT rules and implementing new ones. The difficulty of negotiating major changes in sectors of greatest interest—for example, agriculture and services—may undercut support for future GATT negotiations.

It is widely accepted that GATT has less impact on world trade than it did twenty years ago and faces even more difficulties in the future. GATT rules may cover a lower percentage of trade, but the overall volume of trade is far greater. The content has also changed, meaning that more of what is traded is not covered fully, if at all, by GATT rules (for example, services). For the United States as for the trade regime, GATT is less central than it once was. The developing countries continue to avoid GATT and to promote UNCTAD (albeit with diminishing success on both counts); extra-GATT bilateral and multilateral arrangements have eroded the strength of GATT as the cornerstone of the international trade regime. Yet the MTN codes have expanded the *scope* of GATT rules into the burgeoning realm of nontariff barriers. This analysis affirms, nevertheless, that GATT is still the only *institutionalized multilateral* vehicle for negotiating *overall* regime norms and rules; it also provides the only institutionalized dispute settlement machinery. For the United States GATT has become a *more* important instrument of trade policy per se, particularly for creating rules that extend the scope of a liberal trading order, albeit one whose central norms of nondiscrimination and reciprocity are heavily compromised and in which negotiations have become increasingly complex and difficult (Gilpin 1987: 199–203). GATT also has a greater impact on U.S. trade-related rules, practices, and policymaking processes than it did previously. GATT thus remains an important instrument for U.S. leadership in the international trade regime. It has become a greater influencer of U.S. trade policies and policy processes.

Notes

1. An earlier version of this chapter was presented at the Annual Meetings of the International Studies Association, March 1984, in Atlanta. I wish to acknowledge the generous support of the Roosevelt Center for American Policy Studies and the University of Dayton Research Council, which enabled me to conduct interviews in Washington in 1983–84 and in Geneva in summer 1985. The ground rules for those interviews preclude attribution in most cases. I also wish to acknowledge the assistance of Christine F. Wright in the gathering of material for an earlier draft of this chapter and the helpful comments of Karen A. Mingst, Charles S. Lipson, Mark Zacher, other participants in the Wingspread conference, and Gilbert Winham. Kelechi Kalu provided assistance in analyzing the data on GATT disputes.

2. Division within Congress over the charter of the ITO led the State Department to withhold the charter from ratification because "it contained too many exceptions for other countries and too many obligations for the United States" (Pastor 1980: 97). Congress was not much more receptive to GATT. Prior to 1968 the U.S. contribution to GATT's small operating budget was included in the Department of State budget under international conferences and contingencies to avoid debate over authorization. Through the 1960s members of Congress repeatedly challenged the constitutionality of U.S. participation and extensions of the Trade Agreements Act in 1949, 1953, 1954, and 1958, explicitly stating, "the enactment of the Act shall not be construed to determine or indicate the approval or disapproval by the Congress of the Executive Agreement known as the General Agreement on Tariffs and Trade" (Jackson 1967: 267).

3. This is often disputed by the European Community, especially regarding agriculture but confirmed by OECD studies and by Hufbauer (1983: 333).

4. This view differs from that of European Community members and many other parties who regard the dispute settlement procedures as processes for negotiation (Interviews 1983, 1984, 1985). It has led to American complaints that the GATT proceedings failed to decide who was right or wrong.

5. In 1952 the Netherlands was authorized to suspend "appropriate" tariff concessions to the United States in retaliation for U.S. use of import restrictions on dairy products (Curzon and Curzon 1976: 207). On GATT dispute settlement, see also Hudec (1975).

6. Domestic pressures from the textile interests were not as readily diffused, and the executive branch had to negotiate voluntary export restraints with the Japanese to avoid the imposition of quotas by Congress. The latter would have directly contravened GATT rules. After extending the restraints in 1957, the United States began efforts to seek a multilateral solution to the problem of Japanese and other textile imports in 1959.

7. Such skepticism is hardly new. Indeed, the Office of the Special Trade Representative was created in 1962 precisely because Congress distrusted the State Department's skill in trade negotiations and wanted an agent more responsive to congressional concerns. In recent years Congress has progressively tightened the president's leeway regarding safeguard actions under Section 201 of the 1974 Trade Act.

References

Aggarwal, Vinod K., Robert O. Keohane, and David B. Yoffie (1987). "The Dynamics of Negotiated Protectionism." *American Political Science Review*, 81(2), 345–66.

Blackhurst, Richard (1988). "Strengthening GATT Surveillance of Trade-Related Policies." In Meinhard Hilfand and Ernst-Ulrich Petersmann, eds., *The New GATT Round of Multilateral Trade Negotiations: Legal and Economic Aspects*. Deventer, Netherlands: Kluwer Law and Taxation Publishers.

Brittan, Samuel (1983). "A Very Painful World Adjustment." *Foreign Affairs*, 61(3) (*America and the World 1982*), 561–68.

Camps, Miriam, and William Diebold, Jr. (1983). *The New Multilateralism: Can the World Trading System Be Saved?* New York: Council on Foreign Relations.

Cline, William R., ed. (1983). *Trade Policy in the 1980s*. Washington, DC: Institute for International Economics.

Cline, William R., and C. Fred Bergsten (1983). "Trade Policy in the 1980s: An Overview." In William R. Cline, ed., *Trade Policy in the 1980s*. Washington, DC: Institute for International Economics, 59–98.

Cohen, Stephen D. (1981). *The Making of United States International Economic Policy*. New York: Praeger.

Cohen, Stephen D., and Ronald I. Meltzer (1982). *United States International Economic Policy in Action: Diversity of Decision Making*. New York: Praeger.

Congressional Quarterly Special Report (1962). *The Trade Expansion Act*. Washington, DC: Congressional Quarterly Service.

Cowhey, Peter F., and Edward Long (1983). "Testing Theories of Regime Change: Hegemonic Decline or Surplus Capacity?" *International Organization*, 37(2), 157–88.

Curtis, Thomas B., and John Robert Vastine, Jr. (1971). *The Kennedy Round and the Future of American Trade*. New York: Praeger.

Curzon, Gerard, and Victoria Curzon (1974). "GATT: Trader's Club." In Robert W. Cox and Harold K. Jacobson, eds., *Anatomy of Influence: Decision-Making in International Organization*. New Haven: Yale University Press, 298–333.

——— (1976). "The Multilateral Trading System of the 1960s"; "Rule Supervision and Dispute Settlement"; "Rule Adaptation." In Andrew Shonfield, ed., *Politics and Trade*, vol. I. *International Relations of the Western World 1959–71*. London: Oxford University, 143–283.

Dam, Kenneth W. (1970). *The GATT: Law and International Economic Organization.* Chicago: University of Chicago Press.

Destler, I. M. (1980). *Making Foreign Economic Policy.* Washington, DC: Brookings Institution.

—— (1986). *American Trade Politics: System under Stress.* Washington, DC: Institute for International Economics.

—— (1987). "United States Trade Policy-Making at the Outset of the Uruguay Round." Unpublished paper prepared for the Symposium on Domestic Dimensions of the Uruguay Round, Montreux, Switzerland, March 6–8.

Destler, I. M., and Thomas R. Graham (1980). "United States Congress and the Tokyo Round: Lessons of a Success Story." *The World Economy,* 3(1), 53–70.

Destler, I. M., and John S. Odell (1987). *Anti-Protection: Changing Forces in United States Trade Politics.* Washington, DC: Institute for International Economics.

Dunn, James A., Jr. (1987). "Automobiles in International Trade: Regime Change or Persistence?" *International Organization,* 41(2), 225–52.

Evans, John W. (1971). *The Kennedy Round in American Trade Policy.* Cambridge: Harvard University Press.

Finlayson, Jock A., and Mark W. Zacher (1981). "The GATT and the Regulation of Trade Barriers: Regime Dynamics and Functions." *International Organization,* 35(4), 561–602.

Gardner, Richard N. (1969). *Sterling-Dollar Diplomacy: The Origins and Prospects of Our International Economic Order.* New York: McGraw-Hill.

General Agreement on Tariffs and Trade (selected years). *Basic Instruments and Selected Documents.* Geneva: Author.

—— (1983). *GATT Activities in 1982.* Geneva: Author.

—— (1987). "Conciliation and Dispute Settlement." *FOCUS,* 46(May).

Gilpin, Robert (1987). *The Political Economy of International Relations.* Princeton: Princeton University Press.

Goldstein, Judith (1986). "The Political Economy of Trade: Institution of Protection." *American Political Science Review,* 80(1), 161–84.

Graham, Thomas R. (1979). "Revolution in Trade Politics." *Foreign Policy,* 36(Fall), 49–63.

Haggard, Stephen, and Beth A. Simmons (1987). "Theories and International Regimes." *International Organization,* 41(3), 491–517.

Hudec, Robert E. (1975). *The GATT Legal System and World Trade Diplomacy.* New York: Praeger.

—— (1980). "GATT Dispute Settlement after the Tokyo Round (of Multilateral Trade Negotiations, 1973–1979)." *Cornell International Law Journal,* 13(Summer), 145–203.

Hufbauer, Gary C. (1983). "Subsidy Issues after the Tokyo Round." In William R. Cline, ed., *Trade Policy in the 1980s.* Washington, DC: Institute for International Economics, 327–62.

Interviews (1983, 1984, 1985). Interviews with officials in the Office of the U.S. Trade Representative (USTR), Department of State, U.S. Delegation to the GATT, and the GATT Secretariat, as well as with former officials in May and July 1983, March and April 1984, and July 1985.

Jackson, John H. (1967). "The General Agreement on Tariffs and Trade in United States Domestic Law." *Michigan Law Review,* 66(December), 250–332.

—— (1978). "The Jurisprudence of International Trade: The DISC Case in GATT." *American Journal of International Law,* 72(October), 747–81.

—— (1979a). "MTN and the Legal Institutions of International Trade." Unpublished memorandum for the United States Senate Committee on Finance (May).

—— (1979b). "Governmental Disputes in International Trade Relations: A Proposal in the Context of GATT." *Journal of World Trade Law,* 13(January/February), 1–21.

———— (1983). "GATT Machinery and the Tokyo Round Agreements." In William R. Cline, ed., *Trade Policy in the 1980s*. Washington, DC: Institute for International Economics.

Keohane, Robert O. (1980). "The Theory of Hegemonic Stability and Changes in International Economic Regimes, 1967–1977." In Ole R. Holsti, Randolph M. Siverson, and Alexander George, eds., *Change in the International System*. Boulder, CO: Westview Press, 131–62.

Krasner, Stephen D. (1976). "State Power and the Structure of International Trade." *World Politics*, 28(2), 317–43.

———— (1979). "The Tokyo Round: Particularistic Interests and Prospects for Stability in the Global Trading System." *International Studies Quarterly*, 23(4), 491–531.

Lenway, Stefanie Ann (1985). *The Politics of U.S. International Trade: Protection, Expansion and Escape*. Boston: Pitman Publishing.

Lipson, Charles (1982). "The Transformation of Trade: The Sources and Effects of Regime Change." *International Organization*, 36(2), 417–56.

McRae, D. M., and J. C. Thomas (1983). "The GATT and Multilateral Treaty Making: The Tokyo Round." *American Journal of International Law*, 77(January), 51–83.

Malmgren, Harald B. (1983). "Threats to the Multilateral System." In William R. Cline, ed., *Trade Policy in the 1980s*. Washington, DC: Institute for International Economics, 189–201.

Meltzer, Ronald I. (1976). "The Politics of Policy Reversal: The U.S. Response to Granting Trade Preferences to Developing Countries and Linkages between International Organizations and National Policy Making." *International Organization*, 30(4), 649–68.

———— (1988). "The Deterioration of the GATT Framework in International Trade Relations." In Lawrence S. Finkelstein, ed., *Politics in the United Nations System*. Durham, NC: Duke University Press, 148–74.

Pastor, Robert A. (1980). *Congress and the Politics of U.S. Foreign Economic Policy 1929–1976*. Berkeley: University of California Press.

Preeg, Ernest H. (1970). *Traders and Diplomats: An Analysis of the Kennedy Round of Negotiations under the General Agreement on Tariffs and Trade*. Washington, DC: Brookings Institution.

Shelp, Ronald K. (1986). "Trade in Services." *Foreign Policy*, 65(Winter), 64–84.

Stein, Arthur A. (1984). "The Hegemon's Dilemma: Great Britain, the United States, and the International Economic Order." *International Organization*, 38(2), 355–86.

Strange, Susan (1979). "The Management of Surplus Capacity: Or How Does Theory Stand Up to Protectionism 1970s Style?" *International Organization*, 33(3), 303–34.

———— (1985). "Protectionism and World Politics." *International Organization*, 39(2), 233–60.

U.S. Advisory Committee for Trade Negotiations (1979). *Report to the President, the Congress, and the Special Representative for Trade Negotiations*. Washington, DC: U.S. Government Printing Office.

U.S. Congress, Joint Economic Committee, Subcommittee on Trade, Productivity and Economic Growth (1984). Hearing. *How to Save the International Trading System*, pt. I. 98th Cong., 2d sess. (April 26). Washington, DC: U.S. Government Printing Office.

U.S. Department of Commerce, Office of Trade Policy (1981). *Technical Barriers to Trade*, vol. 4 (September). Washington, DC: U.S. Government Printing Office.

U.S. Government (1984). *U.S. National Study on Trade in Services: A Submission by the United States Government to the General Agreement on Tariffs and Trade*. Washington, DC: U.S. Government Printing Office.

U.S. House of Representatives (1979). *Trade Agreements Act of 1979: Statements of Administrative Action*, pt. II. 96th Cong., 1st sess. Washington, DC: U.S. Government Printing Office.

U.S. House of Representatives, Committee on Ways and Means, Subcommittee on Trade (1981). Hearings. *U.S. Trade Policy.* 97th Cong., 1st sess. (October 28–30, November 2, 3, 12). Washington, DC: U.S. Government Printing Office.

U.S. House of Representatives, Committee on Ways and Means, Subcommittee on Trade (1983). Hearing. *Results and Followup of GATT Ministerial.* 98th Cong., 1st sess. (February 22). Washington, DC: U.S. Government Printing Office.

U.S. House of Representatives, Committee on Ways and Means, Subcommittee on Trade (1986). Hearing. *Requirements of the Manufacturing Clause of the Copyright Law.* 99th Cong., 2d sess. (June 26). Washington, DC: U.S. Government Printing Office.

U.S. Senate, Committee on Finance (1974). Hearings. *Trade Reform Act of 1973*, pt. I. 93rd Cong., 2d sess. (March-April). Washington, DC: U.S. Government Printing Office.

—— (1979a). *Agreements Negotiated under Section 102 of the Trade Act of 1979 in the Multilateral Trade Negotiations.* 96th Cong., 1st sess. (July). Washington, DC: U.S. Government Printing Office.

U.S. Senate, Committee on Finance, Subcommittee on International Trade (1979b). Hearings. *Implementation of the Multilateral Trade Negotiations.* 96th Cong., 1st sess. (February 21–22 and March 19). Washington, DC: U.S. Government Printing Office.

—— (1979c). *MTN Studies*, 6 pts. 96th Cong., 1st sess. (June). Washington, DC: U.S. Government Printing Office.

—— (1979d). *Private Advisory Committee Reports on the Tokyo Round of Multilateral Trade Negotiations.* 96th Cong., 1st sess. (August). Washington, DC: U.S. Government Printing Office.

U.S. Senate, Committee on Finance (1985). *Oversight Hearings on U.S. Trade Policy.* 99th Cong., 1st sess. (November 14, 20, 21). Washington, DC: U.S. Government Printing Office.

U.S. Senate, Committee on Finance, Subcommittee on International Trade (1986). Hearing. *Possible New Round of Multilateral Trade Negotiations.* 99th Cong., 2d sess. (May 14). Washington, DC: U.S. Government Printing Office.

Vernon, Raymond (1982). "International Trade Policy in the 1980s: Prospects and Problems." *International Studies Quarterly*, 26(December), 483–510.

Walker, Herman (1964). "Dispute Settlement: The Chicken War." *American Journal of International Law*, 58(3), 671–85.

Walker, William N. (1976). "International Limits to Government Intervention in the Marketplace: Focus on Subsidies to the Private Sector." London: Trade Policy Research Center.

Winham, Gilbert R. (1986). *International Trade and the Tokyo Round Negotiation.* Princeton: Princeton University Press.

Yarbrough, Beth V., and Robert M. Yarbrough (1987). "Cooperation in the Liberalization of International Trade: After Hegemony, What?" *International Organization*, 41(1), 1–26.

Young, Oran R. (1986). "International Regimes: Toward a New Theory of Institutions." *World Politics*, 39(1), 104–22.

CHAPTER SEVEN

International Food Organizations and the United States: Drifting Leadership and Diverging Interests

Raymond F. Hopkins

Since 1945 the United States has played a pivotal role in launching three international food institutions as well as in developing and spreading new agricultural technology, thanks to its predominance in world food trade and agricultural research. The U.S. role in international food and agricultural organizations, therefore, ought to be one of leadership and influence. Because of the significant stakes it holds, the United States also should be vulnerable to IGO influence in this issue area. Although its share of world grain trade topped 50 percent in the 1970s, surprisingly U.S. leadership in food organizations has declined since roughly the time of the 1974 World Food Conference, and the relevance of these bodies for either assisting or disciplining U.S. policy has shrunk. Instead, relations with the major world intergovernmental food organizations have become increasingly incoherent and inefficient.

This chapter seeks to explain why U.S. leadership has failed and, relatedly, why international food bodies have had little influence on the United States. It will be useful first to provide a brief review of the formation of international agencies in the food and agricultural regime and to relate how U.S. policies have shaped that regime. Second, several explanations for change in U.S. relationships with food organizations will be considered, particularly changes in characteristics of the issue area and the organizations themselves.

International Food and Agriculture Regime Formation

Formal organizations are a central part of the international food and agriculture regime. Some forty bodies in the United Nations system alone deal with international food affairs in areas ranging from research to famine relief (Puchala 1988). Six organizations specialize in food and agriculture; three of these, based in Rome, are the focus of this chapter: the Food and Agriculture Organization (FAO), established in 1945, the World Food Programme (WFP), founded in 1963, and the International Fund for Agricultural Development (IFAD), founded in 1977. The other three important food IGOs are the International Wheat Council (IWC), the Consultative Group on International Agricultural Research (CGIAR), and the World Food Council (WFC; see Kriesberg 1984).

Other IGOs involved in food policy include the OECD and its committees on Agriculture and Development Assistance, the UN Conference on Trade and Development (UNCTAD) and General Agreement on Tariffs and Trade (GATT) with their agricultural trade interests, the World Health Organization (WHO) with its nutrition and food standard interests, and the general financial bodies with a major stake in agricultural investments: the World Bank, the regional banks, the IMF with its "food facility," and the UN Development Program (UNDP; Kriesberg 1984).

The three major institutions (and several of the others) are the result of three waves of international regime building since World War II.[1] Each successive wave has left its legacy on institutional order through the creation of new organizations or changes in established ones. Thus each international food organization has exhibited changing norms and practices as it has responded to changing membership and changing goals among its members.

The three regime-building waves contained distinctive goals: (1) the liberal wave of 1944–60 that aimed at harmonization of commercial interests and the coordination of information standards and research; (2) the development wave of 1960–73 that sought to accelerate the expansion of economic modernization, especially in nonindustrial, poorer states; and (3) the structural conflict wave of 1973–81 in which coalitions of southern or G-77 states sought to control issues, agendas, and budgets in IGOs in order to exercise power and extract resources from industrialized states.

The first wave was led by the United States and was part of the larger effort to establish a liberal and stable world economic order. For agriculture the goal was to harmonize national agricultural policies with free trade principles. A dominant coalition of states in the FAO led by the United States felt it would be desirable to coordinate commercial agriculture policy, establish common standards, share information, provide technical assistance, and address worldwide problems of agricultural surpluses and shortages (U.S. Government 1976). In addition, the Food and Agriculture Organization was to address problems of wartime food trade, nutrition, and famine. FAO was launched by a 1943 planning conference in Hot Springs, Virginia, and began operations in 1945 in Washington near the Department of Agriculture. At the behest of European states, it moved to Rome in 1951. During this period the FAO and other UN specialized agencies developed autonomously within the UN system. Each had its own membership, rules of procedure, and assessed budget.

In the early decades nearly all FAO funds came from assessed contributions. These paid for international services such as the collection and dissemination of information, agricultural research, the coordination of members' policies, and technical advice to governments. Succeeding waves would alter the FAO's functions and sources of funding, as we shall see, but it remains the largest, most central international food agency.

Another organization recreated in 1949 as part of this liberal regime-building phase was the International Wheat Council originally established in 1933 in London. The 1949 International Wheat Agreement gave the IWC substantive responsibility for the first time. As a special, politically distinct commodity agency, its aim has been to stabilize international trade in wheat and occasionally in course grain. By 1960 the international grain agreements effectively lost their price-stabilizing features. Along with UNCTAD and GATT, IWC has vied with the FAO as an arena in which subsequent wheat and grain trade, food aid, and stockholding obligations have been negotiated. Thus in general the IWC has dealt with many of the same issues as has FAO.

The second wave of regime-building reflected the broad effort to strengthen the economic development of "new" states through greater resource transfers. Although the FAO had a mandate to promote international welfare and development in its 1945 charter, its emergence as a major body for multilateral resource transfers to developing countries did not come for nearly two decades. Until the 1960s it served largely as an international clearinghouse and conciliator. Its operating budget paid for a highly respected technical staff in Rome, which monitored worldwide economic and technical aspects of agricultural fisheries and forestries, covered the cost of conferences and workshops, and afforded modest technical assistance.

With the establishment of the UN Development Program in the 1960s, however, and the expansion of World Bank activities in poor countries through International Development Association funds, FAO projects and operational activities oriented toward Third World development expanded substantially, often in cooperation with these and other IGOs. The FAO set up the Investment Centre, whose purpose was to prepare projects (with the collaboration of recipient governments) and then to seek funding for them. FAO staff became project managers for undertakings largely paid for by the UNDP, the World Bank group, and, in more recent years, trust funds provided by dozens of donor governments earmarked for special FAO programs. As a result of these inter-IGO and IGO-governmental arrangements, by the early 1980s over half the annual FAO budget of about $500 million came from UNDP and trust funds, and the FAO was involved in many of the World Bank's agricultural sector loans as cosponsor or technical adviser. In 1984, for example, there were 184 joint Bank-FAO missions, along with cooperative development and evaluations efforts with other development funds and banks. Over the years the United States has been supportive of the FAO trend toward cofinancing and, until it withheld payment to the FAO in 1988, continued to be the major donor to both the assessed budget (25 percent) and the extraordinary budget (over 25 percent).

During the second wave development goals motivated establishment of the World Food Program (WFP) in 1963 under joint UN and FAO sponsorship. The United States and Canada were the prime movers in its creation and donated the majority of its budget. One aim of the WFP was to increase total food aid by creating a multilateral channel that would attract new donors. In the 1950s the United States provided over 90 percent of the world's food aid and Canada, most of the rest. The hope was that the WFP, by attracting new donors, would increase burden-sharing for food aid. Another aim was to strengthen the use of food aid in development projects, a use for which it was especially suited and for which bilateral channels were less appropriate. From a $50 million a year budget, largely funded by the United States and Canada, the WFP grew to handle over $1 billion annually in the mid-1980s with support from over twenty-five donors and with projects in over a hundred countries. In addition to regular development projects, the WFP provides emergency aid both from resources pledged to it and from an international bilateral reserve. Further, it also handles arrangements for some donors' bilateral food aid.

Another new international food organization was established that focused on agricultural research—a basic ingredient for economic development. The Consultative Group on International Agricultural Research was set up in 1972 to coordinate and oversee the work of various research centers such as the International Rice Research Institute (IRRI) in the Philippines and the wheat and coarse grain center in Mexico, Centro Internacional de Mejoramiento de Maize y Trigo (CIMMYT). By 1984 thirteen centers were under CGIAR auspices, and their annual budgets totaled over $175 million (CGIAR 1984). The World Bank hosts their annual budget and program review meetings in Washington; the FAO hosts their Technical Advisory Committee.

The International Fund for Agricultural Development (IFAD), established in 1977, was the final organizational creation of the development wave, though the third wave had already begun. Authorized at the 1974 World Food Conference, IFAD took two years of negotiations to reach the agreed target pledge of over $1 billion for three years' activity. Its purpose is to channel investments to small-scale farmers in developing countries using funds provided by OPEC and OECD states on a roughly 40/60 percent basis.[2]

IFAD's special existence outside the World Bank was justified by its ability to secure large pledges from wealthy Third World OPEC (Category II) countries. IFAD represents a new configuration in North-South collaboration whereby cooperation in financing development occurs in ways that the World Bank or UNDP does not do. IFAD's unique voting system, with 20 OECD states, 12 OPEC states, and 109 developing countries each having one third of the votes, gives formal power to the major contributors while allowing recipient non-oil-exporting Third World states a clear voice. The two donor groups (OPEC and OECD) have control *when* they agree, however. Of $970 million pledged by the three categories of countries, developed oil producers, and others, IFAD received nearly $890 million toward its first three years of work—short only $83 million from Iran. The 1981 replenishment yielded pledges for $1.1 billion and actual contributions of over $900 million in cash and notes.

In the 1970s a third wave of regime-building began. Third World states sought to capture control of international organizations and to channel a greater share of these organizations' budgets to developing countries' needs. This third wave generated conflict as G-77 states sought to reshape international institutions. Because G-77 countries controlled a majority of votes in the main UN bodies, they could use the one-state, one-vote principle to restructure institutions, determine who held offices, and set agendas. The resulting North-South struggle over power and redistribution became fixed with the creation of UNCTAD in 1964 and expanded with the adoption of "new international economic order" principles in 1974. This conflict was manifested in every food organization, particularly in efforts to control organizational resources, policies, and personnel.

In the FAO the G-77 sought to elect or appoint individuals from their own bloc to the secretariats; it urged increased funding for development assistance; and it tabled plans that called for the greater use of government to manage international agricultural activities. Partly as a result of changes and conflicts in FAO, when the global food panic arose in 1973 and leadership and resources were directed toward the aim of averting global food shortages, the 1974 World Food Conference was held in Rome but outside direct FAO auspices in an attempt to skirt the FAO bureaucracy (Weiss and Jordan 1976). Responsibility for the follow-up on resolutions from the conference was given to the ministers of agriculture and finance from major states. For this purpose the World Food Council was established, reporting to the UN Economic and Social Council (ECOSOC).

The WFC is composed of thirty-six member states, with about 25 percent of its membership from OECD countries. Its meetings and the work of its staff are to serve as a high-level coordinating body for ministries of agriculture, providing leadership in the UN system and among member states in solving mutually recognized problems. The council was perceived as a way to check the growing power of the Third World in the FAO, as well as an institutional vehicle that would allow ministries of agriculture to bypass (at least somewhat) cumbersome foreign ministries and UN bureaucracies. However, with an annual budget of $3 million and a professional staff of about fifteen, including the executive director, the council can do little beyond modest lobbying and the promotion of an occasional new idea. In April 1984, continuing a pattern of FAO-led institutional infighting (Fauriol 1984), the FAO director-general urged abolition of the WFC in a report to the FAO's Committee on Food Security (CFS). The proposal was met with strong opposition. Relations between FAO and WFC have recently improved, however, symbolized by the withdrawal of FAO's threat to throw the WFC out of its Rome office space.

The three financially substantial food institutions—FAO, WFP, and IFAD—and the many other minor ones create a complex labyrinth of overlapping jurisdictions. At its core remains the FAO: its staff is over six thousand and its annual budget, including nonassessed contributions, is about $500 million. Unlike the IWC, in which the Soviet Union participates, or CGIAR, which is highly technical and dominated by industrial providers, the FAO operates with little East-West conflict. Aside from partial Soviet-bloc absence, there is a nearly universal membership of 158 states. Consequently it is in a position to be involved in all food issues—production policy, trade, environmental impacts, research, information gathering, and financing of development projects. With a one-member, one-vote formal rule, the overriding cleavage in the FAO is the North-South split. OECD countries supply the bulk of its budget but have exercised diminishing control over its operation in the last two decades. Control in the FAO is worth a great deal, however, because unlike some of the highly specialized food agencies such as CGIAR or IWC, the FAO interacts formally with all national and international institutional players.

The three major food bodies located in Rome oversaw the annual spending of $1.5–$2.0 billion in the mid-1980s. The World Food Program alone in 1985, thanks to responses to the African crisis, had over a $1 billion budget, putting it well ahead of the UNDP and UNICEF as a UN development body. However, budgets fluctuate; growth in real terms for the UN system as a whole has turned negative in the last few years; and the FAO anticipates a 14 percent cut in its regular budget for the 1988–89 biennium. Table 7.1 provides comparable data on budgets, costs of staff operations, and staff size for each of the three organizations. Although it has far fewer information, research, and diplomatic obligations to fund, the efficiency of the WFP based on the ratio of staff costs to total budget is striking.

TABLE 7.1

Budget and Staff Size in Major Food Organizations, 1984–85
(in millions of U.S. $ and number of regular professional and service staff)

	Total Budget	Cost of Operations	Regular Staff
FAO	537	210	4569*
WFP	737	32.4	1122
IFAD	224	18.7	190

Sources: FAO, *Program of Work and Budget* (1986–87); IFAD, *Annual Report* (1985); Maurice Bertrand, *Some Reflections on Reforms of the UN System*, Geneva, 1985.

* Does not include about 1,300 consultants and experts under contract service provisions.

Of course, growth in budgets and personnel does not necessarily mean that the food organizations have been successful in meeting their general goals. For example, little progress toward freer trade in agriculture has occurred. The prevention of famine has been somewhat successful in Asia, but its incidence has increased in Africa. Resource transfers to assist agricultural development in poor countries have declined in the 1980s, and the number of people experiencing chronic hunger has remained static at best (World Bank 1986).

On the less ambitious goals the organizations have fared better. First, a considerable amount of technical research has been accomplished and priorities for research to aid the poorest countries have been established. Second, emergency food relief and humanitarian nutritional assistance, though imperfect, have achieved a remarkable record over the last two decades, especially in the recent African crisis. Third, FAO's information gathering and dissemination on the state of agriculture has established professional standards for the world and the most exhaustive information available. Fourth, services provided by technical staff have proved a valuable global asset. Fifth, FAO, WFP, and IFAD have become important agencies for the transfer of resources, either food or cash, directed at the most pressing problems in developing countries' food systems, notably improving small farmer production and providing nutrition for the poorest. Finally, the FAO and other bodies have served as important mediating bodies, providing forums for multilateral diplomacy and offering good offices in promoting policy coordination.

To what extent can the success and failure of the Rome-based institutions rest with the United States? The United States did play a key role in the creation of each of the three major food institutions, but its relationships with these institutions have not always been close or cordial. Given the dominance of the United States in international agricultural matters, we would expect its influence—positive or negative—to be considerable. We turn, therefore, to an examination of patterns of influence between the United States and the three organizations.

Food Organizations and the United States: Patterns of Influence

The patterns of reciprocal influence between the United States and the Rome food organizations may be analyzed in terms of three distinct categories of organizational activity: (1) promulgation of regime principles and rules, including the role of markets in agricultural policy; (2) allocation of resources directly or indirectly through policy decisions within the IGO; and (3) recruitment of personnel.

As Figure 7.1 illustrates, the analysis encompasses both interactions between the United States and the three IGOs and patterns of influence among IGOs, given that each intergovernmental organization also has the capacity to influence the othes. It also depicts major subunits (executive, legislative, interest groups, and IGO organs), along with their avenues of political influence (votes, budgetary supports, requests for action, and consultations). The principal focus, however, is on the U.S.-FAO relationship.

Table 7.2 summarizes crude judgments concerning the amount of influence each institutional actor and the United States have exerted on each other in each of the three categories. The judgments are based on ten years of participant observation and academic research on these bodies; they are congruent with judgments offered in recent work of others (Talbot and Moyer 1986). The chapter incorporates a few cases that led me to these assessments. Significant influence is claimed to exist when the actions of one actor have actually altered the behavior or outcomes of the other. Clearly specific influence is most readily detected when the United States acts in distinctive ways, as distinguished from the more typical cases

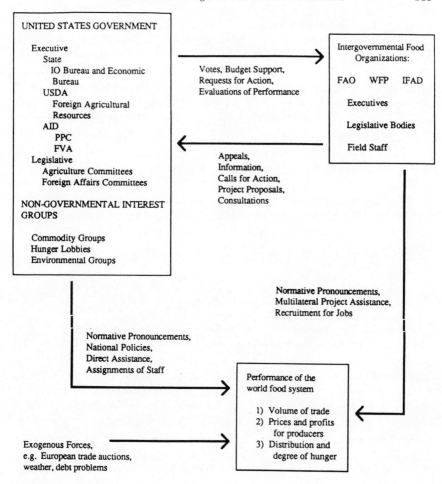

Figure 7.1   Influence Paths among the United States and Major World Food IGOs

TABLE 7.2
Influence Matrix among Three Food Organizations and the U.S. Government

Influence Exercised by	Organization Influenced											
	U.S.			FAO			WFP			IFAD		
	I	A	P	I	A	P	I	A	P	I	A	P
U.S.		n.a.		mod	slt	slt	sig	mod	mod	mod	sig	nil
FAO	nil	slt	nil		n.a.		mod	mod	mod	mod	slt	slt
WFP	slt	slt	nil	slt	mod	nil		n.a.		nil	slt	nil
IFAD	slt	mod	nil	nil	mod	slt	nil	slt	nil		n.a.	

Note: Amount exercised over ideas (I), Allocation (A), and Recruitment of personnel (P) during the 1980s.
KEY: nil; slight (slt); moderate (mod); significant (sig); not applicable (n.a.).

in which the United States is part of the UN "Geneva Group," or acts in concert with OECD or Group B bloc countries. To find occasions when a food agency influenced U.S. behavior, that international agency must have initially acted in ways independent of U.S. preferences and in accord with secretariat or internal goals rather than merely reflecting the interest of its dominant members. Table 7.2 suggests that the FAO and the other intergovernmental organizations have had little influence on the United States in the 1980s, but the United States has had varying and occasionally important influence over them. The two-way influence is clearly less than occurred in the 1950s and 1960s (see Hambidge 1955; Jones 1965).

We now turn to examine interaction of the three IGOs and the United States as depicted in Figure 7.1, looking first at the promulgation of regime principles. In particular, we are concerned with the declining role of the United States in shaping these regime principles and, in turn, being affected by them.

The United States, the Food IGOs, and the Promulgation of Regime Principles

Three issues of principle have bedeviled international agricultural affairs: (1) Should governments intervene to support domestic production and protect farmers' incomes? (2) Should free trade govern international agricultural markets? (3) Should resources for development provided by industrial countries be targeted among recipient countries and projects principally in order to help the poor or to maximize production growth? Although pure principles would not work in practice, the debate among competing recommendations is instructive. Even more to the point is the U.S. position on the actual principles and norms promulgated.

In response to the foregoing issues, the secretariats of the international food organizations have generally argued in favor of reducing the inefficiencies and distortions created by protectionist farm policies of *developed* industrial states but accept government intervention in LDCs. They have favored coordination among governments to regulate international food markets and to reduce world price instability and have urged that the lowest income food-deficit states be targeted for support, rejecting a principle of basing allocations on the "correctness" of a recipient's economic policy.

On all three points the U.S. position has been the opposite of the secretariats'. Indeed, the United States now rejects many of the principles and norms it earlier helped to establish. The United States has opposed such international regime norms as ending hunger through holding international food security stocks, increasing the flow of food aid, and providing greater investment in LDC agriculture. Although these norms were espoused at the 1974 World Food Conference, in various and interrelated ways the United States and other states have ignored them and continued market-distorting practices such as domestic farm subsidies. No inter-governmental mechanisms to control market instabilities have been created despite resolutions calling for them (Hopkins 1987b). World food price instabilities have increased since the 1960s and have decreased in the 1980s only because of changes in the size of U.S.-subsidized surpluses that "overhang" world markets. Finally, food insecurities have grown as the absolute number of people without assured access to minimum food requirements has increased (World Bank 1986). Conflicts between the United States and IGOs over regime principles in each of these three areas—production inefficiencies, stability of food prices, and security of food supplies—will be examined in greater detail.

Regime Principles Governing Production Inefficiencies

International exhortations to encourage efficiency in worldwide pro-duction have not worked. There continues to be overinvestment and wasteful agricultural production in some parts of the world and under-employment of people and resources elsewhere. Farm subsidies encourage inefficiencies in industrialized Europe and North America; farm taxation discourages full production in many developing countries (Schultz 1978).

A major FAO confeence in 1979, the World Conference on Agrarian Reform and Rural Development (WCARRD), drew on a growing consensus of experts on the key barriers to economic growth and develop-ment in the Third World. It enunciated a program of action to achieve greater equity and participation by rural populations through a variety of policies including land reform and small farmer assistance. Progress toward these goals has been modest. Indeed, by the mid-1980s many African states had heeded these norms. There has been no corresponding pronounce-ment, however, on adjustments appropriate in developed country agriculture. The FAO and other bodies have done little to prod industrial-ized states toward "appropriate" policies in this area over the last decade. Although the United States is critical of other developed countries' agricultural subsidies, it has made no move to reduce its own heavy expenditures. So overproduction in rich countries and underproduction in poor countries continue and the protectionist trade pressures arising from this imbalance encourage perpetuation of the situation. Behind the agricultural production inefficiencies lies the failure to achieve significant reductions in trade barriers. Tariff and nontariff barriers limit exports of

American products to European and Japanese markets and exclude from North America and Europe some crops that are grown in both tropical and temperate zones (such as sugar). The United States has made reform of agricultural trade rules a high priority for the Uruguay Round of GATT negotiations and has won reluctant agreement in principle from the EC and Japan for an end to agricultural subsidies (see Karns, chapter 6).

A related consequence of protectionism and agricultural subsidies has been greater volatility and depression of international prices, most dramatically in sugar. There was also a large, costly, and internationally distorting accumulation of dairy and grain products in the United States and Europe between 1980 and 1988. Price instability is the second area of conflict over regime principles.

Principles Governing Price Instabilities

International efforts to reduce price instabilities that have plagued agricultural commodities have been notably unsuccessful. Traditionally tropical crops have been most afflicted, but since 1973 the world grain trade has also been subject to substantial variability. Price instabilities have been compounded by exchange rate fluctuations.

Two schemes proposed in the early 1970s—one for an international grain reserve (discussed by the FAO) and another for a "common fund" (raised by UNCTAD and the FAO)—have fallen by the wayside in large part because of U.S. opposition. Advantages from these schemes were deemed marginal at best for northern countries, and market-oriented ideology came to predominate among policymakers in the United States, especially after 1980.

In the absence of international agreements, minor trade wars have ensued through the use of special trade subsidies to capture or recapture markets with significant effects on prices. In January 1983, for example, the United States made a special government-to-government sale to Egypt of 1.3 million tons of wheat flour. The sale displaced an entire year of expected flour sales from France. The United States used its large food aid program to Egypt as leverage for the sales, and it used discounts to American flour millers selling Consumer Credit Corporation (CCC) stocks well below prevailing prices (that is, U.S. support prices) so that flour to Egypt would be cheaper than European flour. Various soft credit loans have also been used by both Europe and the United States as they compete in a world grain market that has shrunk nearly 40 million tons between 1983 and 1985.

The international grain reserve negotiations were initiated after the 1974 World Food Conference to improve food security and thereby to limit price fluctuations. Initially a 60-million-ton reserve scheme was discussed in 1975. By the time talks collapsed in 1979, the proposal was for a 15–20-million-ton arrangement tied only to wheat. Even this was rejected largely because of opposition from Third World states that found the price ranges unfair (Hopkins 1987b). Since then reserve stocks have never fallen to the historic lows of 1973–75 when they reached about 13 percent of annual world consumption. In fact they reached near historic highs in the 1980s, averaging 24 percent of consumption until 1986. Above 18 percent downward pressure on prices occurs. This was the principal factor accounting for the low world prices in 1984–87 (FAO 1986; Hopkins and Puchala 1979). If grain reserves had been held between 16 and 18 percent of consumption, historical relationships suggest that world prices would have maintained greater parity with other commodities and prevented an erosion of farm incomes and asset values. Supply management failed, however, and the rural sector worldwide has suffered.

Since the collapse of the international wheat reserve talks in February 1979, no significant progress on policy coordination, reduced trade barriers, or common steps to stabilize prices and supply/demand relationships has been achieved. Both Europe and the United States have made small efforts to discourage additional production, but with no direct supply controls applied in Europe. Although a full-blown trade war has been avoided, actions such as the subsidized grain sale to Egypt demonstrate the U.S. unilateral effort to avoid losing its share of its market. In 1978–80 the United States exported over 55 percent of cereal traded in the world market, and the EEC was a net importer. In 1987–88 U.S. exports were equal to less than 50 percent of world trade, whereas the EEC had a growing share of the export market. Total trade in 1987–88 was 196 million tons, a level above trade in the late 1970s but 15 million tons below that of 1980–84, which averaged over 210 million tons (FAO 1989: 2, 26–27). The trade conflict has occurred through unilateral actions, and the only moderating efforts have been bilateral U.S.-EC talks. The United States has perceived no interest (perhaps incorrectly) in coordinating policy through the FAO or other bodies to manage these supply and price instabilities. Essentially the United States has bypassed the FAO. This is a full reversal from relations in the 1946–48 period when the FAO was in Washington and was a welcome partner in setting and legitimating international agriculture policy.

Principles Governing Food Supply Insecurities

In spite of general agreement on the need to reduce insecurities of food supply, both chronic insecurity faced by those in continuing poverty and variable insecurity confronting people whose access to food suddenly fails continue to plague the world (World Bank 1987). Impassioned speeches, dramatic media coverage, and tons of paper and ink poured into international documents have done little to deal with the long-term problem of supply insecurity.

A Cereal Import Facility, established by the IMF in 1981 to supply additional currency to developing countries when they faced unusual requirements to import food, has been little used in spite of major needs that have arisen since then (Ezekiel 1985). The FAO has in fact ignored this effort largely because it was a U.S. initiative outside FAO control and unlikely to provide any organizational advantage to it or its most needy clients.

Declining food security in Africa in the 1975–85 decade suggests clearly the inadequate results of the prodding and encouragement of the international regime for long-term food security measures. The United States, for example, has cut development aid to African countries and withheld its FAO contributions, although the central goal of IFAD is to support long-term, small farmer solutions to food shortages, especially in Africa. The food institutions and major donors including the United States did respond effectively to the Sub-Saharan African famine of 1983–85, almost tripling bilateral and multilateral relief. Food aid was 2.3 million tons in 1981 or 27 percent of all grain imports to the area; by 1985 it was 6.1 million tons representing 51 percent of imports. Although much of the import growth in grains was covered by aid, the need to pay for 6.1 million tons of commercial grain imports by African states with bankrupt treasuries and starving populations pressed hard on countries already desperate (United Nations 1987).

Thus although a norm of preventing starvation was well established by the 1960s and continues to be upheld by the United States, the resources and instruments for satisfying this norm are inadequate, and both the U.S. share and U.S. efforts to encourage burden sharing by others such as the Japanese have been in decline since 1980. In general the international food institutions have not performed well, failing to intervene in time to avert famine disasters. They have not made headway in reducing the total number of chronically malnourished people.

From the foregoing examination of the problems associated with the promulgation of food regime principles it is evident that the conflict between food IGO secretariats and the United States is not the only cause. Other major agricultural states and the IGOs themselves bear responsibility for the failure to achieve security in food supplies, stability in prices, and efficiency in production.

Conversely, the Rome institutions have done well in excluding political issues dealing with Israel and South Africa, for example, from discussions of regime principles, thanks to the recognition that raising them would be counterproductive to the organization's main purpose. Thus although the FAO and WFP have been responsive to many recipient country interests and needs, including states such as Cuba and Vietnam, which are pariahs to the United States, the FAO secretariat especially has worked hard to avoid gratuitous conflicts. By anticipating the negative response of Western donors to largely symbolic challenges expressing the political preferences of Third World countries, FAO was able to avoid direct confrontation over political issues in allocating resources. Only on principles such as sovereign control over agricultural policy and action, production inputs as the key constraint to greater production, and the desirability of larger resources for transfer have the FAO and other bodies openly been at odds with various U.S. administrations, especially the Reagan administration.

As Table 7.2 suggests, the United States has affected the ideas of food agency members but seems unmoved itself by the food agencies. Likewise, the United States has not succeeded in gaining legitimation for privatization by the FAO, WFP, or IFAD, though it has been undeterred from advancing these ideas on a bilateral basis or through the World Bank.

Allocation of Resources

In 1987 the issue of FAO management resources came to a head. FAO budget cuts, U.S. failure to meet its assigned duties, and a decline in ICP funds all contributed to tight restrictions on spending and staff reductions. This policy area of resource size and allocation is of primary interest to the United States and the UN food bodies. The size and conditions of U.S. pledges to the three operating agencies (FAO, WFP, and IFAD) are major factors in their political capacity. The United States has contributed 25 percent of the FAO and WFP regular budgets and about 17 percent of the IFAD second replenishment (1986) pledge. Increased U.S. support for agricultural aid accounted for its initial support of IFAD and contributed to the growth in extrabudgetary allocations by the FAO, which in the mid-1980s equaled about half its expenditures. Now U.S. funding is shrinking relatively and the FAO, as the only food agency with an "assessed" budget, finds itself burdened by the Kassebaum Amendment requiring UN organs to give major contributors more power over spending as a condition for the United States to meet its assessed share. The amendment is seen as an unfair burden in FAO because it was a response to displeasure generated elsewhere in the UN system and by symbolic actions that the FAO had studiously sought to avoid. In 1988 the United States cut its share to FAO below 20 percent, creating a financial crisis, and dropped its support for WFP for 1989–90 from $250 to $175 million, causing a program shrinkage. The Reagan administration proposed still further cuts in contributions to FAO for FY 1989 from roughly $50 to $25 million. This 50 percent cut—the largest of any IGO—reflected the administration's displeasure with the organization and particularly with the reelection of Edouard Saouma as director general (Lewis 1988: A14). In 1989 the Bush administration, though more sympathetic to multilateral bodies, did not change its negative policy toward the FAO.

Exacerbating its funding situation, since 1980 the FAO has lost two interagency battles affecting its resources. The UNDP was ceded the right to implement some of its projects, thus reducing funding through the FAO and other executing agencies. The UNDP also reduced its allowance for overhead or management costs on the remaining FAO projects funded by UNDP. The FAO thus "earns" less. Not surprisingly, the United States is the largest contributor to UNDP. The FAO also lost some guarantees of income in a battle with WFP over the cost of services and the obligation to use FAO expertise. The United States played no great role in either battle, though USAID sided generally with the voluntary UN agencies (UNDP, WFP) while the State Department preferred to remain neutral or press for a peaceful reconciliation.

With respect to allocations among development projects, the United States has not raised serious arguments over FAO projects to countries in U.S. disfavor such as Angola, Cuba, Vietnam, and Nicaragua. Projects in these countries reflect the UN principle of something for every member more than any preference for socialist states. Furthermore, Costa Rica's allocation was three times as large as Cuba's in 1985, for example, though it has only one-fourth the population. We can conclude, therefore, that the relative size of allocations reflects FAO's sensitivity to U.S. preferences.

On similar allocation issues in the WFP, the United States has engaged in ritual-like expressions of opposition, stating that none of its contributions can be used for the projects or arguing that the projects were badly conceived or prepared. It has also raised questions regarding making decisions by consensus. However, rather than create precedents that could backfire, usually the United States has simply abstained or absented itself on "unfriendly" country cases. If consensus were defined as no dissent, the WFP's thirty-member board, the Committee on Food Aid Programs and Practices (CFA), would be faced with a veto situation and would quickly become hopelessly deadlocked. If it meant majority or even 60 percent voting, the United States would lose almost every contest, as it does in the General Assembly. So the CFA has established informal ways to allow dissent to be expressed. Unless the WFP leadership decides to withdraw a project, however, all projects are approved.

One area of controversy between the United States and FAO over allocations has been the size and use of emergency food aid. WFP's normal operations involved projects prepared by staff and national governments, with technical review and advice provided by other bodies, most often in the FAO. Emergency aid, however, though delivered by the WFP, is under FAO authority: the director-general *must* approve the WFP executive director's recommendation. Because emergency food goes to governments, is quick dispersing, requires little accountability, and is a short-term commitment, it is an excellent device for cementing political ties between IGO and governmental officials.

In the 1970s the United States tried to limit the portion of food aid in the WFP biannual budget to be used for emergencies in order to keep development projects from being doled out as diplomatic chips by the director general. The United States feared that emergency aid would be misused and/or would squeeze funds from longer-term development projects. Less developed countries, Scandinavian countries, and the FAO wanted few bureaucratic controls on emergency uses; the United States, Canada, and other OECD countries wanted ceilings. A $45 billion ceiling was agreed on, but implementation came to be a function of FAO/WFP maneuvering and in general the United States did not prevail. This was partly the result of real and mounting food crises, particularly the African food crisis of 1984–85.

Although the United States has lost on issues of who receives allocations of WFP resources, in October 1986 the United States and Canada were able to win major concessions on the types of projects to be submitted. At the twenty-second CFA meeting projects in Grenada, Rwanda, Senegal, and Madagascar were cases in which all food was to be sold and proceeds used for government budget assistance. The United States and Canada saw this as an intrusion into the type of aid they gave bilaterally, a perversion of the original intent of WFP's founding, and asked that the projects be withdrawn. They settled, however, for a promise that WFP would study the principles for such aid, linked as it is to the World Bank or recipient country efforts at "structural adjustment." In the interim the WFP agreed not to submit similar proposals linking food aid to structural adjustment. It is clear that the WFP listens to the United States very carefully and does so especially carefully when other large donors are supportive. Yet in October 1987 a WFP paper defining its past actions (including the four projects listed earlier) was accepted as a basis for continued WFP action.

The whole process of managing projects at the WFP has been influenced by the United States. Until the 1980s FAO was the major source of technical assistance in reviewing and formulating projects on an informal basis. In 1983–86 under an American project manager, a new set of rules for project preparation, largely following USAID patterns, was established with CFA approval. Although the FAO wanted more control and more use of its technical staff in the preparation of projects, the WFP asserted its autonomy, changing procedures for using other agencies' technical inputs. This meant the WFP was free to work with the World Bank or IFAD or other agencies in preparing a project and FAO might not get paid for working on them. The FAO might get only the same courtesy as other UN agencies—that is, advanced circulation and the right to comment during the meeting to approve them. FAO officials, in documents sent to the CFA, called the project cycle proposals "regressive." WFP and FAO were having a modest "war" over other issues of organizational autonomy during the same period, including control of staff rotation and hiring and costing of services.

On almost all issues the United States sided with the WFP. By 1986 the WFP had "won" with new arrangements with FAO giving it at least a portion of what it sought. The project cycle was adopted. On the institutional issues, a special committee of experts recommended changes short of rewriting the basic texts (the constitutions of FAO and WFP), and these were accepted by both WFP and FAO protagonists in light of heavy pressure to end their struggle from most of the OECD countries, including the United States, but not Australia or Canada, which were outspoken warriors on behalf of the WFP.

The most significant budget struggle has concerned IFAD and its ability to secure resources from the United States. The U.S. government was ambivalent on the desirability of this body from its inception. In 1984, at the time of negotiations over a second replenishment, the United States initially offered to withdraw, which would have meant zero resources and, quite possibly, the collapse of the organization. On Capitol Hill the administration (Office of Management and Budget) request was less than half the remaining obligation of $90 million for the first replenishment given to IFAD. IFAD developed strong support, however, by encouraging its natural allies at USAID and USDA. These forces were aided on Capitol Hill by lobbying of Bread for the World, the Hunger Project, and other groups. Senator Hatfield and his staff decided to push for the full $90 million obligated in 1981. It was appropriated and provided to IFAD. The Democratic-controlled House sent a letter to Secretary of State Shultz on the IFAD issue. Even the Republican Senate concurred. When the president and vice president of IFAD came to Washington in 1985 for some modest lobbying, their open luncheon for Hill staffers, usually attended by less than a dozen specialists, drew 150.

The growing food crisis in Africa and IFAD's early success with projects in Bangladesh and Africa, along with a favorable study of the organization's efficiency by a "blue-ribbon panel" chaired by Elmer Staats (retired head of the GAO), also contributed to the dramatic alteration in the mood toward and awareness in Congress of IFAD's situation (Interview with Vice President Donald Brown 1986). By January 1986 the United States agreed to a second replenishment, decreasing its own share among OECD states and accepting a drop in the OPEC members' share along with an increase in the overall OECD share. Other events had contributed by this time to a new attitude toward Third World debt and the role of soft lending even at the U.S. Treasury Department, which then pushed for a full IDA replenishment and accepted the IFAD funding as not competitive with IDA.

Thus IFAD was able to influence the United States and secure allocations to ensure its survival. IFAD had not attempted, however, to influence U.S. trade rules that limit export markets for the very poor country producers the organization finances.

Recruitment of Personnel

Selection of the top leadership of any organization is an important element shaping the character, direction, and accessibility of that organization. This is equally true with respect to the selection of key UN officials, especially those in specialized agencies that operate much like individual baronies in the UN system. By controlling appointments and orders to field and working-level officials, an agency head wields great power. The United States has tried to influence the selection of all the top officials in the Rome agencies. From 1947 to 1959 an American held the director-general post of the FAO and ran it similar to an international version of a ministry of agriculture. By 1975, when Edouard Saouma, a Lebanese, took the reins of the FAO from Addeke Boerma, a Dutchman, the transition to Third World, development-oriented leadership was complete. The U.S.-supported candidate, a Canadian, was soundly defeated.

Given FAO's current membership, the United States has no chance of providing a director-general of FAO or of controlling senior appointments, except to indicate degrees of support for Americans who might be chosen by the incumbent director-general. Of course, this does not mean appointments in the FAO are not an instrument of control or international bargaining. In fact, many appointments, especially of former Third World diplomats, appear to be just that. The United States is below its "national" quota of over 12 percent of appointments and can do little about it.

Saouma instituted a "decentralization" in 1976, creating FAO country representatives as ambassadors to those developing countries with several FAO projects. Representatives and FAO field staff work directly for the director-general and give little attention to the UN principle that all UN field personnel are to be coordinated by the UNDP representative.

Director-General Saouma has also cultivated strong personal ties with most of the permanent representatives of governments accredited to the FAO and has traveled widely to meet heads of state, especially in developing countries. By 1981, when he stood for reelection, there was no open opposition, so thoroughly had he developed personal support throughout the developing world. In 1987, however, Saouma was opposed by Moise Mensah from Benin, assistant president of IFAD and a former official at FAO and the World Bank. Mensah had the official backing of the Organization of African Unity, Japan, many European countries, and Canada. In the election the United States, not historically a supporter of Saouma, did virtually nothing. Faced with competing views at USDA, the State Department, and USAID, the Reagan administration eventually endorsed Mensah late in the process but then did little to promote his candidacy.

Positions in the Rome-based institutions have not been highly sought by Americans in recent years particularly as the attractions of salary and life in Rome have diminished. The United States has exercised only modest control over who gets posts. Most American appointees are recruited through informal professional networks. Even senior posts at WFP, where the United States is generally acknowledged to deserve important representation, are not subject to much direct U.S. control. Furthermore, the politics of WFP-FAO relations have impinged on personnel recruitment. Indeed, in seeking a successor for the project management post, the number three job at WFP, Executive Director James Ingram (an American) nominated an American as anticipated, but not one initially among those proposed by the United States. Even after the United States gave its backing, FAO Director-General Saouma vetoed the appointment and held the job open for over six months as a ploy for U.S. support for his reelection.

In 1986 a decision had to be made regarding the appointment of a new WFP head because the current executive director's term expired in April 1987. Ingram, who had led the WFP into battles with the FAO over autonomy, was very unpopular with FAO, especially with Director-General Saouma. Although Saouma had vowed to "tie his hands behind his back" before signing papers reappointing Ingram, in the end he agreed to the reappointment and announced it at the final CFA meeting of Ingram's first term in October 1986. The turnabout was a result of two factors: united OECD support for Ingram and the onset of an election campaign for Saouma. The swing of the United States behind Ingram was the final necessary condition for this outcome, but the United States had few other options as the moment to take a stand arrived.

Ingram's reappointment gave a sharp focus to the capacity of different organizations and states to influence major decisions and represented symbolically a reward for a hard-working, impersonal management style. It demonstrated further the erosion of FAO control over WFP and the difficulty of forging cross-bloc coalitions.

At IFAD senior personnel have been recruited fairly widely from 44 of the 129 member countries; nevertheless, since its founding a clear understanding exists about top leadership. The president is to come from an OPEC country; the vice president must be an American. In practice much like at the IMF and World Bank, OPEC and the United States consult informally, but each is expected to make a recommendation eventually that will be accepted more or less automatically. Given that the vital element in IFAD funding to date has been negotiations with OPEC countries and the United States, it makes sense that the two top posts go to people most able to work effectively on behalf of IFAD. Other senior IFAD posts, like most of those at WFP, are held by people chosen for experience and competency and to achieve diffusion of national representation.

Working-Level Collaboration

In recent years U.S. government officials charged with liaison to food IGOs have been reactive, even resistant, to the work of the FAO. In other organs they have been more positive but virtually never offered leadership. At the various Rome institutions Rome-based U.S. officials and members of the secretariat collaborate only in highly technical and informal ways. Outside Rome, either in Washington or in the capitals of major developing countries, U.S.-IGO exchanges on food are even slimmer. FAO officials are seldom involved in coordinating aid or working with bilateral aid agencies. To this organizational gap is added the fact that the U.S. governmental and FAO personnel stationed overseas often see themselves serving different purposes. Consequently, influence in either direction is not great.

Since 1981 in particular, the United States has provided little or no leadership in the Rome agencies. This is partly a reflection of the generic style of the Reagan and early Bush administrations, partly a result of competition between international goals and domestic policies, and partly a decline in U.S. attention and resources for global leadership. Yet this U.S. abdication of leadership has not followed on a decline of U.S. relative agricultural capacity but, rather, results from a lack of interest. This may have been compounded by the decline of USDA's influence within the U.S. government. This decline coincides with the shrinking proportion of Americans engaged in farming (about 3 percent), weakening of the farm lobbies, and growing criticism over commodity programs, which, while eating up large budget outlays in the 1980s (over $26 billion in 1986), have not produced sufficient surpluses to permit the USDA to manipulate export markets as in earlier decades.

Thus the three categories of international food agency activity—regime creation, resource allocations, and recruitment of personnel—have not been important to U.S. officials in the 1980s. Correspondingly, U.S. influence in these agencies has declined.

Regime Influence on the United States

It might be argued that the decline in U.S. influence over the FAO and other food organs should correspond with a rise in their influence over the United States. Were U.S.-IGO interactions a zero-sum game, then a rise in regime influence over the United States might particularly be expected. This has not been the case; power arises more often from mutual coordination than from confrontation (Keohane 1984; Lasswell and Kaplan 1950). Thus whereas food IGOs' influence on the United states have been modest and have not grown during the last decade in which U.S. influence fell, on some issues the food regime norms have had an impact. On particular issues of policy and budget allocation, each of the three food institutions was able to exercise some influence over U.S. policy. For example, during the African food crisis in 1983–85, Congress was more excited and generous than the executive branch; members of Congress cited FAO statistics on the food aid need for Africa, whereas USAID and other executive agencies used internally developed, often lower, estimates. Congress concluded by supporting an expanded bilateral food aid delivery program to Africa and augmented multilateral funding. The media attention given this crisis provided greater leverage over public opinion and congressional sentiment to those who supported the policies advanced by the FAO and WFP. Without the favorable predispositions created by this calamity, the modest shifts in U.S. behavior toward positions promoted by these institutions would probably not have occurred.

In addition, as noted, the Reagan administration was turned around on the second replenishment of IFAD in 1986 thanks to strong lobbying from hunger groups, support from key members of Congress, and a few sympathetic bureaucrats, all nurtured to a degree by IFAD.

Aside from these few policy shifts, no U.S. action—whether in stating broad principles, formulating domestic farm, foreign aid, or trade policy, or recruiting personnel—shows evidence of being influenced by the intergovernmental food bodies. USDA and FAO do cooperate a great deal on technical issues, but except in regions of the world where the United States has little commercial interest, the USDA seldom draws directly on FAO data. Basically the United States has a competing data set with FAO, though they do cross-check each other. Thus even the hypothesis that the United States is influenced by international organization data or definition of a situation seldom holds.

Explaining Declining U.S. Influence

Why should U.S. influence have declined? Although the extremely modest influence of the food institutions on U.S. policy has changed little over the years, U.S. use of the Rome-based institutions for its ends has clearly declined over the last thirty years. Two factors provide particularly potent explanations of why this decline has occurred: issue area and organizational changes. These changes have, in turn, affected the quality of American leadership in the food institutions, especially during the Reagan administration. Yet despite this decline, the U.S. government does exercise some control over the Rome institutions, and this too merits attention.

Issue Area

Most actors in the food issue area attach priority to questions of redistribution; Third World economic development rather than the provision of specialized public services has become the top priority. The regime's goals are to reduce poverty; providing information and advice, coordinating research, and mediating agricultural policy coordination are clearly secondary functions. To achieve the goals of the regime, the majority of members are prepared to use government resources to provide needed inputs and price incentives rather than rely on the free market. International commodity agreements are but one acceptable instrument. Both strong state intervention and international commodity agreements have been contrary to U.S. economic liberalism. Because the United States has seldom had many supporters even among developed states, U.S. delegates are not in a position to bargain much over the language of resolutions, the type of approach for projects, or the correctness of government intervention to subsidize inputs or control markets, at least not once the debate becomes public. Most U.S. influence comes from private lobbying well in advance of public discussion among committees or governing bodies. Yet the issues on which U.S. preferences have been overridden have generally been too minor for the United States to threaten to withdraw from one of the food organizations; that threat, nevertheless, is the major source of control left to the United States. In their sum the issues discussed were only marginally consequential for the United States or for the world's food system. Consequently the U.S. promotion of a free market ideology— which, given U.S. farm programs, is especially hypocritical—has not been embraced by the intergovernmental food bodies.

During the 1980s there has been a further ideological shift with renewed interest in privatization. In the Rome agencies there have been calls for greater use of "markets" in addressing food problems (Ikenberry 1987), but the World Bank and IMF rather than the FAO, WFP, or IFAD have been most important in facilitating this ideological shift. The rise of privatization ideology has occurred in food IGOs rather independently of U.S. influence. In developing states the shift is a result largely of bilateral U.S., European, and multilateral bank influence, as can be seen in certain Africa and Asian countries such as Senegal, as well as India and Indonesia (World Bank 1986).

Organizational Characteristics

The organizations based in Rome have been strongly influenced by these changes in the agriculture issue area largely because of the growth in membership from Third World states sympathetic to nonmarket instruments. From a Washington-based, U.S.-led FAO in the 1940s, the food IGOs have become a Rome-based, G-77-swayed set of organs.

In addition, interorganizational frictions and disputes among the various institutions have made the organizations less attractive as instruments of U.S. policy. This past interorganizational conflict between FAO and WFP was particularly evident during the first eleven years of Director-General Saouma's leadership at FAO. Saouma's patriarchal leadership style exacerbated the conflicts.

Since 1985 an era of improved relations among the food agencies has replaced the "war" between the FAO and WFP. This détente promises to reduce the organizational energy wasted by infighting and thus make all the agencies a bit less inward looking. It could also enhance the United States' prospects for reestablishing a position of greater leadership. These bodies' common vulnerability to withdrawal of budgetary support by the United States or other allied states has been responsible for the effort to end internecine IGO strife in Rome. The U.S. withholding of funds from its assessed contributions to the FAO in 1987 and 1988 has severely strapped the FAO and WFP.

The other principal factor is the shift by Saouma from a calculus of power wielding to one of power seeking. For the first time since 1975, the 1987 reelection campaign for the FAO director-general had an undetermined quality about it. The United States, with supporting votes it commands from states in Central America, Africa, and the Pacific—and with its position as largest budget contributor—was potentially the most important vote influencer. Recognizing this, Saouma encouraged the United States to put up a candidate to head the WFP and sought cordial ties with the United States through appointments of Americans and quick responses to requests, as with the rapid establishment of a group to fight the African locust threat in summer 1986. Yet Saouma's reelection in 1987 is a classic illustration of how U.S. domestic politics (notably the Reagan administration's indifference toward UN affairs) led to a failure of influence. In spite of claims of Saouma's mismanagement of funds and use of trust funds for political purposes, the United States took serious action only after his reelection (Pilon 1988).

Domestic Political Factors

Both the changing nature of the issue area, still largely antithetical to U.S. ideology, and the conflicts among food IGOs have resulted in a diminished American commitment to exerting active leadership in the food institutions. Domestic political factors provide additional explanation given that much depends on the attitudes of relevant U.S. governmental actors toward the international institutions.

The diffusion of power in Washington and lack of international experience among the Reagan administration's senior appointees in the USDA contributed to the absence of coordination in U.S. leadership. In the Rome context, where the State Department's International Organization Bureau formally holds sway as interagency coordinator, little collaboration or influence occurs. Recent U.S. ambassadors to the food organizations have brought little diplomatic or professional agriculture expertise to their posts. The trend toward reduced U.S. leadership in the food institutions was particularly marked in the Reagan administration. The ambassadorial post was abolished by the Bush administration. The opposition of the G-77 and multilateral bodies to U.S. recommendations for trade, investment, and marketing strategies have led right-wing groups in particular (such as the Heritage Foundation) to attack the FAO as mismanaged (Fauriol 1984) and, more recently, as the actual cause of the food problem in Ethiopia (Pilon 1988). But not all domestic groups have been negative. The "hunger" lobbies referred to previously support multilateral and bilateral involvement in international agricultural, food, and technology transfers and were very active in securing the survival of IFAD in 1984.

U.S. Agricultural Dominance: The Persistence and Limits of Influence

Because the United States has extensive expertise in agriculture, provides a major portion of food trade internationally on commercial and aid terms, and is a key contributor to financing agricultural development, its influence on the issue area of world food affairs remains pervasive. But the U.S. use of IGOs as a vehicle for exercising influence or legitimating its action is minimal. On minor issues of information sharing and enhancing common epistemic communities of specialists, U.S. interest and influence in IGOs are felt. On major issues the decline in U.S. influence cannot be explained by a decline in comparative base resources in the food issue area but, rather, to a general hegemonic decline that diffused unnecessarily to food affairs and to domestic politics. This situation contrasts with a period of leadership a decade or more ago.

On matters of practical policy and allocation of resources, the United States has been successful in cutting the budgets of FAO and IFAD by reducing its own contributions, but the United States has had little impact on how cuts are absorbed. The U.S. executive branch can still expect and get a number of top slots, but it has been relatively unsuccessful in recent years (with the exception of Donald Brown, vice president of IFAD) in placing Americans of its choice in vacant senior positions. Since the late 1970s the United States had done little to make coordinated and planned use of these positions to influence or harmonize the actions of the intergovernmental food bodies.

Conclusion

Can the United States revitalize some of its latent power in the FAO, WFP, and IFAD? Will the privatization and free market orientation now permeating some development institutions affect the Rome institutions and thus facilitate a renewed U.S. role in the food regime? Will the decline in interorganizational conflict give the U.S. government an added impetus for involvement? With market-oriented philosophies increasingly in vogue, the distance between U.S. ideology and that of many LDCs (who collectively can exercise great power in the food organizations) is reduced. Furthermore, as budget crises occur in the IGOs—particularly the FAO, which has been cut back the most in obligated U.S. funding (not counting UNESCO)—budget support will be increasingly valuable to competing LDC blocs. U.S. influence, even with Saouma continuing as FAO director-general until 1993, can be more effective in shaping regime principles and resource allocations and even getting its preferred candidates into UN posts. To accomplish these goals, however, the United States will need to turn its organizational and financial strengths to such ends.

Notes

1. For a discussion of the utility of using a regime approach to the issue of food, see Hopkins and Puchala (1978: 598–99).
2. The best account of IFAD can be found in King (1985).

References

Bertrand, Maurice (1985). *Some Reflections on Reforms of the UN System*. Geneva.
Consultative Group on International Agricultural Research [CGIAR] 1984. *1984 Report* (October). Washington, DC: World Bank.
Ezekiel, Hannan (1985). "The IMG Cereal Import Scheme." *Report to FAO* (April). Washington, DC: IFPRI.
FAO (1989). *Food Outlook* (May). Rome.
Fauriol, Georges (1984). *The Food and Agriculture Organization: A Flawed Strategy in the War against Hunger*. Washington, DC: Heritage Foundation.
Hambidge, Gove (1955). *The Story of FAO*. New York: D. Van Nostrand.
Hopkins, Raymond F. (1987a). "The Evolution of Food Aid: Toward a Development-First Regime." In J. Price Gittinger et al., eds., *Food Policy*. Baltimore: Johns Hopkins University Press, 246–60.
———— (1987b). "The Wheat Negotiation." In I. William Zartman, ed., *Positive Sum: Improving North-South Relations*. New Brunswick, NJ: Transaction Books, 115–48.
Hopkins, Raymond F., and Donald J. Puchala (1978). "Perspectives on the International Relations of Food." *International Organization*, 32(3), 581–616.
Hopkins, Raymond F., and Donald J. Puchala, eds. (1979). *The Global Political Economy of Food*. Madison: University of Wisconsin Press.
Ikenberry, John (1987). "The Spread of Norms in the International System." Unpublished paper presented at the American Political Science Association meeting, Chicago, September 5.
Jones, Joseph M. (1965). *The United Nations at Work: Developing Land, Forests, Ocean . . . and People*. Oxford: Pergamon Press.
Keohane, Robert O. (1984). *After Hegemony: Cooperation and Discord in the World Political Economy*. Princeton: Princeton University Press.
King, John Andrews (1985). "International Fund for Agricultural Development. The First Six Years." *Development Policy Review*, 3(1).
Krasner, Stephen D. (1985). *Structural Conflict: The Third World against Global Liberalism*. Berkeley: University of California Press.

Kriesberg, Martin (1984). *International Organizations and Agricultural Development*. Foreign Agricultural Economic Report 131 (February). Washington, DC: USDA.

Lasswell, Harold, and Abraham Kaplan (1950). *Power and Society*. New Haven: CT: Yale University Press.

Lewis, Paul (1988, February 23). "U.S. Plans Big Cut in Funds to UN Food Agency." *New York Times*, A14.

Momoh, Eddie (1986). "Beninois to Head FAO?" *West Africa* (June 9).

Pilon, Juliana Geran (1988). "The UN's Food and Agriculture Organization: Becoming Part of the Problem." *Society*, 25(6), 4–10.

Puchala, Donald J. (1989). "The Road to Rome: The Production and Distribution of Food." In Paul Taylor and John Groom, eds, *Global Issues in the UN Framework*. London: Macmillan.

Schultz, Theodore W., ed. (1978). *Distortions of Agricultural Incentives*. Bloomington: Indiana University Press.

Talbot, Ross B., and Wayne Moyer (1986). "Who Governs the Rome Food Agencies?" Unpublished paper delivered at the Annual Meeting of the American Political Science Association, Washington, DC, August.

United Nations (1987). *Africa Recovery*, no. 4 (December). New York: Author.

U.S. Government FAO Interagency Staff Committee (1976). *United States Objectives in FAO*. Washington, DC: U.S. Government Printing Office.

Valdes, Alberto, ed. (1981). *Food Security in Developing Countries*. Boulder, CO: Westview Press.

Weiss, Thomas G., and Robert Jordan (1976). "Bureaucratic Politics and the World Food Conference: The International Policy Process." *World Politics*, 28, 422–39.

World Bank (1986). *Poverty and Hunger: Issues and Options for Food Security in Developing Countries*. Washington, DC: World Bank.

CHAPTER EIGHT

The United States and the World Health Organization

Karen A. Mingst

International cooperation in health issues has a long history. Responding to the nineteenth-century tendency of countries to impose inconsistent quarantine measures, leaders sought increased cooperation largely through periodic conferences on specific diseases. The United States was a frequent initiator and regular attendant at these meetings. Following World War II there was broad agreement among the victors, including the United States, concerning the need to continue this international approach to health activities both to protect the domestic populace from infectious diseases transmissable across national boundaries and to improve the health status of less developed countries. With the establishment of the World Health Organization (WHO) in 1948, members agreed to actively promote and pursue the objective of "the attainment by all people of the highest possible level of health." The undertaking was ambitious especially considering that health in the WHO preamble was defined as a "state of complete physical, mental and social well-being and not merely the absence of disease or infirmity" (WHO 1958: 459).

The purpose of this chapter is to analyze the relationship between the United States and WHO since World War II in terms of how the United States utilized the organization as an instrument of policy and how the WHO influenced the United States.[1] Researchers find that despite the shift in the nature of the tasks addressed by the organization, the relationship has enjoyed remarkable continuity: the utility of WHO for the United States and WHO's impact on the United States have remained rather constant. The government has consistently attached high priority to protecting the health of U.S. citizens and improving the health of less developed populations. The United States has also assured itself of a continuous relationship with WHO by adapting its strategy to avoid direct confrontation. The United States has perceived that it can achieve greater benefits by participating in the international health organization. Specifically, what explains the continuity in the U.S.-WHO relationship? Why has the United States chosen to continue to use WHO as an instrument of policy? What changes have occurred in the relationship? Although WHO was never intended to play a major role in developed "relatively healthy" societies such as the United States, what impact has WHO had on the United States?

The United States and International Health Care:
A Historical Overview

The United States has long participated in international sanitary conferences. Between 1851 and 1903 a series of eleven such conferences were convened. The fifth was held in Washington in 1881 at the request of the government. The purpose behind the American convening of this conference is representative of the national purposes served by such conferences. As Howard-Jones (1975: 45) reports, Congress had approved an act in 1879 "to prevent the introduction of contagious or infectious diseases into the United States." The act required that vessels whose destination was the United States should be in possession of certificates from U.S. consular officials detailing the sanitary history of the vessel. For such a certificate to be given, the U.S. consular official had to board the ship in home port before leaving for the United States. This requirement proved difficult because the ships were in home ports of foreign powers. The United States called the conference to persuade other countries to consent to inspections. Although conference participants did not give their assent to the entirety of the U.S. request, the lesson from the conference was important. The United States convened an international conference to give effect to domestic legislation compatible with its national interest.

With establishment of the Office International d'Hygiène Publique (OIHP) in 1907, the ad hoc international sanitary conferences were replaced by a permanent forum in which the United States participated on a regular basis. The OIHP was to disseminate information on general public health issues, specifically communicable diseases such as cholera, plague, and yellow fever (WHO 1958: 17). Interestingly, a weighted voting scheme was envisioned, though it was never fully employed (Leive 1976: 23).

At the request of the Council of the League of Nations, an international health conference met in London in April 1920. It recommended that a permanent international health organization be established as part of the League of Nations consisting of both League members and nonmembers. It was anticipated that the OIHP would become part of this new international health organization. However, the OIHP had only a formal relationship with the League, remaining a distinct organization with its own secretariat. Furthermore, the functions of the old OIHP and the new organization diverged, with the latter group adopting new methods and expanding its scope of work (WHO 1958: 23–28). The United States opposed the unification of the two organizations, fearing that it would be forced to join the League of Nations if it was a member of the health subsidiary. Hence prior to the creation of WHO, the United States used international health organizations to protect its populace from contagious diseases while assuring its national independence.

After World War II the victors concurred that an international approach to health activities should continue as before. Negotiations were conducted by the Technical Preparatory Committee, which met in Paris from March 18 to April 5, 1946. Believing that the international health activities should have an organizational focus, negotiations centered on only two questions, and these were resolved rapidly. The establishment of a World Health Organization would not preclude the continued functioning of the Pan American Health Organization (PAHO), and non-United Nations members were to be admitted by a single majority vote (Berkov 1957: 53–56). In the former case the U.S. position in support of an autonomous and decentralized approach prevailed, though the specific plan was not U.S.-conceived.

The general purpose of WHO is to be carried out in two ways.[2] WHO provides traditional epidemiological services as emphasized in the earlier sanitary conferences, including monitoring of communicable diseases and international standardization of diseases, causes of death, and biological substances. The organization also provides services to governments in the form of technical assistance for practical projects, health manpower training, and coordination of health programs, including national campaigns to control specific diseases (malaria, smallpox, tuberculosis; Forbes 1980: 119). The United States has found both of these functions compatible with its interests. Protection of the American population from epidemics is of foremost significance, and WHO is seen as instrumental to achieving this protection. Such protection is also more likely to occur if public health services of national governments are expanded. Hence the second objective is fully compatible with the first.

U.S. interest in international health issues and in WHO specifically cannot be adequately explained by national self-interest, however. Both humanitarian concerns and economic motivations have been important considerations, as outlined in the Bourne Report (1978: 43). U.S. battles against malaria and yellow fever grew from its "longstanding cultural tradition of humanitarianism." More recently, the relationship of health to human rights, another part of the humanitarian tradition, has been articulated in official U.S. documents. "Alleviation of unnecessary suffering and ill health in any country is as important a part of respect for human rights as protection of civil and political rights" (Bourne 1978: 43). U.S. interest in economic development has provided added motivation.

> Healthy people and health programs contribute to development in many ways. Since development programs for low-income countries necessarily rely on increased employment and labor-intensive technology, the capacity of the labor force to work and to learn becomes crucial. Illness and premature death reduce the productive potential of the labor force. With good health and nutrition, worker productivity is increased. Good health is also required if education and other investments in human resources are to be fruitful. (Bourne 1978: 174–75)

Given this interest in international health, how has the United States used WHO to achieve its domestic and foreign policy objectives?

U.S. Instrumentality

America's acknowledged leadership in medical research, recognized competence in developing medical technology, and training of public health officials from most member states of WHO has meant that from the outset American policymakers played a key role in setting WHO's agenda and determining the parameters of discussion. Summarizing the early period of U.S. participation in WHO, Jacobson (1974: 210) concluded,

> Of the leading states, the United States is the only one that has consistently sought to take the initiative in programmatic matters. It has proposed for the organization new major courses of action, for example medical research and the eradication of malaria and smallpox. With each such program, and on each occasion its initiative has been accepted by the organization. In the long run, the financing of these activities has been absorbed into the regular budget. Thus, through this process the United States has affected the organization's priorities.

Having such influence over the organization facilitates and expedites use of the organization as an instrument of American policy.

The United States has exercised its influence in WHO to achieve mainly three purposes. When WHO was established, the United States used it to create rules governing the transmission of communicable diseases in order to protect the American population. With these rules firmly in place, the United States began to utilize the information-gathering capability of WHO. Finally with increased American concern for economic development in the Third World, WHO became another instrument for conducting operational activities in the social/human welfare issue area. To a lesser extent the United States has contemplated using WHO for collective legitimation of controversial policies, but such action has generally been unsuccessful.

Rule Making

America's immediate concern with the establishment of WHO was to guarantee continuation of the International Quarantine Regulations, an important set of rules, procedures, and guidelines for states to follow to protect nationals from communicable diseases. Thus the United States urged WHO's adoption of the International Health Regulations in 1951. The general aim of the regulations is "to ensure the maximum security against the international spread of disease with the minimum interference of world traffic." These regulations as modified in 1969 are

> intended to strengthen the use of epidemiological principles as applied internationally, to detect, reduce or eliminate the sources from which infection spreads, to improve sanitation in and around ports and airports, to prevent the dissemination of vectors and in general, to encourage epidemiological activities on the national level so there is little risk of outside infection establishing itself. (WHO 1971)

Nine parts of the regulations identify the following very specific purposes:

(1) *Obligate* member states to have available at ports and airports equipment and personnel necessary to impede international transmission of four communicable diseases (yellow fever, cholera, plague, smallpox) and to deal with any outbreak
(2) *Prohibit* states from taking excessive, largely ineffective measures (quarantine psychology) which may impede international traffic
(3) *Establish* a notification system that provides to WHO epidemiological information and administration measures actually taken

Thus for the United States as for other countries, the International Health

Regulations establish rules to follow in gathering information and reporting about the onset and spread of communicable diseases and to outline the prevailing norms to follow in treating the outbreak.

The regulations were implemented rapidly by states through a procedure proposed and supported by the United States in 1951. At the request of the Senate Foreign Relations Committee, the United States advocated the procedure of "contracting out" whereby the governing body of the organization by majority vote could adopt regulations on certain issues that were immediately binding on members. This obviated the need to submit highly technical international agreements to legislatures for ratification on every occasion (Leive 1976: 25). Rather, specific WHO provisions could be made directly applicable to states, implemented by simple executive action. Hence under Articles 21 and 22, regulations made by WHO would come into force for all members after due notice of their adoption, except for those who register reservations or explicit rejection within a specific period. The World Health Assembly (WHA) would determine if reservations were valid (Gutteridge 1971: 227, 280). Over 120 members have presented no reservations.

The procedures of the International Health Regulations have never been applied in a straightforward fashion. WHO relies on information about the outbreaks of the four diseases as reported by the countries themselves. Occasionally national authorities are loathe to admit the existence of an outbreak that would require implementation of the regulations. Although technically WHO is bound to accept the reports of the national authorities, informally the WHO secretariat gathers information from a variety of sources and seeks to persuade the affected country to act (Leive 1976: 71–82). Both activities are carried out in conjunction with the U.S. Center for Disease Control.

Compliance with the specific provisions of the International Health Regulations is the responsibility of the director-general and a fifteen-person unit in the WHO secretariat. An oversight committee, the Committee on International Surveillance of Communicable Diseases, reviews their work every two years (Leive 1976: 43–44). However, it is the member states who must make the necessary legislative/regulatory changes to conform to WHO directives—and the United States has followed suit.

The United States has also relied on the organization to create other rules and has played a key role in supporting the adoption of several specific procedures that have ensured the smooth functioning of the organization. These initiatives signified American interest in and commitment to the organization. Members could not only specify reservations to the WHO treaty but could also withdraw from the organization upon fulfilling financial obligations (U.S. House of Representatives 1971: 25–26).

With the adoption of these procedural rules, the substantive rules embodied in the International Health Regulations were established for a specific group of communicable diseases. The issue of AIDS (acquired immune deficiency syndrome) has refocused American attention on the International Health Regulations. Should AIDS be classified as a transmissible disease under the regulations? If so, then would AIDS testing at ports of entry and airports become mandatory not only for international travelers but also for refugees and immigrants? To what extent could the International Health Regulations be invoked to prevent states from taking excessive preventive measures, for example, forbidding the entry of an African or discriminating against American travelers? Thus U.S. attention has turned once again to WHO's heretofore noncontroversial International Health Regulations.

Information Gathering

Although the International Health Regulations are a key example of where the United States supported the creation of international rules in order to protect domestic populations, the United States also found WHO consistently useful as an information-gathering source. During the mid-1960s the United States proposed a project for the international reporting of adverse reactions to drugs and provided financial and technical assistance for a pilot project. Twenty of the wealthiest, most economically and technologically advanced countries chose to participate (Kay 1976: 49–50). Again, the WHO-sponsored project was used by the United States to help public health authorities gather crucial information on reactions to specific pharmaceuticals. The technical report series issued by WHO is widely used by the American health community as a source of information on both environmental health topics affecting developed societies such as the United States (for example, recent reports on chlordane, polychlorinated byphenyls, mirex, mycotoxins) and on diseases and therapy affecting less developed countries (leprosy, yaws control, onchorerciasis, and oral rehydration).

On the AIDS issue the United States has supported WHO's efforts to gather information on the spread of the virus. Given that knowledge of infection rates is politically sensitive information, the U.S. government itself would be unlikely to be able to collect such information. The close ties of WHO's secretariat to health personnel in Third World countries and their image of "political neutrality" has expedited WHO's gathering of this information. Such data will be valuable to American epidemiologists trying to trace the spread of the disease and to public health personnel trying to anticipate future health needs.

Operational Activities

The United States has used WHO to support two types of operational activities widely viewed as legitimate areas of WHO's expertise and function. The first is the program of immunization. Given WHO's successful smallpox immunization program that led to eradication of the disease in 1977, the United States has used WHO to support and reinforce childhood immunization programs. Under WHO's Expanded Programme of Immunization, six diseases (diphtheria, pertussis, tetanus, measles, poliomyelitis, tuberculosis) are targeted. The second operational activity is the Special Program for Research and Training in Tropical Diseases (emphasis on malaria, leprosy, schistosomiasis, filariasis, trypanosomiasis, and leishmaniasis) and the oral rehydration therapy (WHO 1982c). The United States has consistently funded and contributed medical expertise to these operational programs.

Since the mid-1970s as epidemiological activities have become routinized (monitoring under the International Health Regulations), some diseases eradicated (smallpox) and better health infrastructure established in some countries, the World Health Assembly, the governing body of WHO, has moved to address the broad issues stated in the organization's preamble and summarized in the Health for All by the Year 2000 Program. The United States has opposed many of the newer tasks. As it has become more of an agenda taker, the United States has found the organization less useful as an American instrument for operational activities in the area of health.

The program entitled Health for All by the Year 2000, announced in 1977, sought the attainment of a level of health that would permit all of the population to lead a socially and economically productive life. The International Conference on Primary Health Care held in Alma-Ata in 1978 led to further delineation of this program with priority given to promoting a better food supply, safe drinking water and sanitation, maternal and child care, immunization, appropriate treatment of common diseases, and provision of essential drugs (Mahler 1981: 3–5). As secretariat personnel explained (WHO 1976: 80–81), "These are different *types* of subjects from those tackled in the past." To at least a few, "health for all" amounts to a call for a "new international health order" with its specifications of the tight relationship between health and development (Bélanger 1983: 260).

The U.S. reaction to the expansion of operational tasks can best be described as schizophrenic. On one hand, support for primary health care had been initiated by the U.S. Agency for International Development (USAID) Office of Health in 1969 and was subsequently referred to in legislation as a "low-cost health delivery system." USAID policy has advocated minimal health services (especially for mothers and children) for a majority of the population at affordable rates without prolonged external dependency. This is consistent with the thrust of WHO's Health for All by the Year 2000 Program (Howard 1981: 7).

On the other hand, the United States has been loathe to accept the implications of WHO's new operational activities for three reasons. First, some of the new policies are aimed at addressing fundamental questions of economic maldistribution, a subject that is, according to U.S. officials, beyond the purview of WHO. Second, to achieve the goals in the Health for All policy, governments in member countries are called on to play an active role in regulating the private sector, including multinational corporations, a policy the U.S. government finds unacceptable. An excellent recent example of the problem can be found in the 1986 World Health Assembly. The WHA declared that tobacco smoking and use in all forms was incompatible with the Health for All goal and called for a global approach to the problem (*United Nations Chronicle* 1986: 101). Such an approach might entail the government's restricting the sales and marketing activities of tobacco companies. Third, the technical superiority of the United States in the medical area is not as useful as an instrument of influence under this reorientation, for the new issues are not technical ones but resource allocation questions.

With the AIDS issue the United States has voiced no serious objections to WHO's operational activities. For example, in Uganda WHO has established an office in Entebbe to conduct epidemiological research and to improve blood-testing and screening facilities. WHO has committed $7 million to these activities for the next five years. Part of the WHO programs include the distribution of two million condoms donated by USAID (Hooper 1987: 476–77). But these as well as other operational tasks of WHO for AIDS are likely to be very controversial, particularly if they are limited to one geographic part of the world.

Collective Legitimation

Efforts of U.S. policymakers to use WHO to legimate controversial national policies have generally failed. In a rare case of U.S. officials attempting such an action, Senator Hubert Humphrey in 1958 tried to persuade the executive branch to seize the policy initiative in WHO by encouraging other delegates to consider a broadened agenda of health programs utilizing research already conducted at the National Institutes of Health. The intent was to legitimate research already conducted by the United States, thus beating the Soviet Union in the propaganda war. In the words of Senator Morse:

I think this a good opportunity for us to go on the aggressive in this propaganda contest with Russia, so to speak. We have a chance to hit her twice. Let's hit her in MSA (Mutual Security Act) and then let's hit her again when we get the World Health Organization legislation before us. (U.S. Executive Sessions of the Senate Foreign Relations Committee 1958, published 1980: 403)

The United States has seldom used or tried to use WHO for such political legitimation activities, however, and the United States will be unlikely to rely on WHO for collective legitimation of an AIDS policy in light of the fact that no American policy currently exists.

The Special Case of AIDS

The AIDS issue provides an excellent test, nevertheless, of whether the United States intends to continue to use WHO as an instrument of policy. Some health officials, including WHO's director-general, are urging WHO to play a major role in tracking the spread of the disease by utilizing its linkages to public health officials in member states. If AIDS is defined as a communicable disease, WHO could be useful as a rule-making body to adopt regulations to slow the transmission of the disease, a task some officials in the U.S. public health community advocate. WHO has been and could be more useful as an information-gathering body, collecting statistics on transmission rates and national government programs. WHO could also engage in operational activities, establishing blood-testing laboratories or disseminating prophylactic devices. Indeed, WHO has begun to mount a campaign in many African countries to educate people about AIDS risks, establish blood-testing laboratories, and undertake other preventive measures (Altman 1987: 13) similar to the program in Uganda (Hooper 1987).

WHO's ability to perform these tasks adequately depends on both increased funding and the availability of epidemiological experts from developed but infected countries such as the United States. The director of WHO's special program is Jonathan Mann, an American. Although the United States has expressed its concern over the spread of AIDS, it has not requested additional funding for WHO to fulfill these tasks. Mann estimates that $20 million is needed for WHO to develop and coordinate programs, with an additional $200 million required for African countries alone ($1.5 billion by 1990). The United States has contributed only $2 million to WHO's AIDS program and another $3 million to various African countries (Harden 1987; Scroggins 1987: 1). This low level of American financial commitment suggests that the United States is not ready to use WHO as an instrument of AIDS policy. So far the U.S. government has been unable to develop either a national policy regarding the content of policy rules surrounding AIDS (should mandated testing occur? should partners of AIDS patients be "tracked" and informed, and employers or schools notified?) or a policy on the federal government's operational responsibilities. WHO is likely to play only a marginal role in the national debate over these issues and, hence, in American national strategy. For WHO to play a critical role in AIDS-related programs in other countries, the U.S. government will need to designate the organization as an important instrument of U.S. policy not only for information gathering but also for the more controversial operational activities.

IGO Influence and Impact on the United States

Although WHO was never intended to play a major role in more developed countries for providing services to governments or organizing programs to control specific diseases, WHO's task of protecting the domestic population from communicable diseases through monitoring of these diseases and providing standardization for epidemiological research is of universal relevance. U.S. health policy has incorporated rules and compliance provisions to meet WHO's standards, though the national standards were often the same as or similar to the international ones.

Adopting WHO Rules

The United States has cooperated with WHO by implementing and enforcing the International Health Regulations, making the necessary legislative and regulatory provisions to comply because they have been beneficial to Americans. To protect the population from the four contagious diseases, U.S. Public Health Service (PHS) officials spend $10 million annually to check 140 million people at airports and ports; PHS physicians stationed in thirty countries check 250,000 visa applicants each year. The cost of compliance and the infringement on sovereignty are low given that serious outbreaks of these particular diseases are unlikely to occur in the United States, making it improbable that the United States would find itself the object of internationally imposed measures. The possibility that the United States would be the object of such measures is what makes the AIDS issue interesting. Thus far, however, the regulations incorporated into the current International Health Regulations have reinforced information-gathering procedures useful to American public health officials in curbing the potential outbreak of specific diseases.

Agenda-Setting

Since the early 1970s WHO members have introduced items into WHO's agenda to which the United States has had to respond. The newly independent countries of Africa and Asia called not only for a new international economic order in the international economic institutions but also for a "new health order" in WHO. Spurred by WHO's successful immunization campaigns, the new majority sought to expand WHO's agenda. On three prominent issues, which it did not support, the United States has resorted to a damage limitation strategy, at times remaining in opposition and at times working to create a minimally acceptable provision compatible with its interests.

The first issue concerns the problems of quality control of internationally sold pharmaceuticals. Between 1963 and the present WHO has considered a variety of measures on quality control, including the establishment of regional testing facilities to monitor the quality of drug imports. The U.S. government, reflecting in part the position of the pharmaceutical companies, has opposed sensitive international regulations in this area. So the United States proposed alternative measures, suggesting that WHO assist in upgrading the technical qualifications of regulatory authorities who could then conduct tests at the national level. As a result WHO advisory personnel assist in training national regulatory authorities. In 1970 guidelines for drug manufacturing quality control were established covering such issues as manufacturing operations, labeling, quality control systems, self-inspection, and reports of adverse reactions. However, the general, often ambiguous nature of these WHO recommendations complicated implementation and enforcement by member states (Kay 1976: 36–45). Furthermore, these recommendations significantly diverged from the stricter provisions envisioned when WHO first discussed the issue—in large part because of American opposition to WHO regulation of multinational pharmaceutical companies. The recommendation therefore gave individual national governments only guidelines for enforcement.

In the mid-1970s the second issue, promotion of milk substitutes by multinational corporations in the Third World, dominated the WHO agenda. It was alleged that artificial milk caused malnutrition and even death in infants. Following WHO's mandate to study the problem, extensive consultations were held with all interested parties to discuss a draft code designed to curb multinational corporation practices in this area (WHO 1982a: 52–53).

In May 1981 the World Health Assembly adopted an International Code of Marketing of Breastmilk Substitutes with the United States alone voting in opposition. The code recommended that member states adopt regulations banning all marketing and advertising of infant formula that discouraged breast-feeding while acknowledging a "legitimate market" for all breast milk substitutes (WHO 1982a: 52–53). Officials of the Reagan administration agreed that many of the code's provisions could not be implemented in the United States because they violated both First Amendment rights and antitrust laws. More important, the administration feared that WHO was becoming an international *regulatory* body (U.S. House of Representatives 1982: 5–9).

On the third issue, the distribution and use of pharmaceuticals in the Third World, the United States opposed WHO's involvement. But over time even the United States responded by offering counterproposals. The issue has revolved around the proper role of drug companies in the Third World.[3] Former Director-General Halfdan Mahler, among others, has denounced "drug colonialism" of the drug companies, charging them with irresponsible promotion practices, including promotion of luxury drugs, failing to provide low-cost generic products, dumping drugs previously labeled dangerous in more developed countries, and engaging in bribery and corruption of both government officials and physicians in the Third World (Silverman et al. 1982: 132–33).

WHO has initiated proposals to curb some of these abuses. For example, in 1978 WHO passed a resolution establishing the Action Program on Essential Drugs. As part of the program, information about drugs has been compiled, the use of generic names encouraged, a list of essential drugs proposed, and a quality control system outlined (National Council for International Health 1982: 4–5). The aim of these activities is to help countries reduce expenditures on drug imports. To meet the health needs of the majority of the population, WHO lists 250 essential drugs most of which are available in generic form and so if purchased in bulk could meet the needs of many (Catsambas and Foster 1986: 30).

Initially the United States opposed these regulatory initiatives and proposed countermeasures. U.S. policymakers invested considerable time and resources promoting these counterproposals. For example, to improve information flow to the Third World concerning pharmaceutical products and regulations, the United States sponsored in 1980 the first International Conference of Drug Registration Authorities. They encouraged the use of WHO's "Certification Scheme for the Quality of Pharmaceutical Products Moving in International Commerce" to counter the dumping charges. To involve the drug companies in preparing for self-regulation, the United States worked with the Pharmaceutical Manufacturers Association to promote establishment of the International Federation of Pharmaceutical Manufacturers Association and reinforce industrywide cohesion (National Council for International Health 1982: 19, 25).

With each countermeasure voluntary cooperation between drug companies and national authorities was encouraged and international regulations discouraged. When the Action Program was approved over U.S. opposition, the United States bargained with officials in Third World governments to try to minimize the impact of the regulations. For example, the U.S. government urged Bangladesh officials to delay implementation of bans on 237 products and prohibition of the importation of 1500 other drugs until agreements could be reached between Bangladesh officials and the pharmaceutical manufacturers. There is some evidence to suggest that the U.S. government even threatened to withdraw support for other WHO programs if any more restrictive codes were implemented (Sikkink 1986: 839). Thus U.S. opposition to pharmaceutical regulation has meant that the regulations passed have been weakened and implementation delayed. In the words of one business official, "The longer these codes are discussed, the more moderate and practical they seem to become" (Furer 1979, quoted in Chetley 1986: 75).

On these critical issues the United States has been forced to respond to issues placed on the WHO agenda on which it would have preferred to remain silent. American responses ranging from active opposition to suggesting counterproposals have been initiated, in large part, by domestic groups.

Mobilization of Domestic Groups

For most issues on the WHO agenda domestic groups have not been active; the public health community has been supportive of WHO. However, each of the three issues described earlier challenged the interests and commercial marketing practices of U.S.-based multinational corporations and led to active involvement of domestic groups in discussion of the issues.

The infant formula controversy in particular mobilized groups on both sides. Companies producing infant formula as well as retail groups such as the Grocery Manufacturers of America contended that the WHO code prevented American companies from engaging in acceptable marketing practices, thereby denying them their rights to free speech and free press (U.S. House of Representatives 1982: 36–39). Members of public health organizations, including the prestigious American Public Health Association, opposed the administration stance, claiming that their expert advice had been ignored. AID Deputy Assistant for Administration Stephen C. Joseph resigned to protest the United States' no vote, arguing that U.S. political credibility and bilateral assistance efforts aimed at population and family planning were irreparably harmed (U.S. House of

Representatives 1982: 2–4; 150–52). Finally, both houses of Congress expressed dissatisfaction with the administration's position, the House approving a motion (301-100) condemning the U.S. vote and the Senate (89-2) urging the administration and American infant food manufacturers to adhere to the new WHO code.

The U.S. no vote has had little negative effect on the functioning of WHO in general or on compliance with the code specifically. For several years the multinational companies skirted the WHO code through a series of public relations measures.[4] The same companies eventually bowed to the pressures of the nongovernmental organizations and agreed to issue company marketing directives consistent with the code. Ironically, during these intensive negotiations WHO and UNICEF assumed a mediating role—a "reconciliation service" (Chetley 1986: 76). In the words of Starrels (1985: 28), that service has "contributed to a more sober, constructive and collaborative dialogue between private industry and WHO." And for WHO, its stature and legitimacy may have been enhanced through its efforts on the issue (Chetley 1986: 139). Although mobilization of domestic opposition did not prove to be a decisive factor in this case, on other issues—in particular that of smoking and use of tobacco—it may have a more significant effect leading to further changes in U.S. governmental tactics.

Changing American Tactics

Confronted with WHO's new operational activities and agenda items, the United States has chosen a strategy of adaptation, making subtle changes in techniques to maintain its influence. Paraphrasing the comments of one top U.S. official, the United States is more discreet and less domineering. For example, every attempt has been made to get cosponsors of initiatives from less developed countries (Interview 1985). This approach is designed to enable the United States to maintain a lower profile, thereby stifling charges of U.S. manipulation of the organization and fortifying WHO's own legitimacy. American officials have worked more behind the scenes to convince countries to support specific measures, building coalitions rather than using threats or financial leverage, though all members and the secretariat remain cognizant that the United States provides 25 percent of the budget (Interview 1985).

An example of U.S. concern with maintaining a less domineering and more compliant image can be seen in the way American officials have worked to respond to the suggested deadlines of the Health for All program. The program calls for national governments to review their respective health systems, develop strategies for achieving Health for All objectives, and submit implementation, progress, and evaluation reports (WHO 1982b). Officials at the U.S. Department of Health and Human Services have been directed to show approval to aspects of the program by finding and supporting suitable projects (Interviews).

Currently although there is widespread consensus among U.S. policy-makers that U.S. strategy and tactics in WHO have changed, there is no consensus on whether the change is beneficial to either domestic or international health interests. Some officials suggest that this alteration in technique is a legitimate response to America's relative decline in power resources. It may well be the only way the United States can operate effectively in IGOs generally and in WHO specifically to get what it wants. In the words of one official, for the United States to accomplish its objectives in WHO, it must carry the "soft stick" (Interview 1985). Other participants lament that the United States is no longer "steering" the organization and criticize the United States for no longer "constructively engaging" it (Interview 1985; U.S. Comptroller General 1977). They contend that the United States could and should take a more active role, as other members "expect" it (Interview 1985). Changing tactics may have enabled the United States to employ WHO as an instrument in more diverse and subtle ways, but they may also have resulted in increased WHO influence on the United States. What factors explain the continuity and subtle changes in U.S. instrumentality and WHO influence?

Explaining Continuity and Change

There has been a high degree of continuity between the United States and WHO compared with U.S. relationships with other international organizations. The United States still uses WHO to create rules designed to curb the spread of communicable diseases, to gather information for epidemiological research, and to conduct the highly regarded immunization program, as well as research and training programs in tropical diseases—all tasks compatible with U.S. objectives. Although the immunization programs were never designed to be implemented in the United States, the United States has been influenced indirectly through its compliance with WHO rule-making procedures (indeed, even strengthening them when deemed necessary) and by participating and even encouraging information-gathering capabilities. This continuity may best be explained by the fact that American medical/scientific leadership is strongly embedded in WHO; with such diffuse influence, the United States has not had to exercise its power in more overt ways. WHO's organizational characteristics, particularly the composition and role of the secretariat, have reinforced this continuity, as has the relative degree of consensus found among a rather small group of U.S. decision makers.

U.S. Power Dominance

Despite the documented decline of American resources and ability to affect outcomes in security and economic matters, American technical and scientific leadership in medical-related fields has persisted. As Bourne (1978: XIII) summarizes,

> We no longer have the virtual monopoly that we once had in medical technology, yet we still possess resources in the health field that far exceed the rest of the world. Our moral leadership and commitment to humanitarian concerns have continued to give us singular acceptance in the developing world. We have resources within the federal government to allow us to provide to the developing world direct support, including technical assistance for the implementation of health care programs. We have unique institutions, such as the Center for Disease Control in Atlanta, which can provide epidemiological support to countries throughout the world. Within the private sector, we possess the capacity to train large numbers of health care personnel either in this country or overseas. We also have in our academic institutions, foundations, and pharmaceutical industry the greatest aggregation of medical research talent in the world.

This widely acknowledged expertise has been inculcated into the norms of many members of the WHO secretariat and delegates to the organization through common medical training.[5] Such common training has led to the establishment of transgovernmental networks among technical personnel in the World Health Assembly (Leive 1976: XII). Many issues are resolved primarily in extensive correspondence between WHO and health ministries, between "experts," rather than through foreign ministries. American scientific leadership in the transgovernmental networks helps to explain why the United States continues to find WHO useful. American expertise is widely used in WHO expert committees and scientific meetings, as well as in providing technical advice to member states.

Of course, U.S. medical expertise is reinforced by American budgetary contributions to WHO, and American policymakers admit that WHO personnel and members are acutely aware of the potential for use of this financial power (Interview 1985). The U.S. assessment for WHO is 25 percent ($62.8 million in the 1986–87 biennium), and it contributes $8 million annually for special programs outside the regular budget. Yet in general promises to augment American budgetary contributions or threats to withdraw funding have not been utilized, though funding has on occasion been delayed. For example, the United States was able to make only a small initial payment to WHO on its 1986 assessment because of a congressionally imposed partial spending freeze on the appropriation. But the United States assured the organization that the reduced payments did not indicate American dissatisfaction with WHO and pledged that more would be paid in late 1987 when the freeze was lifted (U.S. Department of State 1987). There has been little need for the United States to use its financial leverage when its leadership can be manifested in the more diffuse ways described earlier. Although U.S. scientific leadership accounts for much of the remarkable continuity of the U.S.-WHO relationship, desirable organizational characteristics have facilitated that continuity.

Organizational Characteristics

Characteristics of WHO as an organization have acted to reinforce this continuity.[6] Such characteristics include global membership (166 members plus one associate member), specific commitment to health issues, a budget that is the second largest in the UN system after the UN itself ($633,980,000 for 1988–89), and a decentralized organizational structure (with six regional offices). The Executive Board, consisting of thirty-one individuals, includes representatives from the "Big Five"—the United States, United Kingdom, Soviet Union, China, and France—and by informal arrangement each is off the board only one year between three-year terms. The director-general, other secretariat officials, as well as many delegation members are medical doctors. In addition to sharing similar educational and vocational backgrounds, many have been schooled in the American approach to public health.

The organization has had only four directors-general: the first, 1948–52; the second, 1953–73; the third, 1973–88; and the current one, 1988 to the present. The longevity of their tenure and their support by the medical "fraternity" ensure that directors-general are key persons in maintaining WHO legitimacy. The United States has supported each of the directors-general. In fact, former Director-General Mahler has been described by one U.S. official as politically astute, "a master at getting consensus, without being a lackey of the United States" (Interview 1985). Thus as Sikkink (1986: 825) suggests, based on her study of the infant formula code, "the perception of WHO as a technical and professional organization with low politicization increased the impact of consensual scientific knowledge." Because so much of this knowledge has been and is currently derived from American medical research and expertise, general U.S. government support of the organization is affirmed. Given these organizational characteristics, the membership and voting arrangements and the composition and role of the secretariat, all of the principals—including American policymakers—see WHO as a highly technical and competent organization staffed by experts.

In addition, American use of the organization as an instrument of policy has been facilitated by the fact that American nationals hold influential positions in WHO, most important the post of assistant director-general in charge of administrative and financial affairs. This position, currently occupied by Warren Furth (previously by Milton Siegel), has apparently reassured U.S. officials that WHO is both a financially sound and an efficiently run organization. WHO's financial and institutional viability has rarely been challenged. Because the WHO secretariat and World Health Assembly meetings are all based in Geneva, distance circumscribes the amount of daily interaction between WHO and U.S. government officials and usually means that fewer U.S. officials are attentive to the operation. When there is interaction, WHO personnel have been willing to negotiate on specific implementation measures, as they did on the infant formula question. Furthermore, the organization has often acted by simple recommendation and resolution rather than by enacting formal regulations, even though the latter would be appropriate (Gutteridge 1971: 281).

WHO's handling of the issue of Israel's participation illustrates how its organizational characteristics have contributed to a more harmonious relationship with the United States. Although WHO is subject to some of the same pressures as many other IGOs—including the UN, UNESCO, and the ILO—the results have been different. At several World Health Assemblies delegates have sought to isolate Israel by criticizing health treatment given in the occupied territories. In 1976 two such resolutions mustered WHA approval, with the United States either absent or in opposition (U.S. Department of Health, Education and Welfare 1976: 38, 31–32). In the 1977 WHA session a resolution condemning Israel for ignoring previous resolutions and demanding WHO visits to occupied territories was passed over another U.S. no vote. In the 1983 session a resolution condemning health services in the occupied territories was again passed. The United States reacted to these attacks on Israel by voting no on appropriate resolutions condemning Israel and supporting a 1976 report that complimented Israel on health treatment in the occupied zones.

In each case the United States voted against the majority position, voicing its displeasure with politicization of issues viewed as peripheral to the mandate of the organization—the same approach taken in other UN-related IGOs where the Israeli issue has been catapulted to the top of the agenda. Yet neither the supporters of these resolutions nor the United

States has permitted WHO programs and policies to be jeopardized, in contrast to the situation in UNESCO, where condemnation of Israel was one of the justifications for U.S. withdrawal.

In 1989 WHO set aside a Palestinian application for membership—an application strongly opposed by Israel and the United States. With the United States threatening to withhold contributions to organizations giving a seat to the Palestine Liberation Organization, representatives to the WHA voted 83 to 47 to postpone the decision another year. The compromise text by Director-General Hiroshi Nakajima was negotiated so that WHO would not be disabled by a political confrontation (Bollag 1989: 3).

WHO members, at the gentle persuasion of a savvy director-general who informs the WHA of potentially dangerous reactions, have usually agreed to careful wording of resolutions and responses to stop short of ostracizing the United States under the basic consensual norm that health policy should transcend political controversy. Thus the organizational characteristics of WHO, including the technical orientation of the secretariat, transgovernmental networks, and the political savvy of its directors-general and other members on the Israeli issue, have contributed to continuity in the U.S.-WHO relationship.

Domestic Political Factors

Continuity can also be explained by the relative centralization of international health policy in the American government and the high degree of consensus found among relevant U.S. personnel. With rare exception, U.S. decision-making structures and individuals involved with WHO have also been marked by continuity and consensus. U.S. funds for participation are administered by the State Department under the International Organization Bureau Health and Narcotics Programs, and it is that department that oversees the conduct of U.S. activities and the "political" aspects of U.S. participation.[7] At the technical and implementation levels is the Department of Health and Human Services through the Public Health Service's Office for International Health, Office for Multilateral Programs and International Health at the Center for Disease Control in Atlanta. Finally, the AID's Office of Nutrition and Directorate for Health and Population has been involved in multilateral participation because that agency conducts the U.S. government's bilateral health programs. Thus compared with the structures for political or economic policy, the number of different governmental agencies involved is relatively small. Only in the exceptional cases, such as the infant formula controversy, have significant differences developed regarding the content of U.S. policy.

Facilitating the high degree of centralization of international health policy in the U.S. government is remarkable continuity among the most important policymakers. Rose Belmont, director of the Office for Multilateral Programs, Office for International Health at the Public Health Service, has had a sixteen-year tenure, and Neil Boyer, a permanent State Department (non-FSO position) employee, has worked at the same desk for eight years. These two individuals have coordinated U.S. policy with an almost unprecedented degree of consensus. This longevity of tenure is not a recent phenomenon. An AID official previously associated with WHO enjoyed a ten-year tenure.

Yet the continuity of the U.S.-WHO relationship has not been uniform. Changes in the nature of the issue area as defined by a new dominant majority in WHO and opposed by some U.S. government officials have resulted in conflict.

Issue Area Characteristics

Beginning in the mid-1970s the ideology of the numerically dominant WHO coalition began to diverge from the ideology of U.S. liberalism and increasingly tied health issues to the more general issue of "economic deprivation," seeking adoption of new regulatory measures. According to some American officials, such a broadened definition of health exceeded the mandate of the organization; most important, regulatory measures advocated by the dominant coalition described earlier were not only beyond WHO's competence but also were incompatible with American ideology of the efficiency of the unfettered international market. Thus in response to such issues as the infant formula code, control of pharmaceuticals in the Third World, and a program advocating a model code for essential drugs, the United States found itself either in opposition to the majority (infant formula) or trying to forestall adoption of regulations curbing the activities of international businesses. Finding that U.S. opposition in the form of the no vote on infant formula had little substantive effect on the outcome of the debate, the United States chose more subtle techniques to mitigate the effects of proposals before they actually were adopted. The changes in U.S. policy orientation and tactics, then, were responses to changes in the way health issues were redefined in WHO, a reorientation at times at variance with the U.S. conception of the role of an IGO and incompatible with American ideology of health activities being primarily a task of the private sector—a view strongly held by Reagan administration officials.

Changes in Domestic Administration

One explanation for the vehemence of the U.S. reaction to these changes since 1980 lies in the views of key members of the Reagan administration. The administration had been less satisfied with the performance of IGOs in general and very dissatisfied with the fact that there was "too much governmental intervention disguised as international policy coordination" (Keohane and Nye 1985: 149). Thus even though the Reagan administration and every other administration have affirmed their general support of the goals of WHO, they adamantly opposed recommendations or regulations coming from the WHA, which smacked of control over the activities of international businesses. This opposition stems from the ideological commitment to the principle of an unfettered market, staunchly defended in the Reagan administation's approach to economic development in both bilateral and multilateral channels (Templeman and Weiner 1985: 34).

Given the ideological predisposition of the Reagan administration, why did the administration merely alter its techniques of statecraft? Why has the United States not withdrawn from the organization itself as it did for a time in the International Labor Organization and has done in UNESCO? Why was the U.S.-WHO relationship, even during the Reagan administration, different? Two explanations cited earlier deserve reiteration. First, the promotion of better health care remains a goal with which no one disagrees, and the issue area remains highly visible. Because of this the United States has desired to remain in the principal multilateral organization ("where the action is"), advocating its preferred programmatic approach. Second, the WHO secretariat and its directors-general have facilitated the U.S. approach. Although resolutions have passed against the U.S. position, the skillful wording and recommendatory nature have often stopped short of unduly ostracizing the United States and hence jeopardizing WHO's programs for which U.S. financial support is necessary.

In short, the characteristics of WHO, its universal membership, its high functional specificity, high essentiality, and relatively low sensitivity to world political cleavages described so well by Jacobson in 1974 (p. 421) have not substantially changed. The work of WHO's technical committees is widely regarded by the medical community as professionally competent. The presence of members such as Cuba and Nicaragua posed no direct threat to the work of the organization even for the Reagan administration. The United States has not fought funding for these countries even though it has opposed other IGO financing of projects in countries antagonistic to the United States, such as the World Bank in Vietnam and the African Development Bank in Ethiopia. With WHO's highly "desirable" organizational characteristics, the United States has chosen to moderate its techniques of influence, still able to utilize WHO as an instrument of policy for information gathering and limited operational activities, while bearing the political costs of opposing or trying to modify some of its regulatory activities.

Conclusion

In the future the United States may be able to sustain an adaptation strategy. If WHO officials are able to obtain additional funding and personnel for the kind and magnitude of AIDS campaign envisioned, where WHO may become engaged in controversial operational activities, then the U.S. government, already bitterly divided "in house" over the content of an appropriate federal government response, may not be able to invest the energy and commitment to forcing accommodations with WHO. Equally as critical, in 1986 the issue of tobacco was again on the World Health Assembly agenda. At that time the WHA declared that tobacco smoking and tobacco use in all forms was incompatible with the attainment of Health for All. The assembly went further by requesting other United Nations organizations to help curb the spread of tobacco-induced diseases by protecting the health of nonsmokers, and the director-general was asked to ensure that WHO assume an "effective global advocacy role with regard to tobacco and health issues" (*UN Chronicle* 1986: 101). If WHO follows through with the discussion of regulatory measures, then U.S.-based domestic groups, particularly the tobacco companies, would immediately mobilize in opposition. Because both the AIDS and tobacco issues are highly controversial and unresolved issues on the federal government agenda, the U.S. government will be incapable of approaching WHO with effective counterproposals.

Strong American opposition on these issues could result in the United States becoming more defensive, permanently altering the pattern of cordial relations with WHO. As Kenneth Adelman, former deputy U.S. representative to the UN, warned after the U.S. defeat on the infant formula issue, "health groups and corporate enterprises opposing international regulation should have stirred them to muster their forces for the campaign yet ahead" (1982: 16). A more optimistic prognostication would suggest that the salience of the issue area (made all the more manifest by the specter of AIDS) and the institutional legitimacy that WHO has acquired from its past success would avert U.S. alienation from WHO. Although the battle over tobacco is likely to be damaging to the U.S.-WHO relationship, WHO's members must realize that both American financial contributions and scientific expertise are critical for WHO's success and must stop short of trying to regulate the multinational tobacco companies. At the same time, U.S. policymakers must recognize that WHO has been a useful instrument for American policy and that the health concerns of the general population may override the economic interests of a small minority.

Notes

1. Previous research on WHO is surprisingly limited, especially in view of the alleged success of the organization, as well as the recent appearance of several controversial issues on its agenda. Many authors present general accounts of international health issues, devoting a chapter or less to WHO affairs (Basch, 1978; Brockington, 1975; Goodman, 1971). Some exceptions are Allen (1950), Ascher (1952), Pethybridge (1965), Berkov (1957), Jacobson (1974), Hoole (1976), and Riggs (1980). This chapter draws in part on interviews with American government officials conducted in Washington, D.C. in 1985.

2. Actually, the WHO charter lists twenty-two functions (WHO 1985).

3. For a penetrating view from the Third World press of the problem of pharmaceuticals, see Perin (1985: 65).

4. In 1982 Nestlé established the Infant Formula Audit Commission, which was charged with investigating allegations that Nestlé failed to comply with WHO's code of ethics. Specific action taken by the company to comply include redesigning advertising so as not to discourage breast-feeding in less developed countries and restricting free samples of breast milk substitutes to medical personnel. This self-regulation approach adopted by the companies has been fraught with controversy, many groups contending that such action is a public relations gesture and an unacceptable means of implementing the code, particularly considering that the "commission" is funded by Nestlé itself. For an informative overview of the controversy as analyzed by Nestlé, see the pamphlet "The Dilemma of Third World Nutrition: Nestlé and the Role of Infant Formula" (1983). For an analysis of the changes Nestlé has implemented after the WHO vote, see the subsequent pamphlet, "Nestlé and the Role of Infant Formula in Developing Countries: The Resolution of a Conflict" (1984).

5. For a survey of European public health teaching, see Cottrell et al. (1969).

6. For a legal examination of the organizational structures of WHO, see Bélanger (1983).

7. For a particularly critical assessment of State Department involvement in international health policy, see Bourne (1978).

References

Adelman, Kenneth L. (1982). "Biting the Hand That Cures Them." *Regulation*, 6(June-August), 16–18, 35.

Allen, Charles E. (1950). "World Health and World Politics." *International Organization*, 4(1), 27–43.

Altman, Lawrence (1987, June 3). "Key World Health Official Warns of Epidemic of Prejudice on AIDS." *New York Times*, pp. 1, 13.

Ascher, Charles S. (1952). *"Current Problems in the World Health Organization's Program."* *International Organization*, 6(1), 27–50.

Basch, Paul F. (1978). *International Health*. New York: Oxford University Press.

Bélanger, Michael (1983). *Droit International de la Santé*. Paris: Economica.

Berkov, Robert (1957). *The World Health Organization: A Study in Decentralized International Administration*. Geneva: Librairie E. Droz.

Bollag, Burton (1989, May 13). "UN Health Agency Defers PLO Application to 1990." *New York Times*, p. 3.

Bourne, Peter (1978). *New Directions in International Health Cooperation: A Report to the President* (Spring). Washington, DC: U.S. Government Printing Office.

Brockington, Fraser (1975). *World Health*. 3d ed. Edinburgh: Churchill Livingstone.

Catsambas, Thanos, and Susan Foster (1986). "Spending Money Sensibly: The Case of Essential Drugs." *Finance and Development* (December), 29–32.

Chetley, Andrew (1986). *The Politics of Baby Foods: Successful Challenges to an International Marketing Strategy*. New York: St. Martin's.

Cottrell, J. D. et al. (1969). *The Teaching of Public Health in Europe*. Geneva: World Health Organization.

Forbes, John F. (1980). "International Cooperation in Public Health and the World Health Organization." In Todd Sandler, ed., *The Theory and Structures of International Political Economy*. Boulder, CO: Westview Press, 115–31.

Furer, Arthur. "Executive Viewpoint." *Business International* Interview 1 June 1979, quoted in Andrew Chetley (1986). *The Politics of Baby Foods: Successful Challenges to an International Marketing Strategy*. New York: St. Martin's.

Goodman, Neville M. (1971). *International Health Organizations and Their Work*. Baltimore: Williams and Wilkins.

Gutteridge, F. (1971). "Notes on Decisions of the World Health Organization." In Stephen M. Schwebel, ed., *The Effectiveness of International Decisions*. Dobbs Ferry, New York: Oceana Publications, 227–84.

Harden, Blaine (1987). "AIDS May Replace Famine as the Continent's Worst Blight." *The Washington Post National Weekly Edition* (June 15), 16–17.

Hoole, Francis W. (1976). *Politics and Budgeting in the World Health Organization*. Bloomington: Indiana University Press.

Hooper, Ed (1987). "AIDS in Uganda." *African Affairs*, 86(345), 469–77.

Howard, Lee M. (1981). *A Profile of United States Development Cooperation in the Health-Related Sectors*. Report for Office of Health, Bureau of Science and Technology, Agency for International Development, July. Washington, DC: U.S. Government Printing Office.

Howard-Jones, Norman (1975). *The Scientific Background of the International Sanitary Conferences, 1851–1938*. Geneva: World Health Organization.

Jacobson, Harold K. (1974). "WHO: Medicine, Regionalism, and Managed Politics." In Robert W. Cox and Harold K. Jacobson, eds., *The Anatomy of Influence: Decision Making in International Organizations*. New Haven: CT: Yale University Press, 175–215.

Kay, David A. (1976). *The International Regulation of Pharmaceutical Drugs*. Report to the National Science Foundation on the Application of International Regulatory Techniques/Technical Problems. Minneapolis: West Publishing.

Keohane, Robert O., and Joseph S. Nye, Jr. (1985). "Two Cheers for Multilateralism." *Foreign Policy* 60(Fall), 148–67.

Leive, David M. (1976). *International Regulatory Regimes: Case Studies in Health, Meteorology and Food*, vol. 1. Lexington, MA: Lexington Books.

Mahler, Halfdan (1981). "Health for All by the Year 2000." *World Health* (February-March), 3–5.

National Council for International Health (1982). "Pharmaceuticals and Developing Countries: A Dialogue for Constructive Action." Washington, D.C.

Nestlé (1983). "The Dilemma of Third World Nutrition: Nestlé and the Role of Infant Formula." Vevey, Switzerland: Nestlé Corp.

Nestlé (1984). "Nestlé and the Role of Infant Formula in Developing Countries: The Resolution of a Conflict." Vevey, Switzerland: Nestlé Corp.

Perin, Sylvie (1985). "L'Afrique poubelle." *Jeune Afrique*, 1293(October 16), 65.

Pethybridge, R. (1965). "The Influence of International Politics on the Activities of Non-Political Specialized Agencies—A Case Study." *Political Studies*, 13(2), 247–51.

Riggs, Robert E. (1980). "The Bank, the IMF, and the WHO." *Journal of Conflict Resolution*, 24(2), 329–57.

Scroggins, Deborah (1987). "The Global Assault on AIDS." *The Interdependent*, 13(1), 1.

Sikkink, Kathryn (1986). "Codes of Conduct for Transnational Corporations: The Case of the WHO/UNICEF Code." *International Organization*, 40(4), 815–40.

Silverman, Milton, Philip R. Lee, and Mia Lydecker (1982). *Prescriptions for Death: The Drugging of the Third World*. Berkeley: University of California Press.

Starrels, John M. (1985). "The World Health Organization: Resisting Third World Ideological Pressures." Washington, DC: The Heritage Foundation.

Templeman, John, and Elizabeth Weiner (1985). "Reagan vs. the Global Bureaucracy: The Big Stick Is Working." *Business Week* (July 8), 32–34.

U.S. Comptroller General (1977). *U.S. Participation in the World Health Organization Still Needs Improvement*. Report to the Senate Committee on Governmental Affairs, May 16. Washington, DC: U.S. Government Printing Office.

U.S. Department of Health, Education and Welfare, Public Health Service (1976). *Report of the U.S. Delegation to the Twenty-Ninth World Health Assembly*, Geneva, Switzerland, May 3–21. Washington, DC: U.S. Government Printing Office.

U.S. Department of State (1987). "WHO." *Gist* (June).

U.S. Executive Sessions of the Senate Foreign Relations Committee (1958). Historical Series, vol. X. 85th Cong., 2d sess. Washington, DC: U.S. Government Printing Office.

U.S. House of Representatives, Committee on Foreign Affairs, Subcommittee on National Security and Scientific Developments (1971). *Science, Technology, and Diplomacy: The Politics of Global Health* by Freeman H. Quimby, Congressional Research Service. Washington, DC: U.S. Government Printing Office.

U.S. House of Representatives, Committee on Foreign Affairs, Subcommittee on International Economic Policy and Trade and on Human Rights and International Organizations (1982). Hearings, *Implementation of the World Health Organization (WHO) Code on Infant Formula Marketing Practices*. 97th Cong., 1st sess., June 16–17, 1981. Washington, D.C.: U.S. Government Printing Office.

"World Health Assembly Appeals for More Aid to Health Strategies of Developing Countries." (1986). *United Nations Chronicle*, 23(August), 101–2.

World Health Organization (1958). *The First Ten Years of the World Health Organization*. Geneva: World Health Organization.

World Health Organization (1971). *International Health Regulations (1969)*. Geneva: World Health Organization.

World Health Organization (1976). *Introducing WHO*. Geneva: World Health Organization.

World Health Organization (1982a). Biennial Report of the Director-General to the World Health Assembly and to the United Nations. *The Work of the WHA 1980–1981*. Geneva: World Health Organization.

World Health Organization (1982b). *Plan of Action for Implementing the Global Strategy for Health for All*. Geneva: World Health Organization.

World Health Organization (1982c). *Seventh General Programme of Work Covering the Period 1984–1989*. Geneva: World Health Organization.

World Health Organization (1985). *Basic Documents* 35th ed. (February). Geneva: World Health Organization.

• CHAPTER NINE •

Changing Patterns of Conflict:
The United States and UNESCO

Roger A. Coate

On December 31, 1984, the U.S. government officially terminated its membership in the United Nations Educational, Scientific and Cultural Organization (UNESCO). This policy action marked a new low in a long, troubled relationship. Almost from the inception of the organization, U.S. officials' efforts to use UNESCO as an effective instrument of foreign policy had been subject to recurring frustrations.

This chapter analyzes the evolution of U.S.-UNESCO relations in terms of both the nature of U.S. participation in the organization and the effect of UNESCO on U.S. policy and policymaking processes.[1] To what extent has why, what, and how the U.S. government sought to influence UNESCO changed over the past four decades? How best can such change be explained? How has the influence of UNESCO on policymaking in the United States changed, and why? In keeping with the basic theme of this volume, explanation for such changes will be explored in the context of the overall decline of U.S. dominance in the interstate order, as well as factors related to the issue areas with which UNESCO deals, characteristics of UNESCO itself, and U.S. domestic political factors.

As the following analysis reveals, there have been numerous changes with respect to why U.S. officials have attempted to influence UNESCO, what they have tried to influence, and how they have gone about doing so. The decline of U.S. dominance provides only an incomplete and mainly indirect explanation of such phenomena. Characteristics of UNESCO (including most notably the role of the director-general), the nature of the issue area in question, in more recent years the attitude of U.S. administrations, and the nature of American press reporting about UNESCO assist in providing a relatively more complete explanation of the deterioration of U.S.-UNESCO relations.

It is exceedingly difficult to establish precisely the impact UNESCO has had on U.S. policymaking. The substantive concerns—education, science, culture, communications—with which UNESCO has dealt represent areas in which the U.S. government has traditionally played a very small national role. National policies in these areas have generally been viewed by U.S. officials with mistrust and suspicion. In addition, the nature of the responses in UNESCO to various U.S. policy initiatives in the early years appears to have significantly influenced how U.S. officials conducted subsequent participation in the organization. These officials tended to adopt a rather negative and defensive policy posture aimed more at damage limitation than at active attempts to initiate and shape UNESCO programs and policies. This policy posture in turn influenced political processes and outcomes in UNESCO, which further frustrated and alienated U.S. officials. The nature of this dynamic feedback process becomes clearer as we reflect on the evolution of U.S.-UNESCO relations.

U.S. Participation in UNESCO

Unlike many other postwar international governmental organizations, UNESCO was largely European in origin. Active U.S. government involvement in the planning of UNESCO came relatively late. Such action was taken only after it had become clear to U.S. observers that an intergovernmental organization in education would likely be established with or without American participation.[2]

Representatives of the U.S. government joined the discussions at the 1943 Conference of Allied Ministers of Education (CAME) as observer participants. Soon external pressures, particularly from Great Britain, began to mount for more extensive American involvement. In November 1943 the U.S. observer in London cabled the State Department that "we should enter the conference as quickly as possible if we are to affiliate with it at all, because the longer we stay out the less fluid it will become and the more difficult it will be to secure modifications in its organization or objectives" (quoted in Sewell 1975: 61).[3] The American response was vigorous. "Americans, wanting an originating role, tried the gambit of starting afresh" (1975: 63) by bringing before the conference a draft constitution for a United Nations organization for educational and cultural reconstruction.

When the representatives of forty-four governments met in London on November 1, 1943, to establish such an organization, negotiations centered primarily on two alternative drafts: the CAME-U.S. draft and a French version. Following the model of the Institut International de Cooperation Intellectuelle (IICI), the French plan placed a strong emphasis on non-governmental participation. The CAME-U.S. draft was far more statist in orientation, limiting membership to representatives of national states.

The constitution that emerged from the discussions clearly reflected attentiveness to the concerns of U.S. officials, as well as those of the British and French representatives. UNESCO was to contribute to the attainment of peace and global security and world order based on liberal democratic principles "promoting collaboration among the nations through education, science and culture" (UNESCO 1984b: Article 1).

At American insistence, the mandate also encompassed communications by calling on members to "collaborate in the work of advancing the mutual knowledge and understanding of people through all means of mass communication and to that end, recommend such international agreements as may be necessary to promote the free flow of ideas by word or image" (UNESCO 1984b: Article 1, Section 2). Indeed, from the beginning the communications work of UNESCO was a predominant concern of U.S. policymakers.

UNESCO, then, was not initially the conception or initiative of U.S. officials. Creating an effective mechanism for ensuring military security took precedence. Only after it became apparent to American observers that such an organization would emerge did DOS officials undertake a strong initiative to influence the nature of the emerging entity. They made certain that UNESCO would be consistent with an American vision of an acceptable world order and that the organization would be open to U.S. influence. However, there also appears to have been a significant degree of reluctance, especially on the part of French representatives, to accept what Keohane (1984: 137) has termed the "ideological hegemony" of the United States. As will become clear in the following sections, such reluctance did not dissipate with time.

UNESCO as Policy Instrument, 1946–68

When the delegates met in Paris in 1946 for the first general conference, a number of important concerns regarding UNESCO's future had yet to be confronted. Not the least of these was selection of the first director-general. The constitution placed substantial authority and responsibility in this position. The United States assumed that the directorship-general would go to an American.[4]

However, President Truman's choice for that position, Francis Biddle, received little support (Ninkovich 1981: 97–98); subsequently Julian Huxley from the United Kingdom was elected as UNESCO's first director-general. The U.S. delegates were able, however, to negotiate two concessions regarding Huxley's selection. First, his term of office was to be limited to two years. Second, he was to appoint a deputy director-general (an American) who would be responsible for administration, personnel, and finance (Sewell 1975: 107).

Despite this initial disappointment, U.S. officials seemed to exhibit vigorous support of UNESCO in these first years, as reflected in the quality of individuals appointed to represent the United States (such as Archibald MacLeish, William Benton, and Milton Eisenhower). In addition, although participation in UNESCO did not play a major role in U.S. foreign policy during this period, officials did attempt to use the organization as a policy instrument for projecting the American vision of a global democratic order as the raison d'être of the organization's communications mandate.

Beginning in 1946 an attempt was made to get UNESCO to legitimate a U.S. initiative to establish a worldwide radio network, which was to be used as a tool in the struggle against communism. In making such a plea U.S. representative William Benton argued that mass communication was UNESCO's most important area of work (Sathyamurthy 1964: 160). As Sewell reports, however, after 1946 this proposal quietly died. Similar proposals that appeared about 1950 "in turn were dropped before the end of the Korean War, at a time when vocal segments of the American public were turning against UNESCO because of what were frequently termed its communist tendencies" (Sewell 1973: 162).

Such policy frustrations and the circumstances surrounding them were indeed symptomatic of larger concerns related to the U.S. government's participation in UNESCO. "Despite the interest taken by the [State] Department in 1947, its approach to UNESCO through 1949 was largely reactive and negative, more to assure the failure of Communist penetration than American dominance" (Ninkovich 1981: 154).

Yet Washington still voiced high hopes for UNESCO. Speaking to a meeting of the U.S. National Commission in April 1950, President Truman pledged strong support for UNESCO, whose work he termed vitally important. Predicting that UNESCO could be successful in time, he cautioned against expecting success too quickly. "In organizations like [UNESCO] . . . if over a generation or two generations we come close to accomplishing our purpose, we have made great progress" (quoted in Sewell 1973: 162–63). Perhaps Truman personally had reason for optimism. Explicitly building on the development theme in his Point Four Doctrine of 1949, UNESCO had decided to participate in the United Nations' Expanded Program of Technical Assistance (EPTA).

At the same time, however, other important actors in the U.S. government, including William Benton, were upset with UNESCO's perceived unwillingness to face up to the "political issues of war and peace" (quoted in Sewell 1975: 140–41). The first half of the 1950s brought numerous strains to U.S.-UNESCO relations. The Korean War, McCarthyism, and admission of the Soviet Union as a member had important effects on U.S. participation in this organization.

Apparently with little reluctance, U.S. officials set out to mobilize UNESCO and its facilities as propaganda instruments in what became known as the "Korean campaign of truth." One might assume that at this time in an intergovernmental organization such as UNESCO, without the membership of the Soviet Union or its Eastern European allies[5] U.S. representatives would have had little trouble mobilizing support for what was, after all (at least in name), a United Nations action. However, when the special meeting of the Executive Board convened in August 1950 at the request of the United States, the going was not as smooth as U.S. representatives might have assumed or hoped. The second director-general, Jaime Torres-Bodet, moved quickly and successfully to have his own four-point proposal accepted in place of the somewhat more demanding U.S. proposals. Although the content of such action was not fundamentally different from that contained in the American proposal, UNESCO's refusal to adopt the U.S. plan of action had far-reaching effects. "In the United States there was a growth of public frustration with this UN agency which failed to act effectively on a problem with such an obvious solution: that of exposing Communist aggression to all the world" (Sewell 1975: 150–51). This posture was not short-lived, nor was it to be reversed with the passing of this director-general. American disillusionment with UNESCO was perhaps most pronouncedly felt with respect to the organization's budget. In this regard Director-General Torres-Bodet and the U.S. delegation soon found themselves in substantial disagreement. Given the UN's "ability to pay" basis for budget assessments, the U.S. delegation was in a position to threaten and apply negative sanctions in this regard. In large part it was the U.S. delegation's use of such actions that led to Torres-Bodet's resignation at the seventh General Conference in December 1952.

Acting Director-General John Taylor and his "permanent" replacement, Luther Evans, were both Americans. However, the U.S. government–UNESCO relationship remained strained. This time the conflict was centered on attempts by the U.S. government to impose jurisdiction, as it related to alleged disloyalty and anti-American activities, over American citizens in the international civil service of UNESCO.

By the time the Soviet Union sought membership in 1954, the influence and interest of U.S. government agencies in UNESCO affairs in general had begun to wane. U.S. officials had found UNESCO to be a very unwilling and undependable instrument through which to conduct important foreign policy initiatives. The organization had failed to act as the "political" body many of its American supporters had perceived and/or desired it to be. It was in this context that a U.S.-supported British proposal to amend the UNESCO constitution and to transform the executive board into a body of member state representatives was approved. Thus no longer did Executive Board members technically serve solely in their own right as individuals, representing in theory the general conference as a whole. Furthermore, with the admission of the Soviet Union, U.S. officials sought to make UNESCO more of a technical agency than a political body.

With U.S. encouragement, UNESCO rapidly took on a more technical orientation. Early experiments with technical assistance activities expanded in scope as membership composition in UNESCO shifted more heavily toward the Third World. According to former Deputy Director-General John Fobes (1972: 113), "more self-examination of UNESCO's role in development took place in the years 1960–1962 than in all the years after 1946."

With this increased focus on technical assistance came a desire in the United States to fund such activities through special funds (such as the United Nations Development Program, or UNDP) over which U.S. officials could exercise relatively greater influence than was the case with the regular UNESCO budget. This policy orientation was accompanied by U.S. initiatives for greater budget stringency within UNESCO proper. The ongoing conflict over the budget intensified, especially with the appointment of a new director-general, René Maheu, who was determined to expand the scope of UNESCO's development activities even further. U.S. officials found that they were unable to restrain UNESCO's assessed budget at the level they preferred. Finkelstein (1988: 404) relates that Maheu frankly told Assistant Secretary of State Harlan Cleveland "that he would not follow the budget guidelines Cleveland had urged on him."

These policy setbacks fueled a growing sense of indifference toward UNESCO in the 1960s. Governmental and nongovernmental agencies that served as UNESCO's main support groups in the United States found UNESCO's increased focus on development less central to their primary mandates.

In general U.S. initiatives to use UNESCO as an instrument of foreign policy during this early period tended to be focused on three primary areas: regime creation, promotion of operational activities, and collective legitimation of U.S. foreign policies. In all three areas U.S. officials endeavored to build on the liberal ideological foundations incorporated within the UNESCO Constitution and to promote notions of mass media, mass education, and individual human rights.

In this regard U.S. officials participated in the preparation and/or adoption of various standard-setting instruments that were subsequently adopted by the general conference. In addition, American experts played an active role in conducting preparatory studies that contributed to the formulation of such principles. These conventions included the 1948 Agreement for Facilitating the International Circulation of Visual and Auditory Materials of an Educational, Scientific and Cultural Character; the 1950 Agreement on the Importation of the Educational, Scientific and Cultural Materials; the Universal Copyright Convention and its annexed protocols (1952); and the 1958 Convention Concerning the International Exchange of Publications. Of these the Universal Copyright Convention is perhaps the most notable. It was drawn up specifically to enable Americans to participate directly in a universal copyright protection system. It is the only international copyright instrument of worldwide scope to which the U.S. government is a party.

UNESCO also served to provide a mechanism for Americans to participate in the international governance of collective goods, to conduct certain operational activities, and to promote international scholarly cooperation in education, science, and culture. U.S. representatives were instrumental in initiating numerous international programs, such as the Intergovernmental Oceanographic Commission (IOC), which was established in 1960 to promote cooperative scientific investigation of the ocean space, and the International Hydrological Decade, which promoted the transfer of technical advice on water resource management to the Third World. In addition, Americans were encouraged to serve on the permanent staff of the secretariat and to participate as field experts and consultants. Indeed, American expert influence tended to predominate in various UNESCO substantive sectors, especially in education and science.

During the earliest years of the organization, U.S. officials vigorously attempted to use UNESCO to legitimate various foreign policy initiatives. Perhaps most notable were the aforementioned attempts to establish an anti-Soviet worldwide radio network under UNESCO's auspices and to engage the agency in the U.S.-designed "Korean campaign of truth." In both cases the responses from UNESCO and its member states disappointed U.S. officials. As discussed earlier, from the mid-1950s onward a main U.S. concern in UNESCO became the refocusing of the organization's activities to more technically oriented concerns (that is, technical assistance and cooperation). Although they viewed the organization as an undependable instrument for major U.S. foreign policy initiatives, officials actively promoted the legitimation of liberal ideological values.

U.S.-UNESCO relations have been troubled since these early times, but 1969 marks an identifiable turning point. One indicator of a change in participation concerns the nature and tenure of appointees who served as U.S. representatives to the Executive Board. With a series of U.S. board members serving short terms beginning in 1969, U.S. participation became markedly less coherent, more reactive, and oriented toward damage limitation rather than being positive and oriented toward projecting a leadership role. The U.S. National Commission functioned less and less effectively.[6]

UNESCO as a Policy Instrument after 1968

Throughout the 1960s a fundamental element of U.S. interest in UNESCO remained the propagation of the concept of free flow of information through mass communication as part of the liberal democratic order. In general UNESCO's work in communications reflected such interests. Technical assistance efforts in this area focused on building communications infrastructures in developing societies. With the UNESCO-sponsored international meeting of specialists on mass communication and society in Montreal in 1969, however, communications debates in UNESCO's political bodies began to focus on Third World complaints about dependence on communications and information infrastructures centered in advanced industrial societies. Third World delegates charged that a huge imbalance existed in the global distribution of and control over communications resources. Major Western wire services were said to monopolize world news coverage, creating a one-way flow of information. To redress these perceived asymmetries, Third World delegates introduced the notion of a new international information order to the UNESCO debates.

In addition, Soviet delegates began an overt assault on the concept of free flow of information. Delegates to UNESCO's 1972 conference initiated discussions of a declaration on mass media. Although Soviet resolutions in this regard were not adopted, they posed serious challenges for U.S. officials and soon became the primary preoccupation of American participants. Moreover, Soviet proposals tended to become confused in the United States with the Third World calls for a new order.

The American press and most U.S. government officials viewed the call for a new order as an attempt to exert state control over the press and to restrict the free flow of information. In response, U.S. officials, along with other Western delegates, began in 1974 to engage actively in UNESCO communications debates. Contrary to widespread perceptions in the

United States, these American endeavors were generally successful in defending free press interests, and UNESCO programs remained oriented toward Western free press concepts.

At UNESCO's general conferences in 1974, 1976, and 1978 Soviet-initiated draft declarations on the media, including articles that would sanction the supremacy of the state over the press, were defeated. The 1976 proposal did serve to structure the conference debate over the new international information order issue around the topic of free press versus state sovereignty, but in each case the conference took actions that reinforced freedom of the press. In 1974, for example, the director-general was authorized to undertake cooperative measures to facilitate the free and balanced flow of information between industrially advanced and developing societies. Two years later the Nineteenth General Conference, with the strong support of the United States, instructed the director-general to review all of the problems of communications in contemporary society. This he did by appointing the International Commission for the Study of Communications, also known as the MacBride Commission. This U.S. initiative was designed to move future communications debates away from ideological rhetoric and to set the framework for a later program of action—the International Program for the Development of Communications (IPDC).

At the Twentieth General Conference in 1978 Soviet delegates again tried to get UNESCO to adopt a highly restrictive declaration on fundamental principles governing use of the mass media. In fact, a mass media declaration adopted that year called for the free flow and better-balanced dissemination of information, not for increased state controls. To the Soviet delegation's chagrin this declaration was a free press-oriented statement calling for freedom of opinion, expression, and information recognized as an integral part of human rights and fundamental freedoms. The statement argued that journalists must have access and freedom to report information.

The Twenty-First General Conference in 1980 unanimously adopted the report of the MacBride Commission. Debate over a draft proposal to establish a commission for the protection of journalists, however, sent shock waves through the U.S. government and the American press. Moves for the "protection" of journalists were seen as largely being covers for state "licensing," a totally unacceptable concept to proponents of American First Amendment freedoms. The debate surrounding this issue became the exclusive focus of Western news reports about the general conference (Sussman 1984b: 2), in spite of the fact that the proposal never resulted in a formal resolution.

In the minds of many American reporters and government officials, the proposals for a new information order were seen as a Soviet-inspired Third World attack on the free press. To the contrary, as late as 1978 Soviet officials were arguing that there was no need for a new order; the current one based on state sovereignty was sufficient. Furthermore, although UNESCO, including its director-general, was actively involved in defeating Soviet initiatives on state sovereignty over the media, the American press has tended misleadingly to credit UNESCO with proposing such ideas. Moreover, representatives of thirty-three media organizations in the United States, Western Europe, Latin America, and Asia joined together to form the World Press Freedom Committee (WPFC). The main purpose of this new body was to work and speak out against advocates of state-controlled media and other opponents of a private enterprise (that is, "free") press. This group became especially active in monitoring activities in UNESCO and in working to shape U.S. communications policy toward the organization.

In an attempt to turn the communications issue around and refocus it toward a more Western orientation, the U.S. government, along with other Western free press supporters, initiated in 1980 the International Program for the Development of Communications. The purpose of the IPDC was to reorient UNESCO's discussions and actions over communications away from ideological debate over new orders and toward the technical development of communications infrastructure in developing societies. Western financing and technology were to be used to create regional and local news agencies and other communication capabilities.

The IPDC was approved, and a thirty-five-member intergovernmental board to supervise the program was established. Although much of the funding pledged by the United States and other members has not materialized, the program has generally been hailed as a success (Sussman 1984d: 6). For example, the IPDC has assisted with creation of the Pan African News Agency (PANA), which served as the continent's first interregional communications system.

By the end of the Twenty-Second General Conference in 1983 the situation in UNESCO had become even more favorable. Several significant gains had been made by American and other free press advocates. These included a decision to treat the New World Information and Communications Order (NWICO) as merely an "evolving process," not as a series of imposed regulations. In addition, programs to study the watchdog role of the press and to examine governmental censorship were established. Ironically, Western victory in this protracted debate in UNESCO occurred precisely as the main protagonists for the free press position (that is, the Americans) withdrew.

This analysis of the communications debate indicates that U.S. officials had *not* lost the ability to influence policy outcomes in UNESCO effectively. When American needs and interests were clearly articulated and U.S. officials actively engaged in the decision processes of the organization, policy outcomes were largely satisfactory.

UNESCO's programs and activities in the area of human rights represent another case in point. Despite the rhetoric during debates in the delegate bodies about people's rights, the basic approach taken in UNESCO has consistently been compatible with that promoted by the United States. UNESCO has given priority to promoting traditional individual human rights; the notion of people's rights has never attained the status of a program.

The UNESCO program on international human rights was largely U.S. built over a period of several years. U.S. representatives were active in preparing a recommendation concerning education for international understanding, cooperation, peace, human rights, and fundamental freedoms, which was adopted by the general conference in 1974. Americans were also instrumental in drafting the rules of procedure and in defining the mandate of the Committee on Conventions and Recommendations (CR), established in UNESCO in 1978. This body is charged with examining allegations of individual human rights violations in the areas of UNESCO's competence. Important from a U.S. government perspective was the inclusion of machinery to expose Soviet violations of human rights (Buergenthal and Torney 1976).

These policy successes in UNESCO for the United States and other Western delegations did not come about by chance. In large part the outcomes resulted from the active interventionist role played by the director-general. It was Director-General M'Bow who warned that the 1976 Soviet draft resolution was unconstitutional, thus leading to its demise (Sussman 1984b: 9). In 1978 he again interceded to kill the Soviets' main communications draft. A Western-oriented resolution subsequently was approved (Sussman 1984c: 6). In order to achieve such successes, U.S. representatives have had to engage in bargaining and to cooperate with the director-general as well as with delegates of other member states. Yet as we have seen, this had been the case since the early years of UNESCO.

In addition to these post-1968 initiatives in defense of the established communications and human rights regimes, Americans were perhaps the most aggressively engaged in UNESCO's natural science program area (UNESCO 1984a). American scientists as well as government representatives were active in planning and organizing a number of the organization's most important large-scale science programs. The Man and the Biosphere (MAB) program, which was conceived at a UNESCO-sponsored conference in 1968, was officially launched in 1971. Not only did Americans play a key role in creating the program, but U.S. officials remained actively involved in MAB's international coordinating council.

Earth scientists from the United States helped to create UNESCO's International Geological Correlation Program (IGCP), which promotes international cooperation in global geological problems. Since the program's inception in 1973, Americans have gained increased access to foreign mineral and energy resource data and to geological sites such as Siberia that are not accessible under other circumstances. Another important U.S. initiative was the international hydrological program, established in 1974 to provide technical assistance in that area. This program has provided access to information on geographical areas and research results that would not otherwise be available. Americans also remained active in the Intergovernmental Oceanographic Commission, whose oceanographic data exchange has provided Americans, including the U.S. Navy, access to a large amount of important data on oceans, currents, and winds. A 1983 interagency review of U.S. participation in UNESCO's natural science sector underscored the importance for the United States of this information-gathering (that is, intelligence) function (National Science Foundation 1983: 1). U.S. officials have regularly served on the numerous intergovernmental councils that oversee and regulate these activities.

U.S. officials were also active, especially in the early 1970s, in preparing and adopting various standard-setting instruments. These included conventions on prohibiting the illicit exchange and transfer of ownership of cultural property (1970); protecting against the unauthorized duplication of phonograms (1971); protecting the world cultural and natural heritage (1972); and the 1971 revision of the Universal Copyright Convention. The World Cultural and Natural Heritage Agreement resulted largely from a U.S. initiative. After the early 1970s U.S. officials approached the topic of standard setting rather cautiously as the debate in UNESCO's delegate bodies tended more and more to reflect challenges to the established international order—particularly the call for a New World Information and Communications Order.

The outcomes of these communications debates, however, generally reflected U.S. officials' preferences. Moreover, in the years immediately preceding U.S. withdrawal from UNESCO the most contentious aspects of the NWICO were greatly reduced. As reported by the Department of State in its 1983 report to Congress under PL 97-241, the subject of the protection of journalists had disappeared from UNESCO's agenda after 1981. Yet the U.S. government's actions in and "policy" toward UNESCO continued to be predominantly negative, reactive, and oriented toward damage limitation—and then withdrawal. What was the Reagan administration trying to influence in UNESCO, and why?

Disillusionment Turns to Withdrawal

U.S. officials' disenchantment with UNESCO reached a climax in late 1983. In a letter to Director-General M'Bow dated December 29, Secretary of State Shultz formally announced President Reagan's decision to withdraw from UNESCO. The withdrawal was to take effect on December 31, 1984, after a twelve-month waiting period required by the UNESCO Constitution.

Three main concerns with UNESCO were specified by the Department of State (1984b):

(1) excessive politicization of UNESCO's programs and personnel
(2) promotion of statist theories
(3) unrestrained budgetary expansion and poor management practices.

For the first six months in 1984 these general concerns served as the primary justifications for withdrawal. By midyear, however, it was apparent to many observers both inside and outside UNESCO that these concerns were only superficially related to why and what Reagan administration officials were trying to influence by their withdrawal action.

Analysis of background materials indicates that undue politicization, promotion of statist theories, and excessive budgetary expansion and mismanagement were not generally perceived to pose serious threats to American interests in UNESCO (Coate 1988: 10–16). These materials were produced by thirteen separate governmental departments and agencies with UNESCO-related mandates, eighty-three U.S. embassies and consulates, the U.S. National Commission for UNESCO, and numerous nongovernmental organizations at the request of the State Department for an in-depth review of U.S.-UNESCO relations conducted in late summer and fall of 1983.

However, the conclusions presented in the *U.S./UNESCO Policy Review* (U.S. Department of State 1984b) and released by the State Department on February 27, 1984 to justify the withdrawal action bore only marginal resemblance to the recommendations from these bodies. For example, *none* of the reports from any contributing body viewed the situation in UNESCO as warranting withdrawal. Indeed, the recommendation of the interagency working group on science headed by the National Science Foundation (1983: 8) stated that "the scientific benefits the United States derives from participation in UNESCO clearly warrant our continued participation." Though identifying certain "organizational shortcomings" in UNESCO as being problematic from an American perspective, the NSF report focuses much more extensively and critically on problems of funding, coordinating, and managing U.S. participation in UNESCO.

The Department of Education's report (1983: 6–7) on UNESCO's education sector states,

> During negotiations on what the United States considers fundamental uncompromisable issues in education, when we are represented by well qualified negotiators, the U.S. usually prevails. . . . Despite our frustration, most of the General Conference education agenda is not ideological, political or contentious. Even the troublesome standard-setting area represents only a small percentage of what UNESCO does.

UNESCO was said to constitute a stabilizing institutional influence clearly in U.S. interests. In addition, "UNESCO virtually alone maintains the effort to develop effective methodologies for eradicating illiteracy" (U.S. Department of Education 1983: 7). The U.S. Agency for International Development's (AID) report articulated even stronger support:

> UNESCO serves several functions in educational development unique to all other development agencies. . . . No other bilateral or multilateral development agency is equipped or willing to serve in these capacities. For those purposes alone, the U.S. should not cut off funding to UNESCO completely. (U.S. AID 1983a: 2)

The Smithsonian Institution (1983: 2) argued that it was "essential that United States access to UNESCO be maintained and that UNESCO's essential programs not be crippled for want of U.S. financial support and leadership." With respect to UNESCO's communications sector, the USAID report (1983b: 2) concluded, "In sum, basic U.S. interests in communications are reasonably well served. U.S. withdrawal would not enhance the achievement of those U.S. objectives."

In addition, the Twenty-Second General Conference, which concluded just one month before the U.S. withdrawal announcement, was relatively positive from an American perspective. In his report to the U.S. National Commission in December 1983, the head of the U.S. delegation to the conference, Edmund Hennelly, concluded in part that his personal balance sheet showed that the conference had been a "clear plus for the U.S." He evaluated this general conference to have been "among the least politicized and the most constructive from the U.S. point of view in recent memory" (U.S. National Commission for UNESCO 1984: 11).

The State Department's own *Report to Congress* (1984a) under sections 108 and 109 of PL 97-241 in February 1983 provides even a greater challenge to the claim that undue politicization, statist theories, and unrestrained budgetary expansion and mismanagement were what U.S. officials were attempting to influence by withdrawal. These reports concluded that UNESCO's programs for the most part contributed to U.S. foreign policy goals and particular U.S. educational, scientific, and cultural interests; that vigorous continued U.S. participation in UNESCO was essential to protect U.S. interests; and that UNESCO was not implementing any policy or procedure that would justify withholding funds under the provisions of PL 97-241.

The reports also identified various direct and indirect economic benefits to the United States. "UNESCO expenditures which benefit the United States . . . amount to about 40 percent of the value of the U.S. contribution." Such direct expenditures included fellowships, procurement of U.S. equipment, consultants' fees, and payments to American staff. "Similarly, United States prominence in UNESCO's science and education sectors creates markets for U.S. scientific and educational products and materials" (U.S. Department of State 1983b: 5). Viewed together with the seven other ways listed in the reports in which UNESCO membership served U.S. national interests, one begins anew to raise questions about the withdrawal actions.

Why and what were U.S. officials trying to influence in UNESCO? A July 13, 1984, letter from Assistant Secretary of State Gregory Newell to the director-general helps in part to answer such a question. In that letter the assistant secretary redefined the U.S. government's position on reform. Shifting from his previous litany on politicization, statist theories, and budget/management problems, Newell outlined three new concerns that he claimed were of fundamental importance to the U.S. government:

(1) creating mechanisms to assure that important UNESCO decisions and programs enjoy the support of all major groups, including the Western Group;
(2) a return by UNESCO to concentration upon its original purposes; and
(3) the assumption by member states of their rightful authority in the organization, through strengthening of the General Conference, and in particular, the Executive Board. (Newell 1984)

These fundamental reforms point to several primary concerns, which appear to have underlaid the Reagan administration's UNESCO policy.

Administration officials were frustrated at the inability to use UNESCO —and, indeed, the United Nations more generally—effectively as an instrument of U.S. foreign policy. Although attempts to beat back Soviet and Third World challenges to the concept of the free flow of information had been successful for the most part, there appears to have been particular frustration within the administration over the inability to control outcomes in UNESCO. To overcome such a condition U.S. officials proposed various structural changes that would give a very small minority of member states, the primary Western funders, such control.[7] However, such a proposal found little or no official support in UNESCO, even among members of the Western caucusing group, the Western Information Group (WIG).

Other Western delegates argued that such capability already existed. Major UNESCO decisions, including program and budget matters, had been made by consensus since the mid-1970s. A drafting and negotiating group (DNG) mechanism in the general conference served to enable regional groups, including the Western group, to block highly contentious and ideologically inspired resolutions. This concurrent majority system appears to have worked rather effectively in those cases in which relative intragroup cohesion existed in WIG. However, a problem from the U.S. government's perspective seems to have been getting other Western group members to support American policy positions.

Reagan administration officials also wished to purge from UNESCO all political debates that questioned the legitimacy of the established global communications order. The outcomes of such debates seem to have become very obscured in the minds of many high-level policymakers. For example, although such challenges had been consistently turned back as a result of timely interventions by the director-general, UNESCO has more often than not been charged with having initiated or led the challenges (Sussman 1984b). The communications debates were not likely to stop, so withdrawal might well have been seen as the most appropriate unilateral course of action.

In addition, inherent in Assistant Secretary Newell's redefined statement of fundamental concerns was a desire to diminish substantially the relative status and influence of the director-general. However, administration officials were cautious never to publicly attack Director-General M'Bow; to do so would not only have rallied Third World supporters to his defense but would likely have alienated many Western delegates as well.

Finally, it appears that an important indirect target of the Reagan administration's action in UNESCO was the United Nations itself. Soon after Ronald Reagan took office in 1981, administration budget officials took aim at the UN system, especially at UNESCO. David Stockman, director-designate of the Office of Management and Budget (OMB), proposed that the president might wish to consider withdrawing from

UNESCO. Stockman urged such action in the context of an overall retrenchment in foreign aid—especially multilateral aid. Furthermore, he discussed additional cost savings that could be made should the U.S. refuse to pay its legally binding assessments for 1981 and 1982 (Fobes 1981).

Such early predilections were quite compatible with a broader ideological approach taking form in the White House and elsewhere in Washington both inside and outside the U.S. government. According to a former high-level White House adviser who was actively engaged in the UNESCO issue, Stockman was merely attempting to exploit deep-seated anti-UN as well as anti-UNESCO attitudes among right-wing White House officials and advisers in order to slash the budget (U.S. Department of State 1983a).

These anti-UN attitudes were bolstered by an aggressive campaign by the Washington-based Heritage Foundation and other right-wing political groups to get the United States out of the United Nations. The UN was portrayed as an anti-U.S. organization that attacked

> the very essence and philosophical base of the free enterprise system. It is an assault which condemns, almost without supporting evidence, the notion that the dynamics of growth and economic expansion is individual initiative, creativity and the incentive provided by the opportunity of making a profit.
> . . . In repudiating free enterprise, and by ignoring capitalism's record of success, the United Nations and its agencies have raised to the level of gospel the tenets of what is called the New International Economic Order. . . . The tenacity with which the United Nations fights for NIEO at every forum, from every rostrum and in every possible publication and statement is awesome. (Pines 1984: xi)

Moreover, because the UN provides a forum for the articulation of such challenges by member states, there seems to be a belief that if the United Nations were to go away, somehow so might such challenges—"a world without the UN would be a better world" (Pines 1984: xix). It would appear that UNESCO was viewed as the UN system's Achilles' heel. How much of a change does this attitude represent, however?

Changing Patterns of Influence

When comparing the nature of U.S. participation in UNESCO since the late 1960s with that of the earlier period, several important differences and similarities are noteworthy. First, since the early 1970s U.S. officials have been much less active in initiating standard-setting instruments in the UNESCO forum. The primary exception has been in the area of human rights, where Americans remained quite active throughout the decade. On the other hand, U.S. representatives frequently found themselves on the defensive, confronting Third World and Soviet challenges to the maintenance of established international orders and regimes, especially in the areas of information and human rights.

Second, after finding UNESCO to be a difficult forum for legitimating foreign policy actions, U.S. officials were reluctant to use UNESCO for such purposes. Moreover, from the mid-1950s onward U.S. initiatives focused more on the organization's functional mandates, operational activities, and scientific and intellectual cooperation. Since the late 1960s initiatives have focused heavily on scientific cooperation, surveillance through information gathering, and technical assistance.

In the 1980s it appears that UNESCO became a symbol in important U.S. policymaking circles of all that was perceived to be wrong with the United Nations. Withdrawal from UNESCO would send a clear message to member states, as well as to international administrators, that the time had come for serious change in the structures and processes of other UN institutions.

This analysis—as with any brief treatment—can hardly do full justice to the diversity of UNESCO's concerns and, hence, to the variability in its usefulness to different constituencies. Nonetheless, the debates over communications clearly colored the attitudes of both government officials and an influential private group—the media. And because it became the symbol of all that was wrong with the UN, other groups such as scientists could not make their case heard for the value of the organization. UNESCO has always posed unique problems for the United States, however, because it deals with issues that are not within the purview of the federal government's power and, indeed, on which there has often been strong antipathy in the United States to a governmental role. Thus the pattern of instrumentality may not be all that surprising. But what has been the pattern of UNESCO's influence on the United States?

UNESCO's Influence on U.S. Policy

The discussion that led to the founding of UNESCO forced U.S. officials to look beyond the narrow sectoral boundaries that had tended to characterize planning for postwar educational recovery and to look toward the creation of a more comprehensive global order. International educational, scientific, and cultural policy had to be viewed in an integrative manner and coordinated accordingly. To these areas U.S. officials added mass communications.

Moreover, the UNESCO Constitution required the U.S. government to make arrangements for associating the principal American nongovernmental and governmental bodies in these sectors with the work of the organization. The nature that such popular participation should take became a topic of debate. An important element in that debate was the extent to which a U.S. national commission should be associated with and/ or subject to control by the State Department (Ninkovich 1981: 95). When Congress created a large, popularly based national commission by joint resolution in 1946, the nature of its future relationship with the State Department was left ambiguous and never completely resolved.

Frustration with what was perceived as UNESCO's failure to act as the political organization that it was designed to be led to growing U.S. disinterest in UNESCO affairs. The tension between UNESCO's political and functional tasks created an identity problem that compounded the situation. U.S. participation became more negative, defensive, and oriented toward damage limitation.

Over time a dynamic relationship emerged between changes in UNESCO and U.S. participation. As the organization's resources and energies were channeled away from intellectual cooperation, disinterest gave way to alienation toward the organization in some important policy circles. The quality of U.S. participation declined. A void in leadership was filled by an already strong directorship-general.

Many functional agencies in Washington effectively disengaged from UNESCO. After the late 1960s the organization's domestic support base diminished among both professional and civic organizations. These problems intensified as certain issues on the UNESCO agenda, especially those related to the Arab-Israeli conflict and the NWICO, entered the political agenda in Washington.

In 1974 the general conference adopted three resolutions concerning Israel or limiting its participation and granted the Palestinian Liberation Organization (PLO) observer status. These actions and related events generated immediate consternation from various quarters inside and outside the U.S. government. They also led to a congressional ban on contributions to UNESCO until the president could certify that such conditions had been corrected (Section 9[a] [12] of the Foreign Assistance Act of 1974 (PL 93-559]).

The actual crisis was short-lived, and the following year President Ford certified that the situation had been sufficiently rectified to allow funding to resume. The Israeli issue was resolved in 1976 for all intents and purposes with the admission of Israel into the European regional program group. The impact of these anti-Israeli activities on U.S. participation in UNESCO, however, lingered for years. One of the most significant long-term impacts was the change in attitude within the American Jewish community toward UNESCO. Although historically Jewish scientists and educators, as well as other Jewish intellectuals, had been among the most active participants in U.S.-UNESCO relations, many prominent Jews ceased to participate in UNESCO's work after these 1974 actions. Moreover, although Israeli officials in Paris in 1984 privately voiced trepidation over U.S. withdrawal, Jewish groups in the United States generally voiced strong support for President Reagan's action.

The NWICO debates of the mid-1970s also had a profound impact outside as well as within the government. Representatives of a number of media organizations in the United States and Western Europe, for example, formed the World Press Freedom Committee to work and speak out against advocates of state-controlled media and other opponents of a free press. This group became especially active in monitoring activities in UNESCO and shaping U.S. communications policy toward the organization.

The NWICO debates quickly became an obsession with many American reporters covering UNESCO affairs.

> The U.S. news media reported these communications debates at UNESCO as though the ultimate agenda was censorship. . . . Yet, never have any of these elements [licensing journalists, codes of journalistic conduct, monitoring reporting] been approved at UNESCO. Not a single resolution, not a single statement of a top official of UNESCO ever called for licensing, governmental codes for journalists, monitoring of journalistic output, or censorship. (Sussman 1984c: 6)

After extensively documenting American news media coverage of UNESCO activities, Leonard Sussman, executive director of Freedom House, concluded that "American press coverage has reflected the *possibilities* of press-controls, not actualities, and that important distinction has never been made clear" (1984b: 9).[9]

An important point to be made in this regard is that such incomplete and biased reporting, when internalized as an important component of the policymaking process, can have quite a significant impact on policy and policymaking processes. This, indeed, is what happened with respect to the management and conduct of U.S. participation in UNESCO.

Although the outcomes of UNESCO communications debates were relatively positive from an American perspective after 1981, the impact of the communications issue on U.S. policy became increasingly negative. Most notable in this regard was passage in 1982 of the Beard Amendment—Section 109 of the State Department Authorization Act for fiscal year 1982–83, PL 97-241, which prohibited U.S. contributions to UNESCO should the organization implement any policy or procedure that licensed journalists or their publications or restricted the free flow of information with or among countries, or imposed mandatory codes of journalistic practice or ethics. The secretary of state was required to report annually to Congress concerning such matters. Such reports constituted a new formalized agenda item for the U.S. Department of State and Congress.

In summary, then, growing American disinterest in UNESCO during the late 1960s rapidly became transformed into alienation in many policy-relevant circles in subsequent decades. At the same time, however, the proliferation of program activities in UNESCO brought numerous new items into U.S. policy agendas. These concerns became scattered among various governmental bureaus and agencies, as well as numerous non-governmental bodies. As summarized in 1983 by a U.S. AID official:

> Frequently, interested staff members are scattered individuals, not even in a single office of the agency, and their efforts on UNESCO matters tend to be isolated from the main thrust of their agencies, and from the knowledge their agency colleagues have. Moreover, bilateral technical activities that one agency may initiate with UNESCO may escape the notice of the State Department. Thus, the overall impression is of a bewildering proliferation of disparate activities, all of seemingly marginal value. (U.S. AID 1983b)

UNESCO's legitimacy problems in the United States grew.

As a result of the very diversity of UNESCO's activities and of the scattered nature of its constituencies, when Assistant Secretary Newell decided that the United States should withdraw from UNESCO, there was no centralized group to coordinate the opposition. Indeed, relatively few strong protests were heard from American educational, scientific, cultural, or communications constituencies. Not only were a great many of UNESCO's activities viewed as somewhat marginal to mainstream sectoral interests in these areas, but most observers of UNESCO had also been socialized by the American press to view the organization with disregard.

Explaining Change in U.S.-UNESCO Relations

In the foregoing analysis of U.S.-UNESCO relations a number of changes have been identified with respect to (1) what U.S. officials have sought to influence in UNESCO, why they did so, and how they went about doing it; and (2) how UNESCO has influenced U.S. policymaking. Were these changes primarily the product of a relative decline in U.S. "power resources" and an associated decline in willingness and ability to control outcomes? What alternative explanations can we offer? What roles did issue area attributes, characteristics of UNESCO, and/or domestic political factors play in this regard?

Decline of U.S. Power

The decline of power explanation as outlined in chapter 1 does not fit well with the circumstances of the UNESCO case. As we have observed, there was an early and sustained decline in U.S. efforts to use UNESCO to legitimate specific U.S. foreign policy actions. UNESCO was tried and found to be a very reluctant or unwilling party to U.S. efforts to use the organization as a propaganda instrument or to wage an anti-communist struggle. Frustrations over such difficulties helped to feed growing disenchantment and disinterest toward UNESCO in important political circles.

U.S. policy toward UNESCO soon turned rather negative and reactionary. Since the 1960s much effort has been expended attempting to limit potential damage to U.S. policy interests rather than attempting to initiate and shape UNESCO's programs and policies. Such a change appeared long before any substantial decline in U.S. dominance.

In the substantive issue areas of UNESCO's mandate—education, science, culture, and communications—it is not clear that a relative decline in *relevant* political resources actually occurred or, if so, when it occurred. The "power resources"—economic and military—which are the main foundations of the decline of power explanation, are not general political resources of tremendous utility in the UNESCO forum. American scientific, cultural, and communications preeminence in the world appeared to have shifted much less dramatically than in economic and military areas.

Indeed, the data seem clear: when U.S. officials were actively engaged in UNESCO, clearly stating policy preferences on issues that were important to them, UNESCO outcomes were generally compatible with such preferences. The problem was basically one of political will, not capability. The point should be underscored, however, that a clear link does not seem to have existed between this lack of willingness to remain actively engaged in UNESCO and any general decline in relative influence capability. In order to understand better the forces at play in this regard, we need to examine the impact of issue area characteristics.

Characteristics of the Issue Areas

The nature of UNESCO's substantive issue focus seems to have affected the evolution of U.S.-UNESCO relations in several ways. The main foci of

UNESCO involved areas Americans believed were inappropriate issues for national government intervention. Educational and cultural policy were traditionally not federal government activities; therefore American government officials had little experience in dealing with such areas. Lacking national ministries, organizing and coordinating policy to engage effectively in UNESCO affairs requires extraordinary activities and energies, which in the context of a large, complex bureaucracy are difficult to sustain over the long term. Moreover, other elements of UNESCO's mandates focused on subjects that struck at the heart of liberal ideology: individual human rights, free flow of information, a free press. The majority of members in UNESCO, including both Third World and Western European governments, found statist solutions to some of these problems acceptable. However, statist approaches ran squarely counter to American values. When these values were perceived to be threatened, selective attention and energies were focused to deal with the "problem." Such a defensive and reactive posture seems to have had the cumulative impact of creating and then reinforcing an extremely negative image of UNESCO and its activities.

Domestic Factors

Growing ideological differences between UNESCO and the United States were exacerbated by domestic political factors. Changes in administration do not provide the primary explanation, however, for why the nature and effectiveness of U.S. participation in UNESCO had declined markedly over many years, especially after 1968. A frequently told story alleges that shortly after taking office President Nixon scrawled a pejorative note ("Let's gut this outfit") on the corner of a UNESCO-related memorandum (personal communication from former official). Later Nixon appointed one of his wife's relatives, Edward Sullivan, as the U.S. ambassador to UNESCO. During Sullivan's two-year term (1973–74) he attended relatively few board functions, and it was during this period that Arab members were successful in pushing through their anti-Israeli resolutions. Thus the decline of American interest and leadership within UNESCO preceded the debates over freedom of the press.

Nonetheless, the galvanizing issue leading to the U.S.-UNESCO split was the debate over the free flow of information. The image of UNESCO that most Americans received, including many high-level foreign policy decision makers, was that provided by the American press. Fixated narrowly on self-interested aspects of UNESCO's communications debate, the American media produced an image of the organization that was far

from representative or in any sense of the word "objective." As we
have seen, that image was generally a very negative and misleading
one.

Of course, high-level officials have access to other channels of
information regarding UNESCO's activities. Yet experience with the
Reagan administration indicates that such information channels can be and
indeed have been unintentionally or intentionally ignored. For example,
early in the Reagan administration the U.S. National Commission for
UNESCO was targeted for zero funding. Administration officials
apparently did not wish to hear from those parties that were mandated by
Congress to manage U.S.-UNESCO relations.

In addition, the presence of a particular official in a key position was
crucial to the outcome. Gregory Newell, a young former campaign aide
and White House employee, was appointed assistant secretary of state for
International Organization Affairs, and he acted swiftly to make UNESCO
withdrawal "his issue." Newell quietly attempted to isolate and discredit
several leading conservatives who were knowledgeable in UNESCO
affairs, among them Edmund Hennelly and Leonard Sussman. In addition,
Newell so intimidated various staff members within the IO Bureau that
they were afraid to speak out with information they believed the assistant
secretary did not want to hear (Personal interview). Moreover, at least one
important draft document that had been written as part of the UNESCO
review process and which was highly critical of the State Department's
management of U.S. participation in UNESCO was suppressed in the
bureau. Several staff members feared negative retribution by Newell
should the information in the document be made known. For example,
an internal 1983 State Department draft document concluded, "the
U.S. government has not had for many years an articulated set of
goals and objectives which, linked together, constitute a comprehensive policy toward UNESCO" (U.S. Department of State 1983a). Such
a conclusion is consistent with that of a report by the U.S. comptroller
general in September 1979 titled *UNESCO Programming and Budgeting
Need Greater U.S. Attention*. That report concluded, "U.S. efforts
in UNESCO in recent years have been directed more toward political
concerns than with Agency programs" (U.S. Comptroller General
1979: ii–iii).

Other U.S. governmental agencies echoed similar concerns and
criticisms in their contributions to the Department of State's review of
UNESCO. As a congressional staff report concluded, "U.S. management
of its relations with UNESCO over the years has helped bring on some of
the problems UNESCO now faces" (U.S. House of Representatives 1984:
34).

Characteristics of UNESCO

In addition, characteristics of UNESCO as an organization clearly affected changes in the U.S.-UNESCO relationship both negatively and positively. General U.S. dissatisfaction was fueled by reports of serious management problems within the organization as well as controversy over the director-general's management style. The position of the director-general had gained preeminence within the organization with respect to influencing policy outcomes. Throughout the 1970s and 1980s the director-general worked with U.S. representatives to create positive solutions from an American perspective when U.S. officials were actively engaged in UNESCO and made their objectives and desires clear (Finkelstein 1982: 26).

Although American press coverage of Director-General M'Bow might have led casual observers to a different conclusion, former U.S. Ambassador to UNESCO Estaban Torres (1977–79) and Edmund Hennelly, head of the U.S. delegation to the Twenty-Second General Conference in 1983, both considered M'Bow, the director-general from 1974 to 1987, to have been an effective leader (U.S. House of Representatives 1984; Weber 1984: 14). M'Bow demonstrated time and again that he knew well how to use his influence effectively to protect against what he saw as threats to himself and UNESCO (Personal interviews). Although the preeminent position of the director-general was clearly perceived within the Reagan administration, high-level officials did not recognize that M'Bow stood ready and willing to use his substantial influence to protect fundamental U.S. interests as well as those of his other constituencies in an almost totally political way. Instead, administration officials viewed M'Bow as another "evil emperor" out to destroy the American way of life and liberal democratic values (Summary observations from interviews).

Communications debates in UNESCO presented an important challenge to liberal values and became the predominant focus of U.S. participation in the 1970s and 1980s. Yet excepting the IPDC initiative, the U.S. policy posture remained largely negative and reactive. The positive outcomes of the communications debates from a U.S. perspective appear to be related more to characteristics of UNESCO—most important, the active interventionist role of the director-general—than the result of effective U.S. participation.

The primary mechanisms by which U.S. officials have attempted to influence UNESCO have changed over the years. In the early period the main avenues for projecting influence involved the initiation of agenda items (such as the UNESCO radio network, Korean campaign of truth, substantive programs and policy actions) budget stringency, and electoral support of executive heads. Over time U.S. officials have expanded and diversified their mechanisms of influence. Close cooperation with the director-general has been one such mechanism. Legislative mandates linking U.S. contributions to certain conditions provided important leverage on occasion. Such actions appear to have sent a clear message to the director-general and other member states regarding limits of toleration with respect to specific issues such as Israel and NWICO.

Pressure for budgetary stringency in UNESCO has seldom been very effective, however, partly because of the difficulty of attaining Western group consensus. When such consensus was reached within the Western budget group ("Geneva group") in 1984, the U.S. objective of a zero-growth budget was, in fact, met. Director-General M'Bow had made it clear that he would accept such a zero-budget growth, thus perhaps making such Western group consensus possible.

Finally, the U.S. government used what might be called a member state's ultimate source of influence: withdrawal from membership and the removal of its 25 percent share of UNESCO's assessed budget. However, it does not appear that this instrument was well used.

> When the United States announced its decision in December 1983 to withdraw from UNESCO in December 1984, it appears to have had no clear set of goals and strategy for reforming the Organization. . . . Because U.S. objectives were not clearly laid out for UNESCO, many believed that the decision to withdraw was irreversible even though the United States has expressed willingness to reconsider its withdrawal decision if reforms were made. (U.S. House of Representatives, 1985: 5)

On two occasions (December 23, 1983 and February 11, 1984), National Security Advisor Robert McFarlane, acting for President Reagan, had requested the Department of State to develop a clear plan of action and to launch a major campaign to mobilize international support to turn UNESCO around. As the congressional study concluded, however, "there is little evidence that from January to May, the Bureau [of International Organization Affairs] and the U.S. Mission responded to this request, and the U.S. policy in UNESCO did not reflect a strong commitment to reform. Instead, the United States demonstrated ambivalence about its role in UNESCO" (U.S. House of Representatives 1985: 5).

Conclusion

It is difficult to assess the full extent to which UNESCO activities have influenced U.S. policy and policymaking processes. Many new items have been placed on the agendas of U.S. governmental bodies, and the issues and problems of the last decade have differed markedly from those of the early years. Three decades ago U.S. delegates decried the unwillingness of UNESCO to assume its "rightful" role as a political organization. In 1984 U.S. policymakers attacked UNESCO for being unduly politicized. Three decades ago the U.S. delegation supported a move that significantly increased member state involvement in and control over the Executive Board. In 1984 Department of State officials bemoaned statism in the organization. Conversely, however, some issues have changed very little over the years. For example, American delegates have consistently voiced concern over such issues as budgetary growth and program proliferation.

Why the U.S. government used UNESCO and *what* U.S. officials sought to influence have changed over the years. However, a decline of relative U.S. power resources does little to explain such phenomena. For the most part important changes occurred substantially before the decline of the power thesis would have predicted. Alternatively, a number of other factors in combination appear to provide a more complete explanation of the evolution of U.S.-UNESCO relations. These include the nature of the issue areas inherent in UNESCO's mandate and their relation to American liberal ideological values; various organizational characteristics of UNESCO, including especially the role of the director-general; and a number of domestic political factors, including the nature of U.S. participation in UNESCO, the images and attitudes of certain U.S. administrations and their officials, and the highly biased reporting and lobbying by U.S-based news media. The interrelatedness of these factors makes it unwise to attempt to weight them in terms of their relative importance for explaining the changes we have observed in U.S.-UNESCO relations. What does seem clear is that a thorough rethinking of the nature of U.S. participation in multilateral affairs, as well as a recommitment to the principle of international cooperation, is needed prior to taking any action with respect to the future of U.S.-UNESCO relations. These findings suggest that adequate explanations of complex global social processes, such as those investigated in this volume, are not likely to emerge from perspectives that are narrowly grounded in state-centric assumptions of a world dominated by egoistic national actors. The scientific study of international organizations requires that we move beyond such overly simplistic thinking and develop more realistic, process-oriented models that focus on relationships and roles among individuals, groups, and other meaningful action units of world politics.

Notes

1. An earlier version of this paper was presented at the 1985 Annual Meeting of the American Political Science Association, August 29–September 1, 1985, New Orleans; portions of this chapter have also been adapted from Coate (1988). Research activities conducted in this study have been supported by the Byrnes International Center at the University of South Carolina and the Secretariat of the U.S. National Commission for UNESCO. I wish to thank Jonathan Davidson, John E. Fobes, James Holderman, Margaret Karns, Karen Mingst, Donald Puchala, Peter Sederberg, and the numerous other friends and colleagues who have commented on various aspects of this manuscript.

2. The historical material discussed in this section draws heavily on Laves and Thompson (1957), Finkelstein (1984), Ninkovich (1981), and Sewell (1973, 1975), as well as comments by John E. Fobes.

3. Ralph Turner, Dispatch 12183 from London, Attachment Number 1, November 11, 1943, 800.42/306.

4. An informal agreement had been concluded in CAME in which, in exchange for locating the headquarters of the new organization in Paris, the director-general would be an English-speaking person. Although such a qualification did not narrow the field exclusively to Americans, the U.S. representative had assumed that an American should and, indeed, would be selected for the post.

5. Although the governments of Czechoslovakia, Hungary, and Poland had all been members of the organization, each had previously withdrawn. Subsequent to admission of the Soviet government, they rejoined UNESCO.

6. I wish to thank Samuel DePalma and John E. Fobes for their helpful clarifications on this point.

7. For example, Newell (1984) proposed a "procedure for voting on the budget that would ensure that no budget would pass without the affirmative support of members who together contribute at least 51% of the organization's funds." Given the contributions formula used to assess dues, in theory four member states (the United States, Soviet Union, Japan, and Federal Republic of German) and in practice five member states (United States, Japan, Federal Republic of Germany, France, and any one of several other major Western funders) could, in combination, exercise an effective veto.

References

Buergenthal, Thomas, and Judith V. Torney (1976). *International Human Rights and International Education*. Washington, DC: U.S. National Commission for UNESCO.

Coate, Roger (1982). *Global Issue Regimes*. New York: Praeger.

—— (1988). *Unilateralism, Ideology, and United States Foreign Policy: The U.S. In and Out of UNESCO*. Boulder, CO: Lynne Rienner.

Cox, Robert W., and Harold K. Jacobson, eds. (1973). *The Anatomy of Influence: Decision Making in International Organization*. New Haven, CT: Yale University Press.

Finkelstein, Lawrence S. (1982). "The United States and UNESCO: Is the Past Prologue?" Paper prepared for the U.S. National Commission for UNESCO Annual Meeting, Columbia, South Carolina, June 1–3.

—— (1984). "The United States and UNESCO: The Lines Are Drawn." DeKalb: Northern Illinois University.

———— (1988). "The Political Role of the Director-General of UNESCO." In Lawrence S. Finkelstein, ed., *Politics in the United Nations System*. Durham, NC: Duke University Press.

Fobes, John (1972). "UNESCO: Management of an International Institution: Facilitating and Understanding Economic and Social Changes." In Robert Jordan, ed., *Multinational Cooperation: Economic, Social, and Scientific Development*. New York: Oxford University Press, 130–50.

Fobes, John (1981). "O.M.B. Suggestion of U.S. Withdrawal from UNESCO." Memorandum to Members of the Executive Committee and Task Force of the U.S. National Commission for UNESCO, February 1.

Jordan, Robert (1984). "Boycott Diplomacy: The U.S., the U.N. and UNESCO." *Public Administration Review* (July/August), 283–91.

Keohane, Robert (1984). *After Hegemony: Cooperation and Discord in the World Political Economy*. Princeton: Princeton University Press.

Laves, Walter H. C., and Charles A. Thompson (1957). *UNESCO: Purpose, Progress, Prospects*. Bloomington: Indiana University Press.

Massing, Michael (1984). "UNESCO under Fire." *Atlantic Monthly* (July): 89–97.

National Science Foundation (1983). *National Science in UNESCO: A U.S. Interagency Perspective*. Washington, D.C.

Newell, Gregory (1984). Letter to UNESCO Director-General M'Bow, July 13. Washington, DC: Department of State.

Ninkovich, Frank A. (1981). *The Diplomacy of Ideas: U.S. Foreign Policy and Cultural Relations, 1939–1950*. Cambridge: Cambridge University Press.

Pines, Burton Yale (1984). *A World without the U.N.: What Would Happen If the U.N. Shut Down?* Washington, DC: Heritage Foundation.

Sathyamurthy, T. V. (1964). *The Politics of International Cooperation*. Geneva: Libraire Droz.

Sewell, James P. (1973). "UNESCO: Pluralism Rampant." In Robert W. Cox and Harold T. Jacobson, eds., *The Anatomy of Influence: Decision-Making in International Organizations*. New Haven, CT: Yale University Press, 139–74.

———— (1975). *UNESCO and World Politics: Engaging in International Relations*. Princeton: Princeton University Press.

Smithsonian Institution (1983). "Contribution to the U.S./UNESCO Policy Review." Washington, DC: Author.

Sussman, Leonard (1984a). "Access: An American Perspective." Presentation at the Annual Conference of the American Library Association, June 25.

———— (1984b). "A Review of the UNESCO Decision." Discussion with Gregory Newell, Assistant Secretary of State, at the National Conference on "Global Crossroads: Educating Americans for Responsible Choices," Washington, D.C., May 17.

———— (1984c). Testimony before the Joint Hearings of the U.S. House of Representatives' Subcommittee on Human Rights and International Organization and Subcommittee on International Operations, April 26.

———— (1984d). "UNESCO and the New World Information Order." Presentation at the School of Journalism of the University of Missouri, April 17.

———— (1984e). "The U.S. Withdrawal from UNESCO—A Case Study for the Public Relations Specialist." Presentation before the International Committee of the Public Relations Society of America, the International Committee of the New York Chapter of the Public Relations Society of America, and the New York United States Council of the International Public Relations Association, United Nations Delegates Dining Room, April 12.

UNESCO (1984a). *Approved Programme and Budget for 1984*. Paris: Author.
—— (1984b). *Constitution*. Paris: Author.
U.S. Agency for International Development (1983a). *AID Contribution to the Department of Education Statement on UNESCO*. Washington, DC: Author.
—— (1983b). *UNESCO Communications Sector Evaluation: An AID Viewpoint*. Washington, DC: Author.
U.S. Comptroller General (1979). *Report to Congress: UNESCO Programming and Budgeting Need Greater U.S. Attention* (September 14). Washington, DC: Author.
U.S. Department of Education (1983). *U.S. Policy Review of UNESCO and U.S. Participation in UNESCO; Education Sector*. Washington, D.C.
U.S. Department of State (1983a). "Management of U.S. Participation in UNESCO." Internal Working Document, Bureau of International Organization Affairs. Washington, D.C.
—— (1983b). *Reports to the Congress Requested in Sections 108 and 109 of Public Law 97-241* (February 24). Washington, D.C.
—— (1984a). *Report to Congress on UNESCO Policies and Procedures with Respect to the Media Requested in Section 109 of Public Law 97-241* (January). Washington, D.C.
—— (1984b). *U.S./UNESCO Policy Review* (February 27). Washington, D.C.
U.S. House of Representatives (1984). "Summary," Joint Hearings of the Committee of Foreign Affairs' Subcommittee on Human Rights and International Organization and Subcommittee on International Operations, April 25. Washington, DC: U.S. Government Printing Office.
—— (1985). "Assessment of U.S./UNESCO Relations, 1984." Report of the Staff Study Mission to Paris-UNESCO to the Committee on Foreign Affairs, January. Washington, DC: U.S. Government Printing Office.
U.S. National Commission for UNESCO (1984). *What Are the Issues Concerning the Decision of the United States to Withdraw from UNESCO?* Washington, D.C.
Weber, Nathan (1984). "UNESCO: Who Needs It?" *Across the Board*, 21(9), 11–17.
Whitlam, Gough (1985). "Partner or Puppet? The United Kingdom, United Nations and United States." Address to the United Nations Association of Great Britain and Northern Ireland, London, April 13.

• CHAPTER TEN •

The United States, the United Nations, and Human Rights

David P. Forsythe

The relationship between the United States and the United Nations in the field of human rights has proved both complex and ambiguous during the past forty-five years. This troubled and shifting relationship has contributed to the crisis of multilateralism in the United States, a situation in which the United States has questioned the value of many UN programs and indeed its membership in at least parts of the organization.

Perhaps this complex and ambiguous U.S.-UN relationship over human rights could not have been otherwise in its fundamentals, although it certainly could have been in its specifics. The United States was founded largely in opposition to political and religious tyranny and with a strong commitment to economic freedom. Consequently, individualistic civil and political rights loom large, as does antipathy for socioeconomic regulation. But the American political experience, which in the mythology of American political culture constitutes an exceptional beacon for others, manifests a view of human rights different from that of most other nations. This difference is particularly pronounced in comparison with most Second and Third World countries, where communal values rank more highly than individualism and skepticism of unregulated economics is widespread. The United States also stands in contrast to most other democracies of the world, which give less unfettered play to individualism and provide a larger role for the state in socioeconomic matters.

Thus it has been said, "For many non-Americans the most important human rights are not those that Americans regard as paramount" (Bloomfield 1982: 11). Similarly a foreign service officer in the U.S. State

261

Department Bureau of Human Rights commented in an interview, "The United States is so different that it is the last country in the world that should be lecturing others on human rights."

These differences have been reflected in human rights developments at the United Nations. A covenant on economic, social, and cultural rights has been adopted despite U.S. reserve. Many states (especially the authoritarian ones) emphasize (at least in rhetoric) self-determination, combating racism, and promoting economic development rather than protecting a broad range of civil and political rights.

It is important to understand at the outset, therefore, that the U.S. view of human rights is unique. This helps to explain U.S. estrangement from the world (Ungar 1985)—an estrangement intensified by the strong American sense of moral certainty in these matters. Even other democracies do not share some values with the United States. This divergence constitutes the background for periodic U.S. estrangement from, as well as periodic support for, UN human rights activity. More specific factors complicate the picture such as domestic politics, foreign policy alignments, and UN voting patterns.

In this chapter I will use a regime approach to summarize UN activity on human rights, then chronicle the evolution of the U.S. relationship to the core human rights regime over four periods. Because of the nature of the human rights issues, domestic political factors have been particularly important in shaping patterns in that relationship. In the final section I seek to analyze this configurative material systematically focusing both on how the United States has used the UN in the human rights field and how UN activity has affected the United States. I seek to explain in some detail why changes have occurred in both of these aspects, and what the policy implications are for the future.[1]

The United Nations and Human Rights

Since 1945 there has been an explosion in attention to human rights in international relations. Currently more than thirty treaties exist, most negotiated through the United Nations, on a variety of human rights subjects ranging from the general to the particular, from an international bill of rights to rules on the political rights of women (Lillich 1983; U.S. House of Representatives 1983). One way to conceptualize the explosion of diplomacy on human rights after World War II is to use a regime approach (Donnelly 1986: 599–642).[2] One can say that there is a central or core UN human rights regime, as well as several other human rights regimes. An advantage of a regime approach is that it permits exploration of the importance of diplomatic activity beyond that in any one international organization within the regime. The sum total of norms, rules, organizations, and networks making up a regime may be (but does not have to be) more important than a more limited organizational view would indicate.

In the case of human rights, a phenomenon of "nesting of regimes" (Aggarwal 1985) is readily apparent. There is a core UN regime and several regimes beyond that core. Some are regional and extra-UN, as in Western Europe, Latin America, and (embryonically) Africa. Some are global and extra-UN, such as the regime on human rights in armed conflict associated with the International Red Cross Movement. Some are global in scope but particular in subject matter and negotiated through the UN, such as those on refugee or labor rights. The overlapping of related regimes is manifested in fuzzy boundaries (Kratochwil and Ruggie 1986). To illustrate the nesting phenomenon, one can cite the labor regime that revolves around the International Labor Organization and deals inter alia with freedom of association, the right to work, and the right to bargain collectively. It overlaps with that part of the core UN regime dealing with both civil and social rights. The refugee regime that has at its hub the UN High Commissioner for Refugees overlaps with the UN core regime concerning such subjects as the rights to life, to freedom from arbitrary detention, and to adequate shelter, health, and nutrition. Despite such nesting and overlap, this essay focuses on the core UN regime only, but because of the regime approach it does not deal with any single UN agency.

The norms of the UN core human rights regime are defined by the relevant parts of the UN Charter (above all by Articles 55 and 56), by the Universal Declaration of Human Rights from 1948, and by the two general human rights covenants that first entered into legal force for adhering states in 1976; one on civil and political rights and the other on economic, social, and cultural rights. The regime norms contain negative or blocking rights forbidding public authority from such acts as arbitrary deprivation or the right to life, or mistreatment and torture. They also contain positive rights, enjoining those authorities to provide public goods such as free primary education and adequate health and nutrition.[3]

The Covenant on Civil-Political Rights contains a special control agency, the UN Human Rights Committee, made up of independent (uninstructed) experts elected by adhering states. It has the ultimate authority (rarely used to date) to publish its conclusions about state compliance. The Covenant on Socio-Economic Rights is supervised by the UN Economic and Social Council (ECOSOC), which also lacks judicial authority but which has created a special committee to oversee this covenant as well. The UN Human Rights Commission, not to be confused with the UN Human Rights Committee, is part of the regular UN administration and can take action under the Universal Declaration as well as the UN Charter itself; it is made up of states and reports its recommendations to ECOSOC. To the extent that there is an organizational hub for the UN core regime, the commission tends to be that—but incompletely. There is (or was, before budget cuts in the 1980s) a UN Human Rights Subcommisson of independent experts that reports its recommendations to its parent commission. The General Assembly and its standing Third Committee also make recommendations about human rights, as do various other UN bodies such as the Fourth Committee when dealing with decolonization, the Sixth Committee when debating certain legal questions, and even the Security Council when handling the relationship between human rights and peace and security.[4]

Thus there is a set of core norms defining basic international human rights and several largely uncoordinated agencies to specify the rights and duties of different parties. Various nongovernmental organizations are also active in this diplomatic network prodding public authorities into implementing the norms they have endorsed in principle. In Donnelly's terms, by the 1980s the UN core regime had become a "strong promotional" regime (Donnelly 1986). In other terms it was a "tutelary" regime (Ruggie 1983). Both terms suggest that the UN core regime has an indirect rather than direct role in advancing human rights, that its implementation procedures are weak, that it tries to nudge national actors into direct protection steps.

UN agencies and officials associated with the regime can negotiate quietly, undertake studies, provide assistance in the form of education and training, hold public meetings, issue reports, and pass nonbinding resolutions. Although the regime has had only a slight capability to influence states positively, it has had a somewhat greater capability to embarrass. Many serious students have concluded that however weak the UN core human rights regime was, it had nevertheless improved in capability over time.

Only the Security Council, however, can enforce the core UN regime in the sense of giving a legally binding decision and compelling enforcement measures, and this can transpire only in relation to peace and security issues. The council has taken such action only once, when it determined that Southern Rhodesia's unilateral declaration of independence in 1965 constituted a threat to international peace and subsequently voted mandatory economic sanctions. Although the council also imposed a mandatory arms embargo on the Republic of South Africa in 1978, the authorizing resolution did not indicate whether it was denial of human rights that constituted the threat to the peace. Thus although the regime has an exceptional capability to enforce, its normal mode of operation hinges on voluntary implementation by member states (Humphrey 1978).

By the late 1980s the two covenants were legally binding on the more than eighty-five UN members who had deposited their instruments of adherence. Almost forty parties had accepted the Optional Protocol to the Civil-Political Covenant, which permits individual communications to the Human Rights Committee. The United States has never ratified either of the two covenants; thus it cannot vote for members of the committee, be elected to that committee, or authorize U.S. citizens to petition the committee. Nevertheless, the United States is still subject to the Universal Declaration either as an authoritative statement of the meaning of the UN Charter, which the United States did ratify, or as part of international customary law—in whole or in part as determined largely by U.S. courts.

The United States is also party to a half-dozen other human rights treaties beyond the core UN regime, and most of those have a decidedly limited impact on U.S. policy. The United States participates in debates on human rights in all UN bodies comprising states regardless of which human rights treaties it has ratified. Ironically, as a member of ECOSOC the United States is in a position to help supervise the implementation of the Socio-Economic Covenant, which it has never ratified—a situation not viewed with great favor by many states.

More than a decade after the core UN regime came into legal force for about half the UN membership, the general norms of the regime are still being translated into more precise rules. On some subjects, such as civil rights, one of the UN agencies has articulated a precise rule. For example, the Human Rights Committee held that Uruguay had violated its obligations under the Civil-Political Covenant; the UN Human Rights Commission condemned the suppression of labor rights in Poland; and the General Assembly has repeatedly condemned the practice of apartheid. On other subjects, such as socioeconomic rights, the regime remains relatively unspecified. ECOSOC and its relevant Working Group proved exceedingly slow, if not derelict, in delineating the more precise obligations of states parties to that covenant (Mower 1985). This is precisely why a new oversight committee of uninstructed experts was created in the mid-1980s; however, it remains to be seen whether this new committee will make any difference.

The core regime is still evolving; thus the clarity of U.S. obligations under international law, or what might be expected of the United States if its policies were to fit with the regime, varies considerably from one subject to another in the human rights area. A fundamental point is that the norms and more specific rules extant in the UN core human rights regime may influence the United States, whatever U.S. positivistic obligations are under international law. Indeed, in this essay I will stress that particularly Congress but also to lesser extent U.S. courts have been marginally influenced by the UN core regime. This impact of the human rights regime on these two branches has not been widely appreciated.

Conversely, it is evident that the United States has a variety of avenues in international relations and at the UN in which to advance internationally recognized human rights if it chooses to utilize them. It can approach matters positively by seeking diplomatic accommodation, voting for provision of legal experts or training sessions, or providing funds for victims of torture. It can proceed negatively hoping to delegitimate adversaries through critical reports and resolutions, or even withdrawing its presence and/or financial support for operational programs in various UN agencies.

U.S. Policy and UN Influence: Historical Overview

The foregoing discussion, given its brevity, could lead to the impression that the UN core human rights regime is so nebulous and its implementation procedures so weak and chaotic that the entire subject is irrelevant to the United States. Such is decidedly not the case. The relationship between citizen and state is regarded by virtually all states as a matter of vital importance, and in this regard the United States is no exception. Moreover, the UN core human rights regime embodies a philosophy of legitimate public authority; the state that escapes criticism or censure under the regime thereby receives an endorsement of its legitimacy (although there are other sources of legitimacy as well). For these fundamental reasons, as well as for lesser ones, human rights activity at the UN has periodically been important to the United States, whether viewed as an opportunity for influence on others, as a threat to American values, or, rarely, as a source of ideas for the improvement of American society and foreign policy.

It is complex enough to deal with this relationship as a two-way street: U.S. views and influence toward the core regime and the regime's influence on the United States. Complicating the situation still further is the fact that different governmental institutions within the United States have not always viewed U.S. human rights activity in the same way. Thus one has to account for shifts in views and influence in two directions not only over time but also in different institutions at the same time. In this section material is grouped historically from the standpoint of U.S. policy toward the UN; the UN regime's influence on the United States is treated as a subtheme. The impact of the separation of institutions within the United States is woven into both analyses.

U.S. Limited Support, 1945–53

The UN core regime on human rights was never the product of simple U.S. hegemony or dominant power. Although Presidents Roosevelt and Truman and the State Department were sympathetic to including some mention of human rights in the UN Charter, UN policy on human rights in the 1940s was affected by other states and nongovernmental organizations. A number of private organizations as well as several Latin American states pushed for stronger language on human rights at the San Francisco Conference. The final charter provisions on human rights reflected some compromise between the limited generalities preferred by the United States and other Great Powers and the more precise language pushed by others (Lauren 1983; Mower 1979: 5).

Similarly, the drafting of the Universal Declaration of Human Rights between 1946 and 1948 owed much to private organizations, especially the American Law Institute, which submitted drafts. A working copy was prepared by John P. Humphrey, a Canadian and head of the human rights office in the new UN secretariat. A further revision was made by René Cassin of the French delegation to the UN. A number of states participated vigorously in the drafting including Cuba, Panama, Egypt, India, Denmark, and Lebanon (Humphrey 1984).

To be sure, the United States was an important actor in events, especially considering Eleanor Roosevelt's active role in the U.S. delegation to the UN and also as chair of the UN Human Rights Commission in its two early forms. Apparently she played a key role in convincing others to follow up on charter provisions with a single declaration. It seems she followed closely the advice of her State Department managers both in lobbying for most of the articles that were to emerge in the declaration and in making sure that UN human rights activity did not go beyond immediately nonbinding declarations and general resolutions (Johnson 1987: 19–48; Mower 1979). U.S. desires were also apparently satisfied when, in this same period, the UN Human Rights Commission adopted the policy that it had no authority to act on specific complaints or to review particular state practices.

This was the period of Western dominance of the UN, and Washington saw the organization primarily as a channel of U.S. and Western influence over others. In this regard it bears noting that however much the United States was convinced that its political history was a "shining city on a hill" for others to emulate, U.S. officials did not want a really strong UN human rights regime because of the desire to protect Jim Crow laws and other U.S. discrimination from international scrutiny.[5] Hence U.S. diplomacy was designed in part to forestall UN impact on human rights within the United States, even at the cost of reduced influence on others.

The early U.S. policy on human rights at the UN was generally supportive but clearly opposed to precise obligations and powerful international agencies. U.S. policy was part of the international reaction to World War II atrocities and as such was part of the effort to see that they not recur. Yet the United States, like the other Great Powers, was unwilling to create authority and power centers that could really achieve that aim. Professions of support were not followed by provisions for action. A skeletal regime was created, but U.S. independence was protected; violations of rights in the United States were not scrutinized.

Such cautious policies, designed to associate the United States with human rights in the abstract but to block inconvenient international action, were fashioned by the executive with scant direct input from other constituencies. Executive officials did take into account the anticipated views of southern members of Congress and opposed a strong UN human rights regime.

U.S. courts in this political climate could hardly have been expected to thrust U.S. human rights policy into an international framework, and they did not. Indeed the California Supreme Court, in a case that seemed to establish national precedent on these questions, reversed lower court rulings in California (which ran parallel to lower court judgments in Oregon) and held that the human rights provisions of the UN Charter were non-self-executing and therefore not a basis for court judgment without further action by U.S. political branches (Lockwood 1984).

U.S. Neglect, 1954–74

Despite this cautious stance of only limited support for UN human rights activity on the part of the Truman administration, Congress became assertive and hence a major actor on international human rights during the Eisenhower administration. When UN standard setting moved from adoption of the Universal Declaration to drafting the two covenants, the Senate intervened to compel the executive to withdraw in large part from a leadership role on international human rights. Brickerism, the unsuccessful movement for a constitutional amendment restricting the treaty-making authority of the president, was so strong that it forced the Eisenhower administration to eschew major involvement in the UN core human rights regime (Hevener and Whiteman 1988; Van Dyke 1970). This was the beginning of the period of U.S. neglect of UN human rights programs, compelled by the Congress but acceded to more or less willingly by four administrations.

Given both the cold war and McCarthyism, many members of Congress were concerned that the executive was not acting strongly enough in defense of the United States. In the hysteria of the times, numerous charges were made against U.S. human rights activity. The emerging covenants were seen to represent creeping socialism, an assault on the Constitution, and a product of treasonous elements in the State Department and UN Secretariat. It was in this context that Eisenhower and Dulles downgraded the importance of UN human rights activity.

In this era it was clear that American nationalism—in particular a belief in the superiority of traditional American values—dominated any effort to broaden the American conception of human rights or to learn anything from UN proceedings. A key feature of Brickerism was that U.S. law should not be affected by the international law of human rights. The American Bar Association opposed ratification of the two covenants, whose provisions were essentially completed by 1956. A strong movement in Congress against socioeconomic rights, supervision by international authority, expansion of federal authority, and demise of senatorial and congressional roles combined to torpedo any possibility of U.S. leadership in international human rights matters. Defensive domestic politics dominated U.S. foreign policy on human rights. The executive could not consider the UN core regime as an instrument of policy because of the almost hysterical assault on the regime by Congress and the organized legal profession.

Some U.S. diplomacy on UN human rights did exist, but there was less to it than met the eye. For example, the UN Human Rights Action Plan, a U.S. initiative, was actually a plan to cover the retreat of the United States from international human rights (Forsythe 1985a). This plan for continued promotion of human rights through studies and seminars was not seriously pursued and had little impact. The United States took occasional initiatives at the UN on such subjects as forced labor, but U.S. policy overall could be fairly considered as one of neglect.

When the United States supported a UN human rights program during this period it was because that action fit with anticommunism. The United States belatedly recognized the importance of the UNHCR and international law on refugees because that agency proved useful in dealing with Hungarian refugees in 1956 and in highlighting communist oppression (Forsythe 1989).

Thus the Eisenhower administration was marked by a retreat from leadership on international human rights matters. Domestic politics prevailed except where human rights could serve anticommunist goals.

And the courts continued to refuse to use the UN Charter's human rights provisions as a basis for judicial settlement.

Two important trends are evident in the evolution of the UN core regime in the 1960s, one negative and the other positive from the general U.S. view. On the one hand, the increase in UN membership led to a new majority, which in turn took a different approach to many human rights issues. There was much rhetoric directed toward the collective right of self-determination, the "right" to economic development, and toward the human rights violations of South Africa, Israel, and Chile after 1973. Little rhetoric or action was directed toward violations by Eastern European and Third World states.[6]

On the other hand, the UN Human Rights Commission, with approval from other UN organs, reversed its earlier policy of acquiesence and undertook to supervise state practice on human rights in several ways. Beginning in the late 1960s, the commission examined the cases of particular states and did not limit this review to the international pariahs; it responded to nongovernmental complaints in a weak but nevertheless symbolically important way; it initiated the practice of using both working groups and rapporteurs to focus on particular problems (Alston 1983; Tolley 1987).

The Democratic administrations of the 1960s fall into the era of neglect because of the lack of high-level commitment and of new initiatives. No effort was made to associate the United States with the principal documents of the UN core regime. Yet it should be noted that lower-level involvement occurred, and the United States did follow the lead of certain Western European and Third World states in strengthening the UN core regime.

U.S. neglect for human rights, at the UN and elsewhere, was particularly pronounced during the Nixon-Kissinger administration. Henry Kissinger believed that human rights fell within the domestic jurisdiction of states and that the intrusion of human rights into U.S. foreign policy unnecessarily complicated geostrategic calculations.[7] Even when Kissinger used the rhetoric of human rights to counter or quell domestic criticism, an underlying reservation if not hostility remained (Arnold 1980). He reprimanded, for example, State Department officials who broached the subject of human rights in private diplomacy with other governments; and, after giving a public speech supporting human rights, he communicated privately to the target government (Chile) that the speech was only for American domestic consumption (Forsythe 1985b: 25–31).

At the UN, Ambassador Daniel Patrick Moynihan publicly and shrilly complained that human rights activity was being used by totalitarian states to delegitimate the West. U.S. policy on human rights at the UN and elsewhere, argued Moynihan, should be used as a weapon against communism (Moynihan 1978).

Although President Ford spoke more on human rights in his public appearances than did his predecessors, he did so to counter charges of the Reagan forces on the Republican right that Nixon and Kissinger had been too soft on Soviet-led communism and of the Carter forces on the Democratic side in emphasizing the human rights issue in general.

For most of the period of neglect—or at least from 1956 to 1974—the executive branch dominated U.S. human rights policymaking. Neither Congress nor the courts played significant roles on international human rights. Indeed, Congress played a negative role in the issue area.

U.S. Renewed Interest, 1974–81

It is ironic that Congress, having compelled a U.S. retreat from international human rights at the United Nations in the 1950s, compelled their reinsertion on the U.S. foreign policy agenda in the 1970s. Whatever the executive was doing at the UN on human rights throughout the period, there was finally a widespread perception in Congress that human rights was underemphasized in U.S. foreign policy, especially during the Nixon-Kissinger period. This was not so much a congressional concern with U.S. policy at the UN per se as a concern with human rights and ethics in foreign policy more generally. Yet the UN figured prominently in subsequent congressional action.

In 1973 Congressman Donald M. Fraser, chair of the Subcommittee on International Organizations and Movements of the House Foreign Affairs Committee, began systematic hearings on international human rights. These had a major impact on the agenda of U.S. foreign policy. Fraser and his principal assistant, John Salzburg, gave a clear international framework to the concept of human rights. The hearings clearly articulated that human rights meant human rights as defined by the UN core regime, not merely human rights as understood in the American context. It was argued in essays authored by Fraser and/or Salzburg that the United States should use an international definition of human rights, and that concerted diplomacy with others, not a unilateral approach, was important for an effective U.S. policy.[8]

When legislation was subsequently approved on the subject of human rights, much of it referred to "internationally recognized human rights." This was true of three general statutes linking human rights to security assistance (International Security Assistance and Arms Export Control Act, section 502B), economic assistance (Foreign Assistance Act, section 116a), and voting in multilateral financial institutions (International

Financial Institutions Act, section 701). All three acts from the 1970s contained the stipulation that U.S. foreign policy was to be affected by a consistent pattern of gross violations of internationally recognized human rights in recipient states. This language was also incorporated into a number of country-specific statutes, as when Congress required executive certification of progress on internationally recognized human rights in order for U.S. assistance to continue to countries such as El Salvador and Haiti (Forsythe 1989).

Subsequently debate arose as to the meaning of the phrase *internationally recognized human rights*. Testimony by former U.S. officials at the UN (for example, the late Clyde Ferguson) tried to suggest that the phrase in U.S. legislation meant the same thing as the phrase in UN diplomacy, given that the phrase at the UN had been initiated by officials such as Ferguson. A fair reading of the legislative history, however, indicates that some ambiguity remained about the precise import of the phrase. It was clear that the phraseology had come from the UN and that key lawmakers were trying to make U.S. law consistent with UN practice (U.S. House of Representatives 1984: 157-F).

However, when U.S. law tried to specify what was meant by internationally recognized human rights, the examples were always from the civil and political rights consistent with American political history. Congress never tried to specify in legislation a comprehensive definition of the key phrase, but its partial listing of examples referred to torture, denial of due process, arbitrary detention, and the like. Thus it could be argued with some reason that having paid due respect to internationally defined human rights, Congress went on to stress the classic American version of such rights.

Relatedly, there was little interest in ratifying the UN Covenant on Social, Economic, and Cultural Rights (U.S. House of Representatives 1982). Although members of Congress did show interest in basic human needs and in humanitarian relief that could be directly related to socio-economic rights, these subjects were not treated in a framework of rights but rather in terms of morality or national interest or even good economics (for example, one should liberate laborers in South Africa or women in less developed countries because it was good free market economics to do so).

Thus it can be argued that members of Congress in the 1970s were slightly influenced by the UN core regime in their efforts to get the executive branch to take greater interest in human rights. A number of private organizations that were active both at the UN and in American politics served as transmission belts in the process. Members of Congress such as Don Fraser, working in conjunction with these private human rights groups, did take into account UN norms and organizational decisions, though the United States was not legally obligated to do so. Phraseology from UN proceedings showed up in U.S. legislation even while key members of Congress were aware of shortcomings in UN developments (Fraser 1977: 153). At the same time, more strictly American approaches to human rights were much in evidence, and there was clear resistance to those parts of international human rights (economic, social, and cultural) that did not fit so apparently with American experience.

Congress had clearly raised the issue of human rights before presidential candidate Jimmy Carter proved that human rights could be a useful campaign theme (Drew 1977: 36). It is now clear that the newly elected president had no clear conception of the human rights issue (Carter 1982: 144) and that for a variety of reasons the Carter administration never developed a clear strategy (Muravchik 1986: chap. 5; Rossiter 1984). President Carter's personal convictions and domestic politics—not UN proceedings—led to the renewed emphasis on human rights in U.S. foreign policy. UN influence was indirect and marginal.

The Carter administration sought, however, to incorporate international norms into U.S. decisions as never before. The president signed and submitted the two UN Covenants along with other human rights treaties to the Senate. Secretary of State Vance stressed that the United States did accept the idea of economic, social, and cultural rights. One of the administration's first acts was to lobby Congress for repeal of the Byrd Amendment, which violated UN mandatory economic sanctions on Rhodesia—sanctions undertaken indirectly to support self-determination, majority rule, and one-man, one-vote principles. Carter appointees in the State Department reduced U.S. foreign assistance to certain countries because of a consistent pattern of gross violations of internationally recognized human rights, though no such public rationales were given (R. Cohen 1979; S. Cohen 1982). The administration also voted in the Security Council for a mandatory arms embargo on the Republic of South Africa, indirectly because of apartheid. Thus the Carter administration, by design or ad hocery, did move somewhat in the direction desired by Congressman Fraser at the outset of the period of renewed interest in human rights, placing U.S. policy to some degree within an international framework and utilizing multilateral diplomacy.

To be sure, there were other developments, inconsistencies, and clashes between the executive and legislative branches, for the one thing that characterized the Carter policy more than any other was inconsistency. The administration resisted congressional efforts to introduce human rights considerations into the work of the international financial institutions. Against the wishes of the White House, Congress also imposed an economic embargo on Uganda for the human rights violations

of General Amin. When human rights concerns were in conflict with
perceived national security interests in places such as El Salvador, the
Philippines, or Saudi Arabia, they were downgraded. In the last two years
of the administration, particularly after the Soviet invasion of Afghanistan,
political and military competition with the Soviet Union was significantly
upgraded. Even prior to that time Carter had allowed executive branch
lawyers to attach reservations and understandings to the covenants sent to
the Senate, which would have had the effect of preventing any changes in
U.S. law because of international human rights law should the United
States ever complete ratification.

Yet overall one would have to conclude that the Carter team did
demonstrate renewed interest in international human rights as defined
primarily by the core UN regime. There was indeed plenty of domestic
institutional and substantive conflict, and particularly during 1977 and
1978, anarchy seemed to reign in human rights debates in Washington.
Whatever the difficulties of arriving at a consistent and reasonable policy,
it was a time of renewed interest in internationally recognized human
rights.

Relatedly, some important shifts took place in the U.S. courts to
reinforce changes in international human rights policy. In two cases the
federal courts "discovered" customary international law on human rights
and based their legal reasoning on that discovery in important ways. In
Pena-Irala v. Filartiga (1980) the U.S. District Court for the Second Circuit
in New York held that torture constituted a violation of customary
international law. Hence under the Judiciary Act of 1789, U.S. courts
could accept a civil tort claim involving such a claim. In *Pena* the court used
this line of reasoning to afford monetary relief to a victim of torture in
Paraguay whose torturer had come into U.S. jurisdiction. *Pena* also
offered the possibility of other torturers' being prosecuted if they entered
the United States. The district court ruling cited the Universal Declaration
of Human Rights, the UN Civil-Political Covenant, and other international
prohibitions of torture as evidence that customary international law existed
and was binding on the United States even though the United States had
never ratified the treaties in question. The Carter administration, in fact,
urged the court to rule as it did, and public interest lawyers participated on
the winning side.

In *Rodriguez-Fernandez v. Wilkinson* (1980) the U.S. District Court in
Kansas held that an excludable alien from Cuba could not be held in a
maximum security prison without criminal charge; such detention was held
to violate international customary law prohibiting arbitrary detention. The
court looked at the UN core regime, as well as other evidence, in ordering
the immediate parole of the prisoner.

On appeal, the *Rodriguez* case (654 F.2nd 1382, 1981) led to a different use of the international law of human rights. The appellate court in question, in agreeing with the substantive conclusion of the lower court, did not base its judgment on international customary law. Rather, it used international human rights law as evidence of what was required by U.S. municipal law. Thus the appellate court, unlike the district court, found municipal law relevant to the case. But the appellate court still utilized the UN human rights regime in supporting its judgment that the prisoner was entitled to release.

Hence U.S. court systems showed some "slight movement" (Hassan 1983: 85) toward increased use of the UN human rights regime, thus bypassing traditional barriers arising from claims to domestic jurisdiction, nonjusticiability, the non-self-executing nature of some treaties, and the absence of U.S. ratification of important human rights conventions. Attorneys and interest groups interested in further utilization of international human rights norms seized upon the *Pena* and *Rodriguez* cases to press U.S. legal authorities in that direction (Lillich and Hannum 1985; Tolley 1987a). Legal publications and seminars in the American private sector stressed that appropriate protection could be afforded individuals through one of the lines of legal reasoning found in these two cases, which, in turn, were based in part on the UN regime.

Era of Subservience to Cold War Politics, 1981–19?

The Reagan administration, if left to its own preferences, would have simply collapsed human rights policy into anticommunism. The fact that this did not happen quickly and easily can be attributed to Congress. Bipartisan support for a broad interpretation of human rights remained strong. Nevertheless the Reagan administration had sufficient power to alter U.S. foreign policy on human rights despite congressional criticism and concern, so that from 1981 U.S. human rights policy was significantly different from that in the 1974–80 period. For at least the first five years of the Reagan presidency, human rights became subservient to renewed anticommunism. Short-term, politico-military competition with the USSR overshadowed other considerations. U.S. policy toward human rights at the UN reflected this dominant prism—at least during 1981–85—in spite of congressional pressures otherwise.

Early administration statements, as well as the nomination of Ernest W. Lefever to be Assistant Secretary of State of Human Rights and Humanitarian Affairs, made clear that the Reagan team intended to view human rights strictly as a weapon in the ideological competition with the Soviet Union. This most nationalistic of recent U.S. administrations, believing strongly in American exceptionalism, had little use for international definitions of human rights. The Reagan administration was also clearly in the unilateralist rather than multilateralist tradition and thus manifested little positive orientation toward the UN at the outset. A basic view held by many new officials was that Carter had undermined U.S. efforts to fight communism because of broad concern with an internationalist conception of human rights (Davis and Lynn-Jones 1987; Kirkpatrick 1983).

Congressional opposition to these early Reagan orientations, led by the Republican-controlled Senate, forced the withdrawal of the nomination of Ernest Lefever. This was the first act of a drama in which a relatively more pragmatic and cosmopolitan Congress sought to check the ideological impulses of the executive branch. Other acts were to follow on El Salvador, Nicaragua, and Guatemala in Central America; Haiti in the Caribbean; Argentina and Chile in South America; South Africa and Liberia in Africa; and the Philippines and South Korea in Asia. In these and other cases Congress sought to inject considerations of at least some internationally recognized human rights.

The Reagan administration disparaged the UN human rights regime. Official publications such as the annual country reports on human rights conditions around the world and press statements redefined international human rights to reflect traditional American values (Forsythe 1982; U.S. Department of State 1982). Thus socioeconomic rights were discarded. There were attacks on the UN's handling of human rights by Ambassador Jeane Kirkpatrick, among others. The administration showed no interest in Senate consent to ratification of the two UN covenants. It showed no interest in an even-handed approach to human rights around the world but rather sought to block consideration of human rights violations by friendly governments such as El Salvador, Guatemala, Chile, and Argentina.

It can be argued that the first Reagan administration substituted the Kirkpatrick doctrine for the UN core regime as a guide to foreign policy on human rights (Forsythe 1988). Violations of human rights by Marxist states were challenged vigorously and publicly; violations by friendly authoritarian governments were dealt with by quiet diplomacy, if at all. Officials close to the Reagan administration called the UN human rights regime ambiguous, unenforceable, and unworkable; they preferred a crusading American tradition (Muravchik 1986), even if some might call it cultural imperialism.

Some observers saw a shift in U.S. human rights policy in the second Reagan administration (Jacoby 1986). Reagan pledged U.S. opposition to human rights violations whether of the left or right. The United States distanced itself from repression in the Philippines and Haiti and publicly criticized General Pinochet in Chile; it used the UN Human Rights

Commission in an effort to get Pinochet to yield power. These steps raised the possibility of a policy more sensitive to internationally recognized human rights.

Nonetheless, it does not appear that a major shift in human rights policy took place. Rather, in certain places (for example, the Philippines, Haiti, and Chile) Reagan administration officials decided that U.S. security interests would be served by the removal of oppressive regimes to undercut growing power by the extreme left. Both in the Philippines and in Haiti Reagan drifted with the repressive status quo until the eleventh hour despite persistent warnings by members of Congress about impending events.

The overriding concern of the Reagan team remained focused on communist movements around the world. In a few places this primary concern allowed the United States to oppose human rights violations by friendly dictators in order (belatedly) to head off violent rebellion that would jeopardize U.S. security (and economic) interests. There was no fundamental shift from a parochial to a cosmopolitan orientation on human rights or toward increased awareness of the substantive merits of the UN regime. There was no increased reliance on the UN core regime as a primary or independent variable in the making of U.S. foreign policy; on occasion that regime happened to fit with U.S. perceptions of security policy, as in Chile. The speech pledging equal opposition of the left and right was mainly an effort to garner congressional support for the Contra's war against the Sandinistas in Nicaragua. There was no increased executive pressure against human rights violators in places such as Liberia or Pakistan.[9]

During the last two years of the Reagan presidency, when Reagan was politically weakened by the Iran-Contra scandal and when a number of ideologues had left the administration, human rights policy was slightly more moderate or centrist in American politics. There was some U.S. pressure on allied countries such as Panama, Paraguay, and South Korea to improve their human rights' records. This may have been the result of congressional pressures over time, or perhaps of personnel changes in the State Department.[10] Such a shift may also be seen as validation, in indirect and incremental fashion, of the UN human rights regime. A large number of members of Congress had been pushing the Reagan team to take action on human rights in South Africa, the Philippines, and Chile even though this posed some problems in the short run for perceived U.S. security and economic interests. The exact origins of this congressional pressure especially concerning South Africa were not clear but probably lay more in American moralism than in international human rights.

During the second Reagan administration, U.S. courts continued to rely on international standards to decide a number of human rights cases. In the *Cardoza-Fonesca* case (*Immigration and Naturalization Service* 1987) the Supreme Court struck down administration guidelines for standard of proof required for the deportation of an alien; the Court preferred the standard found in the 1980 Refugee Act, which was derived from international instruments on refugees. Conversely, in the *Tel-Oren* case (1984), the Circuit Court of Appeals for the District of Columbia refused to utilize the *Pena* precedent making torture a violation of customary international law. The Court dismissed the case involving a tort claim against Palestinians who had allegedly tortured hostages in Israel.

Most U.S. courts remain uncomfortable with heavy reliance on the international law of human rights. Few American judges and attorneys have the experience to draw on that growing body of law (Tuttle 1978). The Senate's consent to ratification of the Genocide Convention in 1986 may help to break down this judicial caution, especially considering that Senate action was strongly endorsed by the American Bar Association in a complete turnaround from its position in the 1950s. But if the executive branch does not encourage courts to use international human rights instruments, judicial conservatism will certainly be reinforced. And there is no movement in the United States toward greater acceptance of social, economic, and cultural rights whether by the executive branch, Congress, or the courts.[11]

Explaining the Shifting U.S. Relationship with the UN Human Rights Regime

U.S.-UN relationships in the field of human rights have been complex, ambiguous, and shifting. The U.S. position has changed from one of limited support, to neglect, to renewed activism, to anticommunism. There are at least four possible explanations for this changing state of affairs: shifts in U.S. power, changes in the issue area, nature of the regime, and shifts in domestic politics. Although all help to explain changes in patterns, U.S.-UN relations have been more strongly affected by domestic politics than by any other factor. But its power has enabled the U.S. to remain largely peripheral to and aloof from many developments concerning international human rights.

Power

The UN core human rights regime was not the simple product of U.S. policy as the dominant power or hegemon in the early postwar period.

Even when the United States was clearly predominant in military and economic power, it did not play a predominant role in shaping the norms of the core regime on human rights. Indeed, for a time the United States voluntarily surrendered any leadership role in UN human rights programs because of congressional opposition.

Later, as others shaped the core regime in ways that did not wholly accord with U.S. preferences, the United States withheld its endorsement from various conventions on human rights. According to regime theory, the United States might have been expected to endorse the core regime anyway on the grounds that because it could not control matters itself, it was preferable to enter fully into this international regime to maximize U.S. influence and to restrict the power of others. If one does not have the resources to control a situation, compromise is better than defeat.

On human rights issues, however, a "smug aggressiveness" (Garth 1986) has characterized much of U.S. policy. Especially during the Reagan administration and earlier during the height of the cold war, either the president or Congress or both saw the United States as an example for others to emulate. Whether the United States had the power to compel others to adopt its view of human rights was not the most important question. In American mythology, American moral example would substitute for power; for the United States had already discovered "Truth" on human rights (Davis and Lynn-Jones 1987; Schlesinger 1978).

There are at least two ways, however, in which a focus on power helps to explain U.S.-UN relations on human rights. First, voting power within the UN does matter; this is taken up in the section on characteristics of the regime. Second, the United States is not vulnerable to power moves by adversaries who might have wished to coerce the United States into a different view of human rights. The United States could maintain its views in this field and not be subjected to trade embargoes or similar sanctions— although such possibilities seem highly academic when discussing U.S. human rights policies.

Issue Area Characteristics

It has been long noted that power relationships are situationally specific, shifting by issue and issue area (Baldwin 1979). The field of human rights is a unique one, and the nature of this issue area does explain much in the relationship between the U.S. and the core UN regime.

There is probably no subject of international relations on which one finds more durable views than human rights. States do not change their human rights views and policies easily or frequently unless there is a change in the predominant ideology of key personnel. Military regimes may end repression; civilian regimes may revert to repression. But views on human rights and patterns of behavior tend to be deeply rooted in domestic societies, making change extraordinarily difficult to achieve. American governmental principles, including those on human rights, have risen out of the social history of its citizens and stress Lockean liberalism tinged by Adam Smith economics. Such social roots help to explain why the UN core regime has had only marginal influence on the United States—and on many other states as well. After all, Marxist regimes derive their principal legitimacy precisely from the espousal of Marxism as "scientific truth"; to accept an international view of human rights would be to sacrifice a major source of legitimacy.

Furthermore, the subject of human rights pertains to a crucial relationship between state and citizen. It is an extraordinarily sensitive subject not yielded easily by states to international regimes, organizations, or agencies.

Yet paradoxically there has been an explosion of concern with internationally recognized human rights since 1945. States want to do something about *other's* human rights violations. India led the campaign against South Africa's apartheid in the 1940s and early 1950s; India also led the campaign *against* an international treaty on human rights in internal war that might restrict Indian freedom of maneuver when dealing with violence at home (Forsythe 1978). The United States has criticized the Soviet Union for its human rights problems but kept the UN core human rights regime from having an impact on American discrimination against blacks, the death penalty for juvenile offenders, or the treatment of Native Americans. It is the dialectic of such contradictory policies that has propelled the UN core regime to its present status. Most states support the human rights regime but seek to direct its focus elsewhere. It is this paradox, special to the human rights field, that helps to explain why the United States has been inconsistent in its relationship to UN human rights programs. At times the United States has been unwilling to use seriously and constructively the UN human rights channels as instruments of influence, preferring to protect itself from these same international influences that might be strenthened by further use.

In addition, the principle of reciprocity is less important in the human rights field than elsewhere. Parties active in human rights do not approach a state—say, South Korea—by saying "If you treat your citizens well, we will treat ours likewise." Rather, there is frequent appeal to legal and moral obligation, to maintaining respectability in the international community, or to preserving legitimacy in the face of criticism. The fact that the UN core human rights regime contains some norms antithetical to American values explains further ambiguity in the U.S. position.

The American version of Lockean liberalism, as noted at the opening of this chapter, is slightly at odds with the liberalism of other democracies and markedly at odds with the reigning dogmas concerning political economy in most countries of the Second and Third Worlds. Further, the American vision of good government and the just society, plus a history of isolationism and a tendency toward unilateralism, have made U.S. adjustment to the UN core human rights regime difficult for some (for example, Jimmy Carter) and impossible for others (such as Ronald Reagan). Some of the norms of the regime—especially those pertaining to economic, social, and cultural rights, not to mention emerging claims to such rights as development, peace, and solidarity—are foreign to American political philosophy. The many authoritarian states that make up voting majorities at the UN have not inspired great confidence in UN human rights activities in the past by their obvious double standards and lack of procedural due process.

Given that most UN members do not subscribe to Lockean liberalism or laissez-faire capitalism, it is only to be expected that the United States would have some difficulty relating to a core human rights regime emanating from that organization. When the General Assembly declares that Zionism is racism, when the Human Rights Commission year after year debates Israeli violations of human rights but refuses to debate Syrian or Iraqi violations, when there is a vigorous criticism of Pinochet's Chile but a deafening silence about Amin's Uganda, U.S. estrangement from UN activities on human rights is readily understandable. The decline of the U.S. voting position within the UN has clearly affected the U.S.-UN relationship in this context.

Yet other democracies have worked persistently and sometimes successfully to improve the regime, as have other states such as Senegal which, though not manifesting Lockean liberalism, have displayed moderation in politics at home and a balanced commitment to human rights abroad. For example, Sweden and the Netherlands persistently and successfully struggled for a convention on torture in order to refine extant norms and agencies on that subject, whereas the United States displayed great indifference to the entire process (Baehr 1989). The other industrialized democracies have legally adhered to the Covenant on Civil and Political Rights to make the Human Rights Committee, which oversees that treaty, as effective as possible; the United States has stayed aloof.

There is no denying that the core regime incorporates some norms that are alien to American traditions and has sometimes functioned according to undesirable double standards. Likewise, the agencies of implementation are weak in authority and even weaker in power. Yet these characteristics of the regime do not fully explain periodic U.S. alienation. A fuller explanation of those patterns lies in American domestic politics.

Domestic Political Factors

American political culture, incorporating beliefs in American exceptionalism and tendencies toward both intellectual isolationism and unilateralism,
accounts for much in the U.S.-UN relationship over human rights. This
combination of traits was much in evidence during the Reagan administration. It was equally evident in Congress during the period of Brickerism in
the early 1950s. In addition, a vociferous segment of the American polity
has seen any effort at international cooperation as nefarious and sub-
versive. When either the legislative or executive branch has been
dominated by such views, it has been impossible for the U.S. government
as a whole to be responsive to the UN human rights regime or to use it to
any significant extent in trying to influence others.

It is also clear historically that the struggle to govern between the
presidency and Congress has greatly affected U.S.-UN relations on human
rights. Congress forced Eisenhower's retreat from UN human rights
programs in the 1950s, and Congress did battle not only with Nixon and
Ford but even with a somewhat committed Carter administration in the
1970s over the same subject but in exactly the opposite direction. In the
1980s Congress had some influence curbing the Reagan administration and
trying to push it into a human rights policy more compatible with
internationally recognized human rights. It has yet to be fully appreciated
how much Congress has been a maker of policy and a taker of UN
influence in the human rights field.

Private groups have played an important role in the human rights field,
especially after Congress became assertive on human rights matters in the
mid-1970s. There is a wide variety of lobbying groups active in human
rights issues. Many follow UN events closely and work with members of
Congress and/or officials in the executive branch pushing for policies
consistent with UN norms and rules. For example, in the late 1970s interest
groups concerned with human rights violations in Latin America became
"one of the largest, most active, and most visible foreign policy lobbying
forces in Washington" (Schoultz 1981: 75). Groups coordinated activity
through the Human Rights Working Group and the Washington Office of
Latin America. Among the most visible was Amnesty International, an
important conduit of information about the severity of human rights
violations (Schoultz 1981: chap. 2). Some of these groups have also tried to
get U.S. courts to utilize regime norms in their rulings. Others have served
as transmission belts for UN influence on the United States. Domestic
groups (such as the American Bar Association in the 1950s, or business
groups with respect to Latin America) have also opposed placing human
rights on the foreign policy agenda (Forsythe 1985: chap. 4; Schoultz 1981).

Evaluating the impact of such private groups is difficult. Most of the groups aim to make human rights a key component of U.S. bilateral policies and have exhibited less concern for U.S. policy in multilateral institutions. Human rights lobbies are generally less effective when confronted with strong competing interests at stake—national security, anticommunism, corporate profits (Schoultz 1981: 108)—though the issue of apartheid in South Africa has proved an exception. Separation of powers guarantees multiple access points for the human rights groups, but it does not guarantee their impact.

Conclusion: The Past as Future

There is no easy explanation for U.S.-UN relationships in the human rights field over the past forty-five years. Human rights remains a relatively unique issue area. What has clearly changed is that the international community through the core UN human rights regime has expanded norms and rules consistent with the demands of a changing membership. The U.S. response to these changes has been largely conditioned by domestic factors. Separation of powers involving in this case all three branches, each with specific authority on the issue, increases the likelihood of ambiguous and sometimes inconsistent positions. Particularly important is the role played by Congress, the courts, and private groups in transmitting international norms into the American system.

Given the role played by domestic politics, if U.S. policy is dominated in the future by the likes of Brickerism or Reaganism, the U.S.-UN relationship is doomed to extreme difficulty. Likewise, if the core regime is captured by reactionary forces that in the name of human rights try to suppress civil and political rights, there will be nothing but friction. UN activity will have little positive impact on the United States, and the United States will distance itself from UN human rights activities. If, however, U.S. policy is pragmatic and the UN regime itself exhibits a balanced commitment to human rights, there is reason to believe that their relationship can be less troubled than in the past.

During its last two years in office, the Reagan administration took a more even-handed approach to human rights issues in areas such as South Korea, Panama, Paraguay, and, to a lesser degree, Chile. Congress was still assertive and favorably disposed to most UN action on civil and political rights. In the judicial sector, there was at least slightly more reliance on international instruments, however erratic, than in previous decades.

Moreover, the UN regime had shown increased balance compared with the 1960s and early 1970s. Independent rapporteurs and working groups were utilized to bypass the "tyranny of the majority"; both Communist and Third World violations of human rights were addressed to at least some extent; and new norms and agencies were established, as on torture. I am persuaded that despite problems at the UN, the core human rights regime is more balanced and dynamic than previously (see also Donnelly 1988).

At the same time, the UN core regime on human rights remains weak and problematical. Information is disseminated, but authoritative decisions are rarely reached. The proposal to create a high commissioner for human rights continues to be rejected by the General Assembly, and the Subcommission on Human Rights may finally fall victim to budget cuts. Likewise, the U.S. commitment to internationally recognized human rights remains limited and subject to shifting coalitions in Washington.

There are at least some reasons to hope, however, that the relationship may be less troubled in the future than in the past. Yet the characteristics of both the issue area and regime, as well as the primacy of American domestic politics, suggest that the U.S.-UN relationship is unlikely ever to be smooth.

Notes

1. I thank those who commented on earlier versions of this chapter: Margaret Karns, Karen Mingst, Chadwick Alger, Margaret Galey, Charles Hermann, Raymond Hopkins, Harold Jacobson, Stephen Krasner, Mark Zacher, and Jack Donnelly.

2. On conceptual and definitional problems of regime analysis, see Kratochwil and Ruggie (1986). More generally on regimes and coordination, see Keohane (1984).

3. For more detail on the core regime, see Forsythe (1985b) and Tolley (1987b).

4. The International Court of Justice can also provide binding judgments, but it has historically not been given much opportunity to do so because states have not usually consented to judicial treatment of human rights cases. This record indicates how seriously states view the subject of human rights and how reluctant they are to have international organizations pronounce on the relationship between state and citizen.

5. Executive views may have been well founded politically, if not morally, given the fate of the Genocide Convention in American politics in the late 1940s and early 1950s. Truman signed the treaty and submitted it to the Senate, where it was vigorously attacked—and stalled until 1986. One of the (specious) attacks on the convention was that it would open Americans to trials abroad because of actions against various minorities within the United States. Had the Truman administration pushed for a really strong core UN human rights regime, it is likely such an effort would have met the same fate as the Genocide Convention.

6. A vigorous critique is found in Donnelly (1981). But for an effective rebuttal, see Alston (1983).

7. Kissinger, who has left a clearer view on these matters than Nixon, argued that the traditional U.S. approach to foreign policy resisted concepts of power, equilibrium, and stability in favor of moral and legal principles (including on human rights) that were debilitating. See Kissinger (1969: pt. 2). He later tried to reformulate his position (Kissinger 1978).

8. According to a letter from Fraser's principal assistant to me, the 1973 congressional emphasis on *international* human rights stemmed from the mandate of the subcommittee Fraser chaired, the chairman's "strong belief" in the UN and the international law, and the assistant's background in UN human rights affairs. See Fraser (1977: 152), U.S. Congressional Research Service (1977), and U.S. House of Representatives (1974) for further evidence.

9. The case of Liberia, though little noted, was illustrative. At the very time of Reagan pronouncements about an even-handed human rights policy, U.S. foreign assistance increased dramatically to the military government in Monrovia, which was engaged in open repression of its critics. A bipartisan movement in Congress tried to compel the administration to respond to human rights violations. The executive branch saw security interests at stake and thus resisted congressional pressures. When Secretary of State Shultz visited Monrovia in early 1987, he tried to sweep human rights violations under the diplomatic carpet, which intensified the debate in Washington. Congress finally legislated its concerns into the foreign aid bill.

10. It is difficult to be certain about how to characterize Reagan's human rights policy. At times U.S. rhetoric and action were balanced and presented with reference to international instruments on human rights. At other times the old cold war flavor was evident. For example, Richard Schifter, the new architect of human rights policy, made speeches about the Soviet Union and the Helsinki accord that were impressive in their moderation and accurate in their references to Soviet diplomatic-legal commitments. Yet a former Cuban political prisoner was appointed to represent the United States at the UN Human Rights Commission in an effort to give U.S. policy a cold war slant. See U.S. House of Representatives (1986).

11. For the pros and cons of ratification of the two basic UN Covenants, see Lillich (1981). On the U.S. judicial rejection of substantive economic rights, see Good (1984).

References

Aggarwal, Vinod K. (1985). *Liberal Protectionism: The International Politics of Organized Textile Trade.* Berkeley: University of California Press.

Alston, Phillip (1983). "The Alleged Demise of Human Rights at the UN: A Reply to Donnelly." *International Organization*, 37(3), 537–46.

Arnold, Hugh (1980). "Henry Kissinger and Human Rights." *Universal Human Rights*, 2(4), 51–71.

Baehr, Peter R. (1989). "The General Assembly as a Negotiating Forum." In David P. Forsythe, ed., *The United Nations in the World Political Economy.* London: Macmillan.

Baldwin, David (1979). "Power Analysis and World Politics." *World Politics*, 31(2), 161–94.

Bloomfield, Lincoln P. (1982). "From Ideology to Program to Policy: Tracking the Carter Human Rights Policy." *Journal of Policy Analysis and Management*, 2(1), 1–12.

Carter, Jimmy (1982). *Keeping Faith.* New York: Bantam.

Cohen, Roberta (1979). "Human Rights Decision-Making in the Executive Branch." In Donald P. Kommers and Gilbert D. Loescher, eds., *Human Rights and American Foreign Policy.* South Bend, IN: University of Notre Dame Press.

Cohen, Stephen B. (1982). "Conditioning U.S. Security Assistance on Human Rights Practices." *American Journal of International Law*, 76(2), 246–79.

Davis, Tammi R., and Sean M. Lynn-Jones (1987). "Citty upon a Hill." *Foreign Policy*, 66(Spring), 20–38.

Donnelly, Jack (1981). "Recent Trends in UN Human Rights Activity: Description and Polemic." *International Organization*, 35(4), 633–56.

——— (1986). "International Human Rights: A Regime Approach." *International Organization*, 40(3), 599–642.

——— (1988). "Human Rights at the United Nations 1955–85: The Question of Bias." *International Studies Quarterly*, 32(4), 275–303.

Drew, Elizabeth (1977). "Reporter at Large: Human Rights." *The New Yorker*, 53(July 18), 36–62.

Forsythe, David P. (1978). "Legal Management of Internal War." *American Journal of International Law*, 72(2), 272–95.

——— (1982). "Socioeconomic Human Rights: The UN, The US, and Beyond." *Human Rights Quarterly*, 4(4), 433–49.

——— (1985a). "The United Nations and Human Rights. 1945–1985." *Political Science Quarterly*, 100(1), 249–70.

——— (1985b). *Human Rights and World Politics*. Lincoln: University of Nebraska Press.

——— (1986). Review of A. Glenn Mower, Jr., *International Cooperation for Social Justice: Global and Regional Protection of Economic and Social Rights*. *Human Rights Quarterly*, 8(3), 540–44.

——— (1988). *Human Rights and U.S. Foreign Policy: Congress Reconsidered*. Gainesville: University Presses of Florida.

——— (1989). "The Political Economy of UN Refugee Programs." In David P. Forsythe, ed., *The United Nations in the World Political Economy*. London: Macmillan.

Fraser, Donald M. (1977). "Freedom and Foreign Policy." *Foreign Policy*, 26(Spring), 140–56.

Garth, Bryant G. (1986). "Aggressive Smugness: The United States and International Human Rights." *American Journal of Comparative Law*, 34(Supplement), 411–26.

Good, Martha H. (1984). "Freedom from Want: The Freedom of United States Courts to Protect Subsistence Rights." *Human Rights Quarterly*, 6(3), 335–65.

Hassan, Farooq (1983). "The Doctrine of Incorporation." *Human Rights Quarterly*, 5(1), 68–86.

Hevener, Natalie Kaufman, and David Whiteman (1988). "Opposition to Human Rights Treaties in the United States Senate: The Legacy of the Bricker Amendment." *Human Rights Quarterly*, 10(3), 305–37.

Humphrey, John P. (1978). "The Implementation of International Human Rights Law." *New York Law School Law Review*, 24(1), 31–61.

——— (1984). *Human Rights and the United Nations: A Great Adventure*. Dobbs Ferry, NY: Transnational.

Immigration and Naturalization Service, Petitioner, v. Luz Marina Cardoza-Fonesca, No. 85-782, Decided March 9, 1987, *United States Law Week*, March 10, 1987, 55LW 4313.

Jacoby, Tamar (1986). "Reagan's Turnaround on Human Rights." *Foreign Affairs*, 64(5), 1066–86.

Johnson, Glen (1987). "The Contributions of Eleanor and Franklin Roosevelt to the Development of International Protection of Human Rights." *Human Rights Quarterly*, 9(1), 19–48.

Keohane, Robert O. (1984). *After Hegemony: Cooperation and Discord in the World Political Economy*. Princeton: Princeton University Press.

Kirkpatrick, Jeane (1983). *The Reagan Phenomenon and Other Speeches on Foreign Policy*. Washington, DC: American Enterprise Institute.

Kissinger, Henry (1969). *American Foreign Policy: Three Essays*. New York: Norton.

——— (1978). "Continuity and Change in American Foreign Policy." In Abdul A. Said, ed., *Human Rights and World Order*. New York: Transaction Books, 154–67.

Kratochwil, Friedrich, and John Gerard Ruggie (1986). "International Organization: A State of the Art on an Art of the State." *International Organization*, 40(4), 753–77.

Lauren, Paul Gorden (1983). "First Principles of Racial Equality: History and the Politics and Diplomacy of Human Rights Provisions in the United Nations Charter." *Human Rights Quarterly*, 5(1), 1–26.

Lillich, Richard B., ed. (1981). *U.S. Ratification of the Human Rights Treaties*. Charlottesville: University Press of Virginia.

Lillich, Richard B. (1983). *International Human Rights Instruments*. Buffalo, NY: William S. Hein.

Lillich, Richard B., and Hurst Hannum (1985). "Linkages between International Human Rights and U.S. Constitutional Law." *American Journal of International Law*, 79(1), 158–63.

Lockwood, Bert B., Jr. (1984). "The United Nations Charter and United States Civil Rights Litigation: 1946–1955." *Iowa Law Review*, 69(4), 901–56.

Mower, A. Glenn, Jr. (1979). *The United States, the United Nations and Human Rights*. Westport, CT: Greenwood Press.

———— (1985). *International Cooperation for Social Justice: Global and Regional Protection of Economic/Social Rights*. Westport, CT: Greenwood Press.

Moynihan, Patrick (1978). *A Dangerous Place*. Boston: Little, Brown.

Muravchik, Joshua (1986). *The Uncertain Crusade: Jimmy Carter and the Dilemmas of Human Rights Policy*. Lanham, MD: Hamilton Press.

Pena-Irala v. Filartiga (1980). 630 F. 2d 876.

Rodriguez-Fernandez v. Wilkinson (1980). 505 F. Suppl. 707.

Rossiter, Caleb (1984). "Human Rights: The Carter Record, the Reagan Reaction." *Report*. Washington Center for International Policy (September).

Ruggie, John Gerard (1983). "Human Rights and the Future International Community." *Daedalus*, 112(Fall), 93–110.

Schlesinger, Arthur, Jr. (1978). "Human Rights and the American Tradition." *Foreign Affairs*, 57(3), 503–26.

Schoultz, Lars (1981). *Human Rights and United States Policy toward Latin America*. Princeton: Princeton University Press.

Tel-Oren (1984). 726 F.2d 774 D.C. Cir.

Tolley, Howard, Jr. (1987a). "International Human Rights Law in U.S. Courts: Public Interest Groups and Private Attorneys." Paper prepared for the American Political Science Association Annual Meeting, Chicago, August.

———— (1987b). *The United Nations Human Rights Commission*. Boulder, CO: Westview Press.

Tuttle, James C., ed. (1978). *International Human Rights Law and Practice*. Philadelphia: ABA.

Ungar, Sanford, J., ed. (1985). *Estrangement: America and the World*. New York: Oxford University Press.

U.S. Congressional Research Service (1977). *Human Rights in the International Community and in U.S. Foreign Policy, 1945–76*. Report prepared for the Subcommittee on International Organizations, Committee on Foreign Affairs (July 24). Washington, DC: U.S. Government Printing Office.

U.S. Department of State (1982). Report submitted to Congress, "Country Reports on Human Rights Practices for 1981." 97th Cong., 2d sess. Washington, DC: U.S. Government Printing Office.

U.S. House of Representatives Committee on Foreign Affairs Subcommittee on International Organizations (1974). *Report: Human Rights in the World Community: A Call for U.S. Leadership* (March 27). Washington, DC: U.S. Government Printing Office.

U.S. House of Representatives Committee on Foreign Affairs Subcommittee on Europe, Middle East, Asia, and Human Rights (1982). *Hearings: Implementation of Congressionally Mandated Human Rights Provisions*, volume II. 97th Cong., 2d sess. Washington, DC: U.S. Government Printing Office.

U.S. House of Representatives Committee on Foreign Affairs (1983). *Human Rights Documents*. Committee Print, September. Washington, DC: U.S. Government Printing Office.

U.S. House of Representatives Committee on Foreign Affairs Subcommittee on Human Rights and International Organizations (1984). *Hearings: Review of U.S. Human Rights Policy*. 98th Cong., 1st sess. Washington DC: U.S. Government Printing Office.

——— (1986). *Review of the UN Commission on Human Rights*. 99th Cong., 2d sess. Washington, DC: U.S. Government Printing Office.

Van Dyke, Vernon (1970). *Human Rights, The United States, and World Community*. New York: Oxford University Press.

CHAPTER ELEVEN

Continuity and Change in U.S.-IGO Relationships: A Comparative Analysis with Implications for the Future of Multilateralism in U.S. Foreign Policy

Margaret P. Karns
Karen A. Mingst

The last two decades have been marked by a series of episodes in which U.S. commitments to participation in multilateral institutions have been called into question. The difficulties the United States has had with a number of IGOs escalated during the Reagan administration, fueling a debate over whether a "crisis of multilateralism" complemented the general decline of internationalism in U.S. foreign policy. For example, Thomas Hughes (1985–86: 587) has suggested, "International institutions are now perceived to be obstacles—not, as in the past, tools—to the promotion of American foreign policy goals. Accordingly, multilateralism has been challenged by global unilateralism."

Scholars and policymakers alike worry about the implications of the latter for patterns of cooperation and interaction in the international system. Despite a decline in relative U.S. power, the United States still commands sufficient resources to exercise considerable influence, positively or negatively, on international organizations and the regimes in which they are embedded. The United States can also use those resources to pursue its objectives unilaterally or bilaterally, or even on an ad hoc multilateral basis. Hence the choices of U.S. policymakers have major implications for the future of international regimes and the organizations that in many cases provide structures of interaction, decision making, and operational activities.

Although the Reagan administration modified its early antipathy toward multilateralism and even increased support for a number of institutions such as the World Bank and IMF, a potentially more critical problem has emerged in the erosion of support in Congress for upholding American financial commitments to IGOs. The networks of global inter-dependence have continued to grow, but domestic politics remains an important factor shaping the patterns of cooperation among state and nonstate actors. The real crisis may be one of domestic support for U.S. commitments—especially financial contributions—to IGOs, for in fact the dominant theme that emerges from the preceding chapters is the relative continuity in U.S. relationships with many IGOs over the postwar period.

This volume represents the first major effort to address the debate on multilateralism in U.S. foreign policy. The nine case studies of U.S. participation in different organizations have explored a series of questions relevant to the debate over the future of multilateralism:

(1) In what ways has the importance of IGOs as instruments of U.S. policies to create and maintain patterns of international cooperation and to promote American interests changed over time? Has the United States continued to use IGOs to create international regimes and to shape their evolution and transformation? Has the use of IGOs for collective legitimation and dispute settlement declined? Has IGO information gathering gained in importance with increased inter-dependence?

(2) How have the constraints and influence of IGOs on the United States changed over time? Under what conditions has IGO rule making impinged on the United States? Have IGO rules, information-sharing, and agenda-setting functions increasingly affected U.S. domestic processes? In what areas has the United States adapted decision-making procedures in response to IGO agendas and activities?

(3) Why have these changes occurred? Does the decline in relative power of the United States provide the most convincing rationale for changes in IGO instrumentality and influence? Or do characteristics of the issue areas, properties of particular IGOs, and domestic political factors offer more adequate explanation?

(4) What are the policy implications for the United States of these changes in U.S.-IGO relationships? What adjustments in strategy and decision-making processes do the various cases suggest might increase the effectiveness of U.S. multilateral diplomacy?

In this concluding chapter we identify the factors that explain continuity and change in the patterns of instrumentality which may be relevant to future decisions about the role of specific IGOs and of multilateralism generally in the formulation and implementation of American foreign policy.[1] We also examine how the case studies enhance our understanding of the relationships between IGOs and member states' policies and policymaking processes—an important step toward understanding the impact of IGOs and international regimes on collective behavior at the international level. The latter requires the linkage of different levels of analysis, specifically the international and domestic policy arenas.

The nine case studies span three broad issue areas—security, economics, and social welfare—enhancing the richness of understanding and the bases for generalization. Clearly, however, they do not provide an exhaustive examination of U.S.-IGO relationships, nor do they enable us to draw definitive conclusions that changes in patterns of IGO instrumentality and influence are caused by one or more specific factors or some combination thereof. The regularities that emerge across cases may well be a function of the cases selected. The task of comparison is complicated by the way organizations differ in their mix of purposes and functions and in the ways they affect policies and policymaking. Nonetheless, several clear findings emerge from the comparisons:

(1) Over time there has been a continuing utility of IGOs as instruments of the United States for regime and rule creation whereas in no case has an IGO become more useful now for collective legitimation than in the past. IGOs have rarely been of great use to the United States for information gathering and analysis.

(2) IGOs have had increasing effect on agendas for U.S. governmental agencies and officials as well as on domestic group activity. In few cases, however, have IGO-established rules required changes in American regulations, or has the United States been affected by IGO information-gathering or surveillance tasks.

(3) Changes in the characteristics of both IGOs and issue areas have had the greatest impact on the evolution of patterns of instrumentality and influence.

(4) Domestic political factors figure prominently in most of the cases.

(5) The decline of U.S. relative power resources has not been a major factor affecting the patterns of IGO instrumentality and influence.

U.S.-IGO Relationships: Patterns of Changing Instrumentality

As instruments of policy, IGOs may provide forums for legitimating viewpoints, actions, principles, and norms and for coalition building. They institutionalize processes of information gathering, analysis, and surveillance, and decision making and negotiation for rule creation and dispute settlement. They provide collective goods and carry out operational activities.

The case studies reaffirm the key role played by the United States in creating and sustaining the suite of postwar IGOs. Virtually all of the nine organizations depended heavily on American funds, personnel, and technical expertise. By providing material supports to them, U.S. decision makers expected that these IGOs could be used as instruments of American foreign policy. In some cases the expectation was explicit (the UN Security Council, NATO, OAS); in others, more implicit (UNESCO and WHO). In all cases these institutions also provided legitimacy to American policies. Because of the global predominance of liberalism, the United States could rely on these organizations as dependable forums for U.S. influence. Charles Krauthammer (1985: 152) has suggested, "Multi-lateralism was indeed the preferred means for American action—and there was no real restraint on it."

To be sure, the United States has not always been ready to play a key role in world affairs. Prior to World War II, periods of isolation were punctuated by periods of internationalism. Even during the latter, however, the American belief that the United States had a special role in world affairs rarely led it to assume leadership or responsibility. For most of the post World War II era "globalism meant internationalism, which implied support for multilateralism, not unilateralism," support for IGOs, respect for law, and promotion of economic interdependence (Kegley and Wittkopf 1987: 577).

Table 11.1 on U.S. use of IGOs as instruments of policy across the postwar era presents our assessments of the changes elucidated by the respective authors, specifically whether the organization has been more useful, less useful, or about the same utility for the United States in each of the categories of instrumentality: regime and rule creation, collective legitimation, information gathering and surveillance, rule enforcement and dispute settlement, and operational activities. Because some organizations (most notably UNESCO) encompass a variety of programs, it is possible to find an organization being regarded simultaneously as both more and less useful over the last forty years.

The case studies reveal the continuing utility of IGOs for regime and rule creation with increases in three cases, a mixed pattern for two of the organizations within the food regime, and decreases in two cases. The IAEA has increased in importance because of more intrusive and ornate rules on safeguards. The World Bank, beginning with programs on poverty alleviation in the 1970s and continuing with structural adjustment lending in the 1980s, has established new norms for multilateral development assistance. The scope and specificity of GATT's trade rules widened in large part because of U.S. initiatives in the Tokyo Round. The United States seeks to continue that pattern in the Uruguay Round. After a

TABLE 11.1

Changing Patterns of IGO Instrumentality, 1945–88: Categories of Instrumentality

IGO/Regime Activities	Regime and Rule Creation	Collective Legitimization	Information Gathering and Surveillance	Rule Enforcement and Dispute Settlement	Operational Activities
Security-UN, NATO, OAS	0	−	NA	−	0
IAEA	+	0	+	0	+
IMF	0	NA	+	0	+
World Bank	+	0	NA	0	+
GATT	+	−	NA	+	NA
WHO	0	0	0	NA	+/−
UNESCO	−	−	+	NA	0
UN Human Rights	−	−	0	0	NA
FAO/FOOD	+ (WFP)	−	0	NA	−
	− (FAO)	−	0	NA	−

Key: + = more useful
    0 = about the same
    − = less useful
    NA = not applicable

dramatic loss of importance in the 1970s with the end of the Bretton Woods system of fixed exchange rates, the IMF has enjoyed a renaissance in dealing with international debt problems.

WHO was established to create rules governing transmissible diseases, the International Health Regulations. Its importance for rule setting in international health has remained constant and is likely to rise as attention to AIDS increases. UN human rights organs, the food organizations, and UNESCO have all decreased in utility to the United States for regime and rule creation, though the United States still finds the human rights organs useful for occasional initiatives such as the sponsorship in 1986 of a resolution on religious discrimination. The mixed pattern precludes any conclusion that the decline in U.S. relative power resources has either increased or decreased the importance of IGOs to the United States for the creation and maintenance of international regimes. It reinforces the thesis that IGOs play key roles particularly in the *maintenance* of regimes by ensuring continuity and stability in member states' interactions and efforts to increase order and cooperation.

Since regimes provide broad frameworks of principles and norms to guide state behavior, the usefulness of IGOs as instruments for collective legitimation varies directly with their importance for regime and rule creation. Generally the case studies appear to confirm this prediction, for in no case is an IGO more useful now for collective legitimation than in the past (see column 2, table 11.1). The United States has clearly found UNESCO, FAO, the UN human rights organs, the OAS, and the UN less useful for regime and rule creation and for collective legitimation of its policies and interests. The UN was primarily useful during the height of the cold war and the process of decolonization. Both it and the OAS continue to be occasional vehicles for delegitimating the actions of other countries, as in the condemnation of the Soviet invasion of Afghanistan and Iran's seizure of American hostages.

The World Bank presents a special case of the relationship between regime creation and collective legitimation in the coevolution of thinking about development assistance among U.S. and Bank officials described by Ascher (chapter 5). GATT is unusual also in its increased importance for *trade* rule creation but decreased salience for collective legitimation of more general U.S. foreign policy objectives, as Karns (chapter 6) notes. The changing membership in many IGOs has made it more difficult for the United States to muster majorities in support of its foreign policy actions. It has generally proved easier to gain support for resolutions condemning others.

Although IGOs are very important instruments generally for information gathering and analysis, they are rarely of great importance to the United States, which has its own rich information sources, nor has the United States made much use of IGOs for rule enforcement and dispute settlement (see column 3, table 11.1). In three cases, however, IGOs' usefulness for information gathering has increased in recent years (IAEA, IMF, and UNESCO in the science areas up to the point of withdrawal). It has remained about the same in two cases (UN human rights organs and FAO). WHO's utility in this respect has also generally remained about the same, but there is a prospect of significant change with increased attention to AIDS.

NATO's monitoring of the military forces of both friends and foes in Europe legitimates information the United States already has. Statistics on military spending have provided members of Congress with ammunition to argue for greater burden sharing. Information on other states' human rights records gathered by various UN agencies has provided a basis for checking the U.S. government's own information not found in the State Department's annual reports on human rights. In each case competing sources of information are available. The U.S. Department of Defense conducts its own checks on nuclear safeguards and compares these assessments with such private sources as the Swedish International Peace Research Institute (SIPRI). Amnesty International covers a small range of rights, while Freedom House rates civil and political rights exclusively. The U.S. Department of State reports are the only comprehensive assessment.

The United States has tended to place high value on IGO rule enforcement and dispute settlement activities, though the set of case studies in this volume does not illuminate this role (see column 4, table 11.1). The specific focus of these activities has shifted significantly in two of four cases examined: in the IMF from exchange rate stability to conditionality and in the World Bank from infrastructure to structural adjustment lending. The importance of the IAEA (for nuclear safeguards) and UN human rights bodies has remained relatively constant. The United States has long regarded the GATT dispute settlement procedures, in spite of their limitations and slowness, as useful avenues for achieving changes in other countries' trade practices. Under the Reagan administration the number of complaints initiated by the United States increased, but the United States also found itself the target of more complaints from others.

With respect to operational activities, IGOs in four areas—IAEA, IMF, WHO, and the World Bank—have become more useful to the United States (see column 5, table 11.1). For example, in the 1970s the United States funneled more funds through the World Bank and other multilateral institutions, thereby increasing their operational capabilities. This also strengthened their surveillance and enforcement activities. The United States has supported programs such as structural adjustment lending in the World Bank because they have frequently entailed a kind of conditionality —that is, required changes in recipient governments' policies. These requirements have extended into such noneconomic areas as benefits to women and environmental impact.

IGOs remained about as useful in two other cases: UNESCO (up to the point of U.S. withdrawal) and UN peacekeeping. Significant decreases in utility show up in only two cases, and both involve specific programs or tasks to which the United States objected: FAO's work in allocation of resources and food aid and WHO's "Health for All" programs. In general operational activities tend to serve American interests while addressing global problems and to ensure burden sharing in the provision of international collective goods.

Overall the U.S. relationship with UNESCO to the point of withdrawal in 1984 appears the most difficult to evaluate because of the diversity of its activities. UNESCO has been particularly useful for both informational and operational activities in the natural sciences. The United States initiated the International Program for the Development of Communications (IPDC) to improve communications infrastructure and thereby shift attention away from the ideological debate over the proposed New World Information and Communication Order. The fact remains that UNESCO, like the ILO, deals with subjects with a high domestic impact on member states, and the United States has not had a uniform response to such initiatives.

Analysis of the case studies affirms that the usefulness of the more specialized, technical agencies has tended to remain constant over time; yet, as happened with the major economic institutions, changes in international economic relations may result in periods of decreased utility followed by renewed salience. The lack of clear, consistent patterns suggests that policymakers and scholars alike need to evaluate IGOs in terms of the variety of ways they can serve as instruments of policy and what the United States wants to achieve through specific IGOs at specific points in time. Certainly the case studies rebut the hypothesis that IGOs have become generally less useful as instruments of foreign policy. The question, then, is whether there has been any consistent pattern of change in the impact of IGOs on U.S. policy and policymaking processes. Do IGOs impose more constraints now than in the past?

Patterns of Changing IGO Influence

IGOs constrain or influence member states (and other actors) by setting international and, hence, national agendas and forcing governments to make decisions. They subject member states' behavior to surveillance through information sharing and motivate member states to develop specialized decision-making and implementation processes to facilitate and coordinate IGO participation. They create principles, norms, and rules of behavior with which member states must align their policies if they wish to benefit from reciprocity. In addition, international norms can serve to legitimate the preferences of domestic groups, particularly in pluralistic societies. Finally, IGOs help to establish habits of international co-operation, reinforced by domestic groups' support for norms and rules and the creation of bureaucratic stakes in working in and through particular IGOs.

Discovering and verifying whether IGOs have influenced the United States in any of these various ways is a difficult, often elusive task. Changes in national agendas or decision-making processes may be prompted by a variety of factors, only one of which may be IGO influence. The same can be said for adjustments in national policies and foreign policy strategies. The problem is to establish whether IGOs are more responsible for these actions than other factors. Table 11.2 summarizes the patterns that emerge in the nine case studies.

The case studies reveal a few instances in which IGO-established rules have required changes in American laws or regulations (see column 1, table 11.2). For the most part international rules have paralleled American rules in the cases of health and nuclear power regulations. However, the

TABLE 11.2

Changing Patterns of IGO Instrumentality, 1945–88: Categories of IGO Influence

IGO/Regime	Changing Rules and Norms	Surveillance	Agenda Setting	Decision Making and Implementation	Domestic Groups
Security-UN, NATO, OAS	0 (NATO)	NA	+	NA	0
IAEA	+	+	0	+	NA
IMF	0	0	0	NA	NA
World Bank	0	0	+	NA	NA
GATT	+	NA	0	+	0
WHO	0	0	+	+	+
UNESCO	0	NA	+	NA	+
UN Human Rights	+	0	0	NA	+
FAO/FOOD	−	0	0	NA	+

Key: + = more useful
      0 = about the same
      − = less useful
     NA = not applicable

conclusion of the Multilateral Trade Negotiations in 1979 did require a number of adaptations to bring American practices and regulations into conformity with the new nontariff codes. Adverse panel rulings against U.S. trade practices have also required adjustments when the United States wanted to retain its credibility.

The applications by American courts of UN human rights norms described by Forsythe (chapter 10) are particularly intriguing examples of IGO effects on domestic behavior. In this rare instance the judicial branch has applied norms promulgated by international bodies. Similarly, the symbiotic relationship between U.S. and World Bank aid officials resulted in shifts in the direction and focus of U.S. aid programs, responding to the Bank's emphasis on poverty alleviation. In the former case the pattern is one of increasing influence since the late 1970s. In the latter it seems to be relatively constant. The World Bank has served as a think tank for new approaches to development since it got into the development business in the late 1950s.

NATO continues to play an important role in shaping American military strategy and doctrine. WHO's impact, never large, has remained constant. Only in the case of FAO has there been notable decline in the impact of regime norms and rules on U.S. policies. The United States has openly violated two key norms in the food regime by continuing (and expanding) farm subsidies and by refusing to support schemes to limit commodity price fluctuation. The United States is not alone in these violations.

Although increased interdependence should lead to greater transparency of state actions through information sharing and surveillance, the case studies reveal few instances of IGO impact in this respect (see column 2, table 11.2). Only in one does there appear to be increased influence: the IAEA. Since the early 1970s the importance the United States has attached to IAEA's role in preventing nuclear weapons proliferation led it to accept greater surveillance of its own facilities for peaceful uses of nuclear energy and reprocessing.

The case studies show at least constant if not increased effects of IGOs in setting agendas for the U.S. government (see column 3, table 11.2). There is also a pattern of increased influence on domestic groups in the cases of the food organizations, UNESCO, WHO, and the UN human rights organs. Possibly as other countries propose new items for IGO agendas, domestic groups in a pluralistic society such as the United States in some instances respond even more rapidly than government officials because the groups have special interests at stake. For example, when the issues of control of pharmaceuticals and distribution of infant formula in LDCs were introduced in WHO, both proponents of regulation from the public health community and opponents from the business community sought to air their views in congressional hearings (Mingst, chapter 8).

Similarly, introduction of the issues of Israel's representation and international communications in UNESCO prompted vigorous lobbying by the Jewish community in the case of the former and the press and print media in the latter. When the Europeans campaigned in NATO for a "dual-track" response to the building of Soviet intermediate-range missiles in Europe, a variety of groups in the United States mobilized to influence the response, including American military personnel in Europe.

As new agenda items have been added and, in some cases, domestic groups energized, it is logical that U.S. governmental decision-making and implementation processes have been affected. The number of examples of increased IGO impact on the latter cited in the case studies is small (three), but all are in IGOs with rule-creating powers in issue areas of importance to the United States (see column 4, table 11.2). In the case of GATT, for example, most of the changes occurred in the 1960s and 1970s and involved significant adaptations in U.S. trade policymaking and implementation processes that were previously underdeveloped. These included the creation, institutionalization, and expansion of the Office of the U.S. Trade Representative (USTR), the establishment of sectoral advisory committees, and greater involvement of members of Congress in multilateral trade talks. Similarly, U.S. participation in the IAEA has led to adaptations in decision making with the creation of new offices to service the International Nuclear Fuel Cycle Evaluation, safeguards, and technical assistance. In the case of WHO, the changes have been more specifically in

U.S. strategy for dealing with the organization prompted, Mingst (chapter 8) argues, by its continuing salience and by the necessity for adaptation to changes within WHO itself.

The case studies of U.S.-IGO relations in the social welfare issue area evidence increased influence of IGOs on domestic groups (see column 5, table 11.2). In the mid-1970s domestic groups became actively engaged in efforts to influence the executive and legislative branches to emphasize human rights more heavily in U.S. foreign policy. These activities were not, however, triggered by any substantive changes in the agendas of UN human rights organs; rather, they reflected congressional concerns about the lack of attention to human rights and the growth in numbers and activities of nongovernmental groups concerned with human rights. Similarly, increased concern in the mid-1980s about the African food crisis was fueled by the impact on public opinion of extensive media coverage of the famine in Ethiopia. With greater public awareness and concern there was greater attention to the contribution that the food organizations were making. In both instances IGOs' influence augmented the impact of other domestic factors. As WHO has debated more regulatory policies in the health area, however, it has had a more direct role in mobilizing the support and opposition of domestic groups, as Mingst (chapter 8) describes.

The case studies underscore the difficulty of evaluating the effects of IGOs on state behavior. Hence the examples cited of IGO influence on the United States may well be exceptions and not indicative of the increasing impact of IGOs over time. What patterns do the case studies reveal in the timing of changes in IGO impact and utility over the postwar period? In two a pattern of rather steady decline in U.S. use is evident: UNESCO and the organizations in the food regime. Deterioration was evident as early as 1954 in UNESCO; U.S. interest decreased during the 1960s and eventually grew into alienation, resulting in U.S. withdrawal in 1984. Likewise, U.S. relations with the various Rome-based institutions have deteriorated slowly throughout the postwar period, as Hopkins (chapter 7) describes. By the late 1960s the United States used GATT, the UN, and OAS less than earlier for legitimating its objectives and actions. Changes occurred in U.S. relations with the IAEA and WHO during the mid-1970s, whereas for the IMF there is a rather striking parabolic pattern of decreased utility in the 1970s and increased utility in the 1980s. The World Bank's usefulness for sharing the burden of development aid increased in the 1970s; in the 1980s the United States has promoted a greater role for the Bank in structural adjustment and privatization.

What factors explain the patterns of IGO instrumentality and influence? We identified four potential explanatory variables in the introductory chapter: declining U.S. power, characteristics of the issue area and of the IGO, and domestic political factors. How important are each of these?

Explaining Patterns of Change

Table 11.3 shows the relative significance of each of the four factors for explaining change in the patterns of instrumentality and influence for the respective organizations. Because each factor contains at least two dimensions, our evaluation represents a composite assessment of the multiple dimensions.

TABLE 11.3
Sources of Change in U.S.-IGO Relationships: Categories of Instrumentality

IGO/Regime Factors	Decline in U.S. Power	Issue Area Characteristics	IGO Characteristics	Domestic Political Factors
Security-UN, NATO, OAS	+	+ +	+	0
IAEA	+	+ +	+	+
IMF	0	+ +	+ +	0
IBRD	+	+	+	+
GATT	+	+ +	+	+
WHO	0	+	+ +	+
UNESCO	0	+	+ +	+ +
UN HR	0	+	0	+ +
FAO	0	+	+ +	+ +

Key: + + = very significant explanation
    + = moderately significant explanation
    0 = not relevant

Issue Area

Of the four factors examined, characteristics of the issue area have had the greatest impact on the patterns of changing instrumentality and influence in U.S.-IGO relations. In four of the case studies they provide very significant explanations of change; and in five they have had moderately significant effects (see column 2, table 11.3).

Ideology and salience are the two principal dimensions of issue area characteristics elaborated in chapter 1. The degree of congruity in ideology between the United States and the dominant coalitions in IGOs is the first important dimension of the character of the issue area. Although in many IGOs there have been major changes in membership since the early 1960s and, hence, in the dominant coalitions, the same has not been true in four of the cases examined: IAEA, NATO, IMF, and GATT. The IAEA is unique among IGOs, in fact, in the high level of persistent agreement between the United States and Soviet Union on issues of nuclear proliferation. Likewise, NATO members have enjoyed comparative homogeneity of ideology and shared sense of threat.

In several organizations the ideology of the dominant coalition has changed significantly enough from the time of their founding that the United States now finds itself in a minority position. The change from educational and intellectual liberalism in UNESCO and agricultural (economic) liberalism in FAO to greater state control has left the United States opposing many UNESCO and several FAO programs. The same situation applies in the human rights organizations in which the changing view of the majority that human rights should include not only political and civil rights but also social and economic rights has undermined U.S. support for the regime, however shallow that support may have been at an earlier time.

The degree of interest in the work of a particular IGO—that is, its salience—is the second dimension of issue area characteristics. Beyond the obvious high salience of any matters touching on a nation's basic security, interest is likely to vary with circumstances, the priorities of decision makers, and domestic groups. The cases reveal clear patterns of continuity in the salience of the WHO, NATO, and the IAEA to the United States. These organizations have been and continue to be valuable for the achievement of specific goals.

In contrast, U.S. interest in both the IMF and GATT diminished in the 1970s, more in the case of the former than the latter. Changes in the nature of trade barriers and patterns of competition decreased the role of GATT in world trade. These changes occurred in part because the United States lost some of its comparative advantage in trade. It also faced diminishing ability to control financial markets because of the increasing strength of other currencies and diversity of financial instruments. The shift to floating exchange rates in the 1970s cost the IMF its principal role in ensuring exchange rate stability. Yet the debt crisis of the early 1980s thrust a new role on the IMF in the negotiations of debt-refinancing packages and surveillance of debtors' domestic economic policies. Its salience to the United States, other creditor nations, and banks was greater than ever.

These findings suggest that the importance of issue area characteristics in influencing states' behavior has been underestimated. They confirm the hypothesis stated in chapter 1: because the issue area will influence the nature and structure of IGOs in that area, "we would expect the patterns of IGO instrumentality and influence to be more similar within a given issue area than across different areas." We turn, then, to the role of IGO characteristics as sources of explanation.

IGO Characteristics

Three characteristics of IGOs—membership, IGO tasks, and the role and composition of secretariats—are the most relevant dimensions to our analysis. These are heavily influenced by issue area characteristics. In three of the case studies IGO characteristics explain significant changes in patterns of instrumentality and influence; in four others these characteristics provide moderately significant explanations, as shown in column 3 of table 11.3.

Not surprisingly, growth of IGO membership was relevant to change in virtually all global IGOs in which the United States was not insulated by special majorities or weighted voting (except in the UN Security Council). The United States was therefore more protected in the World Bank and IMF with weighted voting in the former case and special majorities in the latter. The "major interests" norm protected the United States in GATT, as did the decision of most LDCs to join UNCTAD, an alternative forum in which they formed the numerical majority and institutionalized one-state, one-vote decision making. However, U.S. relationships with UNESCO and the food organizations, as well as with the UN in security matters, were profoundly influenced by expanding membership. LDCs used their dominance in the food institutions to call for statist rather than free market approaches and to press their pro-Arab, anti-Israel bias in the UN security organs.

Changing membership has had a diverse impact on the types of policy outputs of some organizations and, hence, on U.S.-IGO relationships. Although the United States continued to support information gathering and certain operational activities of WHO, it opposed the increasing numbers of regulatory and redistributive proposals from Third World members. The World Bank responded to changes in its membership by using enlarged Bank funds to advocate redistribution of resources for poverty alleviation. U.S. aid programs followed suit exemplifying the close, symbiotic relationship between U.S. and Bank officials. The plight of debtor nations in the early to mid-1980s forced the IMF to seek support of the United States and other creditor nations and major private banks for a significant role in debt management.

The composition and role of secretariats provide a much better explanation of continuity in U.S.-IGO relationships than of change. The technical expertise of WHO personnel and the seemingly technical orientation of the IAEA and GATT secretariats have largely insulated these organizations from the effects of changing majorities. Commonality of training of U.S. and IGO personnel in the cases of WHO, the World Bank, and the IMF has had a very significant effect on U.S. attitudes toward and close relations with these organizations. As Ascher (chapter 5) notes with respect to the Bank, however, "the commonality of economic ideology that similar training provides . . . does not leave the U.S. government with greater control in any direct sense." In UNESCO both the secretariat and the director general's position became highly politicized in the 1970s. Their ideologies more closely reflected the beliefs of the Group of 77. In the World Bank the increased presence of staff from the developing countries reinforced the struggle for secretariat autonomy from the United States. This struggle for control in which the Bank sought to become a more truly multilateral institution has been an important factor in the changes in the U.S.-World Bank relationship.

In the food regime IGO characteristics are of special importance because of the emergence of a number of competing organizations. In the face of intraorganizational conflicts in the principal organization, FAO, the tendency of the United States has been to create new organizations. With the creation of the World Food Program and the International Fund for Agricultural Development, interorganizational politics have led the United States to retreat from conflict by pursuing a unilateral course of action.

Domestic Political Factors

Domestic political factors are also particularly important in explaining the changes in U.S.-IGO relationships. As Huntington (1988: 455) suggests, "The societal or domestic constraints on the development and use of U.S. power tightened significantly during the 1970s." In seven of the nine case studies domestic political factors provide either a very or a moderately significant explanation (see column 4, table 11.3).

Among the domestic political factors, the separation of powers among the three branches of the federal government figures in seven of the nine studies. Increased tension between the executive and legislative branches and congressional reassertion of power in the post-Vietnam era have affected U.S. relationships with several organizations. With respect to the human rights regime and the World Bank, Congress has taken an increasingly active role, requiring U.S. executive directors in multilateral development banks to evaluate applicants' records on gross violations of internationally recognized human rights in decisions regarding loans. Similarly, in 1984 Congress criticized the executive's handling of U.S. participation in UNESCO. Tensions between the two branches, along with a lack of commitment by either, have led to changes in the U.S.

relationship with the Rome-based institutions. Neither Congress nor the executive branch has apparently wanted to coordinate U.S. efforts in the food areas.

Equally salient have been the growing efforts of domestic groups to influence U.S. policies in certain IGOs. This is in part an outcome of changes in IGO policy actions. As LDC-dominated majorities have pressed for more regulatory and redistributive activities, U.S. groups have mobilized in response. Domestic groups have also pressed Congress and the executive branch to adhere to international norms in the areas of human rights and security.

Domestic groups have not been consistently either supportive of or antagonistic toward U.S. relations with IGOs, however. Hunger groups supported greater U.S. participation in food aid and distribution through all available channels, including multilateral ones. Yet other groups have lobbied against FAO's antimarket orientation. The media led the campaign for withdrawal from UNESCO while scientists, academic groups, and educational groups lobbied in opposition. Although interest groups are an important and active part of the governmental process in the United States, countervailing pressures tend to negate their influence on policy. This conclusion may be skewed by the fact that we have not included the International Labor Organization or the International Telecommunications Union, two of the IGOs that allow for considerable direct participation by representatives of private associations (Cox and Jacobson 1973: 397). Had these organizations been examined, perhaps domestic groups and interests would have played a more direct role in explaining changes in U.S.-IGO relationships.

Prior to the Reagan administration, changes in presidential administrations had relatively little impact on U.S.-IGO relationships. Successive administrations have sustained U.S. commitments to GATT and the IAEA. Yet the Reagan administration took a sharply different approach to most multilateral institutions. Although Coate (chapter 9) and Hopkins (chapter 7) argue that U.S. disengagement from UNESCO and FAO began long before the Reagan administration took office, clearly that administration translated displeasure with UNESCO into withdrawal and scaled back support in response to the food institutions' statist orientation. Likewise, the Reagan administration's commitment to privatization and free market approaches has been antithetical to efforts in WHO to control multinational corporations' activity and to enhance the role of the public sector in health affairs. In striking contrast to the Carter administration, the first Reagan administration's lack of interest in a balanced approach to human rights violations put it at odds with international governmental and nongovernmental human rights organizations. Thus in the 1980s presidential administrations *have* made a difference.

In general domestic political factors may preclude the United States from sustaining consistent policies, particularly in multilateral institutions. Contributing to this is the need for cooperation between the legislative and executive branches, the impact of domestic groups, and the susceptibility of many of the issues—particularly in the organizations examined here—to changes in salience and ideology.

Declining Power

The case studies lend little support to the primacy of declining U.S. power as an explanatory factor for the patterns of changing instrumentality and influence. As we and others have noted, the decline of U.S. dominance thesis is overdrawn. To be sure, the increase in others' power resource bases, including share of votes and contributions to IGOs, has produced a relative decline in U.S. power resources that has been compounded by misperception and misjudgment. Yet as Russett (1985) has suggested, hegemony may be vanishing, but it is not dead. Strange (1987) argues that the United States retains strategic superiority, still dominates the world's production and knowledge structures, and controls world credit supplies. It thus retains "structural power" (1987: 565): "the power to choose and to shape the structures of the global political economy within which other states, their political institutions, their economic enterprises, and (not least) their professional people have to operate." The case studies lead us to concur. Hence changing influence and instrumentality cannot be explained by declining dominance.

The judgments reflected in Table 11.3 (column 1) are based on the fact that in case after case, the authors found that although a thesis of overall power decline explained little, where evident, decline of power resources and control over outcomes in the *specific issue area* explained a lot. This confirms Baldwin's (1979: 193) argument that "the notion of a single overall international power structure unrelated to any particular issue area is based on a concept of power that is virtually meaningless." Several of the studies, in fact, point to little or no change in U.S. power resources and control over outcomes. This also confirms Cox and Jacobson's (1973: 410) conclusion that the rank ordering of state influence in an IGO was seldom if ever identical with the state's power in the general environment. Influence of some states in some IGOs is greater than their power in the environment; with others, such as the United States, influence may be less than their power in the environment. Our studies suggest that the discontinuities between U.S. influence and power may be explained largely in terms of the interrelationships among the other three variables—IGO characteristics, issue area characteristics, and domestic political factors.

The continuing predominance of the United States vis-à-vis the Western European states and the persistent bipolarity in military power explain the continuity of NATO's usefulness and influence. Despite the increased economic importance of Japan and Western Europe, U.S. influence over outcomes in GATT, the IMF, and the World Bank is protected through legal and extralegal devices, including special majorities. U.S. importance as a food producer assures the continuing necessity of U.S. participation in any multilateral efforts dealing with agricultural problems.

As a result of its overall relative decline, however, the United States has had to adapt its strategies for policy implementation in order to control outcomes. This has meant more attention to bargaining in GATT and threats of negative sanctions in the IAEA and IMF. In a number of cases IGO secretariats have taken steps to accommodate U.S. interests because U.S. withdrawal or diminished financial support would severely restrict the work of the organizations. In the case of the World Bank, this pattern has led to conflict between organizational autonomy and U.S. control.

The two instances in which the United States withdrew from IGOs to express its displeasure with the organizations differ significantly. In 1977 the United States withdrew from the International Labor Organization, claiming that a number of political trends were weakening the ability of the organization to fulfill its mission. Those trends included erosion of tripartite representation, selective application of human rights, and increased politicization. Then in February 1980 the Carter administration stated that sufficient progress had been made in reversing the trends to warrant rejoining the ILO (Galenson 1981; Williams 1987: 50). U.S. withdrawal from UNESCO was not limited to any set of conditions for return, however. UNESCO had become the target of a major campaign by the American media and a symbol of all that was wrong with the UN itself. Yet many of UNESCO's activities in education, science, culture, and communications are in areas in which the U.S. government has traditionally played a very small role and in which national policies of other states have generally been viewed by U.S. governmental officials with mistrust and suspicion. Hence it should not be surprising that UNESCO did not become the prototype for dealing with other IGOs even given the Reagan administration's generally negative attitude toward multilateral institutions. As the case studies reveal, "habits of cooperation" reach deep within government. Although there has been no reversal of U.S. withdrawal from UNESCO under the Reagan administration, even that administration found new uses for other "old" organizations and recognized that organizations themselves change.

To be sure, there is a strong streak of "America firstism" that asks why the United States should bear higher costs and burdens than those borne by friends and allies. Why, some ask, should the United States exercise restraint in observing GATT rules when other governments do not recognize norms and rules constraining their behavior? During the early 1980s the antipathy of many high-level U.S. officials to IGOs as well as domestic pressures created a crisis of multilateralism. Yet a number of factors sustained U.S. multilateralism: the proliferation of global problems requiring multilateral solutions; enlightened self-interest, the desire to shape international outcomes and calculations of expected utility; habitual (learned) behavior; the constraints and opportunities provided by international regimes and organizations; pressures from domestic groups and transgovernmental coalitions; and perceived role. Few Americans would willingly choose to conceive of the United States as a "has-been."Although they may recognize that the United States can no longer exercise the kind of dominance it once did, nonetheless for many Americans the preferred and perceived role of the United States is still one of international leadership.

The case studies illuminate patterns of both change and continuity in the two-way flow of influence between the United States and IGOs. They also enhance understanding of the links among IGOs, regimes, and international cooperation.

IGOS, Regimes, and Cooperation

Although many scholars would argue that there are few pressures *for* cooperation in an anarchic system, governments—including the United States—clearly do engage in cooperative behavior (Oye 1986). As Rosenau (1986: 892) argues, "except in the rare instances when systems break down through secession or all-out war, the elements of any social system have to cooperate in order to sustain themselves and the system of which they are a part. . . . As their conflicts intensify, so will their efforts at cooperation."

To explain the roots of cooperative behavior in an anarchic system, many authors have focused on the international systems level, employing the structural theory of hegemonic stability to argue that the presence of a dominant great power is necessary to the formation of regimes and to the maintenance of international agreements over time. The decline of the hegemon is therefore linked to changes in the character of regimes and particular international arrangements and a corresponding reduction in order and cooperation. As suggested by the case studies, this theory adds little explanatory power to assessing the changes in U.S.-IGO relation-ships.

Recently rational choice and game theorists have also puzzled over how patterns of cooperation arise and have suggested the conditions conducive to stable compliance. Their theories have shed light on the problems of choice under certain conditions; they have discussed strategies to alter payoff structures, thereby improving the prospects for cooperation (Oye 1986). Yet these theorists, assuming unified state actors and dominance of an international game, have difficulty explaining organizational forms, scope, or change (Haggard and Simmons 1987: 504–6). They say little about how regimes arise or how they will be institutionalized.

Functionalist theorists explain how patterns of cooperation are sustained even when the conditions that gave rise to them change—mainly why cooperation persists under conditions of declining hegemony or posthegemony (Keohane 1984). These theorists have suggested that actors might alter the context of interaction through institution building (Axelrod and Keohane 1986). "Not only can actors in world politics pursue different strategies within an established context of interaction, they may also seek to alter that context through building institutions embodying particular principles, norms, rules, or procedures for the conduct of international relations" (Axelrod and Keohane 1986: 228). But these theories do not account for differences between issue areas or for why formal organiza-tions exist in some cases and not in others.

In short, as Haggard and Simmons (1987: 496–97) argue, recent regime literature has largely ignored the problems of organizational design and operation. "Most regimes, however, are likely to have at least some minimal administrative apparatus for the purpose of dispute settlement, the collection and sharing of information, or surveil-lance. Complex cooperative tasks require more elaborate and potentially autonomous, organizational structures" (Haggard and Simmons (1987: 497).

In chapter 1 we argued that international organizations provide the formal structure and processes for information gathering and analysis, norm and rule creation, rule supervision, dispute settlement, and operational capabilities that undergird international cooperation. Many of these tasks and capabilities cannot readily be duplicated and sustained with other arrangements. Yet U.S. relations with a number of these formal organizations have been strained, particularly under the Reagan administration when many appointed officials were openly critical of multilateral institutions. Appointments of senior-level officials with no experience in diplomacy, let alone the specialized field of multilateral diplomacy (such as Gregory Newell, the former assistant secretary of state for International Organizations), contributed to the perception if not the reality of a crisis of multilateralism in U.S. foreign policy.

The debate over multilateralism often concerned whether the United States has borne a disproportionate share of the burden and hence costs for multilateral cooperation in specific IGOs. It is hard to escape the reality that U.S. financial contributions do far outweigh those of any other member state in virtually all organizations to which the United States belongs. If the burdens have been unequal, we might ask, have the benefits also been unequally distributed? Has the United States gained less than others in return on its contributions to the creation and operations of international organizations? Many critics of U.S. participation in IGOs would contend that this is so. Russett (1985), however, argued that the gains for the United States have been enormous. Principally, he suggests, "the international institutionalization with regime building . . . helps spread common cultural and political norms, especially among governing elites, helping to achieve consensus on what problems must be solved and how" (1985: 230). Given the set of purposes served by IGOs, successive administrations have found that the "costs" the United States incurs in such formal organizations have been reasonable.

Yet the case studies indicate that IGOs are not the only vehicles for multilateral cooperation, nor are they the only indicator of U.S. commitment to multilateralism. Ruggie (1985a: 19) has pointed out, "in many instances, though not all, governments appear to have more of a problem with specific institutional mechanisms than with the broad networks of policy coordination and collaboration . . . international regimes in short." Indeed, there appears to be a proliferation of ad hoc multilateral cooperative efforts, such as the Group of 5 (G-5, now G-7) in international monetary affairs, the Geneva groups of Western donors, the nuclear suppliers group, the Multi-Fibre Arrangement, and extra-GATT arrangements for autos, steel, and semiconductors.

Ad hoc efforts, however, are fraught with problems. Because they frequently depend on individuals involved, the participants are drawn off to deal with other issues or leave office. For this very reason Huntington noted some years ago (1968) the importance of institution building for political development—that is, for ensuring, among other things, continuity and stability. To be sure, even in domestic political arenas networks of governmental and nongovernmental officials and ad hoc interagency groups will be useful in moving policy along and in ensuring that the process of governance is not blocked. Thus in the international arena in periods of institutional paralysis (or perceived misdirection), informal patterns of organization may ensure that international cooperation does not cease entirely. Over the longer term, however, institutional development is critically important for establishing durable means for managing conflicts and the expanding agenda of international problems.

Yet none of the various approaches to regime theory accounts for the influence of organizational process, bureaucratic politics, and the perceptions, dispositions, and habits of individual decision makers (Rosenau 1986). They do not account for situations in which states choose to create or utilize formal organizations versus ad hoc mechanisms, nor can they evaluate which structures create more stable patterns of cooperation. And they have largely ignored domestic political processes (Haggard and Simmons 1987).

The case studies in this volume suggest that the answers to these puzzles of choice lie in characteristics of the issue areas and organizations, as well as in domestic political factors. This finding stands in contrast with the thesis that the decline of American power is the primary explanation for changes in U.S.-IGO relationships. In particular the case studies illustrate the value of formal organizations that continue to function through periods of decreased salience, even neglect, and are then still available when changes in the issue area—especially the emergence of new problems— lead policymakers to "rediscover" their utility.

What, then, are the policy implications of the changing patterns of IGO instrumentality and influence that the case studies have illumined?

Policy Implications

Some analysts would assert that if the United States found IGOs less useful as instruments and IGO influence on the United States increasing, the United States should either revert to isolationism or continue to pursue more unilateral policies. Serfaty (1987: 18–19), however, describes the devastating implications of the former. "Bitter over its loss of influence and frightened over its new vulnerability, America is now 'coming home,' seduced by an isolationist promise that is at best, irrelevant, and at worst suicidal." Alternatively, Krasner (1982) suggests that unilateralism may be increasingly necessary to cope with an international order that is "messier" and "fragile" because of the absence of a dominant power able to absorb shocks (p. 30). Gill (1986), conversely, proposes that the United States reconstitute itself as a hegemonic power. Calleo (1987) has argued for devolution of the burden of *both* conventional and nuclear defense to the European members of NATO.

Charges of waste and bureaucratic bloat in IGOs grew, however, in the 1980s not only from such ideological opponents of multilateralism as the Heritage Foundation but also from long-time supporters. Such charges, combined with the growth of U.S. budget deficits, have fueled debate in Congress over the costs and benefits of U.S. commitments to multilateral institutions. Contributions to IGOs are easy targets for cuts, particularly when officials in the executive branch have displayed a negative attitude toward their value.

None of the case studies suggests that a retreat to isolationism, greater unilateralism, or withdrawal from other IGOs are desirable responses to changes in U.S.-IGO relations. In the short term the United States could save money and substitute various bilateral or ad hoc multilateral arrangements. Over the long term, however, the absence of institutionalized ways of dealing with problems, of sharing burdens and costs, of creating norms and rules that bind *other* states would become increasingly expensive. It would also represent a rejection at the international level of processes at the core of American domestic politics: compromise, promotion of adherence to norms, and rule of law. Modification of such a strategy could entail reductions in the level of U.S. financial commitment to that of an ordinary state. The United States already adopted this strategy in part by unilaterally reducing its share of IGO contributions. Other states have also discussed reducing U.S. assessments for the UN system to less than 25 percent to limit the capacity of the United States to cripple the system. But decreasing the U.S. share of IGO contributions may have another effect. As one budget expert from a major donor nation has noted, "There is also a fear of marginalizing the American role in the UN" (*The Interdependent* 1988: 3). There are no grounds in the case studies for proposing a lessened commitment to multilateralism in general or IGOs in particular.

Five possible strategies for more effective multilateral statecraft have emerged from the case studies: closer cooperation with IGO secretariats, greater use of transgovernmental networks, "power steering" through special committees, use of ad hoc multilateral groups, and enhanced training in multilateral diplomacy.

Closer cooperation with IGO secretariats.   In cases in which (1) the United States has continued to use IGOs successfully as instruments of policy, (2) IGOs have retained their high salience, and (3) conflicts with U.S. interests have been limited in scope, the roles of executive heads and secretariat officials have been critical. For example, politicization was averted in both the IAEA and WHO through intervention by top secretariat officials; they recognized the danger of unnecessarily alienating the United States. UNESCO officials were not so cautious.

Given the important role secretariat officials have in making the U.S.-IGO relationships smoother, the United States should downplay the importance of voting that it cannot orchestrate and use its continued predominance (in knowledge and resources) to make secretariats sensitive to U.S. interests. Such secretariats would be less likely to jeopardize those interests in fundamental ways. The United States could also promote quasi-secretariat activity, including the use of nongovernmental uninstructed personnel or experts. This has been increasingly used in the human rights organizations and the ILO. The use of more rapporteurs and expert committees strengthens the role of the secretariats, making them more valuable allies for the United States. The selection of some executive heads, in fact, still requires explicit or tacit U.S. consent, as illustrated in the election of Michel Camdessus as managing director of the IMF in 1987 and of Barber Conable to the presidency of the World Bank. In his effort to secure reelection, FAO head Edouard Saouma courted the United States (unsuccessfully) as well as developing countries. Even Director General M'Bow's decision to withdraw from the UNESCO contest can be explained in part by the concern of other participants over the continuing absence of the United States and Britain from the organization and others' threats of withdrawal. Clearly one strategy for the United States is to play a major role (1) in influencing the selection of executive heads and (2) in promoting high-quality American personnel for other key positions in IGO secretariats.

Use of transgovernmental networks. A second, similar strategy would capitalize on the presence of strong transgovernmental coalitions among IGO secretariat officials and representatives of constituencies in the United States and other member countries, such as those found among international health personnel or monetary officials. Such transgovernmental coalitions may legitimate policy changes sought by members; they may act as allies in persuading governments to accept a policy proposal. Yet as Jeane Kirkpatrick has argued with respect to U.S. participation in UN bodies, the United States has generally not utilized transgovernmental networks and coalitions to its advantage. Although it is unclear precisely how transgovernmental coalitions translate their preferences into policies and with what resources (Crane 1984: 401), U.S. policymakers, steeped in a tradition of domestic bargaining, could use similar techniques more frequently both in dealing with conflicting domestic interests and in exercising influence on decision making in other countries or IGOs. We have an excellent example of how such transgovernmental networks composed of officials representing different interests—the International Air Transport Association (IATA) for the airlines and the International Civil Aviation Organization (ICAO) for governmental authorities—used contacts in the U.S. State Department to resist the U.S. Civil Aeronautics Board's attempts to replace the international regulatory regime with an "open skies" regime for airline routes (Jonsson 1986). In another instance U.S. officials worked closely with the IEA Secretariat to establish oil import targets. Their objective was not so much other IEA governments as the U.S. policy process, moderate OPEC countries, and the symbolic importance of IEA setting targets (Keohane 1982). There is no reason why the United States cannot utilize such transgovernmental coalitions and transnational networks to its advantage.

"Power steering." A third option is to take advantage of subordinate organs or committees within IGOs wherein a number of cases in the 1980s decision-making rules were changed to informal weighted voting even though weighted voting does not exist in the general organization. For example, the International Maritime Satellite Organization employs a system of weighted voting in its council based on each member's involvement through investment shares. UNIDO (United Nations Industrial Development Organization) provides for a strong Programme and Budget Committee so that the market economy and socialist countries, if they vote together, have a veto (Williams 1987: 77). Even the United Nations General Assembly in 1986 adopted a device for such "power steering" with the strengthening of the Committee on Program and Coordination (Gardner 1988: 835). The United States ought to capitalize on these trends to exercise greater influence over key IGO decisions. If U.S. representatives were successful in using their influence in such committees to secure steps to trim excess staff and budgetary waste and to increase operational efficiencies, that would allay some of the major concerns of members of Congress which lay behind the Kassebaum amendment.

Ad hoc multilateralism. A fourth strategy is to increase in a prudent fashion the use of ad hoc multilateral entities, or what Yarbrough and Yarbrough (1987) describe as "minilateralisms."[2] In principle the smaller and more homogeneous the group, the easier it is to achieve consensus; that consensus will also represent a higher common denominator and will therefore more closely approximate the policy preferences of the United States. There will be fewer possibilities for coalition building within the group, and, because the focus or purpose of the group is likely to be relatively specific, fewer if any possibilities for issue linkage. The fact that the United States has been a participant in many of the ad hoc multilateral groups suggests that this has been a purposive strategy adopted by the United States in the 1980s.

The relative success of such ad hoc attempts is a matter of debate. Putnam and Bayne (1984) point to the various measures adopted by the advanced industrial states in the seven power economic summits, though practitioners argue that rarely is anything of substance concluded. Some point to the Geneva Group of Western donors as successful at initiating budgetary restraint in the UN specialized agencies (Williams 1987: 86–87), whereas others have seen the group as only exchanging budget and administrative information and incapable of making any decisions (McDonald 1988). The verdict depends on whether such ad hocism is a supplement to institutionalized multilateralism found in IGOs or a replacement for IGOs.

Training in multilateral diplomacy. A fifth strategy would involve training in multilateral diplomacy for U.S. diplomats. As Ruggie (1985b: 355) points out, "Only intermittently does America engage in the kind of political give-and-take at the United Nations at which Americans excel in their domestic legislative bodies—and when we do, we surprise ourselves (but not others) with our successes." Foreign Service officers get no training in this field or career recognition and are usually moved on after a two-year assignment. Ambassadors in the field of multilateral diplomacy are often political appointees with no prior experience or expertise in this field. Jeane Kirkpatrick, when she was U.S. ambassador to the UN, commented that it took fully eighteen months to two years to gain familiarity with the UN and its procedures (Private communication 1984). According to a long-time participant (MacDonald 1988), of the 1000 delegations a year sent to multilateral conferences, fully 25 percent of the 6000 delegates are attending their first conference. There is no continuity on delegations and therefore no institutionalized memory. Changes in training procedures and career recognition patterns would require high-level political and administrative support but could reap long-term and significant benefits in more effective U.S. representation and participation in multilateral institutions.

Politics of Choice

The relative attractiveness of these various strategies for the United States depends in part on organizational and issue area changes. Interestingly, the case studies point to a number of examples of recent IGO changes themselves stimulated by U.S. policies. For example, the IMF has become an important instrument for the United States and other major creditors to help borrower countries restructure their external debt. By adjusting its focus the IMF is once again useful to American interests. Likewise, during the mid-1980s the World Bank has reembraced economic liberalism, emphasizing privatization, structural adjustment, and reduced statism. Because the Bank is a bellwether, these changes are being diffused through other multilateral development institutions, though the food agencies appear to be laggard cases. Yet the decline in interorganizational rivalry among the Rome-based food institutions may augur positively for the revitalization of latent U.S. influence in these institutions as well. Even in the UN security organs where the likelihood of restoring smoother relationships until recently has been predicated on the unlikely scenario that the United States would define its security interests differently, there is evidence of possible change. Interest in international peace-keeping has revived with the creation of UN forces in the Persian Gulf, Afghanistan, and Namibia: this and other UN efforts to solve regional conflicts could well renew American support for the UN (*The Interdependent* 1988: 3).

Such changes in IGOs or issue areas would reduce the likelihood of the U.S. adopting an isolationist or unilateralist strategy. Yet changes in international organizations also make it all the more urgent that the United States consider the foregoing strategies or other steps to ensure that it is where the action is in the future.

The strategy the United States adopts may well be highly influenced by the actions of the Soviet Union. The Russians have not generally utilized multilateral institutions to achieve their objectives and, indeed, have not been members of the postwar economic and financial institutions (GATT, IMF, and World Bank). They have generally kept a very low profile in the social welfare institutions (WHO, UNESCO, and human rights organs). They have, however, been active in the UN itself, utilizing their Security Council veto in the first fifteen years to protect their interests against American-dominated majorities and assuming a more proactive role once the makeup of the majority shifted after 1960. In a September 1987 speech, however, General Secretary Gorbachev signaled that the Soviet Union was ready to work toward strengthening the role of the United Nations, particularly in the area of security. "It will be required to enhance absolutely the authority and role of the United Nations and the IAEA" (Gorbachev 1987: 27). To back up this verbal commitment, the Soviet Union announced that it was paying up its financial arrears of $127 million, including assessments for UN peacekeeping forces long opposed by the Soviet government. Soviet officials have also hinted that the Soviet Union might seek membership in the major trade and financial institutions.

Ironically, it may well be this Soviet initiative that stimulates U.S. policymakers to develop new strategies of multilateral statecraft. As a Stanley Foundation conference report states (1987: 27–28):

> The Soviet Union is moving to make the United Nations the centerpiece of its policy toward the Third World. The United Nations has become a target of opportunity for the Soviets to make the United States look bad: With the United States $414 million in arrears to the United Nations in 1987, the image of the Soviet Union now appears positive.

Thanks to reforms undertaken by the UN in October 1988, the Reagan administration committed the United States to pay its arrears.

Yet the United States still commands far more resources than the Soviet Union to exercise influence, positively or negatively, on patterns of order and cooperation. Over the last twenty years the United States has been responsible for launching an impressive list of multilateral initiatives, including the UN Population Fund (1968), UN Environment Program (1972), UN University (1975), UN Fund for Science and Technology for Development (1979), UN Water Decade (1980), and UN Decade for Disabled Persons (1982). The possibilities for addressing many security and environmental problems would be significantly enhanced by U.S.-Soviet cooperation in multilateral institutions, as the experience of IAEA with nonproliferation attests. Greater commitment to multilateral institutions by the Soviet Union, however, would require U.S. policy-makers to increase the effectiveness of their multilateral diplomacy. More important for U.S. interests especially in economic and social welfare institutions is greater pragmatism among Third World states, for contrary to widely held (mis)perceptions, the latter do *not* tend to support Soviet positions in the UN (Puchala and Coate 1988: 31, 46).

The preferred and perceived role of the United States for many Americans is still one of international leadership, a composite of multiple roles: donor, godfather/protector, and mediator among others (Hermann 1983; Holsti 1970). Whether that role is perceived to involve a significant commitment to multilateralism is unclear, however. Poll data on public attitudes toward the UN, for example, have shown a significant drop in evaluations of the UN's work in recent years yet virtually no change in responses to the question of whether the United States should get out of the UN.[3] The real challenge, therefore, may lie in rebuilding domestic support for multilateralism among both the public at large and, perhaps most important, members of Congress. There has been all too little attention, either conceptually or empirically, to these and other domestic sources of international cooperation.

Regardless of what the Russian do, it is in the U.S. interest to renew its commitment to multilateral institutions. Certainly not all IGOs can be expected to be equally effective as vehicles of cooperation or equally useful for the United States. There will always be persistent tension between the United States and some IGOs, whether because the IGO is concerned with an issue normally not the subject of federal jurisdiction, as in the case of UNESCO, or because U.S. attitudes of exceptionalism persist, as in the case of human rights. Acknowledging the latent tensions does not mean that the United States must retreat to isolationism or unilateralism. In the words of Huntington (1988: 477), "neither isolation or hegemony is natural or possible now, and some gap between capabilities and commitments may be inevitable." In the coming decade U.S. policymakers must decide whether to pursue foreign policy options based on multilateral opportunities and constraints. The case studies reveal to a striking degree the continued, if not increased, utility of many IGOs for the United States, though in a number of instances there were periods of decreased salience and even neglect. Given increased interdependence, technological changes, and the growth in demand for international collective goods, it is also striking that at least in this set of cases, IGOs have not yet had a greater impact on U.S. policies and policymaking processes. This finding indicates that U.S. norms and rules, as well as information-gathering capabilities, for example, are still for the most part at least equivalent to international ones.

Given continuing U.S. influence, the choices of U.S. policymakers with respect to multilateral institutions—to give them centrality as instruments of policy and to accept the constraints they impose—will have major implications for future patterns of interaction and cooperation in the international system. Other states still look to the United States for leadership of major initiatives for international cooperation and now for institutional reform as well. Although others can share the costs, there is as yet no rival for the role of leadership for multilateralism.

Notes

1. This chapter was presented at the Annual Meetings of the International Studies Association, St. Louis, March 29–April 2, 1988. We appreciate the comments of other participants in the panel, Gene M. Lyons, Harold K. Jacobson, and Ambassador John W. McDonald, as well as those from Charles F. Hermann and other contributors to this volume.

2. For further discussion of ad hoc multilateralism, particularly for negotiating settlements of disputes, see Karns (1987).

3. See Gallup Polls (1985). The pattern of responses to two questions are illustrative and particularly striking:

    1. In general, do you feel the UN is doing a good job or a poor job in trying to solve the problems it has had to face?

Year	Good Job	Poor Job	No Opinion
1956	51%	36%	12%
1967	49	35	16
1970	44	40	16
1971	35	43	22
1975	33	51	16
1980	31	53	16
1983	36	51	13
1985	28	54	18

    2. Do you think the United States should give up its membership in the United Nations, or not?

Year	Should	Should Not	No Opinion
1951	12%	75%	13%
1962	9	86	5
1967	10	85	5
1975	16	74	10
1983	12	79	9
1985	11	81	8

References

Axelrod, Robert, and Robert O. Keohane (1986). "Achieving Cooperation under Anarchy: Strategies and Institutions." In Kenneth A. Oye, ed., *Cooperation under Anarchy.* Princeton: Princeton University Press, 226–54.

Baldwin, David A. (1979). "Power Analysis and World Politics." *World Politics,* 31(January), 161–94.

Calleo, David P. (1987). *Beyond American Hegemony: The Future of the Western Alliance.* New York: Basic Books.

"Compromise, Congress, and the U.N. Budget," (1988). *The Interdependent,* 14(1), 1, 3.

Cox, Robert W., and Harold K. Jacobson (1973). "The Anatomy of Influence." In Robert W. Cox and Harold K. Jacobson, eds., *The Anatomy of Influence: Decision Making in International Organization.* New Haven, CT: Yale University Press, 371–436.

Crane, Barbara B. (1984). "Policy Coordination by Major Western Powers in Bargaining with the Third World: Debt Relief and the Common Fund." *International Organization,* 38(3), 399–428.

Galenson, Walter (1981). *The International Labor Organization.* Madison: University of Wisconsin Press.

Gallup Poll (1985). *Public Opinion.* Wilmington, DE: Scholarly Resources.

Gardner, Richard N. (1988). "Practical Internationalism." *Foreign Affairs,* 66(4), 827–45.

Gill, Stephen (1986). "American Hegemony: Its Limits and Prospects in the Reagan Era." *Millenium. Journal of International Studies,* 15(Winter), 311–36.

Gorbachev, M. S. (1987). "Secure World." Printed in Foreign Broadcast Information Service, *Daily Report: Soviet Union,* September 17, pp. 23–28.

Haggard, Stephan, and Beth A. Simmons (1987). "Theories of International Regimes." *International Organization,* 41(3), 491–517.

Hermann, Charles F. (1983). "Superpower Involvement with Others: Alternative Role Relationships." Prepared for the 1983 Annual Meeting of the American Political Science Association, September 1–4, Chicago.

Holsti, Kal J. (1970). "National Role Conceptions in the Study of Foreign Policy." *International Studies Quarterly,* 14(September), 233–309.

Hughes, Thomas L. (1985–86). "The Twilight of Internationalism." *Foreign Policy,* 6(Winter), 25–48.

Huntington, Samuel P. (1968). *Political Order in Changing Societies.* New Haven, CT: Yale University Press.

——— (1988). "Coping with the Lippmann Gap." *Foreign Affairs,* 66(3), 453–77.

Jönsson, Christer (1986). "Interorganization Theory and International Organization." *International Studies Quarterly,* 30, 39–57.

Karns, Margaret P. (1987). "The U.S., the Contact Group, and Namibia." *International Organization,* 41(Winter), 93–123.

Kegley, Charles W., Jr., and Eugene R. Wittkopf (1987). *American Foreign Policy: Pattern and Process.* 3d ed. New York: St. Martin's Press.

Keohane, Robert O. (1982). "International Agencies and the Art of the Possible: The Case of the IEA." *Journal of Policy Analysis and Management*, 1(4), 469–81.

—— (1984). *After Hegemony: Cooperation and Discord in the World Political Economy*. Princeton: Princeton University Press.

Krasner, Stephen D. (1982). "American Policy and Global Economic Stability." In William Avery and David P. Rapkin, eds., *America in a Changing World Political Economy*. New York: Longman, 29–48.

Krauthammer, Charles (1985). *Cutting Edge. Making Sense of the Eighties*. New York: Random House.

McDonald, John W. (1988). Comments at panel on multilateralism in U.S. foreign policy, International Studies Association Annual Meetings, March 30, April 2, St. Louis.

Oye, Kenneth A. (1986). "Explaining Cooperation under Anarchy: Hypotheses and Strategies." In Oye, ed., *Cooperation under Anarchy*. Princeton: Princeton University Press, 1–24.

Puchala, Donald J., and Roger A. Coate (1988). "The State of International Organization, 1988." Academic Council on the United Nations System. Reports and Papers (1988–2).

Putnam, Robert, and Nicholas Bayne (1984). *Hanging Together: The Seven Power Summits*. Cambridge: Harvard University Press.

Rosenau, James (1986). "Before Cooperation: Hegemons, Regimes and Habit-Driven Actors in World Politics." *International Organization*, 40(Autumn), 849–94.

Ruggie, John Gerard (1985a). "International Organization: A State of the Art on an Art of the State." Presented at the Annual Meeting of the American Political Science Association, New Orleans, August.

—— (1985b). "The United States and the United Nations: Toward a New Realism." *International Organization*, 39(2), 343–56.

Russett, Bruce (1985). "The Mysterious Case of Vanishing Hegemony: Or Is Mark Twain Really Dead?" *International Organization*, 39(Spring), 207–32.

Serfaty, Simon (1987). "Lost Illusions." *Foreign Policy*, 66(Spring), 3–19.

Stanley Foundation (1987). Report of the Twenty-Eighth Strategy for Peace, U.S. Foreign Policy Conference, "Multilateralism in U.S. Foreign Policy." Muscatine, IA: Author.

Strange, Susan (1987). "The Persistent Myth of Lost Hegemony." *International Organization*, 41(4), 551–74.

Williams, Douglas (1987). *The Specialized Agencies and the United Nations: The System in Crisis*. New York: St. Martin's Press.

Yarbrough, Beth V., and Robert M. Yarbrough (1987). "Cooperation in the Liberalization of International Trade: After Hegemony, What?" *International Organization*, 41(1), 1–26.

CHAPTER TWELVE

IGOs, Regimes, and Cooperation: Challenges for International Relations Theory

Duncan Snidal

The case studies in this volume can be read with several purposes in mind. First, they provide a rich description of changes in intergovernmental organizations (IGOs) over the postwar years. The cases reveal common patterns, as well as differences, that characterize the role of IGOs in promoting international collaboration. Second, the cases illuminate the relationship between the United States and various IGOs and, in particular, the ability of the United States to achieve its goals by working through IGOs. This has important implications for American policy in a world in which simple patterns of East-West (or even North-South) alignment have broken down and in which American ability to achieve its goals unilaterally is uncertain. Third, we find important evidence on the workings of international cooperation and regimes. Because the cases have been constructed with a deliberate eye toward general issues of international politics, they offer significant insights to contemporary international relations theory. This chapter develops the resulting implications for further theoretical development.[1]

Recent work on international regimes and cooperation provides common theoretical questions and concepts to enable a constructive comparison across cases.[2] The resulting conclusions for regime and cooperation theories are emphasized in this chapter. But the uniformity and level of development of this body of theory must not be exaggerated. Indeed, one reason the case studies in this volume cannot be taken as a strong test of the theory is that the theory itself is not yet sufficiently well specified to be disproved.[3] The cases nevertheless provide important information regarding the applicability of various theoretical hypotheses, as well as important insights for further development of theories on regimes and cooperation. In addition, the empirical evidence presented in this volume addresses broader questions concerning the connection of regime and cooperation theory to its roots in traditional "realist" or power politics understandings of international politics. The result is a direct engagement with central issues of contemporary international relations theory.

Similarly, each of the four explanations considered in this volume for the changing relation between the United States and IGOs touches vital nerves in contemporary international relations theory. The very emphasis on the *role of formal IGOs* as mediators of international politics is both reminiscent of an earlier era in the study of international organization and a precursor of needed work in the current literature. Recent theorizing has been premised on an expansive but somewhat vague conception of international regimes which deliberately deemphasizes the role of formal IGOs (Krasner 1983). Although empirical work on regimes often discusses the role of formal institutions, the theory is not well developed with respect to the specific role, if any, of IGOs in maintaining regimes or promoting cooperation. Ironically the expansive definition of regime has tended to squeeze out the narrower but still important role of formal organizations.

The cases further challenge scholars to investigate the impact of *issue area characteristics*. One part of this challenge is to incorporate the very different substantive issue areas of welfare, economics, and security within a common analytical framework. For example, in contrast to Jervis's (1983) widely cited conclusion that there is no security regime, both case studies relevant to security issues find that formal organizations—especially IAEA and NATO—have had a profound effect on U.S. policy and international politics. This suggests that security is not as different from other issue areas as is sometimes supposed. A second part of this challenge is to incorporate systematic contextual differences within the theory. How do variations in issue area characteristics affect the performance of IGOs and patterns of international cooperation? Although good theory is general and transcends issue areas, better theory seeks to capture such contextual variations across issues.

The case studies also renew the challenge to structural theories of international politics that fail to acknowledge the importance of *domestic factors*. The argument that levels of analysis must be kept separate overlooks the reality of the interaction of domestic and international politics. Accommodating the intrusion of domestic politics into the international arena within a theory based on states as unitary actors remains one of the toughest challenges for contemporary international relations theory.

Finally, the impact of the *decline in American dominance* on international issues and the performance of IGOs addresses the central questions raised by hegemonic stability theory. The case studies move the examination of leadership beyond indirect analyses of the distribution of power resources to a concrete analysis of American behavior across different issues. In doing do they cast further doubt on hegemonic decline as a compelling explanation for recent international politics. More important, the cases point to aspects of leadership not well captured by crude measures of power resources. The resulting view of leadership as a process of coalition building fits more comfortably with an understanding of cooperation as a multilateral problem not always amenable to unilateral solution.

This chapter looks at what the findings of the case studies on each of these four dimensions suggest for future development of the theory of international regimes and cooperation. It begins by examining the special limitations of a set of case studies based on the relation of a single state to the regime, especially when the United States is the largest and most important player in the international system. Next I consider the complications involved in moving from empirical case studies back to theory. Finally, I turn to the four alternative explanations analyzed in the cases and discuss the implications of the findings for theory building. Although I offer no panaceas, some clear lines for development, as well as some continuing quandaries, are apparent.[4]

Limits of Individual Case Studies

In drawing conclusions from case studies, it is important to be clear what they are cases of and what can be inferred from them. Equally important is understanding what the cases do not cover and what they therefore cannot tell us. A central concern is the implications of these case studies covering the relationship of one state to various IGOs for a general understanding of international regimes and cooperation. In addition, we need to consider how an emphasis on change in the case studies may lead us to neglect equally important but constant factors. Finally, the very focus on formal IGOs raises important questions in our search for a general understanding of regimes and cooperation.

The regime and cooperation literatures both focus on problems of coordination and collective action among states. Each contains the implicit premise that international behavior cannot be understood in terms of an individual state's interests without examining others' interests and the interactions among them. Consequently, in discussing the relationship of any one state to a regime, it is important to consider not only the impact of the regime on that state but also the impact the regime has on other states' behavior. The subtlety of these relations should not be underestimated. An example is provided by the role of regimes in information provision. Several studies note that the United States has significant independent capacity for information gathering, and therefore they minimize the importance to it of this regime function. But this function may nevertheless be of immense importance to the United States because *other* countries rely on IGO informational capacities. This reinforces cooperation by reassuring states that the United States and third-party states are cooperating. American acceptance of IAEA safeguards on its civilian nuclear plants was motivated by such considerations. In addition, and regardless of national monitoring capacities, IGOs create information by changing the meaning of certain behaviors. The United States can monitor trade restrictions by itself, but only in the context of GATT can restrictions be interpreted as violations of international agreements. Such interpretations provide the United States with significant leverage in seeking changes in others' policies. Conversely, specific rulings on national environmental policies or safety measures legitimate state actions that otherwise might be interpreted as disguised forms of trade restriction. Thus even if monitoring is strictly national, IGOs help to determine the meaning of what is observed.

Because the case studies focus on change in IGO-U.S. relations, they naturally emphasize change within the international issue as represented by changing issue area characteristics or change in the IGO; change within the United States represented by changing domestic interests; and change in the relation between them represented by declining power. Several limitations should be noted to this quite reasonable research design. First, relevant changes occurring primarily in third-party states may be reflected only indirectly in IGO or U.S. characteristics. For example, Jacobson explains the declining effectiveness of the OAS for American purposes partly by the increased economic strength of other member states (which is captured only very indirectly in measures of U.S. decline) and partly by changing goals of other states (which are not directly captured in the hypotheses guiding the case analyses in this volume). Second, and contrary to an expectation implicit in the design of this volume, the change in U.S.-IGO relations is often exaggerated. Most cases show substantial continuity in basic U.S.-IGO relations, at least since the period of their initial formation. Even where change appears greatest, in the social welfare policy areas, the studies indicate that this is more a reflection of current policies than of fundamental changes in either the IGOs or the United States. Third, an emphasis on change leads to relative neglect of constant factors that are nevertheless important in determining outcomes. Here the advantage of multiple case studies is evident. By examining variation across cases—even when within-case variation is low across time—we obtain additional purchase on how factors such as issue characteristics or leadership affect performance of the IGO and its relations with member states. In this way constant features that could be overlooked in the analysis of any individual case may possibly explain much of the variation across cases.

Finally, the use of case studies necessarily raises the question of whether the cases examined are representative or are subject to "selection" or other biases (Achen and Snidal 1989). For example, how might the analysis change if the sample included the International Labor Organization or other excluded IGOs? Perhaps different experiences of these IGOs would alter our conclusions. This general problem is compounded in this volume insofar as the very definition of regime emerged as a response to potential dangers of concentrating exclusively on formal IGOs. Increasing use of summitry and G-5 consultations for exchange rate and macroeconomic coordination, as noted in the study on the IMF, illustrates the possibility of overemphasizing the importance of formal IGOs by avoiding cases in which they are less important. Similarly, the exclusion of East-West security issues and arms control because they are not formally institutionalized limits, and perhaps distorts, the findings. The wide substantive range of the cases, coupled with the attention of the researchers to informal institutions within particular issue areas, ameliorates but does not fully resolve these concerns.

The United States as a Special Case

Although every case is unique, the United States poses particular difficulties for extrapolating from its relations to IGOs to general understandings of regimes and cooperation. The most obvious aspect of American exceptionalism is its enormous size and influence in the international system. Even after a period of relative decline, U.S. military, economic, technological, and cultural influence is massive. The United States remains by far the most important actor in most IGOs, often the only actor whose participation is single-handedly decisive for the success or failure of the organization. Simultaneously, it is one of the most insulated states and, at least until recently, is better positioned to resist pressures from other states and IGOs. Because it has less need for them (for example, it has never had to rely significantly on IMF resources), the United States has never been tightly constrained by IGOs as have many smaller states.

Its tremendous international influence in turn makes American domestic policies particularly important for international affairs. The case studies are virtually unanimous in reporting the impact on IGOs of the American separation of powers between the executive and legislative branches. The importance of interest groups, including fragmented bureaucracies, also emerges as a key factor in U.S.-IGO relations in some issues. Although other countries have their own domestic political peculiarities, none reverberates as strongly on international politics.

Nowhere is this special role of the United States so apparent as in its pivotal position in the creation of postwar international regimes and their associated IGOs. As the authors of the case studies remind us, the United States alone, or with a small number of supporting states, led in the creation of the United Nations, World Bank, IMF, FAO, NATO and GATT. After attempting unilateral initiatives, it ultimately also took the key role in developing the IAEA. Only in a few instances, including UNESCO and the UN human rights organizations, were other states the driving force, leaving the United States more a reactor to than a creator of the regime. Perhaps it is no coincidence that these organizations have caused the United States the most aggravation in recent years.

American predominance ensures a continuing special relation between the United States and these organizations. This is revealed particularly in its ongoing leadership role, which is largely welcomed by other members in such IGOs as NATO, IAEA, and the World Bank. Elsewhere American leadership increasingly has been challenged by other states, particularly by less developed states with interests different from those of the United States. Considering that many IGOs were designed with American and developed Western country interests in mind, some conflict was inevitable. This conflict has been aggravated, however, by the U.S. conception of its leadership as more of a strictly unilateral than a multilateral affair. For example, the case studies show that the United States has often viewed IGOs as instruments for the collective legitimation of established U.S. positions rather than as settings for the collective development and negotiation of policies under its leadership. The general decline of the rubber-stamping function is hardly surprising and, perhaps, not so discouraging. Indeed, what from an American perspective has been interpreted as a decline in IGO effectiveness is arguably not central to their performance from an international perspective.

An equally revealing aspect of American leadership has been the underlying presumption that IGOs should constrain other states but not the United States. Again, this view was most sustainable for a set of institutions newly designed for further U.S. interests; it was destined to erode with changes in the institutions, in their membership and in U.S.

interests. For example, the United States has found that having accepted the principle of multilateral decision making in IAEA, it cannot return easily to unilateral or bilateral decision making. More generally, and as Karns and Mingst point out in their introductory chapter, effective utilization of IGOs to affect other states' behavior often requires accepting constraints on one's own behavior. Much of its frustration with IGOs reflects America's own difficulties in coming to terms with changes in the U.S.-IGO relationship more than it reflects any significant change in the effectiveness of IGOs themselves.

Finally, in using the American case we should be attentive to implicit intellectual biases in the analysis. Strange (1983), among others, has stressed the U.S.-centered character of the regime and cooperation literatures. The associated bias is nowhere better reflected than in scholarly views of the role of American leadership in international cooperation. Hegemonic stability theory, for example, portrays the United States as unilaterally providing the public good of "cooperation" whereas other states are passive or even cynical beneficiaries of this largesse. Other states, including close allies, have not always shared this perspective or its implicit corollary that "what is good for the United States is good for the world." A related bias is latent in the focus of this volume on the use of IGOs as instruments of U.S. policy. Although it is reasonable that states will use IGOs to pursue their goals (why else join them?), IGOs are not effective for all national goals. Frequently the very purpose of international cooperation is to limit the pursuit of individual national interests for the collective international benefit. Thus the inability of the United States always to use IGOs as effective tools for containing communism, or more generally for proliferating the American versions of liberalism, capitalism, and human rights, should not be confused with IGO ineffectiveness.

These reservations noted, U.S.-IGO relations provide a useful focus for the case studies. The special position of the United States in international politics accentuates the impact of key variables found in the relationship between any single state and an IGO. The ability of IGOs to influence American agendas, and sometimes to constrain American policy, underscores their potentially greater impact on smaller, more interdependent states.[5] The importance of domestic politics in the determination of policies toward IGOs provides a strong challenge to the unitary actor assumption that dominates the theoretical literature. In particular the transparency of the American system of pressure groups, compared not only with closed authoritarian societies but also with more centrally coordinated societies such as Japan, allows clearer insight into conflicting domestic pressures concerning international cooperation. Finally, the

American leadership role, which has been so central to regime and cooperation theory, can be addressed only by looking directly at its relationship with IGOs. Thus although any case is unique, American uniqueness provides useful leverage for the study of IGO-country relations.

Moving from Case Studies Back to Theory

General theory by its nature is selective in the empirical phenomena it seeks to cover. Because it is impossible to incorporate all the rich findings from this set of case studies, we need to be selective in drawing implications for theory. The difficulty of this selection is further compounded here by the different, though not unrelated, levels at which the theory and empirical cases are constructed. Regime and cooperation theory is cast largely at the international or systemic level, seeking to explain structural factors (Keohane 1983), whereas the case studies focus equally on national-level factors and emphasize processes.

Crossing levels of analysis is not in itself a problem and should not artificially constrain the development of international relations theory. It is true that analyses are simpler when restricted to one level of analysis. But a guideline for simplification should not be misconstrued as a firm rule for theory building or empirical research. There is nothing inherently faulty with mixing levels, and it is hard to avoid doing so except in the most simple-minded theorizing. The study of international regimes and cooperation, for example, necessarily combines an analysis (sometimes implicit) of state interests that are nationally determined with an analysis of state interactions in strategic structures that are internationally determined. The same is true of most realist or structuralist analyses of international politics. Even Waltz (1979), who makes a great virtue of keeping levels separate, implicitly crosses levels of analysis in making assumptions about the preferences of states that ultimately must be affected by national-level factors.[6] Of course, Waltz simplifies his analysis greatly by not investigating underlying state preferences and by concentrating on system-level aspects, especially the distribution of power. He illustrates the usefulness but not the necessity of the dictum. Therefore the appropriate question in evaluating how the present case studies mix system-level arguments (for example, concerning U.S. decline) with state-level arguments (for example, about domestic politics) is this: Does the increased explanatory scope of the theory outweigh the loss in tractability or parsimony?

The cases raise important challenges for the theory precisely by transgressing the levels of analysis barrier to reopen the unitary actor assumption that is both the mainspring and weak link of traditional international relations theory. Insofar as unruly domestic politics means that states do not have consistent preferences, conclusions premised on unitary actor models are impaired. In addition, the case studies move our attention from so-called structural characteristics to the underlying processes associated with state interaction. This is nowhere better seen than in the examination of leadership when a consideration of actual U.S. behavior is substituted for a strictly abstract notion of relative power. Similar attention to process is evident in the discussion of IGO operations. The details of these national-level and micro-level processes provide checks on the validity of the system-level theory, point out its significant limitations, and possibly indicate directions for its improvement.

Of course special problems occur in using case studies of micro processes to examine theories of macro structures. A macro structure may have any number of micro processes underlying it and need not provide detailed prediction on this latter level. Tracing micro processes nonetheless provides a considerable challenge for the sensibility of the macro theory. The analysis of U.S. decline and leadership illustrates the possible refinements to the macro theory and its concepts. Nevertheless, some discrepancies between micro processes and macro theory must be expected. Any theory's simplifying assumptions compress and sometimes distort the underlying reality into a more tractable approximation. It may not be desirable or possible to improve the approximation to underlying processes without making the theory unmanageable. The discussion on incorporating domestic politics pursues this point further.

Even when they cannot be incorporated directly into a theory, insights from micro processes provide valuable understandings for interpretation of the theory. They offer a deeper assessment of the theoretical concepts and of the relationships among them. In the case of structural theories, for example, an understanding of underlying processes connects the general claims to the observed behavior of states. This increases the explanatory range of the theory. Micro processes also help to identify relevant contextual factors (that is, systematic factors affecting outcomes but not explicitly included in the theory) and thereby to delimit the theory's range of applicability. The importance of such interpretation should not be underestimated, especially as theories become more formal and correspondingly more arid. Although considerations such as parsimony prevent a theory from covering details of cases, cases and theory are mutually informing. The theoretical propositions that guide the present case studies illustrate one side of this reciprocally beneficial relationship. The remainder of this chapter explores the other side of the relationship in terms of the following question: What do these case studies of U.S.-IGO

relations suggest for the further development of theory concerning international regimes and cooperation?

Theoretical Challenges Raised

To address the implications of the empirical studies for theory, consider a
brief sketch of what the cases show. Karns and Mingst provide greater
detail in the preceding chapter (table 11.3), but the essential evidence on
each of the four main hypotheses is summarized in figure 12.1. The cases
are ordered from "low" to "high" politics in social welfare, economics, and
security categories as defined by Karns and Mingst. This traditional
categorization of international issues usefully organizes the empirical
results of the case studies insofar as it reflects an ascending order of overall
importance of issues to states. But such an ordering is inadequate insofar
as issues typically categorized as low politics occasionally dominate high

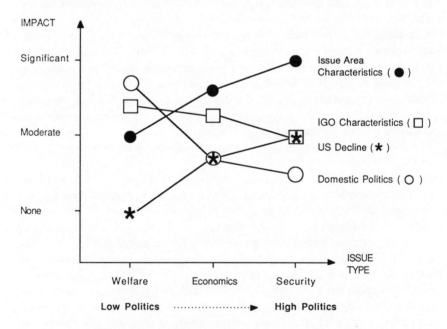

The lines drawn here should be interpreted with caution appropriate
to a small number of data points and fairly loose measurement techniques.
Also, note that "significance" of impact refers to substantive significance
in terms of observed importance of an explanatory factor in various
case studies, not to statistical significance.

Figure 12.1   Impact of Various Factors in Different Issue Types

politics issues (for example, controlling cholera ultimately prevailed over freedom of the seas in the nineteenth century). More important, the high/low politics distinction is misleading insofar as it substitutes substantive categories (for example, security, economics) for analytic categories. I argue in the next section that key analytic similarities across low and high politics, as well as significant differences within substantive categories, circumscribe the usefulness of the traditional interpretation of this ordering as a rigid hierarchy. Thus the high/low distinction can be taken as no more than a very rough guide to the relative importance of issues.[7]

Issue area characteristics are always central and their importance increases as we move from low to high politics. Simply put, when the stakes are higher, basic interests of states are more important in determining outcomes.[8] Conversely, *domestic politics* become less important as international stakes increase. American interest groups are sometimes vitally effective in welfare issues associated with UNESCO, as the media demonstrated in the 1980s, but they play no similarly crucial role in NATO. This suggests that national interest is most clearly defined for high politics and most subject to manipulation in low politics. Similarly, *IGO characteristics* have their strongest impact in low politics issues, though they are not insignificant in high politics forums. It should be noted, however, that the studies exclude East-West security issues where regimes are relatively weak and formal IGOs nonexistent. Finally, *U.S. decline* has had its greatest (though surprisingly moderate) impact in security issues where power considerations are greatest. Changing power resources are less apparent and have less effect in welfare issues.

In all cases the four alternative explanations have had an intermediate impact on the economic issues, reflecting their "middle" position between high and low politics. The key role of issue area characteristics indicates the high stakes states attach to economic issues, whereas the role of IGOs suggests the importance of formal institutions in promoting cooperation on these issues. The greatly expanded importance of these middle issues in the postwar period further lessens the usefulness of any sharp high/low distinction in international politics.

These empirical findings are generally congruent with theoretical arguments found in the literature on regimes and cooperation. This theory is not sufficiently well developed, however, to provide strong hypotheses on all these matters. Thus the cases provide less a test of the theory than an opportunity to explore and challenge it. In this way each of the four explanations of change in U.S.-IGO relations provides interesting material to stimulate further theoretical development. I discuss them in the rough order of their importance in the case studies.

Analysis of Issue Areas

A central presumption of the regimes literature is that international politics can be analyzed in terms of discrete international issue areas such as food or nuclear proliferation. Although issue areas are not always clearly defined (witness the social welfare examples in this volume or the somewhat arbitrary division of tasks between the IMF and World Bank [Feinberg 1988]), it is assumed that they provide adequately coherent units for analysis. It is further assumed that issue areas are sufficiently separate from each other that they can be studied independently. The relation between issues is discussed separately in the theoretical literature in terms of linkage and remains one of the least-developed areas of the regimes literature.

By treating international issue areas as independent arenas, regime theory challenges realist notions that power politics dominates all other issues. The security regime is examined instead as an issue area comparable with economic or social welfare issue areas. This does not mean that all issue areas are equal. Obviously, states find the problems addressed by security regimes of generally greater import than, say, scientific policy within UNESCO. Different degrees of commonality or conflict of interest also affect state behavior. The theoretical literature remains vague, however, in specifying the resulting analytical differences among issues. A central challenge facing regime analysis is to specify these differences systematically, as well as to specify related differences in the impact of key variables such as the number of states or the transparency of their behavior. The resulting analytical categories will be invaluable in promoting generalization beyond the substantive categories offered by high/low politics or issue area descriptors.

The case studies show that issue characteristics are significant determinants of international politics. Changes in regime ideology and salience of an issue to the United States provide the only explanation found to matter in all cases (see table 11.3) and are especially important in high politics. In addition to the longitudinal view of issue characteristics in the individual studies, comparison among cases provides an instructive cross-sectional view. Figure 12.1 shows how the relative power of the four explanations of IGO-U.S. relations varies systematically across the different categories of social welfare, economics, and security (that is, low, middle, and high politics). This provides considerable supporting evidence for an issue area approach to international politics and, through that, suggests avenues for more sophisticated theorizing.

One way to understand the impact of issue area characteristics is through an interest-based approach. The high/low politics dimension approximates the salience or intensity of states' interests. When intensity is high because vital interests such as security are at stake, issue area characteristics and the distribution of power matter most (see figure 12.1). When intensity is lower, domestic politics and IGO characteristics are most important. These findings indicate that the traditional high/low politics categorization, viewed in terms of the intensity of interests at stake, provides some purchase on international issues.

But the high/low distinction fails to capture the "strategic structure" that explains how issue characteristics affect state behavior. Strategic structure refers to the interrelation among state interests, often usefully depicted in simple game-theoretic models.[9] Briefly, conflict of interest is high if states harm one another in pursuing their individual goals, and conflict of interest is low if they inadvertently help one another. The following discussion shows that strategic considerations are more important determinants of international political behavior than are the simple intensity measures represented by the high/low categorization.

Analyzing the configuration of interests also provides, in my view, a more straightforward and powerful understanding of issue area politics than does analysis of the "congruity between the ideology of the United States and that of the dominant coalition within an IGO" (chapter 1: 15). Although the shift from ideology to interest is not unproblematic, many ideological positions presented in the cases are closely connected to state interests as discussed later. The case studies provide additional detail on how American interests intersect the interests of other states. This is important because of the limitations noted earlier with regard to the use of case studies focused on any single country. The relation between American interests and IGOs can be understood only in terms of the strategic relationship (in the game-theoretic sense) resulting from interests of all involved states. Finally, adopting an interest-based approach does not deny the potential relevance of ideology at a deeper level in terms of shaping basic conceptions of interest or interpretations of events.

The advantage of an interest-based approach is evident in the cases. Labeling the consensus underlying IAEA as a "global ideological agreement" (chapter 3: 78), for example, is a somewhat obscure way to describe the high level of common interest among states in limiting proliferation and the nuclear arms race. More important, ideological factors per se are not proximate causes in any high or middle politics case study, whereas the distribution of interests figures prominently in all. A somewhat stronger argument can be made for the effect of ideology independent of interest in the social welfare issue areas. Examples include American pressure for the adoption of free market principles by other states, opposition to state intervention, and growing endorsement of privatization among Third World states (for example, in FAO politics). Sometimes there is a plausible argument that interests are too remote and benefits too uncertain or diffuse for an interest argument by itself to be adequate. But often ideology is either closely related, or subordinate, to interest. Opposition to WHO's expanding regulatory role reflects American liberal ideology but simultaneously serves the interests of U.S. business. American ideological opposition to state economic intervention stops short of dropping its own domestic agricultural subsidies. Likewise U.S. commitment to liberal free trade is sufficiently flexible to allow its participation in nontariff barriers including voluntary export restraints. Even in the American attempt to use low politics IGOs as instruments of anticommunism, it is difficult to sort out ideological factors from the more general strategic interests of a superpower. Finally, ideology matters most where a lack of strong American interest in the IGO creates a vacuum that allows ideology to take over.

A comparison across issues demonstrates how differences in their strategic structure explain much of the politics in the nine cases. The generally smooth politics and "remarkable continuity" of U.S.-WHO relations are largely explained by the near harmony of interests among member states on traditional WHO health issues. High shared benefits relative to program costs create strong incentives for the United States and other countries to work together. The success of IAEA is similarly a result of a strong common interest among states in reducing the dangers of nuclear weapons. By contrast, U.S. difficulties with UNESCO and human rights IGOs are largely attributable to a lack of shared objectives. The same is true for FAO in the more recent period. In both FAO and UNESCO, however, the United States has been able to work compatibly within the relevant IGOs on technical matters when interests coincided more closely. Finally, NATO provides an example of common alliance incentives clashing with individual incentives to let others assume the burden of defense. This has been an ongoing source of friction, but strong common interest has held the alliance together.

Significant changes in states' interests, and therefore the structure of interests, help to explain changes in issue area outcomes. Changing interests may result from the addition or increased influence of new members, from the emergence of new issues, or from changing environmental conditions. Shifts in comparative advantage, the increasing importance of services, the rise of new trading competitors in the Far East, and the emergence of surplus capacity in key sectors all affect state interests in international trade. These developments explain many strains within the GATT framework, especially in conjunction with the increasing resort to nontariff barriers and managed trade. In WHO, proposals for new programs governing international regulation of pharmaceuticals introduce distributive issues and hence conflicts of interest between the United States and developing countries. The general trend in FAO from technical programs to issues involving questions of redistribution of power and wealth from North to South has equally lessened its compatibility with U.S. interests. These changing interests explain much of the recent discord within those organizations.

Finally, the role of the IMF has fluctuated with the interests of key states, especially the United States. The move to a flexible exchange rate system combined with relatively consensual preferences among key Western economic actors reduced the importance of the IMF in favor of informal consultations among major economic actors (for example, the G-5 and G-7) and increased reliance on private financial markets. But emerging interests associated with the debt crisis restored the Fund to new prominence in international financial affairs. Thus changes in interests provide an important explanation for changes within issues as well as for variations across issues.

Accommodating these variations requires theoretical differentiation among the basic contexts presented by cases. Game theory can accomplish this through the use of different strategic structures such as "harmony," "prisoners' dilemma," "assurance," or "coordination."[10] Plausible instances of these game structures are found in the health, trade, atomic energy, and money issue areas, respectively. Of course, a detailed examination of state interests would be required to be sure of these specifications. The variation among games allows issue area differences and similarities to be explained within a common theoretical framework. It encourages the replacement of substantive categories (for example, issue area labels or low versus high politics) with analytical categories. Consequently, if alliance defense has the prisoners' dilemma structure often attributed to it, it may share more in common analytically with a middle politics issue such as trade than with another high politics issue such as atomic energy.

Similarly, strategic structure resolves the seeming anomaly that low politics are often more conflictual than high politics. A relatively sharp focus on highly correlated interests in limiting proliferation through IAEA explains its success despite the intensity of state interests that might otherwise lead to conflict. By contrast, opposed interests in cultural affairs produce conflict in UNESCO even when the stakes are relatively low. Strategic structure is equally suggestive of why budget threats provide compelling levers in UNESCO but not in WHO, even though both are low politics issue areas. Of course differences in the size of the stakes play a role alongside differences in the configuration of interests in determining state behavior and international outcomes.

In addition to examining the different issue areas, the cases indicate the need to consider the impact of other changes within those overall contexts. An instructive example is expanding membership in a regime. This has the dual impact of increasing the number of actors in the issue area and changing the distribution of interests within it. It is generally assumed that an increasing number of actors impairs cooperation for familiar reasons associated with collective action and n-person prisoners' dilemma. But this has not been a severe problem in health or atomic energy issues, suggesting that their different strategic structures entail different implications for changing membership size. In other cases new members disrupt cooperation either by intensifying collective action problems or by introducing a new diversity of interests. Much of the unruliness of international regimes beginning in the 1970s resulted when new members of the international system sought new goals. Finally, the performance of an IGO is dramatically affected by evolving interests of existing members caused by such factors as shifting comparative advantage in trade or changing perceptions of the Soviet threat to NATO. Such examples amply illustrate our need for a better understanding of how shifting interests within issue areas ultimately change international regimes.

Thus the cases demonstrate how interest-based comparisons within and across issue areas lead to an understanding of the development and performance of regimes. The traditional high/low politics distinction offers insight into intensities of interest but is too primitive for most purposes. It is totally inadequate insofar as the configuration of interests among states is of central importance. Here simple game models provide deeper insight, although reference must be made to a wider range of problems than is captured by exclusive reliance on the prisoners' dilemma model (Snidal 1985b). Instead, we need a differentiated theory sensitive to different contexts of international politics and changes within them. Evidence from case studies is invaluable in guiding us toward appropriate theoretical models in posing central questions that need to be addressed.

Putting IGOs Back into Regimes

The regime literature adopts an expansive view of international organization, providing an important corrective to the tendency to take IGOs too seriously as authoritative decision-making bodies. It has highlighted the ability of states to order their relations without strong or formalized central organizations, when self-enforcing agreements provide the basis for successful international collaboration. But in its emphasis on decentralized cooperation, regime theory sometimes understates the importance of formal institutions.

The shortcomings of regime theory in this regard are reflected in the overly simplified abstract game-theoretic description of cooperation within a regime. Perfect knowledge of an issue area and of all states' interests, coupled with assumptions of rational behavior, is presumed to lead to a decentralized outcome that under certain conditions is "cooperative." Regimes are included implicitly through the rules of the game, specification of states' information sets, and resultant state behavior but are nowhere explicitly addressed. The role of institutions in facilitating and maintaining agreements is consequently masked by the simplifying assumptions rather than revealed through them. If the possible outcome is "anarchy" or "cooperation," to pose the typical stylized problem, the game model tells us little about how formal institutions promote a transition from the former to the latter. Although the theory is amenable to a more explicit treatment of institutions, much more work remains to be done in that regard.

Formal institutions are important because many international issues are too complicated for a strictly decentralized resolution to be effective. Large numbers of states with imperfect knowledge of one anothers' interests and capabilities are unlikely to arrive at and sustain cooperative agreements without some form of centralized concertation. At a minimum IGOs provide forums for negotiating agreements, settling disputes, and developing networks of interaction. They define issue areas, thereby restricting the range of interstate bargaining, and set agendas as issue areas evolve. Although many of these functions could be fulfilled through informal conferences or regular diplomatic channels, formal IGOs provide useful continuity for ongoing issues. In addition, certain tasks demand more extensive institutionalization. Collection, provision, and creation of information necessary for successful operation of many international agreements requires a significant bureaucratic establishment. So does the need for professional expertise and technical or research programs. The complexity of international agreements requires ongoing interpretation when applied across a wide range of individual cases. Such tasks can be handled only through an elaborate bureaucracy. In some cases this has led to the development of modest adjudicative and even "legislative" powers for IGOs (for example, WHO, GATT). Even though their operations remain firmly subordinate to the interests of states, somewhat independent IGOs can play an important role in the formulation and implementation of interstate cooperation.

The importance of IGOs to the operation of regimes is clear in the case study chapters. IGO characteristics provide the second most important explanatory factor across the nine cases, as shown in figure 12.1. Not only do IGOs matter in low politics, they are important in economic and security affairs. It is particularly striking that high politics IGOs actually increased in usefulness to the United States during the very period that other IGOs decreased in usefulness for affecting social welfare issues.[11] The studies further demonstrate the utility of existing IGOs in handling emergent problems including AIDS (WHO) and the debt crisis (IMF, World Bank). Finally, several case studies show that IGO influence extends to affecting certain American policies including trade, nuclear nonproliferation, and human rights. Taken together these findings confirm formal IGOs as significant factors in international regimes.

This observed importance of IGOs in different issue areas highlights a set of unanswered puzzles regarding how different levels of formal institutionalization affect the success of different regimes. Although this volume's focus on issue areas involving formal IGOs introduces selection bias into the analysis, several cases nevertheless raise particularly intriguing questions about institutionalization. In security, formal organizations are important for nonproliferation but not for arms control. Is the lack of formal arms control organizations a cause or effect of the relatively low level of success in establishing rules? Or is it irrelevant? Similarly, what aspects of the formal institutionalization of the NATO alliance have been important to its success? Would it have been equally effective as a strictly decentralized effort supported by the closely aligned interests of member states? International monetary affairs is an area in which the merits of formal IGOs versus decentralized cooperation are currently being tested. The recent shift toward informal cooperation among the largest Western states as the basis for macroeconomic and exchange rate coordination challenges the role of the IMF. Yet a contrary shift is apparent with respect to an expanded role for the IMF in debt management. These trends are partly explained by changing issue area characteristics (such as those suggested by the move to flexible exchange rates and concern over private financial market failure, respectively). They are also partly explained by American attempts to maintain control over the monetary area. Clearly the differential performance and operation of regimes under various levels of formal institutionalization need much further attention in regime theory.

The key impact of formal IGOs comes through providing information and changing expectations among states. The cases distinguish several roles for IGOs in this regard, and each is in need of further theoretical elaboration. One role is as forums for bargaining over the creation or change of agreements and for dispute settlement (for example, GATT). These forums contribute to the definition of issue areas, linkage among them, and agenda setting within them. We therefore need to know more about the advantages of broad issue area definitions that expand possibilities for exchanging concessions among states compared with narrow definitions that limit incentives for disruptive bargaining.

A second IGO role is providing technical information and guiding the implementation of programs as seen in WHO, the food IGOs, the World Bank, and the IMF. Under what conditions does expertise create space for partial IGO autonomy from states and what constrains their independent ability to set standards and run programs?

A final but important role is monitoring state behavior to increase the (self-)enforceability of agreements (for example, in IAEA and GATT). This raises central theoretical questions concerning the limits of decentralized cooperation, the requirements for implementing strategies of reciprocity without inadvertently undermining cooperation, and the role of states' reputations. To incorporate these different functions of formal IGOs, regime theory must become more explicit and specific on these key matters than it currently is with its vague references to "improving information" or "lowering transactions costs."

The case studies press regime theorists to be more specific and precise in their theorizing. The broad definition of regimes must be refined further in order for the theory to be fruitfully applied to empirical cases. Because IGOs are among the most clearly defined "observables" pertaining to regimes, there are special virtues in clarifying the various roles of these formal institutions in terms of the theory. Doing so will help to move the study of regimes beyond increasingly sterile definitional debates about regimes (facetiously, is there a pineapple regime?) toward a better understanding of institutions broadly construed.

Domestic Politics

The importance of domestic politics in IGO-U.S. relations varies across issue areas. It is the most important determinant of changing U.S. behavior in low politics issues, as shown in figure 12.1. In addition, in all four social welfare cases IGOs have had increasing influence on domestic interest groups (see table 11.2). By contrast, domestic politics have had a more modest impact on the security and economic organizations studied here. However, frequent executive-legislative conflicts over the use of American armed forces in the post-Vietnam era suggest this finding may result from the particular cases being studied. The observed lesser effect of domestic politics on high politics nonetheless needs consideration.

The importance of domestic politics challenges the unitary actor assumption underlying mainstream international relations theory. But the nature of that challenge needs to be carefully delimited. The unitary actor approach does not assume that domestic politics does not matter, only that it can be summarized in simple assumptions about state behavior or preferences. Findings that domestic politics affects state behavior are therefore hardly surprising. It would be more surprising, and probably nonsensical, if it did not. More important is determining whether domestic politics affects state behavior in ways that structural theories cannot accommodate. The ultimate question is whether the simplifying assumption of the state as a unitary actor can be usefully augmented.

Two separate propositions must be distinguished in examining the interaction of domestic and international politics. The first is that domestic policies dominate state behavior so that international behavior is largely independent of states' international strategic situation per se. If so, the unitary actor assumption is of limited usefulness because international state behavior is determined by the interaction of subnational groupings, even if those groupings are reacting to the "international" environment. The clearest example is the extraordinary influence of the news media, mobilized by a somewhat misplaced fear of a new world information order, in precipitating American antipathy toward and withdrawal from UNESCO. Human rights policy has also been influenced by domestic lobbying groups, though these have been less effective when security or economic interests are at stake.[12] Finally, U.S. policy toward the food IGOs has been influenced by various interest groups, and, as with UNESCO, development of a coherent national policy has been hindered by diffusion of responsibility across governmental agencies. These examples lend credence to the proposition that vagaries of domestic politics on occasion prevail over international factors in setting U.S. policy toward IGOs. It should be noted that in each of these cases, however, domestic groups take command of international agendas only in a vacuum created by a lack of any overriding national interest coupled with a failure of the executive branch to fashion a coherent policy. The unitary actor assumption is impaired whenever domestic politics has this corrosive effect on coherent national policy.

The second proposition is that domestic politics affects states' international behavior in conjunction with—not instead of—international political considerations. In terms of an interest-based approach, domestic factors shape the preferences that guide states in their interactions. This domestic influence need not result in the inconsistency or incoherence typically associated with the intrusion of domestic politics into international policies. Indeed, domestic politics can also be an important source of continuity for international behavior. Such influence is apparent in several cases even though, as noted earlier, this project's emphasis on change in U.S.-IGO relationships leads to an underestimation of stabilizing domestic factors. Many aspects of American security policy, best represented by the forty-year commitment to NATO, are underwritten by a remarkably strong domestic political consensus on core values. This consensus is more fundamental to determining behavior toward NATO than are more publicized and politicized disagreements over the details of the commitment.[13]

Domestic consensus also limits the intrusion of unrelated issues. Although policy toward IAEA has been modified by changing domestic attitudes regarding nuclear energy and criticism of nonproliferation policies, basic agreement on its importance has protected IAEA from attacks by pro-Israel groups. In other cases the technical nature of IGO operations insulates them from domestic politics. Both the IMF and World Bank have enjoyed significant and continuous executive branch support and drawn relatively little attention from domestic interest groups.[14] With regard to the World Bank, Congress has even dampened policy shifts between administrations. In all these cases underlying domestic agreement explains much of U.S. behavior toward IGOs. No serious problems are posed for the unitary actor assumption provided this consensus is maintained.

More troublesome for the unitary actor assumption are domestic politics that produce changing state behavior. Simplifying assumptions concerning state preferences must now be made more complicated to cover contingent (changing) domestic conditions, or else domestic factors must be incorporated directly into the analysis. Of the cases presented here, trade provides the best crucible for examining these matters. Continuing support for GATT across administrations and traditional arguments for trade liberalization have been increasingly challenged by subnational interests. The expanding role of trade in the American economy has made it a more salient domestic issue while a more assertive Congress provides new venues for protectionism. The result has been a proliferation of sectoral demands for trade protection, some with tangible success. To the extent interest groups have repeatedly prevailed over executive branch trade policy, the unitary actor assumption is seriously challenged. But if the executive has maintained its policy (or implemented coherent policy change), then the unitary actor assumption is sustained (although its specific content applied to trade issues may require modification).

What, then, do the case study findings imply for the unitary actor assumption in international relations theory? One alternative is to argue that it is not seriously challenged by them. On security issues, and for the most part on economic issues, U.S. goals and policies are quite consistent over time. Even in trade the American executive arguably has been able to maintain a general coherent trend toward greater trade liberalization. It has made major, short-term sectoral concessions, but it has effectively resisted large-scale, longer-term protectionism. Similarly, the U.S.-WHO relationship illustrates the consistency of American policies on many low politics issues. The United States has been consistent in promoting free market principles and opposing state interventionism. Only in human rights, which under the Reagan administration have been subordinated to security issues, and on certain UNESCO issues, largely peripheral to core American interests, has the United States lacked a coherent policy. This seems to be the exception, not the rule.

Another alternative, still compatible with the unitary actor approach, is to incorporate domestic politics through the changing content of states' preferences. These changes must be systematic. Examples include the impact of party politics or electoral cycles on trade policy, long-term shifts in the domestic consensus on NATO burden sharing, or changing ideological preferences across administrations on human rights issues. Such factors provide empirical elaborations through which the theory can be applied to different cases and interpreted.

The most ambitious alternative is to incorporate domestic politics directly into the theory. Although no logical problem occurs when including domestic political factors in international relations theory, there are severe practical limitations. The bureaucratic politics school amply illustrates how analysis of micro details may obscure rather than elucidate macro considerations. The failure to generalize across cases resulted in largely idiosyncratic analyses that have not culminated in an effect on international relations theory. Putnam (1988) has recently mapped a strategy for a systematic integration of domestic and international politics through "two-level games." Focusing on international bargaining, Putnam assumes states are simultaneously constrained by international factors (that is, what other states will accept) and domestic factors (for example, what will sell at home). He connects his analysis to plausible theoretical insights and provides compelling examples. But the approach is as difficult as it is attractive because it requires a theory of domestic politics. This dramatically increases the complexity of any theory, especially given that the domestic politics of states other than the United States also needs to be considered. Even if a comprehensive theory is not achievable, however, the two-level strategy may provide more systematic insight into the domestic limits of the unitary actor approach.

Thus different strategies for handling the complexities of domestic politics range from summarizing them in simple rules of state behavior to explicit attempts to incorporate them. The onus of the latter approach is not to show that domestic politics matters but to show how it can be incorporated systematically, parsimoniously, and with some generality into international relations theory. This work has barely begun, and it is too early to say if it will succeed. Until it does, the unitary actor assumption will dominate international relations theory, although its proponents have good cause to be cautious and modest about its use.

U.S. Decline: Declining Power or Declining Leadership?

Decline in U.S. power provides the least satisfying explanation of change examined in the nine cases. It explains little of the four social welfare cases and only slightly more of international economics and security. Contrary to prevailing theoretical expectations, IGOs have maintained or even slightly expanded their influence during the alleged period of hegemonic decline. This is a surprising result for a hypothesis that, under the label of hegemonic stability theory, has been granted pride of place in the last decade of theorizing. Rather than leading us to reject the importance of leadership in international politics, however, detailed analyses of the case studies suggest possibilities for rethinking its meaning.

Ambiguities in the concept of leadership are apparent in a comparison of two competing strands of hegemonic stability theory that have coexisted without adequate clarification of the relation and tension between them (Snidal 1985a). One view treats hegemony as coercive, characterized by the imposition of the preferred order of the dominant state on subordinate states. Here IGOs provide useful apparatuses for the implementation and enforcement of hegemonic policies, as well as for their collective legitimation. Declining hegemony offers opportunities for subordinates to change the prevailing order and institutions while the hegemonic state presumably fights a rearguard action to maintain them. The decreasing usefulness of IGOs to the United States for collective legitimation is in accord with this view of hegemony, but the general *increase* in the usefulness of IGOs to the United States for other purposes is not in accord.[15] Thus the coercive leadership perspective provides no compelling explanation of the overall pattern of change in IGO-U.S. relations.

The other view treats hegemony as "benevolent" where a dominant actor provides public goods such as international "order" to other states. Regimes and IGOs are useful vehicles for such action. Politics among regime members should be generally consensual, except for complaints by the largest state about its free-riding subordinates. But declining hegemony pressures subordinate states to pick up the slack in maintaining order. The hegemonic actor should be eager to work with them to this end, although collective action problems make it hard to maintain cooperation. This model is best at describing situations such as NATO and GATT (where the assumption of a public good, or at least the closely related Prisoners' Dilemma structure, is most closely approximated), except that its prediction of regime decline remains substantially unfulfilled. The model is even less compelling for many social welfare issues in which strongly contested conceptions of *the* international public good make an economic public goods model less applicable. The difficulty does not simply arise from differences in issue area characteristics, however, but results from the inherently inadequate conception of leadership as a form of unilateral benevolence.

A more realistic view of international leadership lies between the extremes of coercion and benevolence. It recognizes that interests among states are rarely as coincident as the public goods model requires or as divergent as the coercive leadership model implies. American postwar leadership has neither been simply a matter of bestowing benefits on other states nor one of imposing regimes regardless of others' interests. Instead the United States has had to use its considerable resources—especially the resource of being the key actor in international cooperation—to construct regimes in concert with other states. This has entailed coalition building and bargaining to reconcile interstate differences, as well as careful anticipation and adjustment to changing conditions. The resulting agreements have been truly multilateral, imposing constraints and obligations on all states according to their individual capacities and circumstances.

That leadership depends not only on the possession of significant resources but also on their skillful use is dramatically illustrated by different American experiences in the IAEA and UNESCO. Coate (chapter 9) argues that the United States has always been well equipped with relevant resources for its efforts in UNESCO and has experienced no significant decline in them. By contrast, Schiff (chapter 3) argues that the United States faced an inevitable decline in its resources for promoting its desired nuclear policy as technology spread and the number of nuclear suppliers expanded. Worse, this decline came precisely as American objectives in atomic energy were becoming more ambitious and therefore would seem to require more resources. Yet American success in IAEA has been as significant as its failure in UNESCO.

The difference between success and failure is largely attributable to the quality of American leadership in each case. America was the reluctant suitor at the UNESCO wedding, participating only from fear of being left out. The primary purpose of the organization was foreign to a state with neither a national education nor a national cultural policy. After a brief unsuccessful fling at politicizing UNESCO for its own anticommunist purposes, the United States sought primarily to limit the organization's mandate to technical matters. This left it with a largely negative and reactive posture vis-à-vis UNESCO initiatives, though it has benefited from certain technical programs such as the Universal Copyright Convention and various information collection efforts. This limited engagement in the organization never engendered significant domestic support for UNESCO within the United States, not even a clear home within the U.S. bureaucracy. Finally, the failure to engage in serious coalition building meant that American positions never developed strong international support, not even among its closest Western allies. The net result has been the unhappy relationship with UNESCO, ending in the United States' separation from the organization.

By contrast, the United States has taken a positive leadership role in IAEA. Unable to achieve its objectives unilaterally, it has built coalitions with key states, including the Soviet Union. More recently it has supported efforts to build a consensus with Third World states and has contained its own domestic pressures generated by the Israeli question. The United States has also been effective in working through the IAEA secretariat— as, indeed, it has been effective when it has worked within the UNESCO bureaucracy—and in using outside forums to pressure the organization. Its most extreme pressures have included the possibility of changing or limiting U.S. participation in the regime, but unlike the clumsy withdrawal from UNESCO, these threats have been tied to specific complaints and conditions. Thus U.S. success with IAEA has been attributable to neither its acquiescence nor its unilateral dominance but to its concerted leadership efforts to promote goals through regime institutions.

Other case studies equally illustrate that U.S. leadership depends on a conjunction of resources and initiative. Jacobson (chapter 2) reminds us that the United States never could impose its positions on NATO unilaterally, although with astute negotiations it has consistently prevailed and can continue to do so. Hopkins (chapter 7) shows that food organizations have been much like UNESCO: when the United States seeks to lead, it can, but it has often failed to mobilize its resources to achieve its ends. Kahler (chapter 4) argues that even in its period of predominance the United States bargained to get its way in the IMF. He shows how the decline in formal U.S. voting power has been successfully minimized through logrolled coalitions and the increasing use of G-5 as an alternative forum in which the United States commands a consensus. Ascher (chapter 5) documents the continued centrality of American leadership in the World Bank despite the latter's ongoing efforts to increase its independence and the former's decision to make the Bank a more truly multilateral agency. Thus whatever the decline in its relative resources, the case studies show that the United States retains more than sufficient resources to achieve its goals.[16] What it sometimes lacks is leadership in building coalitions by taking into account the interests of other states.

What does this suggest for theory? Above all it points to the need to broaden the notion of leadership to include coalition building in a multilateral international situation in which states are more equal. Further, it indicates the need to distinguish modalities of leadership according to the strategic structure of interests in different issue areas. Coalition building is easier on many of the traditionally harmonious issues of WHO than on GATT trade issues, in which distribution issues are greater. Opposed interests of consumers and producers in food issues present tougher problems for coalition building. Finally, problems of coordinating international financial policies are largely consensual among the Western economic powers but still require negotiation to accommodate different national interests over large stakes.

Leadership raises related questions about the value of limited membership versus universal membership organizations. When feasible, restricting membership to states with more compatible interests makes cooperation easier. Enforcement of participation is also strengthened by the possibility of excluding noncontributing states. Obvious examples are alliances, regional trading blocs, and small clubs for international monetary coordination. The potential impact of such arrangements has not been worked out in theory, though the cases provide several illustrations in which such arrangements have developed. Finally, we need to know much more about the role of IGOs in fostering multilateral leadership when hegemonic leadership is unavailable. What extent of institutionalization is required for leadership to be effective in different issue areas? How does the viability of arrangements shift with the distribution of capabilities and interests of its membership?

Four Challenges to International Relations Theory

The four hypotheses around which this volume is organized are not wrong, but they are inadequate as currently formulated. The cases support each proposition but simultaneously point out its limitations. The problem carries over to regime theory as a whole. It too can be properly described as insufficiently developed to be "tested" in any rigorous sense. As a result, the empirical evidence provided here can best be interpreted in terms of proposals for further development of the theory. Four main injunctions follow.

Replace substantive issue area labels with analytic labels richer than the high/low politics distinction. The reporting of any individual case naturally attracts attention to its particulars, but the theoretical project demands abstraction from these to general properties transcending individual issues. The high/low distinction illuminates differences associated with intensity but masks more important considerations concerning the configuration of interests. An interest-based analysis of strategic interactions presents one direction of theoretical expansion to correct this deficiency. Similarities and differences across issues are captured in simple strategic structures; key contextual variables such as the number of actors or the distribution of power ultimately must be included in a fuller analysis. The hallmark of successful theorizing is the extent to which different issues can be understood in a common framework.

Restore the analysis of formal institutions (IGOs) to a central place in regime theory. In its eagerness to escape earlier traditions of studying international organization, regime analysis has not adequately explored the impact of IGOs in international cooperation. Doing so will extend the explanatory reach of the theory at the same time that it poses new puzzles concerning the role of centralized institutions in fostering "cooperation under anarchy." Above all it makes us address this question: When is it necessary to organize international cooperation through formal institutions and when will informal negotiations and interactions suffice?

Incorporate understandings of domestic political processes directly into the analysis of international relations. The traditional dodge of hiding behind levels of analysis to avoid central domestic factors determining international politics is no longer enough. Provided they have a systematic effect on international behavior, domestic factors are eminently suitable for theorizing. Building them into international analysis is not a matter of rejecting the unitary actor assumption but of enriching it through greater knowledge of domestic politics.

Broaden the conception of leadership to include leadership of a multilateral partnership for international cooperation. The uneven impact of declining American hegemony is largely a result of its uneven leadership. Important questions about the role of leadership in increasingly multilateral settings are pertinent to understanding the impact of changing international distributions of power. Answers will be strongly influenced by related considerations of the range of interests involved and the role of institutions in orchestrating continuity.

It is difficult (perhaps foolhardy) to predict where theoretical advance is most likely to occur. Issue area characteristics and impact of formal IGOs should be among the most amenable for incorporation into current theory. Each is central to the analysis of regimes and cooperation across issue areas, and both are implicit in regime theory as currently constituted. By contrast, including a broader conception of leadership requires a more substantial revision of current theory. It entails looking beyond the interests of the hegemonic state to consider the needs and demands of other states. Finally, domestic politics poses the greatest difficulty and perhaps the greatest payoff for further theorizing. Whether sufficiently parsimonious characterizations of domestic processes can be linked to international theory will depend a great deal on creativity and no small amount of trial and error. But attempts in all of these areas surely are justified by the evidence presented in this volume.

These four prescriptions for theory have analogous implications for U.S. policy. American leadership must become increasingly a process of coalition building among a wider group of states, as it typically has been with America's closest allies in NATO. This requires greater attention to and understanding of other states' interest and of the resulting strategic structure of issue areas. A need for tough bargaining must be accompanied by a willingness to accommodate others' interests as they accommodate American interests. And because American politics will continue to have its unruly aspects, the executive branch must forge supporting coalitions before international agreements are established and sustain them thereafter. Finally, more serious participation in formal IGOs expands the international influence of the United States and better enables it to achieve its goals, but not without accepting the constraints inherent in effective international cooperation. And perhaps a better understanding of theory will enhance the effectiveness of multilateralism in U.S. foreign policy.

Notes

1. For their valuable comments on earlier drafts of this paper I thank David Forsythe, Leon Gordenker, Charles Hermann, Raymond Hopkins, Ole Holsti, and especially John Ruggie, Karen Mingst, and Margaret Karns.

2. A detailed survey of these literatures is presented by Haggard and Simmons (1987); Oye (1986) and Krasner (1983) are collections of key articles. Keohane (1983) discussed the relation of regime and cooperation theory to the longer-standing realist tradition.

3. For a more general discussion of the limits and virtues of case studies in theory testing and theory building, see Achen and Snidal (1989) and the variously dissenting replies by George (1989), Jervis (1989), Lebow and Stein (1989), and Downs (1989).

4. I use the integrative summary of the basic findings of the case studies presented by Karns and Mingst in the previous chapter as the basis for my discussion. In a chapter speculating about theoretical implications, I have felt more comfortable pushing their data to the limits than they (appropriately) do in their chapter summarizing empirical conclusions. To support my assertions I have relied heavily on the individual case study chapters. Unless otherwise indicated, references and conclusions about particular issue areas are taken from the authors in this volume, even when the citation is only implicit.

5. Care needs to be taken with such claims given that sometimes "weakness is strength, and strength is weakness." The United States might be constrained to support IGOs in certain circumstances or else risk destroying the organization, whereas a smaller state might free ride on the IGO without wider repercussions.

6. Waltz flirts with evolutionary-style arguments in an attempt to locate the tendency for states to seek security within the imperatives of an anarchic international environment and thus avoid crossing levels of analysis. The extraordinarily high survival rate of states, among other factors, makes this unsatisfactory. Regardless, it leaves unexplained why international anarchy is so hostile, unless some reference to the character of state preferences and, hence, almost certainly to domestic-level factors is made. A valuable, though caustic, critique of Waltz is in Kaplan (1979).

7. I thank John Ruggie for useful advice on this point. His criticisms have helped me to clarify the limits of the high/low politics distinction.

8. Issue area characteristics are represented here by "ideology" and "salience" of the issue. The latter is related directly to state interests; the former is related indirectly, as discussed later.

9. I will not introduce game models of international organization explicitly here. A useful introduction on game models is Hamburger (1979); the articles in Oye (1986) illustrate their application to international politics.

10. These terms refer to common 2 by 2 game structures. For a more detailed discussion, see Snidal (1989).

11. See table 11.1 and note 15. This excludes the role of IGOs for collective legitimation. That role has uniformly declined but, as I will argue, is an inappropriate indicator of general IGO effectiveness. For purposes of American foreign policy, of course, this decline is of real consequence.

12. Ole Holsti argues (in correspondence) that the Jackson-Vanik amendment and sanctions on South Africa indicate possible limitations to this generalization.

13. Again, security issues do not always entail a strong, stable domestic consensus. East-West negotiations on arms control and post-Vietnam military policy in the Third World provide instances of fluctuations approaching discontinuity in American domestic opinion. Whether these have rendered American security policy incoherent is an open question.

14. Minor exceptions include congressional attempts to attach human rights conditions to World Bank loans that Ascher reports as "not terribly significant" and congressional Black Caucus opposition to IMF loans to South Africa. Harder to gauge are self-limitations imposed by these or other IGOs in anticipation of possible U.S. domestic resistance. To the extent such factors can be anticipated by IGOs, however, they reflect systematic aspects of U.S. "preferences," even if they are driven by particularistic interest groups.

15. See table 11.1. Excluding collective legitimation, Karns and Mingst report over twice as many instances of increasing IGO usefulness to the United States (that is, eleven pluses in their table) as instances of decreasing IGO usefulness (that is, five minuses). In each of their four other categories cases of increasing usefulness equaled or exceeded cases of decreasing usefulness. Increasing usefulness was especially apparent in the economic issue areas (that is, six pluses versus no minuses) and security issue areas (that is, three pluses versus one minus). The decline in IGO usefulness was largely confined to social welfare issue areas (two pluses versus four minuses).

16. One case in which U.S. leadership has been difficult because of lack of common interests is human rights. Forsythe demonstrates that the United States has never assumed a strong leadership position on UN human rights, largely for domestic reasons. But he argues that if actors maintain their more congruent issue positions of recent years, then a stronger U.S. role is possible in this regime as well.

References

Achen, Christopher, and Duncan Snidal (1989). "Rational Deterrence Theory and Comparative Case Studies." *World Politics*, 41(2), 143–69.

Downs, George W. (1989). "The Rational Deterrence Debate." *World Politics*, 41(2), 225–38.

Feinberg, Richard E. (1988). "The Changing Relationship between the World Bank and the International Monetary Fund." *International Organization*, 42(Summer), 545–60.

George, Alexander L., and Richard Smoke (1989). "Deterrence and Foreign Policy." *World Politics*, 41(2), 170–82.

Haggard, Stephan, and Beth A. Simmons (1987). "Theories of International Regimes." *International Organization*, 41(Summer), 491–517.

Hamburger, Henry (1979). *Games and Models as Social Phenomena.* San Francisco, CA: W. H. Freeman.

Jervis, Robert (1983). "Security Regimes." In Stephen D. Krasner, ed., *International Regimes*. Ithaca, NY: Cornell University Press.

——— (1989). "Rational Deterrence: Theory and Evidence." *World Politics*, 41(2), 183–207.

Kaplan, Morton A. (1979). *Towards Professionalism in International Theory.* New York: Free Press.

Keohane, Robert O. (1983). "Theory of World Politics: Structural Realism and Beyond." In Ada Finifter, ed., *Political Science: The State of the Discipline.* Washington, DC: American Political Science Association.

Krasner, Stephen D. (1983). "Structural Causes and Regime Consequences: Regimes as Intervening Variables." In Stephen D. Krasner, ed., *International Regimes.* Ithaca, NY: Cornell University Press, 1–22.

Lebow, Richard Ned, and Janice Gross Stein (1989). "Rational Deterrence Theory: I Think, Therefore I Deter." *World Politics*, 41(2), 208–24.

Oye, Kenneth (1986). *Cooperation under Anarchy.* Princeton: Princeton University Press.

Putnam, Robert (1988). "Diplomacy and Domestic Politics: The Logic of Two-Level Games." *International Organization*, 42(Summer), 427–60.

Snidal, Duncan (1985a). "The Limits of Hegemonic Stability Theory." *International Organization*, 39(Autumn), 579–614.

——— (1985b). "Coordination versus Prisoners' Dilemma: Implications for International Cooperation and Regimes." *American Political Science Review*, 79(4), 923–42.

——— (1989). "International Cooperation: A Game Theory Analysis of Regimes and Interdependence." Unpublished manuscript.

Strange, Susan (1983). "*Cave! Hic Dragones:* A Critique of Regime Analysis." In Stephen D. Krasner, ed., *International Regimes.* Ithaca, NY: Cornell University Press, 279–96.

Waltz, Kenneth (1979). *Theory of International Politics.* Reading, MA: Addison-Wesley.

List of Contributors

William Ascher is professor of public policy studies and political science at Duke University, and co-director of Duke's Center for International Development Research. His research interests include development policy, political sciences, public administration, and comparative policymaking. He has published two books on political-economic forecasting: *Forecasting: An Appraisal for Policymakers and Planners* (1978) and *Strategic Planning and Forecasting* (1983); and another book on the politics of income redistribution in Latin America: *Scheming for the Poor* (1984). In 1980 he held a Council on Foreign Relations fellowship to study the World Bank's adaptation to the poverty alleviation orientation, and spent that year on the World Bank's Projects Advisory Staff. Several journal articles emerged from that research. Professor Ascher is currently the editor-in-chief of *Policy Sciences* and serves on editorial boards of several other journals.

Roger A. Coate is associate professor of international relations at the University of South Carolina. His work focuses on the theory and practice of international organization and the role of international institutions in world politics. He is the author of *Unilateralism, Ideology, and United States Foreign Policy: The U.S. In and Out of UNESCO* (1988), *Global Issue Regimes* (1982), and is coeditor with Jerel Rosati of *The Power of Human Needs in World Society* (1988). Coate's current research focuses on the political crises confronting multilateral institutions and on the processes by which transnational networks evolve, participate in, and shape global cooperation in specific issue settings.

David P. Forsythe is professor of political science at the University of Nebraska-Lincoln, where he specializes in international human rights and humanitarian diplomacy. His book *Human Rights and U.S. Foreign Policy: Congress Reconsidered* won the Manning J. Dauer Prize awarded by the University of Florida. He is the editor of, and contributing author to, two recent books: *Human Rights and Development* and *The United Nations in the World Political Economy*. Among his recent articles is "Human Rights in U.S. Foreign Policy," published in the *Political Science Quarterly*.

Raymond F. Hopkins is professor of political science at Swarthmore College. He spent part of 1986–87 in Rome on leave studying international food organizations, especially the World Food Program. He is the author of several books and articles on international food policy and food aid, including *Global Food Interdependence* (1980) with Donald J. Puchala, and "The Evolution of Food Aid: Toward a Development-First Regime" in *Food Policy*, edited by J. Price Gittinger, et al. (1987).

Miles Kahler is professor of international relations in the Graduate School of International Relations and Pacific Studies at the University of California, San Diego. His recent publications include *The Politics of International Debt* (editor), *Decolonization in Britain and France: The Domestic Consequences of International Relations*, and numerous articles on international political economy and international relations. Kahler is chair of the Committee on Foreign Policy Studies of the Social Science Research Council. He has been awarded fellowships by the Rockefeller Foundation and the National Science Foundation, and he was a Council on Foreign Relations Fellow at the International Monetary Fund in 1983–84. Kahler taught at Princeton University and Yale University before joining the faculty at the University of California.

Margaret P. Karns is director of the Center for International Studies and associate professor of political science at the University of Dayton, and a faculty associate of the Mershon Center at the Ohio State University. She earned her Ph.D from the University of Michigan. During 1988–89, she was an American Council on Education (ACE) Fellow at Tufts University. She is the editor of *Persistent Patterns and Emergent Structures in a Waning Center* (1986). Her research on multilateral institutions and foreign policy has resulted in several articles, some coauthored with Karen Mingst, as well as the present book. A grant from the German Marshall Fund of the United States supported work at the OECD in Paris in 1985. She and Karen Mingst are authoring a study of the domestic sources of U.S. support for and opposition to the UN for an international research conference on the Future of the UN System in Ottawa 1990.

Harold K. Jacobson is director of the Center for Political Studies of the Institute for Social Research and Jesse S. Reeves professor of political science at the University of Michigan. A specialist on international politics and institutions, he received his undergraduate education at the University of Michigan and his graduate education at Yale University. He is the author of *Networks of Interdependence: International Organizations and the Global Political System*, and is the author or editor/contributor to eight other books. He has also written numerous articles for professional journals.

Karen A. Mingst is associate professor and director of graduate studies in the Department of Political Science at the University of Kentucky. She has published work on international organizations and law, international political economy, and Africa. Her articles have appeared in *International Organization, International Studies Quarterly, Journal of Common Market Studies, Review of International Studies, Journal of Peace Research, African Studies Review, Africa Today,* and *Journal of Developing Areas.* She is the author of *Politics and the African Development Bank* (1990). Dr. Mingst has served as president of the International Studies Association South, and vice-president (1989–90) of the International Studies Association.

Benjamin N. Schiff is associate professor of government at Oberlin College in Ohio. He received his Ph.D. in political science from the University of California at Berkeley. His first book, *International Nuclear Technology Transfer: Dilemmas of Dissemination and Control* (1984) examined the politics of the international nuclear non-proliferation regime, emphasizing effects of the North-South issue on the International Atomic Energy Agency. He is currently working on a book about the United Nations Relief and Works Agency for Palestine Refugees in the Near East. Prior to his appointment at Oberlin College, he was a foreign affairs officer at the U.S. Arms Control and Disarmament Agency.

Duncan Snidal is associate professor in the Department of Political Science and the Graduate School of Public Policy at the University of Chicago, as well as director of the Program on International Politics, Economics, and Security (PIPES). He works on international relations theory with an emphasis on the formal analysis of international cooperation and regimes. His most recent work examines the problem of "relative gains" and demonstrates analytically that relative gains-seeking does not inhibit international cooperation to nearly the extent that has been traditionally presumed.

Index

Acquired Immune Deficiency Syndrome (AIDS) 211, 213–15, 227, 293, 294, 338
  See also WHO
Action Plan Working Group (APWG) 73
Adelman, Kenneth 227
Advisory Committee on Trade Negotiations (ACTN) 156, 160
Afghanistan 274, 315
  Soviet invasion of 7, 50, 52, 274, 294
  Soviet withdrawal from 47
African Development Bank 226
Africa 214
  food crisis 183, 190, 193, 195, 198, 299
  IMF role in 104
  U.S. aid to 190
Agency for International Development (USAID) 128, 192, 194, 212–13, 224, 244
Agriculture Department (USDA) 194, 198
  cooperation with FAO 199
Allende, Salvador 124
Alliance for Progress 49
American Bar Association 269, 278, 282
American Selling Price (ASP) 155, 166
Amin, General Idi 274, 281
Amnesty International 282, 294
Angola 192
Anti-Ballistic Missile Systems, Treaty on Limitation of 32
Antidumping Code 155, 166
apartheid 265, 280, 283
anti-protectionist groups 167, 168
Arab-Israeli conflict 249
  and UN peacekeeping 44, 45–7
Arab states
  opposition to Camp David Accords 46
  and the UN 47
  and UNESCO 253
Argentina 124, 276
Argonne National Laboratory. *See* International Nuclear Technical Liaison Office
arms control 32, 41, 325
  role of IGOs in 33, 338
  See also intermediate range nuclear forces

Arms Control and Disarmament Agency (ACDA) 64, 65, 68, 71, 72, 73, 83
Atomic Energy Act of 1946 57, 62
Atomic Energy Commission (AEC) 61, 71, 72, 74, 75, 83
Atoms for Peace 33, 57, 62, 65, 76, 78
Australia 194
Axelrod, Robert 3
Ayres, Robert 124, 134

Baker, James 103, 111–12
Baker Plan 103, 111, 121
Baldwin, David A. 13, 117, 305
Bangladesh 195, 218
Baldridge, Malcolm 152
Baruch Plan 31
Bayne, Nicholas 313
Beard Amendment 250
Belgium 36, 44, 63, 150
Belmont, Rose 225
Benton, William 234
Biddle, Francis 234
Big Five 222
Bingham, Jonathan 83
Black caucus 107
Black, Eugene 135
Blix, Hans 81
Bloomfield, Lincoln, P. 261
Boerma, Addeke 195
Bourne Report 208, 221
Boyer, Neil 225
Brazil 61, 96, 121, 147, 162
  moratoria on debt payments 112 n.2
Bread for the World 194
Bretton Woods system 93, 108
  institutions 91, 94, 116
  demise of 93, 108, 293
Brickerism 268, 269, 282, 283
Britain 40, 44, 45, 49, 57, 222
  and Bretton Woods institutions 94, 116
  and IMF 95, 96, 105, 110
  and NPT 36
  and UNESCO 232, 233, 234, 312
Brock, William 146
Brookhaven National Laboratory (U.S.) 73
Brown, Donald 202